D1247982

ENGINES
OF
CHANGE

GEORGE C. LODGE

ENGINES OF CHANGE

United States Interests and Revolution
in Latin America

WITH AN INTRODUCTION BY
SAMUEL P. HUNTINGTON

ALFRED A. KNOPF NEW YORK 1970

HN
110.5
A8
L59
1970
~~309.18~~
~~L822~~

THIS IS A BORZOI BOOK
PUBLISHED BY ALFRED A. KNOPF, INC.

First Edition

Copyright © 1970 by George C. Lodge
All rights reserved under International and Pan-American Copyright
Conventions. Published in the United States by Alfred A. Knopf, Inc.,
New York, and simultaneously in Canada by Random House of Canada
Limited, Toronto. Distributed by Random House, Inc., New York.
Library of Congress Catalog Card Number: 75–79338
Chapter 16 originally appeared in slightly
different form in the July 1969 issue of
Foreign Affairs under the title "U.S. Aid
to Latin America: Funding Radical Change."
Manufactured in the United States of America

For Nancy
and
Nancy
Emily
Dorothy
Cabot
George
and
David

OCT 5 1972

PREFACE

This book calls for a new assessment of United States interests, policies, and programs in those regions of the world which are in the process of radical political, economic, and social change. While it focuses on Latin America, I suggest its relevance elsewhere in the revolutionary world, including those communities in the United States in which radical structural changes are occurring or in demand.

It seeks to define the rather fundamental contradiction in United States policy between commitment to change and commitment to stability. It suggests a new formulation of interests and purpose—a new ideology—to replace that of anticommunism, which has lost both its validity and its utility. Accordingly, it recommends some rather specific governmental policy reorganization.

For business, the book considers the implication of continuing structural change on the forms and policies of the United States corporation in the revolutionary world, and makes recommendations for new directions.

My research and writing were done at the Harvard University Graduate School of Business Administration, and for this I want to express my profound appreciation and gratitude to Dean George P. Baker and Senior Associate Dean George F. F. Lombard. My deepest thanks go also to the following colleagues at Harvard and elsewhere who read and criticized all or portions of the manuscript: Professors Lincoln P. Bloomfield, Dwight S. Brothers, Paul W. Cherington, Stanley M. Davis, Lawrence E. Fouraker, Ray A. Goldberg, John D. Powell, John R. Schott, and

Raymond Vernon. Others to whom I am grateful are Warren G. Leonard, vice-president, W. R. Grace and Company; Francisco de Sola, president, De Sola e Hijos, San Salvador; a number of officials in the United States government, especially Viron Peter Vaky, National Security Council, and Amb. Henry Cabot Lodge; and many friends in Latin America.

During the past four years my thinking about the problems of revolution and United States interests has benefited particularly from the brilliance and insight of Professor Samuel P. Huntington, chairman of the government department of Harvard University, who helped me to find a way to place into some kind of order much that I felt intuitively and speculated on experientially. His own masterful *Political Order in Changing Societies* (Yale University Press, 1968) is in many ways the intellectual bedrock upon which this book is built. I also am indebted to Professor Charles W. Anderson of the University of Wisconsin, whom I have known only through his lucid and perceptive book *Politics and Economic Change in Latin America* (Van Nostrand, 1967) which helped me greatly, particularly in finding historical causes for contemporary observations in Latin America. My deepest thanks go also to Bishop Marcos McGrath of Veraguas Province, Panama (now Archbishop of Panama), who not only gave hospitality and assistance to my students and me during our work in his province but also brought the light of his wisdom to bear upon many complexities which before had been for me dark and obscure.

This book would probably not have been written if Alfred A. Knopf had not suggested it and if he and Ashbel Green had not given me help and encouragement. I am also indebted to Maria Wilhelm for her editorial help and to Sarah Webb for her secretarial assistance.

I must share with all of these persons responsibility for what is good and true in this book, but take for myself alone the blame for that which is not.

GEORGE C. LODGE

BOSTON, MASS.
FEBRUARY 1969

CONTENTS

INTRODUCTION

In a decade the prevailing North American perception of Latin America has gone almost full circle. For most of the 1950's the continent to the south was only a hazy image in the American consciousness. After World War II United States attention focused first on Europe, then on East Asia, and then on the Middle East. Latin America, many people implicitly assumed, would continue to exist as it had in the past: an area in which American interests were high but cause for American concern was low. Then came Castro, the Cuban Revolution, the Bay of Pigs, and a shocked and sudden awareness of the new processes of change at work in Latin America. Within a few years, the leading institutions of North American society became oriented toward Latin America. The Alliance for Progress was inaugurated; new military assistance and military training efforts came into being; United States business groped toward a new and different role; private groups and foundations launched new programs designed to promote development and welfare to the south.

It would be hypocritical on our part not to recognize that much of this attention to Latin America was a direct response to a perceived threat of more Castro-like revolutions. It would, however, also be erroneous not to recognize that the United States response to this threat was not solely in terms of strengthening counterinsurgency forces and promoting old-fashioned economic development programs. United States attention to Latin America was infused with the goal and the rhetoric, if not always the reality, of substantial reform. To the dominant groups in Latin

America, the United States offered help for peaceful change—a "revolution in liberty"—as the alternative to the Castroite formula. The issue posed was squarely one of reform versus revolution.

At that time, revolution did seem right around the corner. In Guatemala, Colombia, Venezuela, Peru, northeastern Brazil, guerrilla bands challenged the status quo, each a potential Castro Revolution in embryo. At the same time, the prospects for democratic reform also seemed high. Betancourt, Bosch, Frei, Beleaunde Terry appeared to have the ideological commitment and the popular appeal to inaugurate effective programs for democratic progress. The race between reform and revolution was seen as a close one. Both were possible; one was inevitable.

As the first decade of the Alliance for Progress draws to a close, Latin America seems far different. The probability of revolution has declined markedly. Guerrilla leaders have been killed, their bands decimated; land invasions have declined; nationalism has stymied the export of revolution; the death of Guevara symbolized the end of the revolutionary surge. Ten years of Castro proved him a Cuban rather than a continental phenomenon. The revolutionary intellectuals angrily debate the responsibilities for and the lessons of their failure. The ebbing of the revolutionary surge, however, has been paralleled by the decline in the strength and the progress of reform. The Alliance has gone sour. The reformers have been replaced by colonels or stalemated by parliamentarians. The United States aid effort has declined and been redirected along less venturesome paths. Its own domestic crises of the ghetto and of youth have replaced the crisis of Latin America on the United States agenda. At the Punta del Este conference in 1961, there were, delegates remarked, two left-wing governments in attendance—Cuba and the United States. Almost a decade later, it would appear that the Latin American status quo had frustrated both.

Yet such would be a superficial reading of the situation. For underlying change, modernization, dislocation, and upheaval are facts of Latin American life. It is to these more fundamental forces of change that George Lodge directs attention in this book. That the old order will be undermined and eventually disappear is unavoidable. The question concerns what, if anything, will take its place. In this book, Professor Lodge focuses attention on the heart of the problem of change: motivation and organization. All too often the United States has tended to think of development in terms of more schools, factories, and roads. But these are, in fact, only the extrinsic symbols of development. They are meaningful only when they are the product of motivation and organization. Development, like revolution, requires changes at the psychological and the political level: changes in the motivation of people and in the organization of power. The real engines of change change these, not just the physical environment.

Effective engines of change, Professor Lodge argues, are found among groups that combine local leadership and the ability to achieve access to national power-holders and that create organizations capable of performing a variety of functions: social, economic, political, and inspirational. As he points out, the vicious circle of stagnation in many backward societies cannot be broken successfully by action at just one point. It makes no sense only to build a new school in a village, or only to make available new fertilizer, or only to improve sanitary conditions. Each of these things may be good in itself, but if it is not a part of a process of total change in the community, its results will be frustrating to the villagers and disillusioning to the developmenters. What is required are multi-functional organizations that can, in effect, attack *any* local development problem and that possess the capacity to break the vicious circle of backwardness not at only one point but at many, with the sequence and timing appropriate for that particular situation.

Professor Lodge analyzes the potential sources of change in Latin America, looking at many of the familiar institutions and social forces, such as the political parties and the military. His most fascinating arguments, however, highlight the role as engines of change of two groups that are often assumed to be bulwarks of the status quo: the church and private business. He calls attention to the strength of the progressive movement within the Catholic Church and the crucial role that priests and bishops have played in inaugurating change in Brazil, Colombia, Panama, Guatemala, and elsewhere. Similarly, he points to the revolutionary impact that the development of business enterprises, particularly integrated food production, processing, and distribution operations, can have in promoting change in rural areas.

The great merit of this book is the broad-gauged approach of the author. It is not the technical monograph of the academic specialist; nor is it the breezy survey of the itinerant journalist. It is instead the work of a generalist who brings to his subject an extraordinary variety of viewpoints and experiences. At one point or another in his career, George Lodge has been teacher, politician, administrator, newspaperman. He has had experience with Latin American labor as Assistant Secretary of Labor for International Affairs in the Eisenhower and Kennedy Administrations. He has dealt with Latin American business as a professor at the Harvard Business School and as the leading figure in the organization of the Central American School of Business Management at Managua, Nicaragua. He is familiar with Latin American agriculture through his work with peasant organizations and their leaders and the active role he has played in the Center for Rural Development. He thus brings an unusually diverse background to the study and analysis of Latin America's problems.

His approach to Latin American development is also informed and shaped by the intense personal experience he has had in helping to promote social, economic, and political change in the backward rural province of Veraguas in Panama. There, the leadership of the local bishop and the collective efforts of the peasants have brought into existence a development organization and forty cooperatives through which the local people are assuming control over their own future, despite the opposition of wealthy landowners, on the one hand, and of communist-oriented guerrillas, on the other. Here is a model of successful institution-building clearly relevant to the problems of rural change in other Latin American countries. AID officials and Latin American leaders will do well to study it carefully. It offers a fascinating example of the generation of the organizational engines of change essential for sustained development. The alternative to Che's dream of "two, three, many Vietnams" in Latin America could well be "two, three, many Veraguases." In this thoughtful, stimulating, and perceptive book, Professor Lodge develops a powerful argument to support this proposition and to show why social and human development should be the core concerns of American foreign policy toward Latin America.

SAMUEL P. HUNTINGTON

ENGINES OF CHANGE

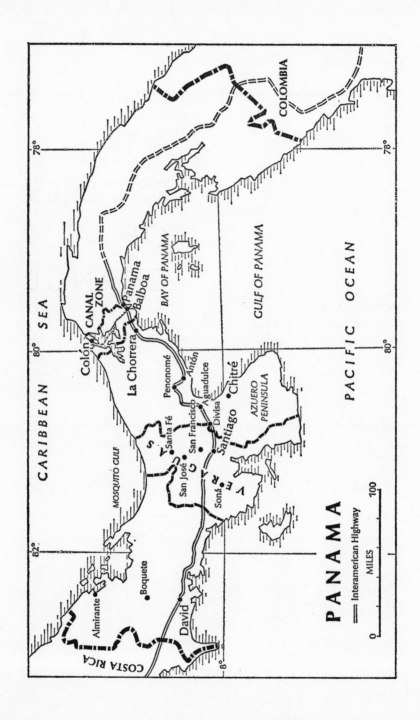

1

THE UNITED STATES AND REVOLUTION

It is troubling and ironic, though probably consistent with the history of nations, that America should at the moment of its greatest power and affluence be at the same time most profoundly in doubt concerning its purpose and direction. Signs of uncertainty and anxiety are abundant.

In Viet Nam we are emerging from a costly and bloody war, the causes of which were rooted in an obscure tangle of history. As a nation we have been bitterly in doubt about the nature and rightness of our commitment. We are uncertain about to whom it was made and why and whether the reasons that prompted it more than a decade ago continue to be good reasons today. We have wondered why we cannot "win," and worried that so much of the fruit of our idealism has been pitted with waste, corruption, and death to the innocent.

The Atlantic Alliance which we forged with the unparalleled generosity of the Marshall Plan has come apart. The grand vision with which we emerged from World War II has soured and seems today to smack of arrogance. European confidence today nourishes itself on resentment and antagonism toward the United States, both its government and its business.

In Latin America the initial vision and spiritual message of the Alliance for Progress have been blurred and garbled; the image of America is once more darkened by the suspicion of commitment to the status quo and, therefore, to resistance to change. Our efforts to promote economic development and political stability have been unsatisfactory. Conversely, one of the most hopeful political developments in the hemisphere, the Christian Democrat movement begun by Eduardo Frei Montalva in Chile and taken up by Rafael Caldera in Venezuela, has come about and is proceeding in several countries quite apart from our efforts. In fact, it appears that part of this movement's virility derives from its political and ideological independence from the United States, as well as its increasing affinity with Europe. And in Peru, Velasco's nationalism thrives partly on opposition to the United States.

Overshadowing all is the awareness that man's technological achievement has given him the awful capacity to destroy himself entirely; that peace, therefore, is not something merely to be sought, but is for the first time in the history of life on earth an absolute necessity for human continuity. Indeed, all other issues pale beside this one. It is becoming increasingly clear that peace —that is, survival—demands radical shifts in old attitudes and structures: integration and synthesis in all areas, social, political, and economic; the identification of new mutualities of interest; the diminution of old boundaries; the merging of nations into regions and regions into a world order. But the pursuit of peace is an oddly unpeaceful process, filled with the ingredients of conflict. Machinery for the resolution of these conflicts is, therefore, of paramount importance, but for its construction we must first be willing to establish a new ideology: a clear ordering of priorities, a determined set of values, a new framework of objectives and purposes.

Our old ideologies, to the extent we have had any, are inadequate. And the traditional pragmatic approach we tend to prefer is likewise proving increasingly sterile and incapable of providing the means and the measures through which we can make the decisions of the future. The programs of other countries are suffering like fates. Soviet communism and the other varieties of Marxian dogma are even more inadequate to the task. But this is small comfort.

Our dilemma would be less critical if change were not so

swift or its demands so radical and penetrating. Political and social change in the world today are often literally revolutionary, and survival depends upon the capacity to understand this and to give it order. The purposes of the United States with regard to such change are dangerously unclear.

Equally important—and this is a revolutionary concept in itself —we must break with the tradition of violence and upheaval that has characterized most revolutions in history. The theory that revolution must be synonymous with bloodshed has been self-perpetuating and will continue to be so as long as men refuse to accept radical change as a necessity, and even as a fairly common phenomenon in living.

This book will examine the nature and process of radical political, social, and economic change in Latin America. The issues of change, it will be seen, are basically philosophical and ideological, and to achieve the radical change the future inevitably demands for Latin America, the region must be understood in these terms and not merely in terms of economic and industrial backwardness.

To begin with, a word of apology and some definitions: This is not the work of an economist or a political or social scientist, or indeed of any other sort of professional specialist. Nor is it the effort of someone with a particular set of bureaucratic loyalties. It is rather the attempt of a random observer, who might pretend to the title of generalist, to collect critical but diverse aspects of today's revolutionary environment in a part of the world very important to us, and to relate them to the interests of the United States. Without being critical of the specialists or of those with policy-making or administrative responsibilities in governmental or entrepreneurial bureaucracies, it does appear that there is room for comment by the unspecialized nonbureaucrat on several counts.

First of all, the radical change we are facing is composed of inextricably connected elements which are political, social, economic, religious, cultural, psychological, and so on. These elements are apt to be distorted if they are isolated artificially for viewing by the high-powered microscope of the specialist. (It must be said, however, that it is from the work of many admirable specialists that much of the following synthesis has been composed.)

Secondly, bureaucracies, whether public or private, are designed of necessity to serve interests and meet challenges at particular moments which quickly pass by. We have long observed that as they grow, they develop within themselves substantial inertia which is apt to make them progressively conservative and conventional, and blind to the need for radical change.

Some of the words and terms of development, change, and modernization are particularly troublesome because they are used by specialists and generalists in many different ways.* I think I should, therefore, state as precisely as possible what I mean by several words which have been subject to various definitions.[1]

By *ideology* I mean a rational and organic vision of the nature and problems of a community in its being and in its becoming which is translated into a working plan often referred to as a *doctrine*. The plan becomes operable through a process we call *politics*, which can be defined as the way in which institutions, their leaders, and their members function.

There is general agreement on *feudalism*, which is quite alien to American economic and culture patterns. It is basically a socio-political system imposed on a rural economy. What is sometimes overlooked is that unlike some hierarchies, feudalism fuses, rather than distinguishes, the military, judicial, fiscal, and general administrative kinds of authority. In Europe and Latin America feudalism has been characterized by the existence of large, practically self-sufficient estates cultivated by peasants for

---

* A word about economists from Dr. Roberto de Oliveira Campos, former Minister of Planning of Brazil, banker, author, businessman, and himself one of Latin America's most eminent economists is relevant: ". . . it may well be said that the crucial issues of Latin American development are motivational and political in nature. Although there is no immediate danger that the economists will join the army of the unemployed, it is quite clear that they have left precious little that is new or unsaid on the mechanics of development. The floor must be given to the social psychologists and the political scientists. We economists must recognize that cross-fertilzation of the social sciences is perhaps the only way for us to regain fertility."

the profit of the owner. The peasants get a very small share of the crops in payment, as well as the use of parcels of land for their own purposes. Few systems have done such a thorough job of arbitrarily controlling a large mass of people.

Most people are in agreement that *revolution* means deep and radical changes in the social, political, and economic fabric of a nation or a people. By "radical change" I mean permanent reallocation of power; for example, recomposition of land-holding patterns, restructuring of credit and market systems, substantially different composition of ruling elites, and the imposition of new criteria for the distribution of wealth. But I want to distinguish revolution clearly from the anarchy, coups, or unorthodox changes in governmental leadership which have been so common in the developing world. Revolution involves the constant change which is proceeding underneath the chaos and the coups, reaching into every phase of work and life. It is an intentional attack on a political and moral order and a conscious effort to establish a new one. It has traditionally been accompanied by violence, but this need not always be so.[2]

This book considers the revolutionary process in Latin America because there it is particularly dramatic. Its outlines are bold and sharp; it is therefore convenient for analysis. The status quo is relatively easy to perceive; the nature, source, and effect of its power are relatively simple to describe. The failure of traditional revolutionaries and revolutionary ideologies—especially communism—is particularly clear. The shape and purpose of new forces which may carry forward the inevitable revolutionary process are increasingly perceptible.

Latin America is also useful because it is a mirror reflecting, at least in part, radical yearnings in other parts of the world: the student new left in the United States and Europe, the Black American, the disappointed Marxist, the disillusioned Communist, the purpose-seeking anarchist. After centuries on the sidelines of the world, Latin America may be on the verge of becoming an extraordinary testing-place wherein the world will see —and perhaps be enlightened by—different revolutionary courses being played out in response to differing choices being made by those who hold power. The courses may be dangerous or sublime:

bloody war, threatening world peace and survival; an intensified continuation of the smoldering, wasteful, aimless, mildly anarchic conflict of the past and a myopic groping for an inexplicit vision; or it may be a more or less consciously directed and organized effort to secure revolutionary change with a maximum of peace, independence, and justice.

It is still within the capacity of the United States to affect which course the revolution follows. We are, however, in grave danger of losing that capacity because of our long-standing refusal to face the contradiction in our policies and programs between change and stability. We have advocated change, but we have generally acted to promote stability. We have in countless ways placed ourselves athwart the inevitable revolutionary process; occasionally, we have been at war with it. Such behavior, if continued, will almost certainly reduce or even eliminate United States influence over the revolution's course and will tend to insure that we are branded its enemy. To be an enemy of the inevitable is a guarantee of defeat; more important, to use our power to impede the revolutionary process in Latin America is immoral by the standards which we ourselves use to judge a good community.

In a real sense the dilemma is ideological. Our long preoccupation with anticommunism has delayed our formulation of an acceptable revolutionary alternative and has diverted us from using our great power and resources to lead in the construction of new structures for a new order. Our principal enemy today is philosophical: it is our own predilection for crisis-oriented pragmatism.

I shall propose radical changes not only in our foreign policy, but in the institutions created to carry it out. Both have become mired in outdated assumptions extrapolated into the future through the workings of tradition, inertia, chance, imperception, and ignorance. I shall make similar proposals for American business. A radical restructuring of American philosophy as well as of bureaucracy is needed if this country is to protect its national interests and contribute to the development of other areas of the world.

I

If the United States is to secure its vital interests in Latin America, it must understand better the nature of revolution in our hemisphere. It must also define and determine more precisely our relationship and commitment to that revolution and revise accordingly the policies and programs, both private and public, which it employs in the region.

Americans have a tendency to suppose that actions speak louder than words, yet the words of John F. Kennedy were perhaps the most important factor in those first years of the Alliance—his assertion that the United States was a revolutionary country, that the American people profoundly supported the irresistible demands of the people of Latin America for radical, social, political, and economic change; that we were concerned only that the revolution be constructive, serving its own highest and noblest ends; and that its independence be protected against those who would subvert it for imperialistic purposes.

"Let us transform the American continent into a vast crucible of revolutionary ideas and efforts," said President Kennedy in March 1961.[3]

This was the galvanizing mystique which helped put his picture in the huts of the interior, in workers' housing projects of the cities, in *tiendas,* gas stations, and schoolhouses throughout the hemisphere. These were the words which could have made our intervention in the Dominican Republic more understandable and acceptable in Latin America. We missed the mark in that instance. Basing our action on the need to save lives and on an ill-defined anticommunism, we were made to appear antirevolutionary. In fact, we entered a chaotic rather than a revolutionary situation, in which the real and legitimate revolution of the people of the Dominican Republic was being endangered by those who were using it for imperialistic purposes. We should have been seeking to protect the independence of the revolution, and we should have said so.

While today our actions and programs are little different than in 1961—they may even be improved—our words, our message, our philosophy, our ideology, are more obscure. Those in the hemisphere who realize the need of constructive revolution, understanding that without it will come the destructive variety, are floundering for leadership and are vulnerable. They will not turn to the source of money or aid, but to where the ideas for a new society shine brightest and clearest.

An observer of our efforts in Latin America in the past decade cannot avoid the vision of a generous people expending considerable material resources in a struggle which is fundamentally not materialistic and which cannot be won without clear and consistent ideological statements and restatements on our part, accompanied by action based on a more precise understanding of the nature of revolution and the consequent requirements of successful development.

I will attempt to show that economic and technical inputs must be preceded or accompanied by the creation of new political and social institutions. Such socio-political organizations would be both mechanisms for the receipt of economic and technical elements and engines of change. They can be built by many different kinds of powers or agents—governmental, nongovernmental, entrepreneurial, social, and cooperative. Material or technical injections falling outside such structures are largely ineffectual in development, except as the vagaries of chance may make them otherwise. The fact is that there is no necessary connection or relevance between economic development and political growth and stability. The conventional American assumption that there is a causal relationship between economic assistance, economic development, and political stability is wrong. As Samuel P. Huntington of Harvard says: "Economic development and political stability are two independent goals and progress toward one has no necessary connection with progress toward the other." [4]

Eduardo Frei Montalva, President of Chile, puts this thought in another way:

> The problem is that what was fundamental to the Alliance for Progress—a revolutionary approach to the need for reform—has not been achieved. Less than half of the Latin American countries have started serious programs of agrarian

reform. Drastic changes in the tax system are even scarcer, while the number of genuinely democratic regimes, far from increasing, has actually declined. In other words, there has been no strengthening of the political and social foundations for economic progress in Latin America. This is the reason why the ultimate objective of the Alliance—the formation of just, stable, democratic and dynamic societies —is as distant today as it was five years ago.

Several experiences indicate that economic progress alone does not suffice to ensure the building of truly free societies and peaceful international coexistence. The problem does not stem solely from the inadequate flow of internal financial resources. What has been lacking is a clear ideological direction and determination on the part of the political leaders to bring about change. These two factors are intimately related and they involve the collective political responsibility of all the members of the Alliance.[5]

Much of our difficulty in South Viet Nam as well as in Latin America has arisen from our failure to act on this principle.

2

It is useful and interesting to put this notion alongside the theory of economic development which Walt W. Rostow sets forth in his farseeing work, *The Stages of Economic Growth: A Non-Communist Manifesto.* Rostow notes a number of requirements for the "take-off" of traditional societies into a period of sustained growth, and says that the critical take-off into economic development requires first what by our definition is revolution or radical change, and, secondly, the creation of a certain kind of "new political, social and institutional framework." [6]

The importance of communism does not lie in its ideology, which has become progressively obscure and unattractive, but rather in the fact that it is a relatively effective (if inhumane) form of power seizure, organization, and control. In the Soviet Union and Red China it can impose a centralized dictatorship with the pervasive kinds of control which are necessary to effect change and create the framework necessary for growth. This

explains why so many of the nations of Latin America as well
as Africa and Asia often find themselves subject to various forms
of dictatorship. The difficulty in Latin America, at least, has been
that few if any dictators have regarded "the modernization of the
economy as serious, high-order political business," nor have they
espoused "radical shifts" in social attitudes.[7]

Latin America's history of failure to establish effective political
institutions that would embrace substantial portions of its population has meant that repeatedly it has confounded the expectations
of traditional socio-economic thinkers. For example, while all
the normal social and economic indicators of growth made it
appear that Argentina was in the "take-off" stage as early as
1935, its per-capita income since that time has been almost
stagnant. There has been little or no change which can be
described as either progress or development.[8]

Rostow also emphasizes the critical role of agriculture in the
development process, noting that "most take-offs have been
preceded or accompanied by radical change in agricultural techniques and market organization." [9] He points out that an increased food supply will be necessary to feed a rising population
and increasing urban concentrations, and to minimize loss of
foreign exchange through food imports. New socio-political
organizations are thus particularly important in rural areas, where
they affect farmers and agriculture.

Dimly, perhaps, we can begin to perceive the snares which
have trammeled the United States in the revolutionary world, in
its foreign aid program as well as in some of its business ventures. We can also begin to see the exciting outlines of broad
new opportunities, new ways and forms, of new possibilities for
the promotion not only of our national interests but of world
order and peace.

First, the snares. American foreign aid began in 1948 with
the miraculously successful Marshall Plan, which injected money
and material into the deflated European structure. The all-important fact was that there was a structure: there were modern
men skilled in the organization of industry and government;
there were cohesive communities with long and tested political
traditions; and there were confident and practical dreamers with

new visions of economic and political integration extending the cohesion across national boundaries to make a new European entity. Exhilarated and inspired by our success in Europe, we sought to extend the formula to the underdeveloped world. It was not long before disenchantment set in. There was no deflated structure to inflate. Either there was no effective structure at all, or that which existed was inefficient, corrupt, or retrogressive— sometimes all three. In general, therefore, our money and material was either wasted or used to foster and sustain a structure, a regime, or an elite which was slated for radical change or abandonment.

The formula was changed to concentrate our aid on "institutional development," that is, education, health, industry, government services, and the like. But this material and moral support generally has solidified the status quo, contrary to the requirements of continuing development; most of the governments through which we distributed our assistance had neither the will nor the capacity to make efficient use of it. David E. Bell, the exceptionally capable administrator of the Agency for International Development from 1962 to 1966, spoke of "the growing emphasis on self-help by aid recipients." [10] But too often "self-help" has been a delusion. To be genuine it requires a level of motivation, organization, and competence which is just not present in much of the revolutionary world. Governments and their agencies, however, have become extremely adept at feigning "self-help." This has led to increasing corruption, a natural result of forcing on an administrative unit expectations which it is incapable of fulfilling. In South Viet Nam we deluged the countryside with everything from tin roofs and schoolhouses to hogs and fertilizer, under the misapprehension that we were strengthening local government in what we liked to think was a "self-help" process. In fact, there was little which remotely resembled "local government" in the rural areas of South Viet Nam—and the same is true of most of Latin America.

A related snare develops out of the use of foreign aid as a means of discouraging violence, disorder, and conflict. Former Defense Secretary McNamara stated our policy in this area most succinctly when he declared in 1966 that there was an irrefutable relationship between violence and economic backwardness. He pointed out that of the thirty-eight very poor nations with a per-capita income of less than $100 a year, thirty-two had experienced important internal conflicts since 1958.

Secretary McNamara's argument that there is a direct relationship between poverty and instability arouses hopes which are bound to be disappointed. Indeed, if one were to attempt a rule relating income to political instability, the record would seem to show that rapid economic growth is a major cause of chaos and violence.

Crane Brinton some years ago showed in his analysis of the period preceding the French Revolution that it was the prosperous middle class which was loudest in its condemnation of the monarchy and which refused to save it by paying taxes.[11] It is not too much to suggest that very similar groups were responsible for Castro's success in Cuba, which as a nation had one of the highest per-capita incomes in Latin America at the time of the revolution.

This is not to argue that economic misery and poverty among large numbers of the population may not be a factor in violence and instability, or may not in fact share some common causes with it. Surely, as in Cuba and South Viet Nam, the vulnerability of the countryside to exploitation by organized revolutionaries is partly the effect of economic want. More important, however, the vulnerability would seem to be the result of a complex set of political, social, and economic factors conspiring to produce among the masses of the people a sense of helplessness, hopelessness, isolation, and depression.[12]

In Asia and Africa, ethnic, racial, and tribal factors as well as the remnants of colonialism would seem to be much greater causes of instability than poverty. Political extremism is also typically stronger in the wealthier than in the poorer sections of a country. In Italy the center of communist strength was the prosperous north rather than the poverty-stricken south. In India the communists have flourished in Kerala (with the highest literacy among Indian states) and in industrialized Calcutta, not in the economically more backward areas. In Latin America communist and other radical movements have been strongest in Cuba, Argentina, Chile, and Venezuela, four of the five wealthiest countries in per-capita income.

Yet communism is not necessarily the principal or even an important cause of revolution and violence, especially in Latin America. The causes are much more profound and varied; communism may have been quicker to understand them and more adept at utilizing the chaos and confusion with which revolution is always accompanied to gain power. But the misconceptions about the simple poverty-instability relationship to which so many United States officials have adhered has caused basic difficulties in executing our foreign aid program and fulfilling our foreign objectives.

The escape route from these snares takes us back to the requirement, cited earlier, for new socio-political receptacle-engines. Their design and operation raise additional questions: In what direction do these engines of change move? What is the nature of the revolutionary environment within which they operate and which indeed they help to form? What are the inevitabilities of the change process? Over what do we, the United States—government or business—have influence? What real alternatives do we have? And perhaps most important, what are the vital interests or objectives involved in making the selection?

THE ENVIRONMENT

2

THE ECONOMY: The Structures of Power and Poverty

To our south are close to 300 million people, increasing at the rate of about 3 per cent a year. About 40 per cent are less than fifteen years old and one half are less than twenty. Within thirty years Latin America will contain some 600 million people, or 10 per cent of the total world population. In 1900 it had about 5 per cent.[1]

These people occupy a land area which is one million square miles larger than the United States and China combined. They come from widely different parts of the world, representing many races. A substantial proportion are Indians, whose ancestors migrated from East Asia more than 10,000 years ago and who established the great Indian empires in what is now principally Mexico, Guatemala, Ecuador, Bolivia, and Peru. Others are Negroes, whose forebears were slaves from Africa. A minority are Europeans, descendants of the Spanish and Portuguese conquerors, and more recent immigrants from Italy, Germany, Britain, and other countries. The majority are a mixture, *mestizos* (Indian and European) and mulattos (African and European).

Population growth has withered real per-capita GNP to an increase of about 1.6 per cent a year since 1960, actually less than in previous years and well below the minimum increase of 2.5 per cent a year which the Alliance for Progress set as necessary for the achievement of its social and economic objectives (see Table

TABLE I

Average Growth in Real Gross Domestic Product
Per Capita, 1961–6

Country	Per Cent
Nicaragua	5.3
Panama	4.8
Bolivia	3.6
Peru	3.2
Guatemala	3.0
El Salvador	2.8
Mexico	2.7
Chile	2.6
Honduras	1.6
Dominican Republic	1.5
Colombia	1.4
Brazil	1.2
Paraguay	1.2
Venezuela	1.2
Argentina	1.1
Costa Rica	.8
Ecuador	.7
Uruguay	—1.5
All Latin America	1.8

Source: Yves Maroni, "Economic Trends in Latin America in the 1960's," Federal Reserve Board staff paper, April 26, 1967, p. 4.

1).* There has been an actual drop in per-capita production of food during the last eight years.[2] Total investment in Latin America as a percentage of GNP has generally declined, and in the past decade or so productivity has virtually stood still.[3]

* Preliminary data for 1968 shows a rise of 5.5 per cent in Latin America's gross national product over 1967, which amounts to 2.5 per cent per capita. This followed two consecutive years when per-capita growth was only 4.3 per cent, or 1.4 per cent per capita. The 1968 increase was due largely to higher exports of the region's major commodities—copper, meat, cotton, and coffee—which can be expected to encounter continuing difficulties on world markets. (CIAP Report, *The New York Times*, February 4, 1969, p. 1.)

Dr. Roberto Campos lists Latin America's most crucial development problems as low agricultural productivity, population growth, inadequacy of "human capital," the control of inflation, and the passing of the era of easy import-substitution.[4]

The twenty-one countries of Latin America abound with stark and dramatic contrasts: 900,000 people exist in the half-life of slime, squalor, and disease around the breathtaking beauty of Rio de Janeiro, while further south in São Paulo some five million people are building one of the chief industrial centers of the world, making more automobiles than all of Russia, consuming more electricity per person than Chicago, and eating in 8,000 restaurants, surrounded by suburban sprawl.

More than 100 million peasants are landless or own plots which are scarcely sufficient for subsistence. In general, 5 per cent of the population owns half of the cultivable land. In some countries land holdings of 250,000 acres or more are not unusual.[5] The decreasing agricultural production requires that more and more food be imported, using scarce foreign exchange and raising food prices (see Table 2). It is not too much to suggest that Latin America will experience starvation of famine proportions within five years if there is not a radical change in the factors which affect food production and distribution.

While the volume of world trade has doubled since 1938, exports of Latin American countries have increased by only some 70 per cent (40 per cent if petroleum products are excluded). Although the region once accounted for 8 per cent of world trade, the figure now is only 6.5 per cent. This situation is partly attributable to the steady decline of world prices during the last decade for such major Latin American exports as sugar and coffee. Debt servicing and profit remittances have contributed to a net capital outflow from the region of some $110 million annually from 1961 to 1966. This reduction in Latin American capital resources compares to a net inflow of about $220 million annually from 1956 to 1960.

Feudalism flourishes in some of its most crippling forms. In the high Andean plains one can still see advertisements for the sale of "50 acres, five horses and 10 Indians." The majority of the people live in grinding poverty, weakened by malnutrition

TABLE 2

Country	Total Production					
	1961	1962	1963	1964	1965	1966
Total—19 Republics	111	114	119	117	130	125
—CAEC*	119	128	135	142	143	142
Argentina	100	102	116	114	104	111
Bolivia	106	104	109	111	109	111
Brazil	114	114	119	109	141	123
Chile	108	103	109	112	111	111
Colombia	106	111	112	111	118	115
Costa Rica*	118	118	117	110	114	129
Dominican Republic	107	109	108	104	101	106
Ecuador	121	121	120	125	132	138
El Salvador*	125	125	139	143	125	131
Guatemala*	117	136	142	140	161	146
Haiti	109	98	90	89	90	85
Honduras*	110	115	116	126	134	124
Mexico	111	121	123	133	143	145
Nicaragua*	123	144	157	197	182	190
Panama	104	103	106	118	136	135
Paraguay	106	112	114	112	116	112
Peru	123	128	127	130	128	129
Uruguay	109	109	115	123	119	110
Venezuela	109	118	134	136	144	150
Other Latin America						
Guyana	121	121	108	116	127	126
Jamaica	110	109	113	120	124	124
Trinidad and Tobago	113	104	111	106	114	113

NOTE: Bulk of production in calendar year shown. P — Preliminary.
Source: U.S. Department of Agriculture, Economic Research Service.

Indexes of Total Agricultural Production by Country
1957–9 = 100

1967	1968P	Per Capita Production							
		1961	1962	1963	1964	1965	1966	1967	1968P
129	132	102	102	103	98	106	99	100	99
150	155	108	113	115	117	114	109	112	112
119	119	95	95	107	103	93	98	103	101
107	113	99	95	98	97	93	93	87	90
127	129	104	101	103	91	115	97	97	96
114	119	101	94	97	98	95	92	93	95
121	125	96	98	96	92	95	89	91	91
136	152	105	101	97	88	88	96	98	106
106	100	96	94	90	84	79	80	77	70
145	141	110	107	103	103	106	107	109	102
139	135	115	111	120	119	101	102	105	98
155	158	106	119	120	115	128	112	115	114
85	89	103	91	82	79	79	73	71	73
137	143	100	101	99	104	107	96	102	103
146	154	100	106	104	109	113	111	108	110
186	197	113	128	135	164	146	147	139	142
138	144	95	91	91	98	109	105	104	105
117	122	98	101	100	95	95	89	90	91
123	119	113	114	110	109	104	102	94	88
97	99	105	103	107	113	108	99	86	87
160	162	98	102	112	110	113	113	117	114
138	138	112	108	94	98	104	101	107	104
116	109	105	103	104	108	109	106	97	88
112	120	103	92	95	88	92	90	87	90

* — Central American Economic Community countries (CAEC).

TABLE 3

Per-Capita Gross National Product
(Constant 1966 prices; in U.S. Dollars)

	Per Capita GNP		Per Cent Change	
	1966	1967[P]	1966	1967[P]
Total, 18 Latin American Republics	411	419	1.3	1.9
Subtotal, 5 Central American Common Market Republics	303	304	1.4	0.5
Venezuela	879	900	−0.7	2.4
Argentina	716	724	−2.4	1.2
Panama	546	579	6.3	6.1
Chile	556	563	3.9	1.2
Uruguay	569	547	1.2	−4.0
Mexico	493	510	4.0	3.5
Costa Rica	405	409	2.5	1.0
Nicaragua	331	333	−0.1	0.6
Brazil	307	313	1.4	2.0
Guatemala	309	308	1.2	−0.3
Peru	295	299	2.3	1.2
Colombia	293	297	2.2	1.4
El Salvador	281	284	2.2	0.9
Dominican Republic	266	264	8.3	−0.6
Ecuador	237	243	1.6	2.5
Honduras	230	231	0.7	0.5
Paraguay	225	225	−1.2	0.0
Bolivia	156	162	4.5	3.8

[P] Preliminary

Source: Office of Regional Policies and Programs, Bureau for Latin America, Agency for International Development.

and intestinal disease, many unable to read and write, resigned to an early death.

Most political regimes are unstable and administrative bureaucracies weak. Large sections of the countryside are beyond the effective reach, control, and, in some cases, interest of national governments. The majority of the people have no sense of participation or representation in the political system.

"In many ways Latin America is a creature of dispersion," writes Dr. Arturo Morales-Carrión, "geographical dispersion, cultural dispersion, power dispersion. It has belonged to the world of the political invertebrates since the Napoleonic times. You cannot deal with it as with the well-rounded coherent power entities—the political vertebrates—in the contemporary period: England, France, Germany, Russia, Japan, even China."[6]

United States business has invested some $10 billion in Latin America, or about 18 per cent of its direct foreign investments. Between 1961 and 1966 United States government assistance to Latin America totaled more than $6.5 billion in grants and loans. While the region has enormous potential resources, sufficient to make it among the richest regions of the world, it is today a caldron of uncertainty. Its order is crucial to the world's order; its peace to ours.

Our interests lie in understanding the forces which are at work in Latin America—their relationship to one another, the pressure which is behind them and the targets ahead; in measuring carefully without myth or preconception, freed as far as possible from extraneous and irrelevant experience, what is inevitable and what is susceptible to influence. It may seem arrogant to suggest that we must measure our influence, but to do otherwise is to be like the foolish ostrich.

I

The distance and gaps which separate Latin America's communities and countries from one another, regional disparateness, remoteness, and isolation contributes greatly, as Morales-Carrión has said, to the disintegrated state of Latin America. Apart from a reasonably complete and integrated air system, transportation in Latin America is inadequate or nonexistent. There are three major transport systems in the region, in Mexico, southern Brazil, and Argentina. Secondary systems exist in Chile, Venezuela, Colombia, Peru, Cuba, and Uruguay, and are being formed in Central America and Northeast Brazil. Though some of these systems are linked with one another, there is little traffic between them. Most of the goods traffic in Latin America is between cities and their adjacent countrysides, ports and inland localities, or ports and other continents, principally Europe and North America. The Andean spine and the jungles of the Amazon and southern Panama are serious natural obstacles to a coordinated continental transport system.[7]

Although air transport is more expensive than other forms, its use is increasing rapidly because so much time is saved. In the early days of the construction of Brasilia, many building materials were flown in. Meat is transported by air to Caracas from remote ranches in the *llanos* of Venezuela, and cement, machine parts, and beer are flown into areas of the Peruvian *selva* not served by road, rail, or river. Sears, Roebuck has even found it economical to fly mattresses from Panama to other outlets in Central America.

Total length of rail lines in Latin America is about one third of that in North America, but tonnage handled is far less—48,000 million kilometer-tons for all of Latin America in 1961, compared with 96,000 million for Canada and 822,000 million for the United States. Some 80 per cent of that tonnage was accounted for by Argentina, Mexico, and Brazil. Almost all rail lines in Latin America are single track and many are of different gauges, which makes train service inconvenient and slow. It takes four days and nights, for example, to go by train from La Paz to Buenos Aires, a trip which can be made in a few hours by plane.

While many Latin American countries in recent years have embarked on extensive road-building programs (Brazil's being one of the most ambitious in the world), the number of commercial vehicles in the region is only slightly more than that of Canada, which has less than one tenth as large a population. In spite of impressive total lengths of roads, very few of them are paved and many cannot be used during the wet season. A considerable proportion are one lane, like the one-track railroads, so that traffic has to go in different directions on alternate days.

The Pan-American Highway, now complete except for a section between Panama City and Colombia, will join the principal road systems of Latin America. Although it is quite unlikely that it will be used as a commercial throughway, the highway does provide good transport within countries and has encouraged some international linkages, particularly in Central America. It has also served as a starting place for feeder roads into the countryside.

Transport and transport policy become crucial when we consider the problems of regional integration and the development of a Latin American common market. For example, in 1968 exports and imports among Latin American countries were only 7 per cent and 10 per cent, respectively, of total trade.[8] It is also important because of the gaps and strains which exist between rural and urban segments of the population.

2

Today about half of Latin America lives in towns of more than 2,500 inhabitants, the figure going to well above 60 per cent of the population in Argentina, Chile, and Uruguay. This is a much higher proportion of urban dwellers than exists in Africa, India, or China, and is not far below that of Japan and the Soviet Union.[9] Furthermore, projected growth rates indicate that by 1970 the population of Latin America will be predominantly urban.[10] In 1960 the region had nine metropolitan areas with a population of more than a million. Today there are 18 and by 1980 it is expected that there will be 26, ten of which will have more than 2.5 million people.

Latin Americans are leaving the countryside for the cities, partly because, incredibly enough, they can get more to eat there. Although urbanization is normally assumed to indicate increasing prosperity, industrialization, and modernization, this does not appear to be a correct assumption for Latin America. In even the more advanced countries only 10 to 15 per cent of the labor force is employed in industrial enterprises of five or more workers.[11] This compares, for example, with 26 per cent in Belgium, which is substantially less urbanized than those Latin American countries. The nice assumptions that urbanization and industrialization lead to greater access to education and thus to increased social mobility do not seem to hold up under examination either, as was proved by the most intensive study yet made of social mobility in a Latin American city (São Paulo).[12] In spite of the fact that São Paulo's industrialization and growth have probably outpaced that of any other city in Latin America, the study could find no evidence of an acceleration in the rate of upward social movement since the turn of the century. It should be noted, incidentally, that "education," which may flourish in the cities and is certainly a primary goal of development efforts everywhere, does not necessarily effect either social or economic change.

The cities are swelling because the countryside cannot support its people. They are being inflated artificially while they still lack the resources, organizations, or institutions to absorb and utilize the influx. Slums, for example, are growing in most places at five times the rate of new low-cost housing. It had been generally assumed that these vast armies of idle urbanites would become sources of violence and political agitation. Again, Latin America has surprised its observers. The striking, if not shocking, characteristic of urban migrant slum-dwellers is their lack of complaint and political action. Despite the appalling squalor in which they live, migrants apparently experience a comparative improvement over what they had known in the countryside and have higher hopes for their children's future. This phenomenon helps to explain the political conservatism of Latin American cities and, perhaps indirectly, the comparative radicalism of its rural areas.[13]

Latin America's rural malaise and urban artificiality may well arise from its colonial history. In contrast to cities in the United States, for example, Latin America's cities were founded and grew long before the outlying countryside was settled or cultivated. The region was from the start an urban civilization, devoted primarily to the exploitation of mineral wealth, with only the most superficial attention being given to the cultivation of land. Insofar as the land was developed, it was by landowners, many of whom lived in the cities and operated their vast holdings through others. Land settlement was therefore apt to be casual and disorderly. Towns did not grow around farming communities but rather were way stations on the routes between principal cities. Furthermore, the culture of these cities was imported from Europe, forming an artificial overlay, smothering the genuine indigenous culture which might have formed had the development process been more balanced.

3

Another debilitating cycle of causes and effects has produced a shortage of capital available for investment in Latin American countries. Perhaps the most serious problem, economically as well as politically and psychologically, is the flight of capital from the region. It is estimated that anywhere from $8 to $10 billion of Latin American money is kept in foreign banks or invested in the United States or Europe.[14] These funds, which may easily equal ten years' financial assistance from the United States under the Alliance for Progress, are urgently needed, not only for entrepreneurial ventures, but also to finance roads, land reform, schools, and hospitals.

Much of the drained money is in the baggage of dictators or former dictators and their entourage. Rafael Trujillo, who admitted to no special talent for business, amassed a fortune during his thirty-year rule in the Dominican Republic which is estimated to have been among the five or six largest in the world.[15] Little of this was invested in his homeland.

More insidious than the work of recognized villains, however, is the quiet but persistent action of Latin America's wealthiest and most respected citizens who take their money from where it was made and put it in other countries where they think it will be safe. They trust neither their governments nor their countrymen; they see no wrong in bleeding their already bloodless communities; they are, therefore, presumably ready to jump themselves and to follow their money to safety abroad when and if that too becomes necessary. That a leading elite of any community should be so motivated raises the question as to whether the political entity of which they are an important part can legitimately be called a nation.

We are not now talking of the surreptitious actions of a few; we are describing, rather, a general characteristic of the Latin American oligarch, which has a major impact on government policy. The very threat of increasing the flight of capital is sufficient to cripple even the strongest government and frighten it from making much-needed reforms in taxation, for instance.[16]

Another cause for the scarcity of capital in Latin America is the disadvantageous terms of trade. The prices which the region can effectively place on its agricultural exports are decreasing, while those on the manufactured goods it must import are rising.

When the Alliance for Progress was launched in 1961, it was hoped that United States private investment in Latin America during the decade would total $3 billion, or about $300 million in new investments each year. But the advent of Castro and the accompanying strife and instability has caused this investment to drop sharply below expectations. In 1961 it was $173 million. In 1962 there was a net outflow of only $32 million. This trend was aggravated by Brazil's expropriation of the International Telephone and Telegraph Company and the American and Foreign Power Company in 1962, and by Argentina's cancellation of the contracts with the Argentine Petroleum Authority, under which foreign oil companies were developing that country's oil resources. While these actions may have fulfilled campaign pledges, kindled the fires of nationalism, and provided superficial solace to the demagogues, it is as yet hard to perceive any benefit to the people of the countries concerned. In 1963 the trend reversed, with a net inflow of $78 million, and United States investment has continued upward since then, reaching $191 million in 1967.[17] The improved situation resulted partly from such movements toward political stability as the victory of Rómulo Betancourt's reform government in the Venezuelan elections of 1963, despite Cuban agents' attempts at sabotage; and the rise of reform-minded governments in Chile and Colombia. In general, however, as was cited earlier, more capital regularly leaves Latin America than comes in. Much of the outflow is in the servicing of United States loans.

In Mexico too, in spite of a vigorous program of "Mexicanization" and numerous associated constraints, the climate for investment has been improving steadily, because Mexico has had the confidence and political strength to define clearly the criteria and priorities by which it will assess foreign investment. These are subject to change, and a foreign company can count on few guarantees, but at the same time it can be relatively confident of Mexican cooperation if its operation is consistent with Mexican needs: if it is providing goods or services which are essential and if the capacity and resources it brings are scarce locally. Food processing, for example, enjoys a most favored position in Mexico today.

In addition, substantial impetus to new investment has been brought to Latin America through the imaginative organization of foreign capital by the Atlantic Community Development Group for Latin America (ADELA). Stimulated by Senators Jacob K. Javits and Hubert H. Humphrey, ADELA was formed in 1964 under the leadership of Standard Oil of New Jersey and FIAT of Italy. It has been responsible for the investment of more than $70 million in development projects. Participating companies include IBM World Trade Corporation, Sybetra S.A. of Belgium, the Swiss Bank Corporation, Ford, First National City Bank, Coca-Cola, Chrysler, Dow, Dupont, Caterpillar Tractor, Deere, U.S. Steel, Gulf Oil, Seagrams, Midland Bank Ltd., Commerzbank A.G., and a Japanese consortium.[18]

A more subtle but extremely important cause of inadequate capital in Latin America is the traditional and persistent neglect of agriculture. Failure to use its vast land resources efficiently or effectively has resulted in immeasurable waste, required the use of scarce foreign exchange in order to import foods, stimulated recurrent cycles of inflation, and perpetuated archaic political and social institutions and relationships.

A different aspect of the capital problem is revealed in the phenomenon that the rich are getting richer and the poor are getting poorer. An annual increase of 4 per cent in the gross national product over and above population growth is considered extremely high in Latin America. Very few countries have met the goal of 2.5 per cent set by the Alliance for Progress. Nevertheless, let us apply a theoretical 5 per cent growth rate to Brazil and the United States. To the Brazilian who is subsisting on $150 a year, if we assume equal distribution, it means a $6 increase. To the North American, however, who receives $3,000 a year it means a rise of $120. Obvious as this may be, it reflects something which is not so obvious: namely, that to measure development in such rough terms as GNP is misleading if not completely fallacious. Not only is the wealth gap increasing between Latin America and the industrial north, but it is also increasing between the rural and urban sections of individual countries.

4

Deeply entwined in Latin America's development dilemma is the vicious circle of problems associated with trade. Most Latin American countries are heavily dependent upon one or two commodities for the foreign exchange which they increasingly need in order to buy from the industrial world the manufactured goods that they cannot produce at home. The prices of these few commodities—coffee, sugar, copper, and the like—are subject to radical and rapid fluctuations in world markets; the overall trend of these fluctuations has been and is likely to continue to be downward. Latin American leaders, fired with a sense of injustice at this state of affairs, are convinced that the international trading system is stacked against them—and they want it changed.

Latin America is, of course, not alone in this dilemma. Dr. Raúl Prebisch, a Latin American economist and secretary general of the United Nations Conference on Trade and Development (UNCTAD), contends that prices for the farm and ore products which the poor nations as a whole sell to the rich have fallen 12 per cent since 1957. At the same time, the machinery, transport, and technical equipment which industrial nations sell to the underdeveloped countries have risen in price. The result has been a 16 per cent decline in the balance of trade of the poor nations in ten years. This means that the payments received by them for their products has fallen 16 per cent in terms of what they must pay for their purchases abroad. In ten years this has caused a drop of more than $13 billion in the earnings received by the poor nations for their exports.[19]

Other factors complicate the problem for Latin America, whose share of world exports fell from 8.6 per cent to 5.9 per cent between 1956 and 1965.[20] The instability of foreign markets for raw materials has caused widespread and often unpredictable unemployment and inflation. Investment in industries producing primarily for local markets has been low, causing prices for local commodities to be high, keeping worker incomes low, and retarding industrial growth and productivity. Many Latin American export industries are controlled by foreign companies, and this fact, added to the helplessness which Latin Americans feel in the face of the international trading system, produces a particularly debilitating condition of frustration. This shows itself generally either in hopeless resignation or in irrational anger, but rarely in a continuing determination to take the radical and painful steps at home requisite to remedy the situation. A poignant example is the case of Chile, which is heavily dependent on two United States copper companies for its export earnings. In 1964 Chile projected exports valued at $520 million, of which $450 million was copper ore. In other words, in that year 87 per cent of Chile's export receipts depended upon copper. If the price of copper were to drop 10 per cent, Chile would lose $45 million in purchasing power. During the 1950's, the United States decision to stockpile copper badly distorted the Chilean economy and later caused serious hardship.

To give some other examples: Colombia derives roughly 63 per cent of its export earnings from coffee; Bolivia, 53 per cent from tin; Brazil, 43 per cent from coffee; Ecuador, 52 per cent from bananas; Honduras and Panama, roughly 50 per cent from bananas; Venezuela, 92 per cent from petroleum; and Chile, 83 per cent from copper. Mexico has the most diversified exports, with cotton being dominant and accounting for about 13 per cent of the total.[21] Peru's exports are also relatively well balanced, fish meal and copper accounting for 23 per cent and 27 per cent, respectively.

Latin American politicians and businessmen have besought the industrialized countries, particularly the United States, to guarantee markets for traditional export commodities at what they call "just prices." But, as Lincoln Gordon points out: "If these guaranteed markets were to be for products in stagnant demand in the industrialized countries, this would amount to an inefficient and quite inequitable form of barely disguised aid. . . ." [22] It would also, in effect, be subsidizing and thereby supporting and solidifying the inefficient and archaic land and agricultural systems which are becoming increasingly unacceptable politically.

While Gordon does not minimize Latin America's trade difficulties, he refutes the frequent allegations of the "constant deterioration of the terms of trade," arguing that they have actually improved by 10 per cent since 1962 and "have been remarkably stable during the past three years [i.e., 1964–7]." He contends that most Latin Americans have been "singularly backward" in taking advantage of existing market opportunities in the more industrialized countries. Those who experiment with new products try to find markets at home, and governmental policies discourage the expansion of exports.

Gordon hopes that the attitudes induced by economic integration within Latin America, with its pressures for greater competitiveness and cost consciousness, will be reflected as well in greater export efforts for nontraditional products in world markets. There are no panaceas for the Latin American trade problem; neither commodity agreements nor preferential arrangements by themselves offer comprehensive solutions. Gordon says: "The only satisfactory long-run solution lies in development itself, in the industrialization and agricultural modernization and diversification of the Latin economies, with priority for the production at competitive costs of items in growing world demand." He believes that the natural and human resources of the continent should make this perfectly feasible and advocates "objective joint analysis of obstacles and remedies rather than . . . doctrinaire confrontations invoking abstract principles of equity." [23]

This prescription, while perhaps rational and wise, provides small comfort to Latin Americans, who see themselves weak and vulnerable in any such "objective analysis." More deeply and darkly, they see that their difficulties are rooted in the inadequacies of their political, economic, and social structures and in the pain and fear of changing those structures.

Policies designed to increase exports and decrease imports of manufactured goods have had unfortunate secondary effects.

There has been, for example, a widespread adoption of import substitution, accompanied by high protective tariffs, often climbing as high as 500 per cent. In many cases this policy has fostered high-cost, inefficient industries which are effectively insulated from the energizing effects of real competition. While they may flourish for a time, the small market for their expensive products is quickly satiated and they invariably languish, with substantial unused capacity. The export of manufactured goods from Latin America has also been deterred by the tariff structures of the advanced countries. Although raw and partly processed materials generally enter these countries duty free or at low duties, manufacturers bear high duties.[24]

The demands of world trade and markets on Latin America raise a host of questions: Where will the managerial and technical skills and the capital required for new industries come from? What will these new industries most likely be? If they are in part related to agriculture, and to food production, processing, and packaging, as regional needs would seem to suggest, what will be the effect on land systems, on the elites, on political power? Finally, what are the requirements to make the revolutionary impact of a solution to Latin America's trade dilemma a peaceful and constructive one? More on these questions later. Let us return now to the characteristics of the economy of Latin America.

5

It is customary to refer to these characteristics of the Latin American economy as "problems." But of course whether they are perceived as such depends on where the viewer sits. For the *campesino* in his remote village the problem may be a need for rice during the drought, medicine for a dying child, a new woman to bear him another, or liquor to drown his troubles. For the oligarch the problem may be the maintenance of what he has or the subtle determination of what he must concede. For others the problem may be adverse economic statistics, growth rates, or revenues. For still others the problem may appear as the threat of communist incursion or the expansion of profitable markets.

The mere identification of a characteristic as a "problem" presupposes a desire and an agreed direction for change, which cannot be presumed. If when we speak of problems, we also speak of their solution in terms of progress or development, then we are not only presupposing change, but also change in a certain direction, toward a particular objective; we are assuming further that there are generally recognized criteria by which the success of change can be measured and priorities determined.

Sometimes, North Americans unconsciously speak of development and its problems in terms of the distance between what exists in Latin America and in the United States. That the Latin American may not see his problems or his development in this way tends to confuse us; if by chance he does, it may be still more confusing.

Two examples will illustrate:

The national universities of Latin America are for the most part troublesome places, hotbeds of student protest (as they are everywhere). They are usually inefficiently managed, with part-time faculties who are frequently absent from their classroom, attended by part-time students with little discipline or intellectual zeal; removed from and distrusted by the status quo and often by the United States embassy. A good deal of United States assistance in one form or another has gone to Latin American universities, most of it based on the proposition that the universities suffer to the extent that they differ from institutions of higher learning in the United States. Consequently, teams of professors are sent from the United States to show the light to their Latin American counterparts. The results are understandably disappointing to all concerned. As we shall see, a more fruitful approach requires perceiving that the university's problem lies within the context of its relationship to its surrounding community. The superficial difficulties mentioned above are only symptoms of the fact that the Latin American university has become drastically isolated from the society which it is supposed to serve, and thus its critical function is left largely unperformed.

A second example of fallacious "problem" perception is embodied in the phrase "revolution of rising expectations" and similar phrases which imply that there is a great desire for "improvement" on the part of the poor. We tend to perceive the Latin American *campesino* as a somewhat seedy version of Benjamin Franklin, imbued with the Protestant ethic, eager for profit, hungry for education, straining at the bonds which tie him. This of course is by no means the case and ignores the fact that the majority of people in the United States have from the country's founding sustained an almost incredible level of drive and confidence. As a consequence of this misinterpretation, for example, we build scores of schoolhouses in Latin America, fill them with teachers and textbooks, and then are surprised and dismayed when education, the acquisition of knowledge, frequently does not result.

The scarcity of motivation and confidence in Latin America can be understood if we look further into some typical characteristics of the environment.

The Isla San José suburb of Guayaquil, Ecuador, is a rapidly growing community of close to 50,000 persons, most of whom came to the city because life in the countryside had become unbearable. The municipality of Guayaquil, the industrial center of Ecuador, aided by civic-action units of the Ecuadorian army, created Isla San José by dumping garbage in a marshy area on the edge of the city. Day after day yellow trucks with the Alliance for Progress seal on their sides unloaded the city's refuse to make the streets of the new community. The plan called for the army afterward to pack the garbage down and cover it with dirt and gravel. But the army didn't come. For six months prior to the time of my visit, the people of Isla San José had been living in crude shacks on streets piled five feet high with live garbage. Vultures and children fought for scraps of food; insects were so thick that one had to wear a handkerchief to keep from inhaling them; the sidewalks, gutters on each side of the garbage heap, ran with yellow ooze; rats were abundant; typhus was rampant and there were occasionally outbreaks of cholera.

Some thirty Peace Corps volunteers lived in this community, attempting to organize the people, help them find work, give them hope, and seek to bring the services of the city to them. Water was theoretically delivered in city or army water trucks and sold to the inhabitants of Isla San José. The city water line ended in a thin, shaky pipe about a mile away. The volunteers regularly implored the army's civic-action unit to bring the gravel fill and pack down the streets. Nine times promises were made and nine times they were not kept. The volunteers were seriously threatened by the dread Chagas bug, which infests the bamboo canes that are used for building huts in tropical areas such as Isla San José. At the time there was no known cure for Chagas's disease, which induces a fatal fever. One Peace Corps volunteer went to jail defending a neighbor against what he considered to be an unreasonable police assault. The local bully had tried to throw the volunteer's friend off his miserable spot of garbage-strewn land; his neighbor had resisted, and the bully, a man of some influence even in such surroundings, had put the police on him.

There are many such places. In spite of the fact that Venezuela is in the forefront of the reform and development movement in Latin America and has the unique benefit of large governmental revenues from the oil companies, more than 40 per cent of all dwellings in Caracas have no immediate access to water.[25]

One of the most appalling slums in Latin America is the Hollywood section of relatively prosperous Panama City. Located almost across the street from the lush green lawns and clinical cottages of the Canal Zone, it contains some five thousand families living in rotting shacks that are built on rickety platforms over a fetid swamp. Hollywood's population is expanding at a rate which far outstrips the low-cost housing efforts of the Panamanian government and AID.

Why do the *campesinos*, the peasants, come to places like this, which surround almost every Latin American city? The reasons are many and varied, but some quick answers illustrate some of the complexities of "development."

"There is no food in the countryside," I was told.

"But the land is green and fertile. I have seen it," I replied.

"But that land belongs to the great landowner. It is not mine," was the reply. Or "We have no money to cultivate it, no money for seed, no way to get our produce to market. We are sick and tired."

The *campesino's* land, if he has any which he can legally call his, is small and barren, and the number of persons it must support grows quickly. In general, Latin American per-capita agricultural production was less in 1966 than in 1958.[26]

In Peru half the people live on barter alone and 80 per cent of the other half earn only the equivalent of $53 a year. Some one hundred families own or control 90 per cent of the national wealth. Sixty-five per cent of the population are officially called illiterate, with many more undoubtedly qualifying; 45 per cent have never seen a doctor. Chronic hunger prevails, caloric intake averaging 1,200 a day against a minimum need of 2,400. Life expectancy hovers around forty-four years, as compared with seventy in the United States.[27]

Even in progressive Chile a recent estimate indicates that a quarter of all personal income was earned by less than 3 per cent of persons in the upper-income brackets; whereas at the other extreme about 55 per cent of the population received less than 16 per cent of all income. Less than 8 per cent of families in El Salvador receive over half of the country's total income, whereas 61 per cent receive only one fifth of the total. As recently as 1960 in Venezuela about one eighth of those receiving income got half the total; 45 per cent about one tenth of it. From 1950 to 1964 in Guatemala, though the gross national product increased, the per-capita income of the rural population, which is at least 66 per cent of the country, dropped from $87 a year to $83.[28]

One could add to these statistics those on mass unemployment (and even more extensive underemployment, especially in rural areas), and serious and continuing inflation in many countries, which in Brazil, for example, raised the cost of living 40 per cent in 1966.

The dimensions of poverty are not decreasing; they are expanding rapidly, as is the gap between the rich and the poor. Increasingly, and in many areas for the first time, the gap is causing profound and activating resentment. An eloquent statement of this resentment is found in the diaries of Carolina Maria de Jesus, a Negress living in one of the shanty slums of São Paulo: "The merchants of São Paulo are playing with the people just like Caesar when he tortured the Christians. But the Caesars of today are worse than the Caesars of the past. The others are punished for their faith and we for our hunger. In that era those who did not want to die had to stop loving Christ. But we cannot stop loving eating."

No problem is more serious in Latin America today than that of land, its use, its ownership, productivity, and development. Food production must increase if famine is not going to succeed today's widespread malnutrition. Some consider this a technical problem, soluble by the utilization of better seed, fertilizer, and machinery. Some see it as arising from political decisions to give priority attention to industrialization. Others view it as a socio-logical and cultural problem caused by lack of education and training. And still others feel it is fundamentally an economic problem, with deep roots in the plantation-based economies of many Latin American countries.

I shall argue that the food and land problems of Latin America, like the region's problems in general, are composed of an inextricably interconnected series of ideological, political, social, economic, and cultural factors; and that the initial attack on these factors must be motivational and organizational.

The output of agricultural workers in general is extremely low in most of Latin America. If we let 100 equal the productivity of an agricultural farmer in Italy, for example, the relative figure for Argentina would be 91, for Panama, 54, Colombia, 45, Venezuela, 32, and Guatemala, 21. The United States figure would be 286, Canada, 199, and France, 132.[29] As with many such measurements, however, the actual situation is worse than the figures indicate, because the bulk of Latin America's agricultural crops is produced on the relatively efficient sugar, coffee, cotton and other commercial plantations, which means that the productivity of domestic food crops by small farmers is consider-ably below the figures given.

The economic consequences of Latin America's declining capacity to feed itself are obvious. In 1966 Chile had to import $157 million worth of food products at a time when the Frei government was trying desperately to control inflation. This re-quired an expenditure of 18 per cent of the country's scarce foreign exchange earnings on imports like wheat, milk, meat and other foodstuffs which Chile is perfectly capable of producing.[30] President Frei has estimated that $100 million of Chile's current food imports could be grown at home.[31]

Insufficient food production produces a condition of creeping starvation throughout the countryside of Latin America. The supposition that those who live on the land always have enough to eat is plainly untrue. The big, fertile tracts of land are largely inefficiently cultivated and used except where they may be producing crops for export—and a very small percentage of the earnings from those crops return to the rural population. These tracts, and those used for grazing, are being expanded in many countries, eroding the small family subsistence plots which were inadequate to begin with and are relatively unfertile. Rapid population increase is further diminishing the food supply. Though in many Latin American countries fruits may be plucked from the trees this is hardly a sufficient dietary base.

Most of Latin America's productive land is in the hands of a few very large owners in the form of *latifundias*. The remainder is distributed in a wide variety of patterns among many small landowners, tenants, sharecroppers, and squatters. In all, only 30 per cent of Latin America's arable land is under any form of cultivation.[32] Some of the large estates are farmed efficiently, but because of their immense size it is often possible for the owner to draw a satisfactory income from them without bothering to use the land effectively or to help or encourage his tenants to do so. In many cases the estate has been handed down from generation to generation. Frequently the owner lives in the capital city and may rarely visit his property. Having invested little capital in it, he expects little income from it. The landowner is often happy to sell his land if he can get a good price from the government. Otherwise, he may keep it in a general state of torpor, waiting for the value of the land to increase by virtue of population growth and the development of the economy as a whole. This results in underutilization of labor, soil, water, and other resources. Actually, the land is often not so important for the wealth it brings as for the political power, prestige, and security which it entails.

Another tenure system is the *minifundia,* or small holding, of perhaps four or five acres, whose owner is not linked to or dependent on the *latifundia* for land, employment, or resources. The small farmer in this system, however, is frequently dependent for credit and market access on a collection of money lenders, storekeepers and merchants, who in one way or another may be influenced or controlled by the large landowner. In some areas—coastal Ecuador, Indian regions of the Andes and Guatemala, and parts of rural Mexico—there are communal or semi-communal systems of land tenure with groups of small cultivators jointly owning and operating a piece of land. The following figures, necessarily imprecise, tell the dramatic story of Latin America's land distribution.

In Latin America as a whole it has been estimated that less than 10 per cent of present land holdings cover 90 per cent of the land. Figures indicate that in Argentina in 1960 36.9 per cent of the cultivated land was controlled by some 500 owners of large *haciendas.* In Brazil 5 per cent of the people control some 60 per cent of the land [33] and 10 million out of 12 million farmworkers own no land at all.[34] Nicaragua is probably unique in that one family, the Somozas, are reputed to own or control, directly or indirectly, about 75 per cent of cultivated land. Similarly, in Peru 82.6 per cent of the land is owned by some 7,200 people. The remaining 17.4 per cent is held by 841,401 persons, none of whose property is larger than 5 hectares. More than a million Peruvian farmers own no land at all.[35] One family has an estate as big as Rhode Island, and one *hacienda* is a third the size of Cuba.[36] That Peru has been the scene of continuing agrarian revolt is not surprising.

A report from the cacao region of Brazil indicates "that it is invariably the same men who are in the cacao production, who are in the directorates of the banks, in the top organs of the cooperatives . . . and at times in the export houses. On the other side these very firms are also owners of the cacao plantations." [37] They are also influential politicians, livestock owners, and merchants, and invariably are tied directly or indirectly to cacao by-product industries.

Chile and Colombia have in recent years conducted energetic

programs to provide for more equitable distribution of land. In Chile, however, it has been estimated that 6 per cent of the people still control about 21 per cent of the land. In Colombia, some 750,000 *campesinos* have no land at all, while 325,000 others hold plots averaging less than one acre each.

It is argued by some that transforming traditional agriculture in order to increase agricultural productivity is dependent upon an increase in economic opportunity and the acquisition of useful skills and knowledge. This represents a naïvely bland and imprecise perception of reality.

Virtually every country in Latin America has what it calls a land-reform law, in many cases passed under the pressure of the Alliance for Progress. Generally speaking, the laws are meant to increase agricultural productivity, to assure greater employment opportunities (especially in rural areas), and to relieve social tensions by improving the distribution of property and income. The matter of land reform thus involves at once political, social, and economic change. It is economically and socially important to give land to the peasants in such a way that they are encouraged to produce more on it. It is also important to take land away from the oligarchs in order to reduce their political power and provide the basis for greater popular participation in the political process. Strange things have been included under the heading of land reform. Some programs involve the distribution of relatively unfertile government land to the squatters who have traditionally cultivated it, largely for mere subsistence. This means the squatter—now an owner—has to pay taxes on what before was free, and his poverty is increased.

Some change is so desirable or necessary politically and socially that its productive and economic results can be virtually ignored. The nationalization of oil by the Mexican government in 1938, for example, was for many years economically disastrous —in fact, production has never equaled the 193-million-barrel level recorded in 1921.[38] Nationalization in this case was a political imperative for the government of Lázaro Cárdenas in 1938, playing an important part in the welding of modern Mexico out of the chaos of revolution. Food production, however, is too crucial a need for any country to be able to afford the political gains of land reform without insuring an increase in or at least the maintenance of production levels.

Thus, the dismembering of large land-holdings and their distribution to the peasants is only the most rudimentary part of agrarian reform. More profoundly, land and people must be so organized that gains in justice, civic rights and political power are matched by increases in production. To this end, a wide variety of patterns have been and are being tried in Latin America, including the state farms of Cuba, various communal and cooperative farms, governmental settlement programs, encouragement of the relatively small family farm, and large-scale commercial farming. The purpose of all these efforts is to some extent the same: to bring modern technology to bear on agriculture in a way which is culturally and politically acceptable, so as to increase and improve food crops.

It is becoming increasingly apparent, however, that before modern technology can be effectively introduced, substantial portions of the old economic, political, and social structure must be destroyed and new structures built. For example, different market and credit systems must be established before new varieties of seed and fertilizer can be effectively introduced. A farmer has little desire to produce more and better food if he cannot sell it at a reasonable profit, nor can he obtain the products of modern technology on a continuing basis without access to credit which he can afford.

Again Mexico provides an interesting example. Land redistribution was a high aim of the Mexican Revolution and began in earnest in 1935 during the presidency of Cárdenas. Since that time, about half the country's farm land has been redistributed by the government to small rural communities known as *ejidos*, varying in population from one hundred to several thousands.[39] The rest of the land remains in private hands.[40]

That the ejidal land-reform system is far from the perfect model is attested to by the fact that agriculture is today the most serious problem of the Mexican government. In the words of a high-ranking Mexican official, 50 per cent of the people in rural Mexico are worse off today than they were before the revolution.

In fact, by far the most prosperous agricultural areas of Mexico are the large, privately owned commercial farm areas of the north which exist often in violation of the revolutionary restrictions on farm size. The government has recognized the heavy dependence of the Mexican economy on these private farms and has helped them in many ways, including the provision of irrigation systems, modern equipment, fertilizer, and improved seed. This policy caused Mexico's agricultural production to double between 1945 and 1957, while the population grew by 40 per cent.[41]

Venezuela, Bolivia, and Cuba—with Mexico—are Latin American countries which have undergone the most extensive expropriation of property. Since 1958, when Rómulo Betancourt and his Acción Democrática Party overthrew the dictatorship of Pérez Jiménez in Venezuela, some 140,000 *campesino* families have been settled on about three and one-half million hectares of land acquired from both public and private sources.[42] Venezuela's program, however, is a moderate one, and much of the arable land continues to be in the hands of a few. Three kinds of land may be taken: uncultivated acreage; plots cultivated by renters, sharecroppers or day laborers; and land being used to graze livestock that is suitable for more intensive agriculture. Land is paid for in cash and bonds and at the current market value, which makes the program acceptable to most landowners. In effect, the reform law says to the landowners: "You must either cultivate your propreties intensively and efficiently or sell them to the government." [43] And perhaps most important, the program is adequately financed by the country's revenues from its huge oil resources.

Land reform was the primary promise of the revolution of 1952 which placed Víctor Paz Estenssoro's Movimiento Nacional Revolucionario (MNR) in power in Bolivia. Land was distributed as private property to the new owners, although the Indians (60 per cent of Bolivia's population) chose to farm it according to their traditional patterns of communal ownership.[44]

As is perhaps understandable in a revolutionary society, lands of loyal MNR supporters, however large and unproductive, tended to escape expropriation. But the axe fell heavy on oppo-

nents of the regime. "The agrarian reform in Bolivia," said
Alberto Ostria Gutierrez, ". . . had as its primary objective the
economic ruin of the adversaries of the regime, whatever the
size of the property they owned." [45] Once the *latifundia* was
even partially destroyed, Bolivia's problem became one of *minifundismo*. In one sense, the revolution reinforced subsistence
agriculture. It did not build a new agriculture designed to fit a
national economy. The reform also failed to equip the new small
land-holder with the education, capital, and marketing services
needed for greater productivity.

Historically, Bolivia's Indians have probably been the most
exploited and mistreated in Latin America. Condemned to serfdom on the land or drafted through the *encomienda* system for
work in the tin and silver mines, where they died by the thousands, they lived in conditions of slavery and inhumanity. It is
not surprising that the Indians developed a distrust of white
men and their ways. Nor is it surprising that neither in past
times nor today does the Bolivian government have anything
but marginal control over most of its lands and people.*

Land reform, in a sense, was the spontaneous result of the
revolution of Víctor Paz and Hernán Siles, which overthrew
the existing power structure in Bolivia, seized the mines, and
swept the country into chaos and confusion from which it is
still reeling. In early 1952 the Indians, provided with arms and
ammunition by a revolutionary element of the military, immediately turned against the landowners, and within a year most of
Bolivia's *altiplano* (high plateau) was converted into independent
Indian communities, the hated *hacendados* having fled for their
lives. In a way, the government merely legitimized what had
already happened and extended it somewhat. But the new
government felt obliged to assert its political influence on this
chaotic situation and dispatched various sorts of political "patrons" to take the place of the old landowners. The government

---

* Che Guevara's failure in 1967 to arouse peasant following in Bolivia may,
however, indicate that the revolution gave to at least some peasants sufficient
reason to believe in the possibility of representation by government, so that they
were unwilling to accept the offer of change from a Cuban stranger.

also formed rural *syndicatos* (unions) which functioned for a time alongside the traditional Indian hierarchical organization. In most places these *syndicatos* have since crumbled, leaving the Indian structure intact.

Government land programs in Bolivia since the revolution have been of two kinds: colonization and community development. The objective of colonization was to encourage the peasants to leave the unfertile plains of the Andes and settle in the sparsely populated, rich tropical and semitropical lands of the Alto-Beni and Oriente. Although this migration has proceeded naturally quite well, with three or four thousand families a year moving off the *altiplano* into the valleys below, the government-planned colonization efforts have been largely unsuccessful and in some cases positively disastrous. In 1959, for example, the Bolivian (government) Development Corporation moved six hundred families into the Alto-Beni. Technicians of the BDC had drawn up impressive plans, calling for this new community to produce rubber, cacao, and coffee. Hopes were high and many promises were made. But when the families arrived at their new home they found virtually nothing but a patch of wilderness. While they struggled to survive, they were charged for housing and other community needs, so that in 1968 each family was not only still poverty-stricken but was also some $1,000 in debt to the government. They set about growing the only crops they knew how, principally dry-land rice. They consumed most of this, and what they sold was mortgaged in advance to storekeepers and middlemen to whom they were in continual debt bondage. Though some of the more ambitious members of the group grew cacao, there was no ready access to a market; and roads to the community still are usually washed out. Thus they exist— isolated, remote, embittered, with no sense of community or of hope, launched paternalistically by a father whose chief role today is that of debt collector.

The Bolivian community development program aimed at providing educational, housing, and agricultural assistance to peasant communities has been somewhat more successful. In spite of many difficulties, it probably stands as the outstanding govern-

mental effort of its kind in Latin America. For this much credit
must go to the United States AID mission and the Peace Corps
in Bolivia, as well as to local officials.

An Indian community is governed by a council of elders who
rule not by vote but by consensus, following pre-Spanish Inca
political patterns. Lengthy discussions are held; all views are
heard; and then, with the help of some ceremonial beverage and
under the pressure of fatigue, agreement is reached. These
communities existed beside and within the Spanish-imposed
hacienda and *encomienda* systems, and when the latter were
destroyed, beside and within the government's short-lived peasant
unions. The Indian socio-political structure obviously persists,
and finally both the Bolivian government and AID have recognized the desirability of respecting it. Even then assistance was
not easily bestowed. At first the government and AID brought
middle-class white technicians—agronomists and the like—to
assist and advise the peasants. They were completely unacceptable because of the history of experience which the peasants
had had with such "outsiders" and the suspicion that they were
political agents of the government.

To find the source of genuine leadership for the development
of an Indian community is not easy. Frequently, there are a
number of leaders who have become so by traveling up a traditional, semireligious ladder. Everyone knows who the leaders
are and who they are going to be. The highest-ranking of them
is in charge of the fiestas, which are semireligious ceremonies
characterized by the consumption of enormous quantities of
ritual liquor. Others may oversee irrigation or judicial processes.
They may or may not have skills generally associated with technical modernization. Matters are further complicated by the
deep divisions between the Indian communities and the towns,
which are populated largely by *cholos* or *mestizos,* "outsiders"
who traditionally have exploited the Indians unmercifully.

A former Peace Corps volunteer now working with AID and
the Bolivian community development program told me: "In the
beginning, we selected a man from a village without consulting
the elders, sent him to school for training and then returned
him to his village. The local leadership felt threatened by this

'bright young man' and it ostracized him. Almost to spite him, they built themselves a schoolhouse—without allowing his help —and went into town and bought a tin roof for it themselves. The trick is to find who the leaders are and then select young men for training with their approval. One Indian boy so selected did not return to his village after having received training, but the local leaders found him more than a hundred miles away and told him that his whole family would be expelled from the village if he didn't come back and pass on the knowledge he had acquired." Another example of sociological oversight which initially hampered the program was the regulation that a peasant youth who has received his training must return to his village and make a grievance survey to discover local needs. Such an action ran directly counter to the tradition of local authority which is vested in the council of elders. But if the council on its own decided it wanted a project, it would produce both money and work.

More than 60 per cent of Bolivians live in this type of traditional community. Most speak only the Indian tongues of Quechua or Aymará. It is not surprising that in 1966 AID was having substantial difficulty with its training material for community development, as it had been developed in Pakistan and translated into Spanish only. The argument which I was given at the time—that "what's good in one place is good all over"— didn't seem to be holding up.

Although Bolivian statistics are sketchy, the best indications are that agricultural production declined sharply in the midfifties. There is evidence, however, that in recent years it has been increasing, partly because of the national wool program, also a joint operation of the Peace Corps, AID, and the Bolivian government. Incredible as it may seem, until 1965 only 1 per cent of Bolivia's six million sheep were sheared, and $2 million worth of wool was being imported annually. The new program has greatly increased the incomes of rural sheep farmers, once they were persuaded that they would get their sheep back as good as new after they had been shorn.

Perhaps the most successful single rural development program in Bolivia, however, is one associated with the radical social-action wing of the Catholic Church. It is called DESEC (Centro Desarrollo Social y Económico) and was started in 1963 by a French layman, Jean de Meure. By 1968 it had organized more than two thousand families in seventy multiservice cooperative enterprises in five regions of the country. DESEC, like many similar organizations in Latin America, is sponsored by DESAL (Desarrollo Latinoamericano) in Santiago, Chile, which is run by Father Roger Vekemans, S.J., a Belgian sociologist.

Another country in which land reform has been extensive, Cuba, appears to be having many of the same problems of incentive and motivation that plague the agriculture of the Soviet Union. After an initial spurt in agricultural output in 1959 and 1960, production has been diminishing. As of 1961, 59 per cent of agricultural land was in private ownership, 28 per cent in state farms and 13 per cent in some 630 cooperatives. In the first years after the revolution, the production of tobacco, rice, corn, and bean crops increased, largely because of the conversion of inefficiently used cattle-grazing areas into arable land. Sugar production rose spectacularly from 1958 to 1961, then fell disastrously thereafter. The Cuban regime itself has frequently criticized the inefficiency of its collective farms, and yet there are indications that more and more private land has come under state direction. A principal problem seems to be Castro's ideological commitment to paying workers a flat wage without regard to their output.

Wherever one looks at land development efforts it seems apparent that the most difficult and profound problems go well beyond the mere acquisition and redistribution of land. It is frequently difficult for the central government to know the most propitious and beneficial manner and form in which the land should be distributed to its new owners, and many different approaches are tried.

A second type of difficulty arises from the crippling distortions and obstacles in Latin America's market and distribution systems. It is difficult for peasants to get their goods to market; roads are scarce and frequently are impassable during rainy weather. Middlemen cause the farmer's return for his produce to be minimal and the cost to the consumer high. Credit systems are

distorted and exploitative; most peasants live and work in a
state of continual debt bondage to a *tienda* (store) keeper, mill
owner, landowner, or loan shark. Government credit agencies
in general have limited their services to the small and affluent
fraction of the people. Without access to credit it becomes
difficult, if not impossible, for the peasants to buy the seed,
fertilizer, and equipment necessary to farm their new land effectively.

A third difficulty involves the peasant himself, his attitude and
motivation, his hopes and his fears, his competence and ability.
This category is perhaps the most solid of the obstacles to be
overcome in trying to bring about effective rural change.

Even if these problems are somehow solved in a particular
land area, will the process begun continue and extend to other
areas? Will it become institutionalized and broadly accepted?
If not, there is no real land reform in a national sense. For
rural change of any sort to be effective, lasting, and beneficial,
it must be preceded or accompanied by the development of
rural organizations which will be capable of handling all the
problems and obstacles which we have just listed. Only if there
is an indigenous organization, firmly rooted in the rural area
concerned, can it be ensured that government influence will be
properly directed, reasonably prompt, appropriate, effective, and
continuing. Only with organization can the peasant confront
effectively the market and credit structure around him. Only
with organization can he begin to control his environment and
know and exert his power. But even when peasants do organize,
problems frequently arise, because their organizations invariably
seek a variety and a degree of change which those who hold
power, government or otherwise, will not accept.

"Several times a year on Saturday nights, the peasants of the
Valley of La Convención at the eastern base of the Andes in
southern Peru used to foregather in the sprawling, dusty plaza
of this tiny market town. They would start coming around mid-
night, the men marching six abreast in sandals cut from old
rubber tires, and shouting 'Tierra o muerte!'—'Land or death!'
They carried no weapons, although the barefoot women who
followed them, some with infants bound to their backs in shawls,

had rocks bundled in their wine-colored homespun skirts. The men wore faded brown ponchos and floppy sheepskin hats. Their next day's lunch, pieces of yucca and salted meat, was tied inside sweat-stained sashes around the waist." [46] So Norman Gall begins his description of the peasant revolt in the Peruvian Andes which led to a crackdown by the Peruvian army in 1964.

The Indian sharecroppers, agitated by university students from Cuzco, the old Indian capital of Peru two hundred miles away, were striking to end the feudal land system of La Convención. Policemen and landlords were ambushed and killed, and the peasants gained *de facto* ownership of their subsistence plots, two thirds of which were too small to feed a family. The remaining landlords had to scour the highlands to find migrant workers to harvest the crops.

Turmoil continued until the army imposed stability. In March 1966, President Fernando Belaúnde Terry was able to announce: "We have beaten the Communists once and for all. We are sure they won't be back." The United States can claim some credit for the victory because thousands of Peruvian Rangers have been trained at United States Army schools and the United States has contributed more than $120 million in military aid to Peru.*

A somewhat comparable situation prevails in Northeast Brazil, where the leading figure in the quest for revolutionary change is Dom Helder Camara, the archbishop of Olinda and Recife. Dom Helder points out: "Unfortunately, the rich in Latin America talk too much about reform and label as Communists all those who would enforce it. This is easy to understand; the rich in Latin America go on holding 80 per cent of the land on the continent. Often they control Parliament and have the intensity of their idealism and hope in the future gauged by the bank deposits kept in their names in the United States and Europe."

Two of his priests, Father Antonio de Melo Costa and Father Paulo Crespo, have organized about thirty-six peasant unions, embracing 150,000 peasants, into what is known as SORPE (Serviço de Organização Rural de Pernambuco).[47] Their four

* There is obvious irony in the anti-U.S. stance of the current military regime and an interesting contrast in its apparent commitment to land reform.

purposes are: to press the government to enforce the minimum wage laws in the sugar mills; to encourage the establishment of small industries, handicraft and vocational training schools; to avoid external aid ("We do not wish to become beggars"); and, most fundamentally, to change the basic land structure of the region by breaking up the huge sugar properties into family-sized farms which can be run with the assistance of various types of cooperatives. This last purpose is, of course, profoundly revolutionary, carrying with it radical implications for the political, social, and economic life of the Northeast and of Brazil as a whole. It is plain that powerful groups will continue to oppose SORPE's fulfillment in every way that they can. For Father Crespo and Father Melo, however, a change in basic structures is essential for the achievement of anything that can legitimately be called development. But as Dom Helder says: "If I hand out food and teach children to read, then I am a saint. But if I concern myself with underlying problems of reform, then I am a Communist." [48]

To appreciate the extent of the problem confronting Latin America's peasants and those who are trying to change their condition, it is interesting to look at the results of an investigation conducted by CIDA (Comité Interamericano de Desarrollo Agrícola). It was found that there were serious and widespread violations of minimum wage laws in Northeast Brazil, where "feudal traditions are still very strong." Sharecroppers or workers living on the plantations generally have to work one or more days per week either free of charge or at greatly reduced wages as "homage" to the landlord. In the state of Ceará it was found that wages were only 50 per cent of the legal wage rate. In Ecuador's Sierra, it was reported that wages are "more a fiction than a reality." Not only are Indians' wages—a few pennies a day—not paid punctually, but they are not paid at the agreed-upon rates; or wages are not paid in cash at all but in kind. The CIDA reports from a number of countries are filled with lurid accounts of exploitation and cruel treatment of *campesinos* by landowners, of private police forces and bands of strong-arm men used by the *latifundistas* to keep the peasants in line. One powerful landlord, a close relative of one of the country's leading politicians, burned down the homes of his tenant farmers, who were agitating for higher wages and seeking to organize a union. He used bulldozers to shut the irrigation canals with which they watered their subsistence plots, and posted guards to prevent the workers from opening them at night.

"Whoever speaks in favor of the *liga* [peasant union] can expect to be shot at any moment," reported one Brazilian *campesino*. "None of us are safe. A shot can come out of the dark, from one of the *capangas* [the landowners' strong-arm men]." Another said: "This has no end. Violence begets violence. We will not retreat and the owners will not either. There is no remedy. Now it will go to the bitter end when one or the other wins." [49]

One of the characteristics of rural labor in Latin America is that the worker has no simple, fixed, or sure relationship to his employer and his work. He performs a variety of tasks under a variety of arrangements, with constant shifts determined by the crop, the season, the will of the landowner, and other environmental factors over which he has no control. He is subject to call and dismissal without notice. This, combined with the insecurity of his own land tenure, his extreme poverty and malnutrition, and his tradition of hopelessness, makes it extremely difficult for the Latin American *campesino* to contemplate change or to organize any exercise which could be characterized as development.

Furthermore, the rigidities and unbridgeable gaps of the social and political structure prevent what might be regarded as normal, gradual change on the part of the landowners. In most instances they are so far removed from the peasant, and so adjusted to their way of life, that they see little cause for change. Those organizations, factors, and forces which in more fluid societies tend to force change gradually are simply not present, and the influence of the power elite has traditionally insured that government will not do the forcing.

The chances of peaceful change in rural Latin America can only be assessed as slim. The rigidities are too great, the barriers too high, the existing processes of change too slow, and power too polarized. The Venezuelan exception, due to a combination

of enormous oil revenues in the hands of the government and
Acción Democrática's extensive rural political organization, does
not seem likely to be repeated elsewhere, except perhaps in Chile.
Indeed, Venezuela and Chile's very success makes them prime
targets of those forces to whom peaceful change and national
independence are repugnant. It is no accident that Cuban
guerrillas in the first instance and the Communist Party in
the second have had these two countries high on their list for
years.

3

POLITICS: Problems of Legitimacy and Integration

Everything has been tried: efficient dictatorship and corrupt dictatorship, the militarism of animals in uniform and the militarism of intelligent men, anticlerical and exploitative liberalism, clerical and paternalistic conservatism, false revolution and authentic revolution. All have failed (except the authentic revolution in a few countries). The masses remain submerged, power remains in the hands of the landowning oligarchy, the standard of living of the masses sinks while a minority's existence improves. None of the systems that have been tried has been able to bring progress to Latin America.

The only thing that has not been tried is democracy, real democracy, democracy that is at once political, social, and economic, that is government of, by, and for the people.

Víctor Alba[1]

The political and social systems of Latin America are compatible with and in many ways the progenitors of the economic characteristics described in the previous chapter. A few persons in a few elites wield the controlling influence. Power is polarized. At one end of the political spectrum it is collected into one or more of several conglomerates: the landowners; the old commercial groups; the new entrepreneurs; the traditional Church and the new; the old military and the young; trade union leaders; government bureaucrats and technicians.

Among these groups there exist varying strains and tension. Generally, they are in conflict, but with rare exceptions they have managed to contain their conflict within certain stable boundaries. Although the mixture and dimensions of power within and among these groups has changed somewhat, on the whole control has remained remarkably consistent. The frequent coups or—from a United States point of view—unorthodox shifts in governmental control so characteristic of the region actually change the situation very little. Rather, they represent normal and relatively inconsequential shifts within and among the ruling power groups, in conformity with unwritten but governing rules and understandings.

At the other end of the political pole are the groups with revolutionary intentions, whose purpose is to eliminate the opposing conglomerates of power. Here we find some familiar labels: Communist, Marxist, Trotskyite, anarchist, Maoist, Castroite, and the like. But also we find revolutionary nationalists and radical priests who are none of the above. These groups are also in conflict, united only in the sense that their purpose is radical structural change. Some believe that change must come speedily; others, the communists in particular, believe that change is less important than Moscow's international interests. The record of revolutionaries in general has been lackluster, except in Mexico, Bolivia, and Cuba, where revolution has had a profound impact. Often the revolutionary's protest is shrill and superficial, unsupported by effective organization. In the communist case effective will is also lacking. Invariably, when revolutionary movements arise, its leaders are seduced by the ruling elites and absorbed by—or, as it were, sieved in to—the structure. The regime makes promises of reform but little change takes place. If a revolutionary organization manages to maintain itself and to threaten continued change, it is usually set upon and declared an enemy of peace and order. Its leaders are either exterminated or exiled.

In between these political extremes exist roughly 70 to 80 per cent of the people. One estimate has it that no more than 10 to 15 per cent of the population reads newspapers in Latin America.[2] This seems plausible, given overall literacy figures of about

30 to 40 per cent. It is relevant to note that newspapers, like radio and TV stations, are owned or controlled by one or another power group and speak for that group without apology. The vast majority, then, belong to no elite, no interest group, no organization, and in many cases to no real community. They are without access to power. They lack a sense of nationality or identification with the state; they regard the government with fear, suspicion, or indifference. They neither expect nor receive representation from those whom they elect (if they vote), and they are largely convinced of the unalterable nature of their political condition. This group between the poles thus lives in a socio-political void or vacuum. A number of forces are moving to fill that vacuum; but at the moment the vast subgovernment of organizations, pressure groups, and interest associations, vital to government in Europe and North America, is dramatically absent in Latin America.

It is even difficult to say that there is an effective or cohesive class structure. There are those with power, those aspiring to it, and those who are quite certain they will never have it. "The most difficult task in studying the Colombian middle class," wrote Vernon L. Fluharty, "is to find it." [3] Those aspiring to power, who might normally be thought of as belonging to a middle class, are far from united in their purpose or organized in their attack. All they want is what the elite has got. They are essentially conservative, hoping that by being so they will gain admission to the power groups; once there, they become identified with whatever group has admitted them. "There is nothing more conservative than a poor conservative with hopes of becoming a rich one," said Fluharty.[4] "Even the revolutionary, if he makes the grade, gets corrupted," said a Panamanian friend.

The result of this vacuous socio-political condition appears to outsiders as political instability, in the sense that regimes come and go frequently and often with little reference to democratic constitutional forms. During the last decade "popularly elected" governments were denied or ousted from the palace in Guatemala, Honduras, Brazil, Argentina, the Dominican Republic, Bolivia, Ecuador, El Salvador, Peru, and Panama. Not many years before, elected regimes were deposed in Venezuela, Chile, and Colombia.

It would be wrong, however, to suppose that this familiar pattern of instability reflects any structural change or is in fact revolutionary. In nearly every case, though the faces in the palace changed, the holders of power remained very much the same. In a larger sense, then, the political system of Latin America is not so much unstable and changeable as it is paralytically stable, incapable of or unwilling to institute change either within itself or in the surrounding economic and social environment.

What of government? In spite of the gross limitations which the system places on effective action for change by government, progressive thinkers in both Latin America and the United States persist in the notion that the way to national development is by increasing the burden upon government. The traditional argument of the modern liberal and the socialist that the government ought to play a larger and more beneficent role in economic activities rests, of course, on the assumption that government has both the will and the power to do so. The traditional liberal often has what can only be described as an innocent notion that government per se tends to be on the side of the people. In some places this may be so. But in Latin America it can by no means be assumed.

Latin American "democracies" are administratively overburdened, and even today their influence, control, and identity in vast reaches of their lands is slight. And yet, through the Alliance for Progress we ask and expect them to take on more; and in effect pay them to tell us that they are doing so. The real question is not *ought* government to do more but *can* government do more? And when, and how? If the answer is that government can, but not for a long time to come and not until other political effects are felt first, then we must ask ourselves what other political engines must be wheeled into place to carry these countries through the inevitable and radical change which they face.

The importance of precise answers to this question is clear

to the foreign aid program of the United States. It is equally, if not more, relevant (but less clear) to American business because the United States corporation is generally a remarkably efficient organizer of change, which means automatically that it is a political engine of great importance. And yet much of both our government and business thinking in Latin America is built around the false assumption of an effective national government somewhat comparable to our own which can be relied upon, assisted, strengthened, guided, or whatever. We are repeatedly dismayed, even made resentful, by the revelation that such an institution may not be present.

I

Most poignant and profound in the drama of Latin America is the recurring cry which has echoed through history since the conquistadors: "Who are we? What is our name? Of whom are we heirs? What is our purpose?" Such institutions as there may have been are in decay. The old patterns of rights and expectations, of obligations and responsibilities, of duties and privileges, are disintegrating. The hierarchical rigidities are in a state of continuing dissolution. The old ways are crumbling, but new ones are not yet come. Anxiety and insecurity abound, with their associated traits—lack of initiative, low levels of motivation, petty belligerency, quick resentment, and lack of trust. The Latin American, like Hamlet, ponders his nature, asking himself: "What am I: white, Negro, Indian, *mestizo,* European, something that partakes of all this, or something distinct?" [5] There has been no satisfactory answer, only deep political and spiritual torment, a search for legitimacy, a longing for a vision. It is hard to find in history a region or people so intensely afflicted.

But why is this anguish so keen in Latin America? Is not the United States as well made up of people from many different nations and races, many varied cultures and political systems? The United States is unique in the history of nations in many ways, none more important than in the breadth and variety of its political organization, governmental and nongovernmental. We have contrived a vast and complex web of interest groups and

social forces which have more or less assured access to power
and influence for most of our people. Such organization and
access are rare in Latin America. Furthermore, the political
system of the United States was formed as the organization of
its people took place. It had built into its very design, while still
in creation, the capacity to make one nation out of many groups,
to break down social, political, and economic barriers, to produce
homogeneity. The principal failure of the American political
system has been the role thrust on the Negro, who historically
has been systematically excluded, denied power and influence,
and kept in isolation and anxiety. We can see many similarities
between the Negro minority in America and the poor majority
of Latin America in the relationships they share with their
environment.

Few regions of the world have been more rudely treated by
the workings of man and history, more teased by fate, more
victimized and plundered, more defiled, than Latin America.
Nowhere is the helplessness of the individual more dramatic.
With strange and terrible historical consistency we are regularly
forced to acknowledge that the vast majority of Latin Americans
have always been essentially without influence; that they have
been slaves to forces over which they have had no conceivable
control. It is as though the region and the majority of its people
were snared in an awful cage constructed bit by bit by generations of men out of many parts; a cage of baffling complexity,
the key to which was lost before it was completed.

Since the days of the conquistadors, Latin America has willingly or unwillingly accepted a succession of foreign political
forms. Its political history reflects an attempt to adopt the European or United States version of the nation-state. Full-blown,
the model was transported from across the sea and from the
continent to the north with the trappings and paraphernalia of
presidents and parliaments, congresses and senates, and the ringing phrases of liberty, freedom, and democracy.

Essential to the model, however, were certain conceptions of
"nation" and "state" and the combined notion of the nation-
state.[6] While we tend to use the words "nation" and "state"
interchangeably, they are quite different concepts historically.

The concept of the state is relatively clear and simple. It is the center of political authority. This authority can be vested in one man or a small elite, in landowners, in the military, or it can rest upon the will of the majority. In any case, it is a state, legitimized by the values of society. There are, therefore, quite clearly states in Latin America. The concept of nation, on the other hand, is considerably more complex and doubtful. The nation came only after the authoritarian European state, in the first instance, found itself in serious jeopardy at the hands of feudal lords, foreign armies, the new middle class, and peasant masses. The nation was in essence a community, a national community, embracing all parts and people over which the state claimed jurisdiction. It came to be the political mechanism which set the standards of legitimacy for the state and its powers, which in turn then became a "nation-state."

The leaders of the newly independent states of Latin America were captivated by the ideological grandeur of this new form, this nation-state, and they therefore adopted it. But—and this is all important to our discussion—it did not emerge. It was not the result of political, social, and economic working in Latin America itself; it was not the naturally selected political device for dealing with the particular problem of the Latin American community.

Once adopted by those who held power, the nation-state was accepted by those who did not. Acceptance came without question from the apathetic masses of Latin America. Acceptance came also from foreigners, as long as their interests were protected. So without any significant opposition the sham nation-state, a phony copy of what Europe and the United States had developed after centuries of experience, agony, and bloodshed, was transported to Latin America. In a sense, the region's history for the last 150 years can be seen as a rather unfocused effort to fabricate a foundation of legitimacy for this transplanted model.

A basic question is why colonialism in Latin America failed to have the integrating effect which it had in North America. For one thing, the Spanish conquests in the New World were hardly colonies at all; they were integral parts of Spain. While theoretically the king's supremacy was absolute and all-encompassing, his will was left to be carried out by a sometimes un-savory and self-serving collection of officials, agents, and priests. Thus was Latin America introduced to the state, whose authority was far greater than its capacity to enforce. The Spanish mon-archy, instead of integrating and solidifying its American king-doms, contributed to their disintegrated development under a collection of isolated semi-autonomous chieftains whose authority was unlimited and whose responsibility was often guided only by the requirements of personal gain.

A second distinguishing feature of Spanish rule in the New World was the prominence which it gave to cities as opposed to the countryside or to large, integrated political units. The Spaniards, in the tradition of the Romans before them, exalted the city as the principal unit of political, social, and economic life.[7] Spanish policy did anything but stimulate independent political, social, and economic systems within the colonial units, which were later to call themselves nations. When independence came to Latin America, therefore, it did not serve to cut loose a group of more or less self-sufficient and politically integrated states which could then go their separate ways. Rather, it forced "a rending and tearing apart of the systematic substance about which social and economic life was organized."[8]

The wars of independence which cut the ties of Spanish America with Madrid were not in themselves revolutions, in the sense that we apply that word to the vast, radical, and permanent structural changes which shook Russia, France, England, and the United States in the eighteenth and nineteenth centuries. Rather, they were the beginning of a long, slow process of politi-cal addition which very gradually has accommodated within the political system more and more of the region's power groups.

While the Indian, without question, had the most bitter grievances against the Spanish rule, he played a minor role in the battles against the Spaniards.[9] And indeed, except in Mexico and Bolivia, he has played a minor role in the revolutionary process since. The *mestizo* played a more substantial role, but he suffered exclusion from both worlds—Indian and white—whence he sprang. With torn soul he was denied full privileges in either his father's or his mother's community. The chief leaders of the wars of independence were the Creoles, the pure-blooded Spaniards or Portuguese born in America. While the foreigners from Europe were enjoying the pomp and luxury of the vice-regal courts and episcopal palaces, the Creole developed the "robust consciousness of being no longer a Portuguese or a Spaniard but an American." [10]

As the colonial years wore on, he chafed increasingly under the rule of the ceremonial transients from abroad, and as the several wars came to an end, the Creoles found themselves well entrenched, in charge of lands, ports, and commerce, well placed in the social order.

The centralist, urban-oriented doctrines of the old regime lingered on, although from time to time spokesmen for a more federal order appeared. For the most part, political leadership fell to that strong man or *caudillo* who could muster sufficient support from the various concentrated sources of power: the military, the landowners, the Church, and more recently, the labor unions and the university.

The state in Latin America thus became the tool of the powerful. It protected them and their property and fostered their economic system and their social ways. It supported, for example, the inefficient cultivation of huge tracts of land of single crops designed for easy export. The state served to control, if not to curtail, effective economic competition. And most important, it was detached from meaningful social or economic involvement with the nation as a whole. While its existence was felt in the cities, it left the countryside remarkably untouched by its influence or succor, firmly in the hands of those few who owned the land.

As the old structures melted and new ones emerged in the fires of democratic revolution in Europe and the United States, the challenges to traditional authority had immediate appeal to the *criollo* elite of Latin America. But, to be an effective form of national government, constitutional democracy requires more than the replacement of traditional leaders by new ones, however modern their outlook. The working of democracy does not depend so much on the substitution of new elites as it does on the responsiveness of leadership to the remainder of the community.

This principle, in turn, rests on the presumptions that the community is so motivated and organized as to attract and enforce the continuing and effective attention of the state to its needs and priorities, that the community has the power to make the state conform to its will, and that the state is so composed that it must respond. It is apparent that these prerequisites for effective constitutional democratic government were more or less in place in Europe and the United States before democracy was tried. It is equally apparent that Latin America adopted democracy well before the prerequisites for its success were there.[11]

2

In most of Latin America the state's authority, reach, and sense of identification are limited to a rather small radius around the major urban areas. In the countryside it is often either disregarded or looked upon with fear and suspicion. There the *latifundia* or its equivalent exists as a virtually self-contained and self-sufficient political, economic, and social unit. Where the *latifundista* does not hold sway, there are a variety of other rural dwellers—the small landowner, the tenant farmer, and, perhaps most numerous of all, the squatter and occasional farm laborer. These groups are largely detached from both the nation and the state. The state is also seriously restricted in its ability to collect taxes, halt the outflow of badly needed capital, control the military, or reflect the needs of the community in political, social, and economic progress.

While the social system of Latin America has feudal aspects, the Latin American landowner has lacked feudalism's saving grace: He has no loyalty to a higher authority, king or liege; he is not tied to the nation's interest or community's welfare by traditions or commitment or interest. He is in this sense above the battle, without need to become immersed in the business of government. Lacking in the *esprit de corps* of a governing class, he has neither the capacity nor the desire to lead the populace, from whom he needs little and feels permanently detached.[12]

It is not surprising that such an attitude toward and notion of the state has produced dictators, most recently, Trujillo, Perón, Pérez Jiménez, and a score of others. Accepted, often

sought after, and sometimes even longed for after he has been
put down, the dictator offers the promise of that predemocratic
integrative absolutism of which Latin America was prematurely
deprived. He pretends to being the harbinger of national integration and purpose, the man who will speak with the voice of
the people to make the shattered pieces of society whole. Once in
power, however, he and his friends are invariably struck by the
enormity and the thanklessness of the task, compared with the
easy gain at hand. With little responsibility to use public resources for public purposes, the dictator gains much through
control of the state.

The political leadership which has thus developed, however,
has not been without quite exceptional talent and dedication. Its
failure to create a state which could in turn build a nation is not
so much a reflection on its competence, character, or purpose as
it is of the historical sequence by which the environment was
developed and the nature and timing of events. Furthermore,
the Latin American state has been largely denied the opportunity
of rallying the nation for war or for defense against aggression.
This defensive function, of course, has played an extremely
important role in the integration of power and in the national
development of the United States, the countries of Europe,
Japan, India, and, indeed, of all true nations. Latin America,
in so many ways cursed by history, has been largely insulated
from the great wars of the world and has been remarkably free
from serious war between its own states. Its fondness for what
seem to us rather superficial militaristic trappings, its relative lack
of nationalistic heroes and its exaggeration of those wars it has
had are signs of this inadequacy.

Perhaps the principal opportunity which the Latin American
state has had to arouse the nation for resistance to external
intervention and influence has been provided by the United
States, both its government and business. Our intervention has
served as a partial substitute for the crisis of war.

One can argue that United States intervention in Mexico,
for example, was a primary, perhaps even essential, ingredient
in that country's nation-building process, which has gone further
than that of any other country in Latin America. The nationali-

zation of the foreign oil companies in 1938, for example, nationalized far more than oil. It helped to galvanize a nation, and today few would deny that the act was politically necessary, even though in many ways it was economic folly and, at least by Anglo-Saxon lights, judicial hanky-panky.

In the Dominican Republic the nation-building efforts of the Social Democratic Party have been substantially and perhaps fortuitously strengthened because of the United States intervention in 1965. And if we can assume that Cuba is becoming a nation, surely United States government and business can take some perverse kind of credit for the achievement.

It is intriguing to note that Castro's Cuba may be rivaling the United States in providing a threat of intervention against which national solidarity can be forged. Perhaps the best example of this was the Venezuelan elections of 1964, when Cuban terrorists sought to disrupt the orderly transition of government from Betancourt to Leoni. Cuban-supported guerrilla activity has continued in Venezuela since. This continuing source of danger to the nation has without question been a nationalizing factor. Che Guevara's effort in Bolivia might have had a similar effect in that unusually disintegrated country if it had not fizzled so soon.

Then too, the Latin American state, by ironic windfall, was spared much of the struggle of nationalizing development by the coincidental expansion of international demand for its raw materials in the second half of the nineteenth century, owing to the Industrial Revolution. Latin America was provided with a ready-made bonanza prosperity for a few without having to undertake the tough task of building a modern, diversified internal economic structure. World demand for its products— coffee, sugar, cotton, bananas, copper, zinc, iron, and oil— reinforced and sustained the patterns of land use and labor which had been developed in colonial times. And these patterns linger on today, atrophying as world demand and markets change, while pressures grow for the long overdue development of modern industry and agriculture and for efficient internal market and credit systems.

The state was also diverted from its national role by the fact that commercial development in Latin America became so clearly a function of foreign enterprise. The economic role of the state became that of serving the domestic status quo and attracting complementary foreign investors and entrepreneurs. The interlocking of Latin American states with foreign economies and entrepreneurs brought strength and wealth to a few people, but it has done little to solve the problem of national integration and political development for the people in general. The ironies and dilemmas are numerous. Are the people and nation of Brazil truly served if special trade benefits are arranged which have the effect of sustaining the world price of sugar and thus fostering existing structures of sugar power—political, social, and economic—in Northeast Brazil? Are the people of Colombia and the nation as a whole helped by world concessions which tend to continue and solidify the strength of coffee power? Is it better to make the multiple commitments to change which are necessary to diversify, to undergo the agony and thus to weld a more realistic national framework? Is it better to come rapidly to revolutionary transition or to continue to develop slowly, frequently wandering down the blind alleys of the past?

Increasingly, Latin Americans are asking these and similar questions. The distortions and imbalances which characterize the region's relationship to the rest of the world—and particularly to the United States—are finally exposing Latin Americans to the dreadful disparity between their own way of life and the model of modern Western society which they thought they were emulating. Honest and serious Latin Americans are seeing with increasing clarity that alongside the societies of Europe and the United States which they had sought to follow, their experiments in nationhood seem in many ways to be a dismal, purposeless failure. They are looking inward at themselves and their countrymen; looking backward at their historical roots; looking forward to new forms of community which may be more consistent with reality. Sociologists, such as Colombia's Orlando Fals Borda and Brazil's Cándido Mendes, are holding up the mirrors in which for the first time they can see themselves and their societies accurately reflected. The Christian Democratic movement in Chile, Venezuela, the Dominican Republic, and elsewhere is in the political forefront of this self-examination.[13]

But today's nationalizers face a more complicated task than

their predecessors. In one way or another, here and there, the nationalizing process has been haphazardly working. Interest groups, social organizations, political parties, are beginning to form the means of wider political participation, bringing into the light of power the true requirements of the people, creating alternative sources of influence and power which are competitive with the traditional satellitic arrangement of the oligarchs and the state which they permit. And so a new picture is being painted of what the Latin American nation-state must be. The lines and colors are blurred and obscure. The forms are shadowy and dark. The picture may seem menacing and dangerous; but perhaps for the first time it is at least legitimate and genuine.

Consider the nature and forms of protest. Until very recently, Latin American protestors tended to view the deficiencies of their social, economic, and political systems in very much the same way as did their European counterparts. The adoption of the irrelevant European model extended even into the area of protest against the model itself. Latin American protestors have dubbed themselves with the familiar European titles: socialists, fascists, communists, and so on. Increasingly, however, protest is taking a distinctly Latin American form.

The Peruvian APRA* movement is perhaps the earliest case in point. Víctor Raúl Haya de la Torre, its founder and leader, as a student was appalled by the inadequacies of the Peruvian political system in meeting the needs of the nation and its people. He rebelled, was exiled, and turned naturally to Marx and Lenin as the authors of the most familiar and convenient models of discontent at the time. In the early 1920's, however, Haya broke with his doctrinaire Communist colleague, José Carlos Mariategui, insisting, with what was at the time remarkable and original insight, that Marxism-Leninism was designed for modern, industrial Europe and befitted Latin America little better than what was in place. In Peru it was hard to find much of a proletariat that could be vested with the powers of government. So Haya sought in the Indian culture of Peru the cultural roots from which he felt political legitimacy must spring. *Aprismo,*

* Popular Revolutionary Alliance for America (Alianza Popular Revolucionaria América)

the APRA ideology, developed and remains as a kind of ideological amalgam, its significance being that, imperfectly and for the most part unsuccessfully, it sought to develop an indigenous Latin American political philosophy and purpose.

The APRA is one of many similar modern movements of nationalistic reform in Latin America. Without question, the most successful was that culminating in the Mexican Revolution. Others include the Estado Novo (New State) of Vargas in Brazil, Peronismo in Argentina, the Movimiento Nacional Revolucionario (MNR) in Bolivia, and Acción Democrática in Venezuela. Some have been more successful than others; some more heroic, more democratic, more indigenous, more lasting.

All were born in frustration and nurtured by the continuing irrelevancy of historical governmental forms to the surrounding reality. The tragedy is that these movements have created so little change. Except in a few cases—we must keep mentioning Mexico, Bolivia, and Cuba—the new order has replaced very little of the old; in a sense, the old patterns are being repeated.[14]

Today the Latin American state has the form and trappings of modernity—social laws which are among the most progressive in the world, land-reform statutes on every hand, administrative titles and officialdom reflecting every sort of revolutionary goal, all having been inflated, encouraged, and given technical nourishment by the United States. At the same time, behind the façade the fundamental structural flaws, vacuums, inconsistencies, and distortions lie like slothful monsters. We penetrate and we see that constitutional rights are aspirations, not inviolable guarantees; that labor legislation is a pious hope, not an enforceable code; that but a tiny fraction of the people have the means or motivation with which to organize themselves for exerting influence or showing power; that the governmental form in place is not so much democracy (if by democracy we mean government of, by, and for the people) as it is oligarchy—government by, of, and for the powerful.

There can be no doubt, however, that access to the oligarchy is increasing. One observant Latin American told me: "As new groups and individuals organize and gain power they are sieved, or put through a screen, as it were. Those who are harmless are admitted; those who carry danger with them are offered rich incentives to alter their course; they generally submit and are thus admitted safely; a few—a very few—are incorruptible and remain outside. These are the agents for the extension of democracy in our countries; our hope is with them."

3

The principal challenge faced today by governments in Latin America is the intensification of national economic and political integration. Upon the achievement of this depend industrialization, export diversification, regional integration, political continuity, the development of a national community, and more. At the moment, most Latin American states appear unable and in many ways unwilling to effect this integration.

The difficulties which they confront in doing so are formidable. There is the problem of the integration of the foreign enterprise into the national economy, with the related questions of support, concessions, regulations, control, and selection. There are various laws, programs, and policies by which countries encourage or discourage foreign enterprise and investment. There are requirements for local control, as in Mexico and Venezuela in some cases (e.g., insurance). But when we look more closely we find that when the state or the oligarchy wants to it can alter or circumvent the application of the law. Whatever the integration technique or law may be, it is substantially influenced by two juridical concepts which are distinct from our own: the states residual ownership of mineral rights and the "social function of property." These concepts reflect Latin America's political origin in absolute monarchy, with its notion that property is not a right of the individual to be protected by the state, but a trust from the domain of the sovereign to be used for the benefit of society.[15] Success of such a governing philosophy presupposes a king or a state that knows precisely what is for "the benefit of society" and a society which is willing to accept the sovereign's judgment. This in turn requires clear notions regarding political goals and objectives which are prerequisites to the formulation of criteria by which good and bad foreign investment may be determined. But, as we have seen, the Latin American state and its surrounding political society are singularly weak in making such formulations.

In recent years Latin American policies with regard to foreign investment have consisted mostly of an intricate set of tax, trade, and tariff regulations designed to encourage domestic industries to produce at home what had been imported and to diversify and increase exports. This has been essentially a tinkering process on the part of an increasing number of economic technicians. These integrative efforts have been only marginally and superficially successful, for they leave the fundamental socio-political structures unchanged. For example, it seems entirely clear that Latin American poverty is at least as much a function of the internal distribution of the returns of trade as it is of world market conditions. There is a real question whether adjustments designed to help primary product producers do not perhaps limit and postpone the time when the nation as a whole can be an independent, competitive and prosperous participant in the world economy. Import substitution industries thrive until they saturate the small market for their products. They then tend to languish, utilizing a small percentage of their capacity. Local power groups, whether it be the coffee, cotton or sugar growers or those with need for political patronage, tend to distort the state's economic policies and programs for their own ends. Government itself becomes involved in a variety of activities for which it has neither the administrative nor the technical capacity. These include railroads and other public utilities, public works, housing and construction programs. Corruption and inefficiency tend to blur achievements and undermine general confidence.

A related problem of national integration facing the Latin American state involves the organization of agriculture and its incorporation into the national economic and political system. Few states have the will or capacity to undo and reform the rural-urban tangle of land tenure patterns, technical deficiencies, credit distortions, market obstructions and lack of processing and distributive facilities.

The difficulty is not simply with the central government itself or with its regional and local outposts; it involves as much the lack of trust and identity which the people feel toward government, the remoteness of the *campesino* in the field from the palace. It is unreasonable to expect the isolated individual to be able to comprehend and put to use the machinery of government. The world of courts, lawyers, government offices, and technical agencies is a distant and confusing one to most Latin Americans, which he is unable to penetrate without organization, costly assistance, and mental preparation.

The striking characteristic of the Latin American government or state, then, is not its power to intervene in the economic, social, and political life of the country; but rather its remoteness and detachment, its lack of a constituency. Thus, government in the region tends to be a bureaucratic and administrative formation, detached from the majority of the people, answerable to several relatively small conglomerates of power, seeking justification, purpose, and meaning in the ideology of democracy, but being continually reminded that the stuff of democracy is not present in its domain.

Perhaps most important, this relationship—or lack of it—of the Latin American government to the individual makes the government singularly incapable of changing the structure of the community. If development in Latin America is merely another word for change, then it becomes apparent how limited most of the governments are in being able to pursue it. As we have seen and will see time and again, what is offered as "development strategy" by economic planners—industrialization, export promotion, trade preferences—often adds up to a system for using state power to adjust relationships within the existing structure with the effect of strengthening that structure. The strategy is generally less a plan for change and integration than a format for adjustment in order to maintain the existing economic and political system, which is threatened by a multitude of imbalances and distortions. The fact that development so obviously requires change in those systems seems to elude the planners.

Obtaining and keeping political power in Latin America appears to many North Americans to be a confusing, unstable, and unpredictable process. Regimes come and go with no particular relationship to elections. Seemingly irrational violence is common. And yet, as Kalman H. Silvert has pointed out, the political process in Latin America is in a sense quite stable and predictable.[16] Although the patterns of the political process are unfamiliar to those who are used to the traditional ways of constitutional democracy, there can be no denying that they repeat themselves with remarkable regularity and consistency. The intervention of the military, the *coup d'état,* terror, exile, and oppression are as much a pattern there as our Presidential and congressional elections; and there is a certain stability in predictability. The process is only unstable and confusing if we insist on looking at the political systems of Latin America as though they were the constitutional democracies which they pretend to be.

I was in Guatemala in March 1963, during the transition from President Idígoras Fuentes to Colonel Enrique Peralta Azurdia. The event was remarkably orderly and efficient. It consisted of a parade from the army barracks to the airport which lasted about half an hour. I watched from the hotel window as children cheered and waved flags. When I returned home, my wife expressed concern, having read of "revolution in Guatemala." In fact, of course, this was not revolution, but a familiar method of transfer of power. Nothing substantial had changed. There was only a different man in the presidential palace. Power in Guatemala remained pretty much where it had always been, and it continued to be wielded for very much the same ends. The system worked smoothly, but it was not democracy.

Another of the more expeditious barracks revolts was that of Fulgencio Batista on March 10, 1952, which returned him to power in Cuba. Batista's forces began their take-over at precisely 2:43 in the morning and within an hour and seventeen minutes had obtained complete control of the government. By 8:30 a.m. President Carlos Prio and members of his cabinet had taken refuge in the Mexican embassy. But nothing else had changed.[17]

When the military leaders of Argentina made General Juan Carlos Onganía president in June of 1959, he assumed office with more power than any predecessor. He used it to make a clean sweep, dissolving Parliament, state and municipal governments, political parties, even displacing justices on the Supreme Court.

And yet there was hardly a murmur of protest. A reporter on the scene commented: "No constitutional government has ever been laid to rest with so little fuss." [18] Since then, Brazil, Peru, and Panama, among others, have followed suit.

These are by no means special cases. While every country in Latin America is, of course, different, the regional commonalties significantly outweigh national specialities. Even Costa Rica, which boasts one of the region's most democratic regimes, has had unorthodox shifts of government marked by violence in this century, and there is no certainty that violence will not come again.

The Latin American dictator is, as a rule, sensitive to his need for a political base, and he expends considerable time and effort rallying support for himself, bargaining with power groups and seeking to manufacture a consensus. Nicaragua, for example, has been ruled for almost fifty years by perhaps the only dynasty in recent Latin American history. Yet no one familiar with the political strategy of the Somoza family would deny the ability, skill, and foresight with which it worries, cajoles, and manipulates consent.

Generally, in Latin America, elections do not involve substantial proportions of the population, organized in a meaningful way. In many countries there are strict limitations on the right to vote. Of Brazil's eighty-four million people, only about thirteen million are eligible to vote in national elections.[19] Apathy is also a serious limitation, as well as lack of organization of voters by political parties and pressure groups. Without political organization the individual finds it hard to believe that he can affect his political surroundings. He is confirmed in this belief by the fact that the results of elections are by no means always final or definitive. As a result, in Latin America as a whole about 20 per cent of the citizens are registered on the voting rolls.[20] Those who actually vote are generally far fewer.

For the most part, elections are a measure of the strength of one particular power element, generally a political party or a charismatic leader, which unlike other power elements depends for its existence upon popular support. Election results are a definite consideration to the other power contenders in the society, who weigh them and determine to what extent they will accept them. Unlike ours, Latin American elections are, therefore, tentative rather than final resolutions of choices. Whether the elections will be definitive may depend on a complicated process of negotiating, bargaining, and rule-making between the elected group and others who control substantial power.

In 1964, for example, Arnulfo Arias claimed to have been elected president of Panama. Some say he undoubtedly was the people's choice. More important groups than his, however, were unwilling to accommodate the power structure to allow his entry and Marco Robles became president. In 1968 Arias ran again, was elected overwhelmingly despite diligent efforts by the oligarchy—of which he is a somewhat unruly member—to defeat him, and was allowed to hold office for eleven days. Then his efforts to control the country's military caused the National Guard to throw him out. He sought refuge in the Canal Zone, where he constituted a singular embarrassment for the American embassy. The whole sequence was rich in irony. Few Latin American military units have received more training and assistance from the United States Army than Panama's. With none, it might be presumed, do we have closer relations. It is, therefore, hard to conceive that the National Guard would have refused if in the name of constitutional democracy we had urged it to allow Arias to continue in office. Apparently, however, we made no such request. Perhaps we felt it would be undue intervention in the affairs of a foreign country, or perhaps we feared that Arias would make some unwelcome changes.

The tragic history of APRA in Peru is perhaps the most dramatic example of a political party which consistently won elections and just as consistently was prevented from assuming power. Even its combination with Belaúnde's Acción Popular Party to secure his election ended in his ouster by the military in 1968. The reason seems to have been the fear of the military that its aging archenemy, Haya de la Torre, might be elected in the approaching elections of 1969.

Under such circumstances, one might well ask, why bother with elections? Why are Latin American nations usually so conscientious about holding them regularly and on time? The answer is that they are recognized as being an essential device for measuring a certain brand of power which emanates more or less from the people. The fact that elections are only one element among many which determine the final allocation of power does not mean that they can be ignored or avoided.

Some Latin American regimes, of course, find it unnecessary to hold elections. During an interview on the subject in 1959, Fidel Castro's view was reported as follows: "You talk about elections and democracy, but the whole history of Latin America demonstrates that this democracy has been a farce. . . . How can you talk about democratic elections in which only minorities participate? . . . There can be no true democracy without social justice, without a social revolution, and the so-called democratic systems in Latin America will not allow social justice. . . . If I called elections today I would win by an overwhelming margin. But to plunge Cuba today into an election campaign would paralyze the process of social revolution." [21]

The Latin American political system involves a continuing negotiation of power. It is like a game in which the players at the table generally include: various elements of the military or the police, often opposed to one another (as in Honduras in 1958); men of great wealth, who themselves are divided among the older contenders and the newer groups; political parties and their leadership; the charismatic *caudillo* or boss, who may have his own personalistic party; the Church, divided between the old, aristocratic hierarchy and the new, radical, socially active priests and bishops; in some countries organizations of workers, urban and rural; and university leaders, students, and faculty. There are other players at the table, too, who come and go according to their interest. Of these, the foreigner is perhaps most important. He comes in many forms and sizes: a division of marines; aircraft carriers off the beach; the ambassador; the foreign company with a large investment to protect—a mine, land, oil wells; the entrepreneur who brings access to technology, markets, or money; the bank; the international organization; the terrorist and the guerrilla.

The table sounds crowded with players. But probably 80 per cent of the people of most Latin American countries have no place to sit, no cards to play. Access to the game is difficult, though not impossible, as we shall see.

The game involves some rough rules, manners, and ceremonies. New players are admitted when they can demonstrate that they control sufficient power to be worth recognizing, as long as they do not jeopardize the position of existing players. Once in, they are committed to observe the gaming or negotiating rules and process, or else they are expelled. Although the game proceeds within a rigorous context, there is room for play. That is to say, university students can revolt, throw bombs, and wreak havoc up to a point; then the government has an accepted right to step in. But if the government steps too hard, is otherwise generally offensive, or is weak and on the way out anyway, then other players at the table—the military, for example—may seize the opportunity to move in and replace it.

Violence is an important part of the game, for it is a dramatic way of presenting power, showing determination to use it, and testing the commitment and power of other groups. The damage which rioters can do is often a good measure of the strength, determination, purpose, and competence of the authorities. Tanks outside the palace gates do not necessarily have to shoot to force the president out. The guerrilla in the hills is often as much a phantom as he is real, but whichever he is, he affects the game.

The rules of the game are only vaguely related to what we call the constitutional process. They are primarily a set of understandings and commitments made by the players, sometimes tacitly, sometimes explicitly. This character of the system is best illustrated in the "learning process" through which Latin American reformist movements pass after achieving power. This is related to the screening or sieving process by which new elites are admitted. The reformist movement, in its early stages, is outside the effective political arena. Initially, it seeks power, calling for radical structural changes, revolutionary in character. It is not so much asking for a place at the table as it is seeking to overthrow the table and change the game: foreign business must be nationalized, the power of the military curtailed, land distributed to the peasants. The election then becomes useful as a means by which the movement can demonstrate and others can gauge its power in a measurable way. The existing players need to decide whether to accept this new power. Acceptance depends on the understandings or rules which the new player is prepared to make and accept. Generally, at this point the new movement starts using a different vocabulary. "Evolution" replaces "revolution," and there is well-rounded talk about all parties working together for the good of the poor people. The structural factor is eliminated from its advocacy of change.

Acción Democrática in Venezuela is an example of a movement which had to learn how to play the game the hard way. In 1945, AD demanded instant reform, speaking of action against the military and the oil companies. They thus violated the existing rules, were expelled, scourged, and chastened. When the party returned in 1958, it spoke in much more "reasonable" terms about the changes it sought. Even the oil companies hailed this staunch organization of the "democratic left."

Another example of the game in play was Guatemala in 1954 when Jacobo Arbenz, one of the very few democratically elected presidents of Guatemala, attempted to weaken the army, give land to the peasants, and collaborate with the Communists. He was promptly forced to give up his program by a combination of domestic and foreign power groups.

When the system becomes hopelessly snarled and deadlocked by the contending powers, the *caudillo* or strong man steps in —a Rojas Pinilla in Colombia, a Velasco Ibarra in Ecuador, an Odría in Peru, a Perón or a Trujillo. Typically, at least for a time, he is beloved by the excluded poor whom he persuades he is representing at the gaming table. In reality, he is admitted by the elites who, acting voluntarily or involuntarily, accept him as a tentative way of resolving a crisis. Sometimes, when he has served his purpose, he is disposed of, often to be kept waiting in the wings for the next time the normal functioning of the system fails. But sometimes his ambition and ability allow him to gain sufficient control of all power contenders so that he lingers on for many years and even for generations, as in the case of the Somoza family.

Even to speak of "resistance to change" in Latin America is

apt to mislead and distort the true and distinctive nature of the political system. Charles Anderson describes the system as "one that permits new power contenders to be added to [it] but is so designed that older political factors are not eliminated, one that is—if one can accept a most surprising use of the term—more 'tolerant' for political participation than are the political systems of the advanced Western nations." [22] This is a most original and subtle idea which deserves careful thought. If Latin America has achieved a distinctive type of political method, which we might call the Tolerant Oligarchy, those who are interested and involved in the region and its growth and development must design their approach accordingly.

Among other things, Latin America may have devised a system which is peculiarly resistant to revolution. We have already seen that the region avoided the massive restructuring of the great democratic revolutions of Europe and North America, which effectively eliminated all power which could not base its claim in popular consent. Latin America thereby evaded the catharsis of revolution, which flushes out the old and legitimizes some new varieties of power while prohibiting others; and which establishes new and more explicit values, purposes, standards, and criteria. Rather, the region has adopted or acquired consecutively a unique kind of political amalgam: divine-right monarchy, military authority, forms of feudalism, and constitutional democracy. All exist side by side, none entirely legitimate or illegitimate, none definitive.

All along we have had to except from the general rule the three Latin American nations which have undergone true revolution by our definition—Mexico in 1910, Bolivia in 1952, and Cuba in 1959. In all three instances profound structural change did take place; and certain historic power contenders were eliminated. Foreign investments were nationalized as part of an "anti-imperialistic" ideology which was aimed at eliminating external economic and political influence, as well as at unifying the nation. Agrarian reform was of high priority as a means of eliminating the power of semifeudal groups and modernizing the political system; and each country made a point of curtailing the influence of the military in political affairs.

Upon closer analysis, however, there is a question as to whether the classic lines of the old process are not still visible. Indeed, one wonders if the postrevolutionary system does not remain what we might call a Tolerant Neo-oligarchy. Has Cuba, for example, really undergone land reform, or has it merely transferred the power capability deriving from land to different hands, to a different group within an essentially oligarchic framework? And is military influence truly curtailed? Land reform in Mexico is surely not what the revolutionary leaders had in mind. Land power seems to have devolved to the state Ejido Bank and to the large commercial farmers, who exist more or less in violation of the revolutionary norms. In Bolivia the great tin mines are nationalized and the land is reformed, 5 million hectares having been distributed to some 152,000 families. *Minifundismo* has replaced *latifundismo*. But the effects of these revolutionary acts on the political process are not at all clear.

Anti-imperialism was the battle cry of the Mexican and Cuban revolutions, and yet in both nations foreign power is once again a strong force on the national scene. The Soviet bloc is unquestionably a factor in Cuba's political processes, and Mexico is welcoming back foreign investors and entrepreneurs, offering myriad concessions. (In Bolivia, the issue of foreign intervention was strangely absent. There the United States not only financed the revolution but was a profound and continuing influence on its course).[23]

Similarly, signs of the old ways are visible in their political processes. Mexico's ruling political conglomerate, the Party of the Institutionalized Revolution (PRI), looks astonishingly like a new model of the old classical oligarchical pattern. PRI was formed during the revolution and has been reorganized periodically since to make it the continuing and changing embodiment of Mexican power. Since its beginning in 1928, it has overwhelmingly won every election just as predictably as did the oligarchic Democratic Party in Mississippi—before George Wallace. It has done more, however. It has provided a dynamic, flexible arena for the continuing inclusion of new power contenders and for the negotiation of new rules and understandings concerning the allocation and uses of power. For the PRI the

principal problems of political conflict are not with opposition
parties so much as with different groups within its heterogeneous
self. The President of Mexico has increasingly become a moder-
ator, using his authority to maintain balance and loyalty among
the power contenders of the PRI.

The result, according to Raymond Vernon, is that "in a real
sense . . . the strength of the Mexican president is a mirage.
. . . In his ceaseless efforts to achieve unanimity, in his concern
to extend the reach of the PRI the full distance to both the
right and the left, he is held to a course of action which is zig-
zagging and vacillating when it is not blandly neutral." [24]

Although the historic political power processes of Latin America have unusual resiliency, there can be no denying the radical,
profound, and permanent nationalizing effects of the revolutions
of Mexico, Bolivia, and Cuba. The effects of the Mexican
Revolution, for example, have been well described by Seymour
Martin Lipset in his essay on "Values, Education and Entrepreneurship" in Latin America.

"The Mexican Revolution transformed the image and legitimate political emphasis of the nation. It sought to destroy the
sense of superiority felt by those of pure Spanish descent by
stressing the concept of *Mexicanidad,* and by a glorification of
the Indian past. . . . Though Mexico clearly retains major
elements of the traditional Latin American system, it is the one
country which has identified its national ethos with that of
equality and an open society. And with the sense of a collective
revolutionary commitment to growth and egalitarianism, one
finds that business activities, which are sanctioned by government approval, are presented as ways of fulfilling national objectives." [25]

Furthermore, a recent study of sociological changes in Mexico
found that "there is evidence that the Revolution, by reducing
the level of affluence and power of *cacique* (chief) families
and by redistributing *hacienda* lands, has had a considerable
psychological impact on the population in the direction of
strengthening attitudes of independence and initiative, and, conversely, reducing those of submissiveness." [26]

In Cuba and Bolivia also, revolution brought to the people

unprecedented pride and unity, destroying in the case of the latter the traditional barriers which deprived the Indian of equal rights and opportunities. As in Mexico, it gave to the poor and landless of both countries new hope, new power, and new confidence.

It is necessary, however, to distinguish among the three revolutions as to their effect on political stability and the creation of new political institutions. Mexico—and apparently Cuba— emerged from revolution with perhaps the most stable political institutions in Latin America. Bolivia plainly did not. The old revolutionary party and its leaders fell into disarray and discredit, and were forced in 1965 to give way to military rule. In spite of the changes it wrought, the revolution created few if any lasting institutions. It destroyed the old order but provided no clear replacement. Bolivia's most significant political organizations, the mineworkers' and other labor unions, have been regularly used as means to power by one or another political figure, but they have not been institutionalizers of the revolution as they were in Mexico through the PRI.

Huntington suggests several causes for this disparity in political effect of the revolution in Mexico and Bolivia.[27] First is a difference in levels of violence, and thus in required mobilization of power. The Mexican Revolution cost a million lives, including those of almost all its leaders, as well as the economic dislocation of the country for several decades. What Trotsky called "the overhead expenses of historic progress" were extraordinarily high.[28] But in the fury of this exhausting struggle new and tough political organizations were formed and tested, and their rivals eliminated. In Bolivia, on the other hand, only about 3,000 were killed and the costs were much lower.[29] Furthermore, the United States was eagerly at hand to finance the transition, providing Bolivia with more than $150 million from 1953 through 1959. Since then, the country has received grants and loans from the United States totaling $400 million through 1964. Thus, Bolivia was by no means exhausted by the revolution. Plenty of appetite for violence was left. Tried and tested revolutionary organizations were not created; rival claimants were not eliminated. Indeed, the revolution was so painless that it hardly produced heroes, at least not in the Mexican or Cuban sense.

Secondly, none of the leaders of the revolution was able to get a secure and reliable hold on the important labor organizations of the country, particularly those of the miners and the peasants, which had been formed before and apart from the revolution. In Mexico, on the other hand, labor came to power with and as a part of the revolutionary party.[30]

Thirdly, the Bolivian Revolution failed to produce political stability and national unity because of the marked and unusual absence of antiforeign nationalism. There were relatively few foreign interests in Bolivia before the revolution. The owners of the three great tin mines were all Bolivian. Nationalization of the mines thus produced none of the foreign protest that was so valuable to the political formation of the Mexican nation in the 1930's. Huntington concludes: "The Bolivian Revolution . . . raises the issue of whether a complete revolution is possible in the absence of both a significant prerevolutionary foreign presence and a significant postrevolutionary foreign intervention." [31]

The Bolivian Revolution was undoubtedly further weakened by the intervention of the United States and its insistence upon applying economic criteria to what were essentially political problems. By forcing "austerity" and "stringency" in the 1950's on the infant revolutionary regimes it probably insured their failure. In addition, it would seem that the United States must be held to some degree accountable for the downfall of the Paz Estenssoro regime in 1965 at the hands of General René Barrientos, who had been Paz's vice-president. Prior to 1960 the military would have been far too weak to overthrow Paz, but between then and 1965 Bolivia received $10.6 million worth of military assistance from the United States. With that, the army became the most effective political institution in the country.[32]

4

There is little doubt among political leaders of Latin America that the pressures for change are mounting and multiplying and that in one way or another these pressures will have increasing impact. A variety of engines are moving to fill the vacuums and voids between political power and the majority of society. They are traveling at different speeds, in different directions, and are fueled from different sources. The future of the hemisphere will be largely determined by what combinations and balances of these engines are successful.

Latin America and the United States confront these engines and the pressures for change which they embody equivocally, acknowledging their existence, but sometimes wishing and occasionally expecting that they will somehow stall or break down. Development planners and business entrepreneurs have been reluctant to face the existing environment boldly and realistically in all its complexity. They have been particularly reluctant to acknowledge its historic structural flaws, preferring to plaster them over with self-deception in the interests of achieving short-term objectives. This process has been going on a long time. Those who have advocated not rocking the boat have been persuasive. But it is apparent that population increases, food shortages, growing political awareness, the transistor radio, are threatening the boat as never before. The time for change—structural, revolutionary change—is running out.

The most fundamental problem is perhaps ideological in that it concerns the necessity of a vision about what sort of a community the Latin American states are going to achieve. What are its purposes going to be, its priorities, its values, and its standards for the allocation of power? This is a vision which has historically been blurred and distorted, a reflection in a series of warped mirrors.

But also fundamental are the courage and foresight with which many are prepared to view the engines of change which are moving.

"What we have to face," said the late Bishop Manuel Larrain of Chile, for twenty years the most forward-looking prelate of Latin America, "is the hard, painful birth of a new civilization. The danger arises if we do not become aware of this event, and if we cannot give guidance to all the dynamic drives stirring up in our continent." [33]

There are those who say: "Change need not be radical, structural, or revolutionary. The things that need doing can be done by an extension and perfection of the existing order." Characteristic of this group are the *latifundistas,* representing the sugar, coffee, and cotton interests; the dictators, military and civilian; and some Americans.

Others say that the change must be radical and structural; that existing systems are neither modern nor worth preserving. But such change can proceed in a gradual and evolutionary way, the way of peaceful revolution. This is the doctrine of Latin America's most gifted and dedicated political leaders —Betancourt, José Figueres, Lleras Camargo, Eduardo Frei— whose skill, patience, and endurance the world must admire.

A third group, however, says to the gradualists: "You are fooling yourselves. The archaic power groups are too strong. You cannot move them peacefully. You think you have changed things and then they slip back. Look at Brazil and Argentina today, after the ineffective efforts of Goulart and Frondizi, not to mention the efforts of Juan Bosch in the Dominican Republic. Revolution is needed, no matter what. If violence comes, then it will come, and with it the blood, the agony, and the heroes out of which nations are built. Let us move in the great tradition of Zapata, of Castro and Guevara."

4

THE CULTURE: A Crisis of Purpose

Before Kwame Nkrumah's statue was smashed from its pedestal in Accra, Ghana, several years ago, it had written across its base: "Seek ye first the political kingdom and all other things shall be added unto it." [1]

So too, as we have seen, it could be said that whatever Latin America may seek in terms of economic development, the political dilemmas must first be resolved. Political revolution which transfers power from those who do not have sufficient will to those who do is often the forerunner of development. In more integrated and representative communities, of course, there are other ways of performing the transfer. In the political economy of the United States, for example, the financial system acts as a continuing revolutionary pressure, providing power to innovators and withdrawing power from those whose will or capacity is no longer harmonious with the public need or will. [2] In Latin America, on the other hand, the financial system, dominated by a few very powerful groups and many small moneylenders, solidifies traditional ways and prevents change.

In whatever way a society chooses to allocate power, the choice is essentially political, having to do with the nature and purpose of the political structure. If there is dissatisfaction with the present arrangements of power in Latin America, the nature of the change becomes essentially a matter of political alternatives.

The question then arises of the desired direction and objectives of change. What are to be the purposes of power, of society, and what will be their connection with the individual? What will be the new standards by which power is allocated? What are the values by which the community will measure itself? What is the ideological or visionary context of this change?

These are fundamentally questions of culture and values; of the ends of society as determined by those in control and the means used to achieve those ends and to train the young in their continued achievement.

I

We must start this brief review of the cultural and value characteristics of Latin America with a short look at history.

The best guess is that Latin America was first settled by hunters and berry gatherers from East Asia about 10,000 years ago.[3] It is estimated that by the time of Columbus there were some eleven million people distributed among the Aztec, Mayan, Incan, Chibcha, and lesser nations of what was to become Spanish America. Another two million or so were in what is now Brazil. During the next three centuries, a small group of Europeans came to Latin America, not more than several hundred thousand at the most, during the entire colonial period from the early sixteenth to the early nineteenth century.[4]

The Spaniards generally settled where there were existing concentrations of Indians; the Portuguese preferred uninhabited areas, to which they brought large numbers of Negro slaves from Africa. Later, the Dutch, French, and English came, settling particularly in the Caribbean area, also bringing with them considerable numbers of slaves.

The impact of the Europeans was appalling. Within a few decades 90 per cent of the Indians of the Caribbean Islands were destroyed, mostly by Old World diseases. The Indians of Mexico, Central America, and the Andes were reduced by 20 to 30 per cent over a somewhat longer period of time.

Even so, by 1570 only just over 1 per cent of the population of Latin America was of white European origin, and about the same proportion was Negro. By 1650 more than 80 per cent were still Indian, with most of the rest of mixed blood. By 1800, in a total population of 20.5 million, the breakdown was as follows:[5]

	Spanish Areas	Brazil
	(In Millions)	
Whites	3.3	0.8
Mestizos	5.3	
Indians	7.5	0.3
Negroes	0.8	1.9
Mixed (mainly Mulattos)		.6

Today there are four nations in which the Indian predominates: Guatemala, Ecuador, Peru, and Bolivia. There are eight nations in which the *mestizo* is in the majority: Mexico, Honduras, Nicaragua, El Salvador, Colombia, Venezuela, Chile, and Paraguay. Then there are those nations in which Negro blood is mixed with sizeable *mestizo* populations: Panama, Cuba, the Dominican Republic, areas of Colombia and Venezuela, and the coasts of Honduras and Nicaragua. Haiti is virtually entirely Negro. Brazil's racial pattern is distinct, being about 50 per cent white European with the rest a variety of mixtures. Three countries are predominantly white European: Argentina, Uruguay, and Costa Rica.[6] In general, however, it seems reasonable to estimate that Latin America is more Indian and Negro than it is white European.

From this cultural setting comes the recurring question and the agonized cry: Who are we? Where do we come from? What dreadful, bloody, inconclusive mixture is our history and our legacy?

Let us look briefly at two sides of the question; first, at that heroic, cruel, and greedy handful which made Latin America a part of Western civilization—whether it liked it or not. Spain in her golden age was one of those rare political phenomena: a nation without doubts. She had an absolute sense of mission which represented a happy coincidence between the needs of the king for gold and political influence and the needs of the Roman Catholic Church for believers. In fact, in colonial Latin America the Church belonged to Spain much more than Spain belonged to the Church. This union of political and economic ambition with spiritual values was formed and solidified in Spain prior to the days of the conquistadors during eight centuries of conflict with the Moors. In Spain the roles of soldier and priest came to be glorified and made in many ways inseparable.[7] So it came to be that in Latin America "there was a monk in every helmet and a knight in every cowl," to use John Mackay's felicitous phrase from his remarkable book, *The Other Spanish Christ*.[8] It was quite natural for an elite, so formed and taught, to denigrate manual labor, or even business and banking, as a vile sort of employment fit only for Jews, Moslems, Protestants, and other "misfits."

"The Spaniards who shared Columbus' adventure were educated in the following three principles: First, it is pleasing to God to kill and rob unbelievers; second, that warriors and priests form the noblest social classes; third, that work is debasing, and that the land belongs to the crown and the nobility who conquer it, and to the Church which sanctions and shares its possession." [9]

There were, of course, saintly exceptions, none more so than Father Bartolomé de Las Casas, the great and noble Dominican monk whose successors are today one of the vital hopes of Latin America. Father Bartolomé wrote of the *encomienderos*, who enslaved the Indians for work in the mines or on their lands: "They go about clothed in silk, not only themselves but their mules, and, methinks if the silk were wrung, blood of Indians would ooze from it." [10]

Much has been written about the "Spanish personality," that dominating force which cowed thirteen million people and overcame unbelievable physical hardships. Salvador de Madariaga describes the individualism of the Spaniard as "an insatiable acquisitiveness and lack of a social instinct, an innate dislike to be bound together by obligation or mutual consent." He says that "the Spaniard feels patriotism as he feels love, in the form of a passion where he absorbs the object of his love and assimilates it. He is not dedicated to his country; rather he feels his country belongs to him." [11]

An Argentine sociologist, Carlos Octavio Bunge, observes that this "creole arrogance," acquired from Spain, is actually an extreme form of egotism and a principal trait of the South American psychology. It quickly justifies the use of force and violence, as in the motto of the Republic of Chile: "Where reason fails, let force prevail!" (*Por la razon o por la fuerza.*)[12]

This highly personalized view of patriotism has its parallel in the Spanish view of justice. Neither expediency nor mercy triumphs over justice, but friendship can prevail over whatever law or justice may ordain.[13]

This, in brief, is the culture and values which the civilized West brought to the primitive, weak Indian masses. Generations of Latin Americans have raged against this imposition, sometimes effectively, as in Mexico, where the revolution was ignited and enlightened by the Indian and his heritage. The same protest also was the foundation of Haya de la Torre's APRA movement. Haya wrote: "Indo-America is the expression of the new revolutionary conception of America which, having passed through the period of Spanish and Anglo-Saxon conquests, will create a definite political, economic, and social organization on the national base of its workers, who represent the tradition and the race of the exploited indigenous masses. . . . The new revolution in Latin America will be with an Indian base and orientation, with the native conscience and subconscious expressed in an economic and social renaissance." [14]

A similar belief is held by Miguel Serrano, for many years Chilean ambassador to India and a distinguished author. He believes that there must be a basic readjustment of point of view before a truly South American civilization can develop. Latin America must get rid of the illusion that its civilization is basically Western—a branch of European culture. Serrano believes South America must stop turning toward Europe for guidance, that it must find its own spiritual roots in its own continent, and literally reject the West. "We live like aliens in our own continent; we are spiritually rootless because we have never interpreted our own landscape or drawn spiritual values from it." [15]

Serrano's rejection of the West may seem to some fanciful, but it is a vivid reflection of the sense of cultural illegitimacy and historical alienation which are so pervasive in Latin America. Then too, there may be truth in what he says. Nobody knows, of course, where the South American Indian came from. The best guess, as we have said, is Asia, but a more fanciful theory has it that he sprang from a race that existed before the Flood—from Atlantis or the submerged continent of God-wana.[16] But the theory of Asian origin and Serrano's sense of linkage to the East has had a haunting appeal for me ever since a trip to the Bolivian *altiplano* several years ago, during which I visited several Indian communities. It so happened that I had just returned from South Viet Nam, where I had also been to several rather remote villages. Suddenly, in that high Andean wasteland I felt the presence of some primordial and mysterious linkage between the two—Asia and America. It seemed to me that the collection of huts in the midst of which I stood was but a stone's throw from the highland village of Viet Nam where I had so recently been. I am no anthropologist, but several similarities struck me particularly. Both the Viet Namese and Andean communities were ruled by a council of elders who were selected according to a seemingly similar semireligious hierarchical system. Both communities were dominated politically, socially, and economically by a rigid, semireligious (essentially animistic) doctrine or ideology. In both, the ruling council of elders was chosen according to an internal, traditional hierarchical ladder. Alcohol played an important part in the ceremonial rites of both. And in both, the haunting music of a remarkably distinctive pipe, called a *samponas* in Bolivia, could be heard. This instrument is composed of two rows of six pipes each, tied together. Some of the pipes drone with a monotonous, bagpipe-like sound, others play the melody. Most striking, however, was the fact that in both, the village council reached decisions, not by voting, but by coming to a consensus in a way which is most obscure to a Western democrat. In both, land was held communally, divided and distributed on an annual basis according to a bidding process. This was a means of revenue for the village, as well as a way of coping with migrants, or in Viet Nam with the swarms of refugees which for centuries have plagued that tortured land. In both, oddly and quite by chance, I happened to see a carving of a creature that was half animal and half man, and was told that he was the god to whom they prayed for rain. The differences were largely that the Bolivian village was more primitive, the rain god more crudely carved, the ceremonies and religious rites more wild, the old practices more fixed. The land-bidding practice in Viet Nam was becoming a thing of the past, for example, albeit the fairly recent past. Life in the Andean village seemed to resemble a description by an old man of the traditional ways of rural Viet Nam long ago. Perhaps this is what Serrano meant when he said: "A strange legendary spirit floats over the surface of the land, as though it came from another world. It seems to tell of a land where man was once a god, or at least the equivalent of the gods, a total man in harmony with his natural surroundings." [17]

Before leaving this intriguing question of East or West, we should remind ourselves of where a somewhat related inquiry led Professor F. S. C. Northrop, Sterling professor of philosophy and law at Yale Law School. In *The Meeting of East and West*, Northrop describes the inside patio of the building housing the Secretariat of Public Education in Mexico City. Covering an entire and exceptionally lengthy city block, the building in former days was a Catholic convent, but modern democracy and newer philosophies have put it to secular use.[18] On the walls of the patio are frescoes by Diego Rivera, depicting the history of Mexico, glorifying the Indian and "holding up as a human value the application of science to the natural resources of the country." [19] On four vertical flat surfaces specially placed in each corner of the patio are four figures: Quetzalcoatl, Las Casas, Plato, and the Buddha. Quetzalcoatl, "the plumed serpent," was the major deity of the precolonial Aztec inhabitants of the valley of Mexico. He is considered the founder of their agriculture and industry. Father Bartolomé de Las Casas is generally regarded as the man who taught the Indians how to assimilate the Spanish language, art, and religion, and to make it express their own spirits.[20]

The reasons for the presence of these two figures are obvious, but why Plato and the Buddha? Northrop reminds us that in Plato's philosophy there are two "ground principles": the rational, mathematical, formal principle; and the intuitive, immediately apprehended, emotional, aesthetic principle. The first Plato called *logos;* the second, *eros.* Eros has to do with the female; it is warm and passionate. Logos is identified with the male, cold and objective. These principles are basic to the symbolism of the Christian Church. The female Virgin is the emotional, passionate person, and the doctrinal, rational person is the male Christ, representing the unseen (because only rationally known) God the Father.[21]

But, as Northrop observes, Plato quite arbitrarily branded the aesthetic, emotional principle as evil and the male rational principle as good, and his distinction has had a lasting influence on the Christian religion in the West, whether Catholic or Protestant.[22]

Northrop derives from Plato the fact that the Protestant Church does not recognize the symbolism of the Virgin and that it tends to be afraid of vivid colors, the passions, and emotions. Even the Orthodox Catholic says that the Virgin is not divine in her own right. In Latin America, on the other hand, the Virgin assumes an importance of her own and in many churches she has a place of equal rank with Christ. Northrop interprets this as being an acceptance of the passion principle and a neglect of the rational principle.

The Spanish soul of Latin America thus took the emotional, aesthetic female component of life, which Plato had identified as one of the two irreducible principles of all things, and made it good. The same compassionate, aesthetic component is found in the good and divine in the philosophy and religion of the Orient, and Northrop speculates whether Plato's female ground principle might not have come to him from the East.[23]

This acceptance of the principle of compassion explains why the Buddha rather than the Christ figure appears with Quetzalcoatl, Las Casas, and Plato, and also why the intuitive compassion of the Virgin and the Buddha are so much more dominant in Latin America than are the coldly rational Protestant religion and culture of the North.

Northrop deepens this basic cleavage between North and South, East and West, in his discussion of John Locke, whose philosophy still is the foundation of the ideology of the United States, as set forth in the Declaration of Independence and the Constitution. For Locke, unlike the Spaniard, emotions and passions were not intrinsic parts of man's nature, "but merely data like colors and sounds toward which . . . man takes merely the attitude of an observer." As such they were regarded as "secondary and tertiary" qualities.[24] "The really important things were either the material substances with which the businessman or the engineer, 'with his feet on the ground,' concerns himself during the six workdays of the week; or the blank, purely spiritual, intrinsically unemotional, introspectively given mental substance with which in a meeting hall, preferably without colors or sounds to disturb him, he communes on the Sabbath." [25] How different is this from the values inherent in the masses of people gathering to worship at the shrine of the Virgin of Guadalupe!

The cleavage becomes still wider when we consider Locke's theory of government, upon which our political system is based. It establishes above all else the inviolate rights of the individual. Indeed, the only reason for the existence of government, Locke held, was to protect the individual and his property. The strength of United States attachment to this principle is attested to by the ideological turmoil which our pragmatic deviations from it have caused. That we have increasingly found it necessary to place human rights and the public welfare above individual property rights is plain. But we have tended to regard such doings as somewhat anti-American, if not subversive.

If our Lockean beginnings have caused us ideological trauma, they have made it even more difficult for us to perceive the irrelevancy of his principles of government and the primacy of property rights to people who do not understand or believe his philosophy. It becomes additionally absurd to apply those principles to peoples, most of whom own no property for their government to protect. It should be remembered that when the American democracy was formed, the vast majority of our citizens owned property. This has never been the case in Latin America.[26]

This principle of the primacy of property rights over human

and social needs is at the heart of much misunderstanding and tension between the United States and Latin America.

The first great test case in this regard came in Mexico when the Cárdenas government in 1934 became exercised over the fact that during the Diaz dictatorship practically all the oil resources of Mexico had fallen under foreign ownership. In their first attempt to resolve the problem, the Mexicans founded their appeal on Woodrow Wilson's oratorical contention that "human rights are above property rights." [27] This was not the last time that Latin Americans found wide discrepancy between our lofty moral sentiments and our more fundamental ideology.

The Mexican government went on to base its right to take over the oil property owned by United States corporations on two points. At the Pan-American Conference at Montevideo in 1933, the American nations agreed that aliens should enjoy all the rights of each nation's own citizens; therefore, taking over the properties of American citizens for a remuneration specified by the duly constituted democratic Mexican government was considered an application of the Montevideo principle, since the citizens of the United States were to be treated in precisely the same manner as similarly situated Mexican citizens.[28] The truth of this statement is evident in the expropriation of the large *haciendas* of Mexico at that time.

Secretary of State Cordell Hull's response was that aliens are entitled to certain minimum protection under international law, regardless of what a nation may do to its own citizens. He insisted, also according to international law, that this minimum includes "both human and property rights." In doing so the Secretary, as Northrop points out, was simply upholding our traditional theory of political and economic value (the supremacy of property rights), and denying the right of the Mexican government to a different theory.[29]

We might like to think that this issue arose with communism, but it is far deeper and more historic. In fact, it is at least as old as Plato and the Buddha.

2

For all the vast infusion into Latin America of Western culture

—technique, money, and matter—this culture has obviously remained remarkably superficial. The region has been left with ever-increasing questions about itself and its purposes. In many ways this superficial application of culture has probably prolonged a sense of insecurity and lack of confidence. Despite its intrinsic rational good sense, Western culture's main effects may well have been to corrupt, distort, and paralyze.

Everett E. Hagen points out that while contact with Western technical knowledge is a requisite for economic growth, "forces quite independent of the degree of contact determine whether a nation uses that knowledge." For technical knowledge to result in the change that we normally call development, it seems there must be certain cultural, political, and social receptacles or mechanisms in place; there must be a framework of values which dictates the purposes and priorities to which technique and matter are put. If this receiving and implementing structure is not present, technique and matter will have only a haphazard effect. To illustrate his point Hagen compares the four great Asian nations. From 1600 to 1900 Indonesia and India had the most contact with the West—including the most Western investment—China had an intermediate amount, and Japan very little.[30] But of these four countries Japan made the earliest and most rapid development. The parallel to Latin America seems clear.

Hagen also stresses another cultural misconception which has affected our understanding of change, namely, our belief that the present low-income societies can advance technically by simply imitating the technical models already developed in the West. This has proved to be an ethnocentric and incorrect concept, because the success of management methods depends on a changing complex of attitudes toward personal relationships, toward manual-technical labor, and toward the physical world.[31]

3

There is no doubt that Latin American creativity, initiative, and attitudes toward work continue to be heavily influenced, if not dominated, by values implanted during the colonial period.

A weak drive to achieve is plainly closely related to two important aspects of the Latin American value system which have been identified by Talcott Parsons and elaborated on by Seymour Lipset. Parsons noted that individuals in Latin America were likely to be judged not on the basis of abilities and performance so much as in terms of inherited qualities, or what he called "ascription." Latin American society is reluctant to employ a general standard against which to measure individuals; it prefers to respond to some personal attribute or relationship in a "particularistic" fashion.[32]

Lipset goes on to say that in such a "particularistic-ascriptive" system morality converges around the acceptance of traditional standards and arrangements. He finds an emphasis on expressive rather than instrumental behavior, and little concern with the behavior of external authority so long as it does not interfere with expressive freedom. Lipset feels that such systems also tend to emphasize diffuseness and elitism, that the status conferred by one position tends to be accorded in all situations, so that if one plays an elite role (as, for example, that of a landowner), he is respected generally.[33]

Obviously, Latin American countries differ among themselves as much with respect to culture and values as with other matters. However, it is clear that the similarities are sufficiently large to make a regional analysis useful. For example, Uruguay, which is probably the most developed and most democratic nation in Latin America and presumably the least traditional, has much the same contemporary value patterns as the others. Aldo Solari, director of the Institute of Social Sciences at the University of Uruguay, points out that particularism is a very important phenomenon in Uruguayan society. Here as elsewhere the prevailing system of selection of employees for government or private enterprise is based on kinship or membership in a certain club or political faction, on friendship, and so on.[34] Equally strong in Uruguay are ascriptive patterns, placing substantial importance on such matters as family, family obligations, and prestige.

The formation of social elites according to these patterns has some striking effects. Consider the matter of creativity, work, and initiative. One cannot help but note among certain of the traditional elites in Latin America a reluctance to cope with the material or technical problems of life. The rundown *latifundia* is a manifestation of such an attitude. Hagen's explanation for this characteristic is interesting. He says that every person who enjoys a position of privilege in society must in some way justify it to himself in order that he may be comfortable with his good fortune. "If he has gained it by his abilities, justification is easy." If he has gained it by the accident of birth, however, he "is forced to feel that it is due him because he is essentially superior to the simple folk." Therefore, he feels that he owes it to himself, his family, his position, and his elite to be more refined, in contrast to the grubby masses.[35]

Perversely, the oligarch's disdain for manual labor has trickled down the social ladder so that, for example, "almost every Brazilian has the same attitudes towards human toil that are the legacy of slavery. They consider working with the hands degrading and the mark of inferior social position; in fact, a stigma to be avoided like the plague. A popular saying in Brazil is that 'tabalho e para cachorro e negro' (manual labor is for the dog and the Negro)." [36]

Around these patterns has developed Latin America's own particular culture of oligarchy, a word that has been so ill used by demagogues, Marxists, and sloganeers that it has become suspect. But in all truth and precision it is hard to find a replacement for oligarchy in describing the economic, political, social, and cultural systems of Latin America. They are indeed dominated by, and designed to serve, a ruling few.

The culture of the ruling few attaches value and prestige to the ownership of land. The chief families of Latin America remain those whose wealth was or is derived from the land and whose status to a great extent is measured by it. Repeated attempts at land reform have done little to change the situation. Even in "democratic" Uruguay, which has long been dominated by the city of Montevideo, power, as Lipset points out, is concentrated in old land-owning families.[37] To be sure, as we saw in Chile and Peru, the prestige of land may often be mixed with at least some of the money made by the entrepreneur in industry is invested in land, which gives him the prestige which he may otherwise lack.

Such is the case even in Argentina, despite the influence of its cosmopolitan showpiece, Buenos Aires. An Argentine study reports: "Insofar as the entrepreneurial bourgeoisie moved up in the social scale, they were absorbed by the old upper classes. They lost their dynamic power and without the ability to create a new ideology of their own, they accepted the existing scale of social prestige, the values and system of stratification of the traditional rural sectors. When they could they bought *estancias* (ranches), not only for economic reasons, but for prestige, and became cattle raisers themselves." [38]

The culture and values of Latin American businessmen and entrepreneurs reflect the same patterns of ascription and particularism. Experience that the Harvard Business School has had in conducting management seminars in Central America has revealed certain traits often found in the Latin American businessman. These are:

Reluctance to delegate power or authority to those who are not in the family.

An inclination to value prestige in society more than profits.

Unwillingness to allow personal authority to be challenged or overruled by group decision.

A view of the enterprise as a family and the manager as its paternal benefactor.

A preference for personal and informal rather than impersonal and contractual arrangements with employees and business associates within or outside the firm.

An emphasis on personal feelings, inner worth, and spiritual reward rather than maximum profit.

Aloofness from and boredom with the pragmatic, materialistic, and technical.

An aversion and disdain for competition and preference for the arrangement of sales, pricing, and product policies by the power groups involved.

A short-range rather than long-range view of business opportunities, with a strong preference for quick, high profits from sales to a small and relatively wealthy market.

Avoidance of risk as bad per se, with the family disgrace of bankruptcy being the ultimate disaster.

Particular consciousness of risk because of economic and political instabilities.

Frequently, one finds a Latin American firm which grows until the founder runs out of relatives with which to fill top staff positions. It then crumbles at the edges, as it were. Upon the owner's death the enterprise is expected to pass to his son and heir. This often seriously cripples the organization if the son is a ne'er-do-well, not interested in business, or just plain incompetent. When outside managers are hired, they are known as *hombres de confianza* (men who can be trusted), and their loyalty may be significantly more important than their ability.[39]

In a later chapter we shall be looking in more detail at the Latin American entrepreneur. It is appropriate to mention here, however, that his lack of trust for those outside the extended family is a particularly significant bar to effective enterprise. It leads to fear and suspicion on his part and to lack of cooperation and sense of participation on the part of his subordinates. His paternalistic view toward his employees also complicates his personnel relationships, particularly as his workers' demands for independent organization and collective contracts become stronger and more effective.

Distrust of outsiders extends to reluctance to permit investment in the firm. Lipset points out that many Brazilian industrialists feel the sale of stocks to the public literally involves a loss of property. A Brazilian market research survey found that 93 per cent of entrepreneurs interviewed "had never thought of selling stock in their enterprise." Stock markets in Latin America have been singularly unsuccessful, for the simple reason that the most important joint-stock companies are owned by kin-groups who prefer to handle transfer of stock as a purely domestic matter.[40]

These attitudes and values of businessmen in Latin America, part of the culture of oligarchy, are inseparable from the economic and political characteristics which we have already discussed. They depend upon and in turn encourage an unintegrated nation, a state which is controlled by the oligarchy, unorganized and unmotivated masses, an economy dependent on export of crops and mineral resources which again are essentially controlled by the oligarchy. It is strange to find, therefore, prestigious Latin American intellectuals, many of whom are vocal in protest against the oligarchy, providing the essential philosophical and ideological support for many of its attitudes and actions, particularly as far as business and technology are concerned.

The entire body of Latin American thought and literature is replete with rejection of the values of North American industrial society. Rare is the intellectual who concludes that technological change, modern management and industrial practices, and entrepreneurial initiative represent worthwhile values. Indeed these are often identified with the United States and are included as part of the fat target of Yankee imperialism. This ambivalence between the intellectual's desire for change and yet resistance to it on value grounds manifests itself in many ways, with varying result. It is at the very heart of anti-Americanism; it also, ironically, accounts significantly for the failure of communism in Latin America. The Latin American intellectual *pensadore* has tried to interpret the whole reality about him, seeking its roots in the past and looking with grave concern into an unknown future.[41] He is suspicious of the expert and the specialist.[42] Ortega y Gasset, himself a brilliant Spanish intellectual, spoke of "the barbarism of specialization," and Harold J. Laski, who had unparalleled influence in Latin America (as well as in Asia and Africa), wrote similarly: "The expert, I suggest, sacrifices the insight of common sense to the intensity of experience." [43]

Idealism is all-important in Latin American thought, being "the intellectual perspective which gives pre-eminence in human and social life to the role of ideas over economic or material aspects." [44] This peculiarly subtle Latin American doctrine of aversion to pragmatism and matter goes under the heading of *arielismo,* having been set down first by a Uruguayan author, José Enrique Rodo, in a short book called *Ariel,* published in 1900. The book is in the form of an address by Prospero to his students. He compares Latin American values to the spirit of Ariel and the pragmatic, utilitarian United States to the mon-

strous Caliban. He calls the youth of Latin America to follow
"the sweet and serene image of my Ariel. . . . Ariel is reason
and higher sentiment. Ariel is that sublime instinct for per-
fectibility. . . . Ariel triumphant signifies idealism and order
in life, noble inspiration in thought, disinterest in morals, good
taste in art, heroism in action, delicacy in customs."

It is useful once again to contrast Latin America, in its search
for tradition, with Japan, as R. P. Dore has done in his notable
essay on the subject.[45] Dore points out that in building up its
self-image a nation seizes on those features which supposedly
differentiate it from its major international antagonist. The
Japanese could differentiate themselves from Americans (for the
better, they felt) by contrasting their tight family system and
loyalty to the emperor, with Americans' selfish individualism.
But Latin Americans could not find a basis of superior com-
parison in terms of family, political, or legal institutions, so they
fell back on the "spirit." Since the North Americans they saw
were businessmen, they built up a materialist/spiritual di-
chotomy, heaping scorn on their northern neighbors' pursuit of
technology and profit and placing *arielismo* on a revered pedestal.

Thus we return to a point touched on in the last chapter with
respect to the political system, namely, that the leadership for
innovation, change, enterprise, initiative, in Latin America comes
from those who are misfits in the existing order, or social
"deviants," as Lipset calls them; whereas the entrepreneurs of
North America come largely from groups which possess traits
placing them inside the central structures of society.[46]

Immigrants have taken the lead in establishing most Latin
American industry: Arabs (known as "Turcos" in Central America), Jews, Italians, and Germans. The industrial centers of
Medellín in Colombia and Guayaquil in Ecuador were founded
by those who were excluded from the prestigious "arielistic"
elites of Bogotá and Quito. Among 32 outstanding Mexican
business leaders studied by Raymond Vernon, 14 had a foreign
paternal grandfather.[47] In São Paulo, Emilio Willems reports,
521 enterprises out of 714 surveyed were owned by recent immigrants.[48] Other Brazilian studies have shown the striking change
wrought in a rural community near São Paulo by a small, low-

prestige, outcast Protestant sect known as the Evangelistas. Many other examples could be given of the innovative role of the deviant or misfit. Just as many could be offered of discrimination against him by traditional society, which treats him as an alien in its midst. Only Uruguay and, to a lesser extent, Argentina would appear to be free of elitist discrimination against the immigrant innovators.[49]

In their own summary of the problem, Fathers Houtart and Pin have concluded: "When the different Latin American countries will have worked out a truly original synthesis of the values they have received from the outside and those which they draw from their own vigorous cultures, they will then be ready to make a creative contribution." [50]

4

What of the educational system which fosters, preserves, and feeds this culture and these values? It should come as no surprise that education in Latin America serves the culture of the ruling elites and reflects the values of the traditional landed oligarchy. The doctrine of *arielismo,* the disdain for manual labor, for the technical, the pragmatic, for industry and commerce deeply affects the educational orientation of the students. The elementary and secondary educational systems are designed to prepare the youth for higher education in the humanistic culture of the old upper class. Emphasis is on the study of law, the humanities, and the social sciences. And efforts to change the curriculum encounter stiff resistance. President Carlos Lleras Restrepo of Colombia, for example, complains that secondary school students are "studying the same courses as in the 19th century." [51] Florestan Fernandes, a Brazilian sociologist, says that the "democratization" of education has meant "spreading throughout Brazilian society the aristocratic school of the past." He writes: "Education has remained impermeable to economic, social and political revivalist influences. Misunderstanding and contempt of popular education has subsisted, and the excessive prestige enjoyed by the humanistic culture of the old upper class, as patrons of a corresponding type of anti-experimental book-learning, has been perpetuated. The school continues to be an isolated institution divorced from man's conditions of existence and specializing in the transmission of bookish techniques, potted knowledge and routine intellectual concepts. Formal education, in a word, is guarded from any impact that would adjust it to the constructive social functions which it should properly carry out in a society aiming at homogeneity and expansion." [52] These inadequacies among others drove some 100,000 Brazilian students to protest in the streets during 1968, facing guns and imprisonment.

Latest figures show that in 1965, 71,000 students graduated from all Latin American universities, according to the Economic Commission for Latin America. Their choice of major studies were distributed as follows: medicine, 28.1 per cent; humanities, 21.2 per cent; law, 13.4 per cent; social sciences, 13.3 per cent; engineering, 11.3 per cent; natural sciences, 5.6 per cent; architecture and art, 4.3 per cent; and agricultural sciences—which perhaps in terms of community needs is the most important— 2.8 per cent. Higher education is thus making its least contribution to that economic sector in which close to half of the people of Latin America are involved.[53] And there is no mention at all of administration—either public or private, government or business.

Textbooks are inadequate and insufficient. Research is rare, especially in the social sciences. This is particularly serious, because it means that increasingly the university becomes detached from the community and its problems. With insufficient capacity, or finances to carry on research, the university exists in an atrophied condition. That this isolation in a state of unreality contributes to student unrest and anxiety is natural.

In fact, it is possible, without being cynical, to suggest that if the interests of society are not being served by the Latin American university, at least the short-run interests of those in control of it are. Much as it makes noise and blusters, the university as of now is incapable of producing much change in Latin America, and therefore is in reality a perfectly acceptable threat to those at the political gaming table who hold the chips. That the future will be different is certain, but how much and how quickly it will be different is not so certain.

In speaking about the university and the small percentage of students who complete its curriculum satisfactorily, we must realize that we are discussing an almost infinitesimal proportion of the population. Latest figures for all Latin America show that only 14 per cent of the child population attend primary school, and that the population over age fifteen has had an average of less than 2.2 years of primary instruction. Sixty-three per cent of secondary school students in 1960 were enrolled in academic courses. The balance was distributed as follows: business (elementary clerical and bookkeeping), 15 per cent; normal schools, 10 per cent; industrial training, 9 per cent; home economics, 2 per cent; and agriculture, 1 per cent.[54]

Even in developed Mexico the figures are equally appalling. Former President López Mateos estimated that "of every thousand children who manage to put their feet on the first rung of primary school (on the same base, 460 never get even that far), only one reaches the last grade of the professional school. . . . During the course of the first six grades . . . no fewer than 866 fall by the wayside. . . . In summary, through the course of the sixteen grades that comprise a complete educational scale, 999 abandon their studies and only one finishes." [55]

Latin American countries spend roughly $70 million a year on education, or about 2 per cent of the close to $4 billion spent by the United States.[56] More than 50 million adults are still illiterate (as are half of the population of fifteen and over) and the number is increasing. Half the more than 14 million children of primary school age are not in school, and the dropout rate continues to be steep.[57]

There is nothing particularly new or controversial about the fact that such conditions exist. Many have said that education is the primary problem in Latin America; that it is an absolute prerequisite to change. Millions of dollars have been invested in schoolhouses, teacher training, and textbooks. Teams of distinguished professors have been sent from the United States to spruce up Latin America's universities and cajole them into being more like Harvard, Yale, or Michigan State. Some of the medical and scientific schools may have been improved, but general change has been pitifully slight.

Furthermore, we are beginning to get the frightful inkling that some of our cherished preconceptions about education may be wrong. We have been led to believe by Thomas Jefferson and others that education is the backbone of democracy; that it is the cradle of initiative, self-reliance, enterprise, and the other virtues of the Protestant ethic; that it is the light of understanding and truth, shining into the darkness of ignorance. But education may also involve the solidification of existing values, the inculcation of oligarchical principles, the deadening of individuality, the extension of despair and frustration. Which definition applies has nothing to do with the school building, and perhaps not much to do with the teacher or with the textbooks which may be stacked in the warehouse. The definition and significance of education is a function of the society, its values and its culture, its expectations and its needs. Education can affect culture and values, but only if it is clearly designed to do so. The critical factor is therefore neither the amount of education, nor the bricks and mortar invested, nor even the number of teachers trained or textbooks provided. The critical factor is what is being taught, what is the content? Is it relevant to the student? Does he perceive its relevance? Can he use it in the society at large, or is his way blocked no matter how "educated" he may be? Do environmental constraints so smother student and parent motivation for education as to make it virtually impossible under any circumstances?

5

VERAGUAS: The Environment in Microcosm

*By the Divine Will I have placed under the
sovereignty of the King and Queen an Other
World, whereby Spain, which was reckoned poor,
is to become the richest of all countries.*[1]
> Christopher Columbus,
> First Duke of Veraguas

I have scanned the Latin American environment and
viewed it as if through the large end of a telescope. I have listed
its characteristics, and from time to time have allowed my bias
to show, subjectively referring to these characteristics as problems. But I call them problems because I presume that they are
in one way or another obstructing varieties of change which in
turn are desirable in both nature and direction. I am thus further
assuming some standard of values, some criterion by which
change is determined and toward which it is aimed.

I have attempted an environmental synthesis, extending back
in time and casting a shadow on the future, including many
elements which are economic, political, social, and cultural. This
has been a description, as it were, of an Indian blanket seen from
far away, its design and colors dimly perceived. To penetrate
further, to see more clearly, we must turn the telescope around
and view in magnification one small square of the blanket.

This will be Veraguas Province, Panama. Here we shall see
in dynamic display most if not all of the elements of the Latin
American environment discussed so far; their relationship to one
another, the ties and the links, the tensions and repulsions, the
voids and the vacuums. We can then better understand the

forces which are moving to change these relationships and to fill the vacuums.

Panama itself, by many measurements—geographic, economic, social—is characteristic of Latin America, despite its unusual beginnings at the hands of Theodore Roosevelt, the phenomenon of the Canal, and its consequent special relationship to the United States. It is, of course, small, with a population of only 1.3 million people. But comparing it with the other eighteen republics of the region, one finds that Panama is economically and socially near the average, although a little above average in most measurements of standard of living, national product, literacy, education, health, and life expectancy.

I have chosen Veraguas as my example because of my particular familiarity with the region. Since 1963 the Harvard Business School, under a contract with the AID, has been helping business leaders of Central America and Panama establish a center for research, graduate training, and consultation in management. This has grown into the Central American Institute of Business Administration, known as INCAE, located near Managua, Nicaragua. Since rural management is particularly important in Central as well as South America, a project was begun in Veraguas in 1964 under my direction to study the nature and problems of rural change and the relationship of those problems to the manager or entrepreneur.[2] In Veraguas we found ourselves working alongside Bishop Marcos G. McGrath,* one of the extraordinary leaders of the radical social-action wing of the Catholic Church in Latin America, vice-president of the Latin American Bishops' Council (CELAM), and a prominent scholar and theologian. Bishop McGrath saw Veraguas as typical of rural Latin America, and therefore particularly useful as a place in which to design and test new procedures for change and development in the region.

When he first went to Veraguas Province in early 1964, Bishop McGrath found it virtually neglected by governmental development agencies. Communist groups were active, especially in the remote and mountainous interior. Within three years the movement which he started, the Center for Study, Promotion

* Bishop McGrath was appointed Archbishop of Panama in February, 1969.

and Social Assistance (CEPAS), had established forty cooperative groups for purposes of increasing production and improving
the credit and marketing position of the *campesinos;* an overall
multiservice cooperative organization; vocational training and
agricultural schools; a radio station; and a training center capable
of housing and feeding sixty persons. The CEPAS organization
and its associated groups today directly affect some thousand
persons, and indirectly influence thousands more. The Communist organization is dead and the province has unquestionably
been changed in many other ways.

Veraguas, located about 150 miles west of Panama City on
the Interamerican Highway, is one of the central provinces of
Panama (see map). It is bordered by the Caribbean Sea on the
north and the Pacific Ocean on the south. Isolated and remote,
Veraguas has little contact with the capital city, and its people
lack any real sense of belonging to a nation. Those in the
province who have heard of the Canal, for instance, feel it is
very far away indeed.

Long neglected by the Panamanian government and business
community, Veraguas has languished in unproductivity. It is the
seat of power of two or three families who own most of its fertile
land, but who have little interest in the welfare of the province
and its people.

During the 1950's Communist leaders began organizing in
the province. Their purpose was not to change it substantially,
but rather to keep it weak, vulnerable, disorganized, and dissat-
isfied, a useful base for guerrillas who could be landed on and
supported from its virtually unpopulated Caribbean shores.

With a population of approximately 150,000, the province has
roughly one tenth the national total. Santiago (population
10,000) is the largest town and the provincial capital.* Soná
(population 4,000) ranks second. Both towns have grown since
1930, when they numbered 2,200 and 1,700, respectively. But
nearly 90 per cent of the population is to be found in the countryside outside these two centers. Between 1950 and 1960 the
population of the province grew by 23 per cent (compared to
an increase of 34 per cent for the nation as a whole), rural por-

* Its population is increased by approximately 4,000 students when the local
normal school is in session.

tions of the province growing somewhat less than the provincial average.

Veraguas is divided into eleven districts, from Santa Fe on the Caribbean to Montijo on the Pacific. A diversity of population groups lives in this area. In the north, there are some 2,000 Guaymi Indians. Most of the commercial, professional, and educated inhabitants reside in Santiago and Soná. The remainder of the population consists mainly of *campesinos*, living in a variety of settlement patterns.

There are several larger rural towns (population about 1,000) such as San Francisco and La Colorada, which are in constant communication with Santiago and are influenced by it in a variety of ways.

Outside the larger towns, and generally throughout Veraguas, are small villages inhabited by 30 to 150 families. These may be the seat of a school district and have a chapel, one or two *tiendas* (small general stores), a few water pumps, and perhaps a dance floor. While a few huts may be concentrated around a clearing, most are scattered within a radius of one to three miles. Outside the *campesino* communities live numerous isolated family groups consisting of as many as ten members. Usually, these families are poorer than other *campesinos*, none of their members has attended school, and they are highly superstitious.

Although some communities are near the Interamerican Highway and others are on secondary roads, many can be reached only by rutted dirt roads, occasionally passable by Land Rover but much of the time only by horse or on foot. In the rainy season, sudden cloudbursts turn such roads into dangerous rivers. As a result, there is only irregular communication between Santiago and many of the communities.

It would require several volumes to describe adequately the characteristics of Veraguas. I shall concentrate on those I refer to as problems. It is important to note that there are differing views of the problems of Veraguas; by some, the problems are considered to be the extent to which the area differs from a rural county in the United States; for others, the problems are determined by the extent of Communist control; for still others, by the voting patterns of the population; and for some, by the province's economic growth rate and the revenues which can be secured within its borders. If one were to ask the Veraguan *campesino* whether these are his problems, it is hardly likely that he would agree, or even understand the question.

I

The topography of the province is varied. Flat grazing land in the south and central portions extends to rolling hills which give way to large mountains in the north. It is a harsh area. The topsoil is thin and mostly lateritic, rich in minerals but poor in organic matter. Oxidation of the minerals produces a hard top layer. While the scrub vegetation appears lush, the soil is generally poor for cultivation of crops. The fertile topsoil that does build up is eroded each year by heavy rains which last from May to mid-December. The rains are sometimes so violent that most *campesinos* find it necessary to dig drainage ditches around their stick-and-thatched houses to prevent them from being washed away. Rainy and dry seasons alternate, but the climate is hot the year around, with an average temperature of 80 degrees. Efforts to cultivate the area are hampered not only by poor soil but by the presence of a large variety of insects and other pests.

Campesinos are for the most part marginal, subsistence farmers. They are marginal in that a decline in the price of rice or corn in the national market has grave consequences for them; they are the first to suffer when demand falls. They are subsistent in that little excess production is ever available for sale. A year of bad weather, for example, can have catastrophic effects. A late rainy season in 1965 caused the rice harvest in Veraguas to be small and late. The following year heavy rains flooded some of the seeded areas. As a result, in both years, many families were forced to purchase their rice and thus were less able to buy meat, fish, and other high protein foods. Since most of the children are undernourished, flu viruses and colds spread quickly in the villages, and mortality rates are high. Under these conditions, it is not surprising that the *campesinos* are sometimes termed "static" and are hesitant to introduce any changes which they feel might jeopardize their already tenuous state.

The problems associated with land use are many and varied. A *campesino* practices slash-and-burn agriculture. In the early part of a year he cuts down a hectare or so of forest or scrub, lets it dry in the hot dry season following mid-December, and burns it off during March and April. After clearing the remaining logs, the farmer seeds rice and corn by making a hole in the ground with a digging stick and dropping in four or five seeds. The holes are made at two-foot intervals, but seeds are not planted in rows. The crops are weeded twice, in June, July, or August. To weed, the *campesino*, using a short machete, stoops over and makes his way around the field cutting the weeds at their base or slightly below ground. A *campesino* may also plant cane in the field during July, and subsidiary crops such as yucca, beans, squash, and tomatoes are, invariably, planted in among the rice. August through November is the time of rice harvesting. The harvest is made by a group of men and women working together, advancing across the field and cutting each of the rice spigots, stalk by stalk, with a small hand knife. The other crops are harvested as they ripen. A second crop of corn may be planted in September or October, to be harvested in December or January. If the land is fertile, the field will be used the following year. In most parts of the province, land now supports only one year's usage. It is then left to grow back for several years, a new area is cut down, and the cycle is repeated.

The agricultural system of the *campesinos* is heavily labor-intensive. The only capital requirements are those of a machete, hand knife, and seed. To cut down and seed a hectare of land in rice, corn, and sugar cane requires 150 working days. Since most household heads work about one hectare, a considerable portion of the year is not utilized. To be sure, *campesinos* are busy throughout the year repairing their houses, purchasing food in Santiago, recuperating from illness, or working for cash, but one of the problems of Veraguas is subemployment in the agricultural sector.

In years past, *campesinos* were more self-sufficient and less dependent upon consumer goods. Most of them still raise enough rice and corn to meet their needs, but rising capital investments, costs, and shortage of land have forced many out of raising cattle or hogs. The significance of this change has not been so much loss of cash income as loss of meat (protein) available for consumption. At present meat prices of forty cents per pound, the purchase of just one pound of meat requires roughly half a day's wage. Wealthier families share a pound or two of meat once a week, while poorer ones may have meat only once a month. To the basic diet of rice and corn, most *campesinos* add beans to supply "energy."

Campesinos have little ability or incentive to sell agricultural goods on the national market, where historically, they have never been a major force. This situation is combined with their growing dependence as consumers in the market. Once they made clothes and hats, slaughtered their own cattle, were their own midwives, invented stories, and devised their own amusement. Today they are tending more to buy clothes and meat, depend on professional medical help, and listen to transistor radios. With cash income levels ranging from $50 to $350 per year, however, *campesinos* are caught in the trap of being dependent upon consumer items, but lacking the means to purchase them.

Under these conditions the principal resource available to the *campesino* is the land from which he squeezes a living. Over the years, however, the destructive practice of slashing and burning the scrub has caused a great deal of erosion, particularly devastating since the land was not fertile in the first place.[3] In addition, wild grass has grown back in areas that were once forest, meaning that less land is regenerated by lying fallow, or by being naturally fertilized by rotting tree leaves. At the same time, the large cattle owners and cane growers in Veraguas have been slowly moving their fences outward, leaving the *campesino* less land on which to grow corn and rice. Because less forest land has been available to the *campesino* for seeding by his techniques, he has been forced into a poorer position in which he is less able to provide for his basic necessities. Thus the notion that rural people are always able to feed themselves has become increasingly false.*

Land ownership is equally complicated and often obscure. Many of the deeds extend back to colonial times, with no clear record of ownership rights since then. For example, a wealthy Panama City businessman was interested in contributing some of his Veraguan land to CEPAS for use as a cooperative farm. His father had bought what he thought was about a 20,000-hectare tract of land, supposing there was gold on it. There was none, and since the land was of no real value, the businessman had never visited nor taken any interest in it. He was unable to collect rent from those using the land because of the administrative problems involved; rent collectors who ventured into the area were physically molested. When *campesinos* farming this land were asked who owned it, they replied that the government did. When CEPAS had identified a 3,000-hectare tract it considered suitable, a search for the deed was made. The deed revealed that the land had been owned first by the heirs of Christopher Columbus, who was, indeed, the first Duke of Veraguas. In the early nineteenth century the land was taken by General José de la Fabriga. Since that time, about forty other persons, some politically prominent, had acquired some claim to the land and used it as leverage to maintain political control and influence. The president of the republic had to intervene to settle the businessman's right to give the 3,000 hectares to CEPAS. As it turned out, the land was of such poor quality that it was of only marginal value to CEPAS. In general, it is becoming depressingly clear that in Latin America there are not the vast reaches of unused fertile lands which were taken for granted until quite recently.

Of the 22,000 farms which the 1960 census reported under cultivation in Veraguas, almost 70 per cent were less than ten hectares in size. Our observations would indicate that most are

---

* Even in advanced Mexico an agricultural expert recently estimated that "20 per cent of Mexico's cultivated lands are worked by pre-Hispanic methods of cutting and burning without benefit of plow and oxen." Another says that less than 1 per cent of the cultivated land is worked with the aid of tractors.

substantially smaller than that. Only 9 per cent of the farms are owned outright. These, however, occupy more than one quarter of the arable land. While some land is held and farmed under a variety of leasehold and tenancy arrangements, the largest portion is occupied and farmed by squatters.

Relationships between the peasant and the land he farms are thus obscure and vague. Many *campesinos* of Veraguas have some sort of tenant or sharecropping arrangement with a large landowner; some grow sugar cane which they sell to a nearby sugar mill; others work seasonally for wages, cutting sugar, weeding, or performing other agricultural work. The striking fact about all these relationships is the overwhelming insecurity of *campesinos* within them. Such contracts as exist are invariably oral and concluded informally. The *campesino* rarely understands them, and the employer can easily cheat him or cancel the agreement at will without fear of prosecution. The bargaining power of the employer or landowner is controlling.

The arbitrariness of the landlord, the plantation owner, or the mill owner, is a perpetual sword of Damocles over the *campesino*'s head. Without contracts, guarantees, or insurance, without political power or access, without organization or representation, he is entirely vulnerable.

Near Veraguas there is a sugar mill which buys cane in season from some one thousand *campesinos* in Veraguas. The formula and agreement by which they are paid for their cane is a mystery to the cane growers. The mill affects and in many ways controls the lives of these farmers. Economically, they are becoming increasingly dependent upon the mill, as their subsistence crops of rice and corn diminish. This is partly due to the mill's policy of loaning them the use of a mill tractor, providing that they do not plant rice and corn with their cane. The practice increases the value of the cane, but denies the farmer his subsistence food. The mill also supplies credit to the farmers who serve it, and thereby it gains a measure of almost indefinite control. It also affects the farmers judicially: A dispute about land or damages is invariably settled by the mill's representative. The mill obtains about two thirds of its cane from farmers in Veraguas. The other third is grown on its own land. Several years ago workers on its land and in the mill factory joined the Sugarworkers Union of Panama and sought to bargain collectively with the mill. This the mill refused to do in no uncertain terms. Thus, the mill also has a paramount political effect upon the *campesino*.[4]

Panama's Agrarian Reform law represents one attempt to help the *campesino* find a less amorphous status, but the problems of applying and enforcing the law are many and complicated, and surely are not peculiar to either Veraguas or Panama. Although the purpose of the law is to allow *campesinos* to buy the land which they actually farm at a reasonable price and over a period of time, only about 1 per cent of the province's land has been affected by the land-reform program, which was instituted more than a decade ago. For a *campesino* to take advantage of the Santiago agrarian-reform office, he must first know of its existence, which many *campesinos* do not. He must understand the law and the function of the office. He must make the trip to Santiago; have a request formulated orally or in writing; and be prepared to make three or four return trips to get action. It is not surprising that land reform is a slow business, when it is considered that illiteracy among *campesinos* runs close to 90 per cent; that bus fare (when the roads are passable) costs at least fifty cents per round trip, half a day's wage (and in addition a day's work per trip would be lost); and that the authority whose assistance he is seeking may well be obligated to the adversary in the proceedings in one way or another.*

Difficulties in land reform, however, are not entirely due to application of the law. In 1965, for example, the land-reform agency drew up plans and parceled out land to the inhabitants of one community on the basis of straight lines drawn on maps. Unfortunately, the *campesinos*, using their system of slash-and-burn agriculture, were accustomed to having small pieces of seeded and resting land spread throughout the community. *Campesinos* of that community were still arguing in 1968 over who had the right to a piece of land worked for many years by one man suddenly deeded to another. Those who were given

---

* In this connection I should like to state that I am not criticizing the individual public officials in Veraguas, many of whom are competent and dedicated. They are part of a system which greatly restricts their best efforts.

a block of relatively poor land or a piece heavily cut through by an existing road were also unhappy.

About ten years ago, in another community, land was purchased by the land-reform agency from its prior owners at the relatively high price of $30 per hectare. Since then, distribution plans and selling prices have not been settled by the agrarian-reform agency. While government land is supposed to sell for $6 per hectare,* the agency appears to be attempting to recoup its original investment of $30 per hectare. In the meantime, delay of the agency's actions has permitted one large landowner to move his fences slowly onto more and more *campesino* land, causing innumerable fights over the resulting reduction of land available for peasant use. Thus, the key issue in Veraguan land reform is not the laws themselves, but their application.[5]

2

Although distribution of land is a crucial problem, Veraguas is also characterized by a lack of infrastructure. Its principal thoroughfare is the two-lane concrete Interamerican Highway. Only a few all-weather roads extend off it; gravel and sand ways reach other towns, and beyond these are mud tracks. Electricity is available to only a small fraction of the province's inhabitants, and its high cost seriously discourages the introduction of even small new industries. Communications by telephone and telegraph are poor and expensive, with one telephone for every five hundred persons. There are considerably more transistor radios. To notify a relative of a death, a *campesino* often finds it quickest and most dependable to place a message on the radio, hoping that it will be heard.

Public and freight transportation by small passenger bus (*chiva*) is reasonably good but expensive. A ride of five to ten miles, for example, punctuated by many stops and delays, costs at least twenty-five cents. While the system works relatively well for transporting small quantities of agricultural goods—a live chicken or a sack of yucca—from a farm to Santiago, it is only with the greatest difficulty and at high cost that the farmer can

* The $6 price is for the first twenty hectares. After that, the price rises according to the amount purchased.

take any substantial quantity of produce to market. Moreover, it appears that rice buyers in Santiago use this situation to their advantage. Knowing that a *campesino* pays heavily in time and money to transport his unmilled rice to town, and that it would be an almost unbearable hardship for him to take the rice back with him and an impossibility to store it, the buyer can get virtually any price he asks. The *campesino,* who is usually heavily in debt and in need of cash, has little bargaining power and generally takes what he can get.

Under such circumstances it is understandable why business in Veraguas is small both in capital invested and number of persons employed. Enterprises employ an average of 2.5 persons. Rice milling is the only substantial manufacturing industry in the province.* In 1965 new business investment in Veraguas totaled $213,000, but new investment in rice milling in the same year totaled $240,000, which means that there was an actual disinvestment of $27,000 in all other businesses. Sixty-four per cent of invested capital in the province is in commercial enterprises; of these, 84 per cent are small food stores.

A limited variety of high-priced consumer products is available in the shops of Santiago and Soná, with the variety smaller and the prices higher in the outlying villages. Prices of certain items such as onions, tomatoes, potatoes, and milk are markedly seasonal. The price of one hundred pounds of rice, for example, may rise from $8 in November to $11 in July or August. The great variety of fruits bestowed by nature, and occasionally cultivated by *campesinos* in an offhand manner, scarcely reach the market because of the small quantities produced, high transport costs, and lack of market facilities. Foods imported from the United States, such as bacon or canned soup, are marked up as much as 50 per cent in Veraguas, while locally processed items, such as tomato paste, pork and beans, or ketchup, sell at twice the market price in the United States. Readymade clothing and shoes sell at United States prices, but the quality is inferior. *Campesinos* usually buy cloth from the United States, often imported "seconds," to make their clothes.

The businessman of Veraguas has little sense of community.

* The sugar mill referred to earlier is in a neighboring province.

The village *tienda*-keeper often seems to have leadership qualities, partly because of his more exalted economic position, his greater education, and his business acumen. But in spite of his potential, the *tienda*-keeper—or any other businessman— rarely has the will or capacity to lead his neighbors.

Bishop McGrath managed to prod the Santiago businessmen into some community action. The Santiago Lions Club, after a fist fight had split it into two factions, was reunited at a small party given by the bishop in July 1965. Also under his leadership, this club joined with the local 20–30 Club, the Chamber of Commerce, and other local organizations, and in a combined effort with two Peace Corps volunteers (and, more recently, the national government and AID), the group has established a vocational school in Santiago for training auto mechanics, electrical repairmen, and construction workers.* At its opening in June 1966, more than 200 applicants vied for the 60 available places. Today the school accommodates more than 200 students. Two more schools have now been established, also with community initiative and sponsorship, in the small towns of La Mesa and Soná. These schools offer a three-year course for graduates of primary schools. The Ministry of Education has viewed them with special favor, not only because the community support reduces demand on the government budget, but also because the schools' close connection with the community insures that their curriculum will be designed to meet local needs. Students of the schools, for example, rebuilt forty broken refrigerators (obtained from AID), which are now in operation in local hospitals. They have also built benches for rural schools, in many of which children ordinarily sit on the floor. Furthermore, the pattern of local initiative, support, and commitment followed by government assistance has a salutary effect on political structures and relationships.

Despite considerable available and unused manpower, there are few skilled workers in the province. Moreover, though there

* It is interesting to note that Emilio Batista, the able young director of the Santiago Vocational School, who was considered a dangerous leftist a few years ago, was last year elected president of the Panama (National) Association of Private and Public Vocational Schools and is now thought of as a model community leader.

are a number of native products and a few skilled artisans, there
is no handicraft industry. Thus, vocational training is a vitally
needed innovation in a school system which has traditionally
emphasized university-oriented course material in its lower grades
and then allowed less than 2 per cent of its population to achieve
this higher educational goal. The problem in Veraguas now is
to develop new industries and construction to employ the increasing number of vocational school graduates so that they will
not join the migration into Panama City and swell the rank of
the disenchanted unemployed.

3

The *campesinos* in Veraguas are impoverished and deprived in
virtually every respect: wealth, culture, education, and health.
With illiteracy hovering around 90 per cent,* there is a lack
of educational facilities and teachers. Available education is of
poor quality and generally irrelevant to the life of the *campesinos*.
In a sense, education is less hobbled by the lack of teachers and
facilities than by the unwillingness of the *campesino* parent to
encourage his child to attend school regularly, on time, year after
year, and to study—in short, to value his education. The parent
finds it hard to understand why his child should learn to read
and write and work with numbers if his livelihood is to be secured by putting a stick in the ground, planting rice seed, and
harvesting it on land which may be taken from him at any time.
The *campesino* father has no reason to hope that education will
open to his son a life which is different from his own. Education—that is, the acquisition of knowledge—is a function of
motivation and aspiration; some vision of change is required
before education becomes relevant and useful—in Veraguas or
the urban black community of the United States.

Veraguas has an unusually high proportion of one-room, dirt-
floor huts, often housing four or more persons, without latrines,
electricity, or potable water. The province has one doctor and
one nurse for each 10,000 inhabitants and .9 hospital beds for
each 1,000.

* Panama's claim of 78 per cent literacy is thrown into question by the facts
in Veraguas.

Peasant communities are rarely more than an agglomeration of houses spread over the countryside. While these may include a chapel or school, the typical community has no real focal point. Some *campesinos* frankly state that they prefer to live alone. Men often choose to work alone in the fields, not trusting others to do a good job on their land.

Although family groups form the backbone of society, they are brittle. Marriages are rarely formal or legal; it is not unusual for a man to have had two or three "wives." Children usually stay with their biological mother, but sometimes grow up under the care of a near relative. Men accept responsibility for their immediate family household group, but rarely contribute any support money to their offspring from a prior "marriage." Until sugar cane was planted in some areas, there was no permanent investment to hold people to one spot. In consequence, movement from house to house, from house site to new house site, and from village to village is common. These characteristics have helped create a lack of cohesion and internal organization in peasant communities.

There are few historical community groups or traditional leaders. Group decisions and election of and faith in leaders are foreign to the *campesinos* of Veraguas.* Social sanctions, the key to effective group functioning, are also lacking. To be sure, *campesinos* criticize one another and members of the larger society, but the criticisms are indirect. Names are not used and remedial social action is neither suggested nor taken. No leader stands forward to accept responsibility for a situation.

The splintered political life of a peasant community is a result of many factors. Nominally, at least, peasants are a part of the larger political and legal structure of Panama. In the countryside, however, government structures are minimal. The

* This irrelevance of government to the *campesino* is seen in many other countries and settings. In their study of the Colombian *Violencia*, the civil strife in which 200,000 out of a population of 14 million were killed during the last thirty years, Lipman and Havens concluded that "the majority felt that their government was powerless to end the illegitimate use of force which constitutes the *Violencia*." (Aaron Lipman and A. Eugene Havens, "The Colombian Violencia: An Ex Post Facto Experiment," *Social Forces,* December 1965, Volume 44, pp. 238–45.)

peasants are governed immediately by a *"regidor,"* who is appointed by the mayor of the larger district. In practice, the *regidor* has little power, is generally unpaid, and has little desire to enter into or solve disputes between members of the community. Most disputes between *campesinos* must, therefore, be taken to the district capital or to Santiago if they are to be resolved.

Traditionally, power has flowed downward from Panama City to Santiago and from there to the countryside. Votes are purchased from *campesinos* for cash, drink, or promises of government highway jobs, or, in extreme cases, they are obtained through armed threats. Some *campesinos* carry a marked ballot secretly into the voting booth along with the clean legal one. Exchanging one for the other, they emerge from the booth and deposit the marked ballot. They then give the clean ballot to a political agent in return for cash. The agent takes the clean ballot, marks it, and the process continues. In effect, the relation between voter and representative is not based upon popular representation, but upon the exchange of a vote for immediate recompense. The notion of popular representation is replaced by the concept of a short-term contract. The responsibility of elected officials to their constituents does not extend beyond their brief transaction at voting time. Some politicians even view it as their right to recoup vote-getting expenses of their election during their term of office. As a result, Veraguas is not truly represented in the governmental structure of Panama, and, therefore, it benefits little from that structure. While some of the public officials are very conscientious, many are uninterested in and uninformed about the peasant populace. A respectable percentage of the government's budget is supposed to be spent in Veraguas, but the fact is that little of it reaches the people of the province. A $6,000 item for a clinic in the village of San Francisco has been in the budget for seven years. Each year the money is spent, but no clinic has been established.

As we have seen with respect to land reform, the several government agencies in Veraguas have been traditionally remote from the *campesino* and his problems. The rewards for working closely with the *campesinos* are slight, and government jobs are often obtained on some basis other than qualifications for the position. The *campesino* may make several futile trips just to talk with a government official who pays hardly any attention to him. In recent years CEPAS has had some success in its numerous attempts to stimulate technicians and officials of government agencies to reach and help the peasants of Veraguas, but it continues to have trouble penetrating the screen of indifference.

In consequence, the *campesino* has little or no sense of political participation. He has no immediate community structure or larger national group with which to identify. Politics and government for him are a system of contractual favors, far removed from concepts of justice, participation, or representative democracy. In his studies of rural Colombia, Dr. Orlando Fals Borda has recorded many of these same *campesino* characteristics: "An attitude of extreme resignation is one of the results of the [peasant's] complete trust in God . . . the consequent behavior is that of negative stubbornness, *a lack of desire* to improve conditions, especially if this effort goes beyond the nearest boundaries of physical, mental and financial capacities." Fals Borda goes on to relate how the sequence of history has piled layers of inhibitions, restraints, and pressures on the people. He speaks of the "elite-made" culture, which for the most part has "impoverished the peasants." In general terms, otherworldliness, reserve, and hypocrisy were greatly emphasized, the first by the Spaniards and the other two by the Indians themselves after the conquest. Resignation, docility, and fatalism were the natural "results of the settled, unbending conditions created during the colonial times. Finally the republican period fostered individualism through chaos and civil war (the *violencia*) and political fanaticism through a fuller exploitation of docility." [6]

4

There is no doubt that the *campesino's* culture and mentality present many impediments to change or development. His lack of skills, not only agricultural and technical, but also in decision-making, is perhaps fundamental. The process of economic decision-making can be viewed in terms of the information individuals gather, the conceptual system into which the in-

formation is fitted, the skill with which individuals make decisions, and the value systems by which options are chosen. On
all four points, the decision process of the *campesinos* of Veraguas
Province is in striking contrast to that employed in more developed areas of the world.

A peasant has no systematic way to gather economic information; in fact, he has no concept of information-gathering. In a
small community, all kinds of information are passed at once.
Talk of the coming harvest is mixed with conversation about
an iguana hunt, a recent adventure in drunkenness, the latest
crisis in the village, and the danger of rats to the rice harvest.
There is no qualified and available source to which people can
turn for information on which to base decisions, nor do *campesinos* make an attempt to pull together what information they
do possess.

Moreover, the conceptual system the *campesino* does have
seriously limits the introduction of change. The concepts behind
a slash-and-burn technique of agriculture are foreign to the
ideas of modern agriculture. It was found, for instance, that a
number of men in one village, although not making use of
available tractors and insecticides, had obtained fertilizer for
use on their sugar cane crops. Why this innovation was accepted
while others were not was a puzzle until explanations were
sought from several men. They said that in the older days the
forests were thicker. Thus, when they cut down the forest on
a piece of land and burned it off the fire was stronger than it
was now. The fire in turn burned the top of the earth and left
a heavy deposit of ashes. They believed that the heavy fire made
the land richer and the crops better twenty years ago. They failed
to recognize that the land was used less intensively twenty
years ago and that dead leaves of a forest might have enriched
the inert soil. They concluded that fertilizer had the same effect
as ash from a good fire—it made the land strong—and they were
willing to adopt the innovation of fertilizer because it was no
challenge to the basic conceptual system behind the slash-and-
burn technique.

Campesinos also lack the skills to judge and manipulate information and to plan ahead. Most can add, but not on paper.

As far as we could tell, no peasant has ever kept economic records. In a recent survey, some *campesinos* did not even know the size of their most important harvest—the rice crop. Presumably, it was used until the supply ran out.

Associated with a lack of planning is the system of values by which *campesinos* select from various economic options. We have little precise information on the values which *campesinos* try to maximize. Although they are aware of saving money in consumer purchases, few attempt to set out rational criteria in making business choices. As one *campesino* who used a tractor said: "We have never thought in terms of making a profit." At best, they try to minimize the immediate costs of their farming, thus prohibiting use of tractors. Others wish to avoid risk, which effectively excludes new techniques. It would be absurd to say that *campesinos* have no wish to live a more comfortable life, but since their means for doing so are limited, most settle for a subsistence level of agriculture. They aim only for the certainty of enough rice, corn, and yucca to last the year.

Change for the *campesinos* is further hampered by their fatalistic attitudes. They believe strongly in personal luck or destiny as the main factor in material success. God is seen as controlling every aspect of existence, while man only lives out his destiny. Some persons are born lucky, others are not. The effect of this philosophy is that the world is seen as undirected and unorderable, for man does not and cannot control it by his own efforts. Success or achievement, therefore, is brought not by hard work or intelligence but by luck.

The *campesino* outlook can be illustrated by two examples. Whenever an individual talks about what he will be doing the next day, he invariably adds: "If God grants it." This is recognition of God's immediate power, and if an individual does not so recognize it, he may be struck "sick," or worse, before he is able to realize his plans.

The second example is the national lottery, which creates undying interest and fervent excitement. Scarcely a week goes by that a man does not buy at least one ticket for the Sunday drawing. The lottery, of course, is pure chance. However, numbers to bet on are chosen from dreams or license plates; one man even divines numbers through playing cards. He explains that persons have to have faith in him, that he has faith in God, and that good numbers will appear. He is reputed to be quite successful.

Short of good luck, change is regarded as either impossible or dangerous. Most peasants say of themselves: "We are the poor people," using the permanent rather than the impermanent form of the verb "to be." They feel they are experiencing not just a temporary decline, but a permanent state.

Having this conviction of poverty, *campesinos* lack any strong desire to make the most of their resources. Often, for example, they could plant more seeds or cultivate more land, but they do not. They rarely compete for the few cash-paying jobs which are available to them. Even if they have the time and the money to go to Santiago, very few *campesinos* seek out government extension agents or sugar-cane mill inspectors who could help them. Within peasant communities there is little urge to "keep up with the Joneses."

While this lack of motivation is due partly to the *campesino's* belief in destiny and to the general pressures of his environment, it also may be due to his inner core of individualism. His world is a small one, intensely centered about himself and those immediately around him. The world outside is vague and obscure. Although he has names for even the smallest section of his community, he often confuses the capitals of neighboring provinces with the actual province name. It may well be that lack of cooperation, groups, and leaders, and the fragmented structure of communities are due in part to the self-centered nature of the *campesino's* world. This in turn may be one of the reasons that *campesinos* often do not seem to respond to "the demonstration effect." Agricultural extension agents are repeatedly disheartened by the unwillingness of a peasant to emulate the practice of more progressive or competent neighbors. Of course, this problem is also related to the peasant's general position in society.[7]

This individualism makes it hard for the peasants to find their place in the surrounding society. They are neither a lower class nor an autonomous Indian entity; yet they share certain char-

acteristics with both. Like a lower class, they are at the bottom
of the economic ladder. They share the political and religious
values and traditions of the society. Unlike a lower class, however, the peasants of Veraguas are without power or influence
to affect these values and traditions.

As is the case with an Indian group, peasants are often nearly
independent economically, although they are steadily becoming
less so as they lose more and more of their subsistence plots.
Unlike tribal groups, however, Veraguas peasants have no
ongoing social systems which guide their lives in communities.
They possess no legal or political power in their communities.
Their sense of allegiance to a locale is weak.

It is this anomalous, middle position of *campesinos* in Veraguas that keeps them limited, weak, and vulnerable. They are
the "poor people" in one sense, at the bottom of a society of
which in another sense they are not fully a part. At most, a
peasant boy can hope to grow up to be a local schoolteacher,
assistant to a mayor, member of the police or truck or tractor
driver. No one from his stratum rises further. Unlike Indian
groups, peasants do share the values of the surrounding society
which define what are favored positions, but as with Indians,
access to these positions is completely blocked.

The passivity of the *campesinos* is a characteristic frequently
noted by development workers trying to rouse group or individual interest and action. Suggestions made by an outsider are
generally met by a blank expression. The outsider scarcely
knows whether his ideas have been understood, whether they
have been stated incorrectly, whether the listening *campesinos*
disagree—or whether what has been said has gone beyond
them. It is this passivity, so much a result of the *campesino's*
position in society, which ironically restrains him from changing
the status quo.

Campesinos not only see themselves as being poor and accept
their role, but also accept no blame or responsibility for it. In
their view, it is not their fault, but rather that of the larger
society, that their life is as it is. This attitude is, of course, self-
defeating and permits the rest of the society to blame *campesinos*
for not accepting responsibility for their lives or acts. In terms

of the larger society, of which they are a part, *campesinos* lack
personal dignity.

The *campesino* is thus an increasingly expectant nonmember
of a society with which he has none of the socio-political ties
and relationships upon which any set of meaningful expectations must be based. He is the helpless wanderer in a socio-
political void; the mute, anonymous statistic which baffles economists and planners; the target of guerrillas looking for a secret
home; the threat to all those who hold power; the menace and
at the same time the means to all that is comprehended by
development, peace, and tranquillity. He lives in a world which
invites radical change to a degree which can only be defined as
revolution.

5

It is from this dismal web of multiple impoverishment that
many of the most enterprising Veraguans migrate to Panama
City, never to return. There they acquire a miserable shack in
one of the growing shanty towns and enter the half-life of
prostitution, scavenging, and idleness on the slimy margin of
the city. An estimated five million Latin American families are
now in these circumstances, and the number is growing rapidly,
outstripping both the capacity of the state to provide housing and
of industry to provide jobs.*

Panama City is a particularly dramatic example of this phenomenon. Panama has received a relatively generous annual aid
package from the United States—something on the order of
$30 million in recent years—with the hope that a stable en-
vironment for the Canal will result. As of 1967–8, most of this
money was spent in or near the capital city, much of it for low-
cost urban housing. Nevertheless, the slums grow. There almost
seems to be some perverse magic at work: the more money, the
more slums. Meanwhile, the capacity of the neglected countryside to employ and support its population decreases while its

---

* Lima's shanty towns, for example, grew from 10 per cent of the city's population in 1958 to 20 per cent in 1964. Rio de Janeiro's *"favelas"* are increasing
three to four times as fast as the city itself.

birth rate soars. And so the specter of famine walks with ever-surer tread.

The obvious question comes: Why not intensify agriculture and increase rural employment opportunities so as to improve the condition of life in the countryside and stop the urban migrants before they leave home? This, of course, is a considerably harder task than constructing houses, laying sewers, or building roads. For the modernization of the countryside inescapably requires radical change in political structure and institutions. "Development is much more than a matter of encouraging economic growth within a given social structure," Robert L. Heilbroner has written. "It is rather the modernization of that structure, a process of ideational, social, economic and political change that requires the remaking of society in its more intimate as well as its most public attributes." [8] Development is change. In Latin America it is revolutionary change.

6

It is plainly unacceptable to argue that the people of Veraguas should be left to themselves, or that the poverty and misery in our own back yard should be eradicated before we look elsewhere. There are compelling moral reasons requiring those who have to share with those who have not for the sake of both; national boundaries are not justifiable barriers to human concern. It is increasingly apparent that the neglected, vulnerable, chaotic rural areas of the world are tempting havens to neo-imperialists and predatory powers, who find such places convenient bases for war. We need no reminder of the dangers of escalation which accompany such wars and, therefore, of their threat not only to freedom and national independence, but also to the peace of the world and the survival of mankind. If the world is going to be able to feed itself and to build strong and integrated economies capable of supporting growth and higher standards of living, the orderly, efficient, and just utilization of land resources is imperative.

The United States has, therefore, a vital interest in the Veraguases of this world. Promotion of their development is urgent, and indeed a number of efforts in this direction are under way in the province. These efforts, however, bring problems of their own, some of which are as significant as those which the efforts are intended to solve. For example, if weak governmental administrative units are asked and expected to perform tasks of which they are essentially incapable, and if this performance is a prerequisite to the receipt of money or goods, then falsification and corruption will almost surely follow. If the conviction of Veraguan *campesinos* that their lives are controlled by "outside" forces is reinforced by establishing in their minds the hope that government agencies have come to solve their problems, then their initiative, self-confidence, and capacity for community action will be further retarded and their development impeded. Or if their expectations of help from "outside" exceed what actually arrives, the result will be deepening despair and disillusionment. So far, most governmental efforts made to help Veraguas have had negative effects. And if Veraguas is a microcosm of a society, it is unfortunately also a microcosm of inept attempts to solve problems.

The Panamanian government began its efforts to aid the *campesino* by establishing in 1960 the Reforma Agraria, which was designed to survey and sell land to those *campesinos* who held valid claims. Panamanian law requires that land not being used in some productive manner be given up for government reallocation, and that peasants living and working the same piece of land for seven years have a legal right to that land. But effective land reform must await the development of real, local political institutions and organizations. These are necessary in order to determine the optimum size and dimensions of land allocation in any particular community. They are also necessary to provide and introduce new skills and competence regarding land use and agricultural production; to reorganize the market and credit systems; to insure that the newly landed *campesino* is brought into the national political, social, and economic system with adequate protection and representation; and in general to provide the *campesino* with the motivation necessary for any change at all.[9]

In 1968 some technical help was available through DAP (Divulgación Agrícola de Panamá), the rural extension agency of the Ministry of Agriculture, Commerce and Industry (MACI). DAP's purpose is to form cooperative and agricultural clubs; to teach farm techniques and home improvement, and to stage community fairs. Important as DAP's mission is, so far it has had little effect on the *campesinos* of Veraguas. The two agents who staff the DAP office in Santiago have the use of a Jeep, but they are reluctant to visit the remote rural communities. Although they are supposed to work with formal and informal community groups, these are scarce; and those which do exist, such as CEPAS cooperatives, rarely receive effective help. The greatest difficulty seems to be the lack of enthusiasm which the DAP agent has for his job. If this does not result in inaction, it frequently produces careless activity.

For example, once an agent encouraged a *campesino* to undertake a chicken project to produce eggs. The agent came to help build the chicken coop, but he seemed to be more interested in being seen helping *campesinos* than in accomplishing the end in view. When the coop was finished, baby chicks were brought out to the *campesino* so that he could raise them into laying hens. Of more than one hundred chickens, however, over fifty turned out to be males. Then it was found that a number of the females did not lay eggs; but it was several weeks before a veterinarian was brought out to inspect the batch and identify the nonlayers. In the meantime, the *campesino* had to pay the continuing feed costs.

In many ways, the most significant government agency in Veraguas is the Instituto Fomento Economico (IFE), the local Economic Development Institute. This semiautonomous government department is responsible for all development programs beyond the jurisdiction of other agencies. Among other things, it maintains price supports, administers a rice mill in Santiago, and, most important, is supposed to offer credit to farmers in areas where other credit facilities do not exist. But IFE is a bit like the World Bank: It is happy to lend money to those who are well equipped to repay it. All but the wealthiest and best-connected *campesinos* are thus effectively barred from its benefits. Furthermore, even if the money were readily available, it is doubtful that many *campesinos* would seek out the service because they are fearful of the burden of debt and they also object to the idea of interest. In other words, the requisites for receiving monetary and technical help do not exist among the *campesinos*. The receptacles for making such help useful are not in his community.

Another government service should be mentioned briefly: the Unidad Sanitaria (Health Service), which is supposed to provide low-cost health facilities and services to the *campesinos*. In Veraguas this organization is truly a phantom, rarely if ever functioning. On the one occasion when it did, it was for the purpose of taking the census.

If Panamanian agencies have failed to reach the Veraguas *campesino*, the "outsiders," especially those from the United States, have done little better. AID has given support to several rural development projects in Veraguas, including the Santiago vocational school, primary schools for *campesino* children, and revolving credit funds for CEPAS cooperatives. It also supports the operations of many of the Panamanian government agencies. It is not clear, however, that increased AID assistance in Veraguas would be necessarily beneficial if it were to follow the pattern of agricultural assistance sometimes found in other countries.* For example, in one Latin American country, a highly trained agricultural technician sent from the United States, a seed specialist, was there to assist a *campesino* with his tomato crop. The *campesino* was reluctant at first to use the fertilizer and seed offered by the technician because the farmer, operating on the margin of existence, viewed any change as a dangerous risk. Finally he cooperated, however, and as a result his crop was bigger and better than before. But the rains washed out the road to his farm so that many of the tomatoes rotted in the field because the truck to take them away could not get through. When it arrived, it was, of course, the same truck as before, owned by the same local interests who controlled all the transport in the region. The market system was also the same as

* Criticism of AID here is not aimed at the AID mission in Panama or at any of its personnel, but rather at the objectives of the agency, and the doctrine and means by which it seeks to implement them. The problem is in the AID system, and not with individual missions or personnel. The facts given are as of early 1968.

before, with the result that the actual return to the farmer was not appreciably different. When the visiting expert suggested that the farmer continue on his own the following year, purchasing fertilizer and better seed, the farmer's face went blank. The credit system, unchanged by the expert's visit, precluded obtaining funds for such purchases. The expert departed, leaving the farmer more convinced than ever that change was a dangerous thing.[10]

As we train more and more specialists in the United States, it places a heavy burden even on our own managerial structure to integrate, organize, and utilize these specialists effectively. Generally speaking, we are set up in both our private and public sectors to do this, although there is some reason to believe that we are short of capable generalists. If this is a problem in the United States, it is of course even more acute in Veraguas, where the United States trained specialist is nearly useless, or even demoralizing, unless he is carefully supervised by a generalist or is part of some generalizing organization or institution.

AID's effectiveness is also limited sometimes by its seeming predilection for programs that will result in tangible material projects. Schools and latrines, for example, being regarded as essentially "good things," are constructed with little regard for their contribution to the growth of long-term development institutions. Frequently, the long-term effect on the people of such material inputs is minimal.

The very word "project" or "program" connotes a concrete, tangible item. We think in terms of monuments—bridges, schools, centers, or irrigation ditches. Lip service, of course, is always given to the goal of reaching the people and to "self-help," but all too often the end project, in Veraguas, remains just a project, substantially irrelevant to the people.

When we do speak of people, it is in terms of training them to take care of the project, or changing them to fit around the innovation. The mistake is that we do not begin with the people, with their social, political, and economic needs, and with the prerequisites necessary to the fulfillment of those needs. A schoolhouse does not necessarily result in education.

Problems in the organization of AID itself also sometimes

hinders development efforts. AID, being located in Panama City, operates principally through Panama City organizations and the national government. As we have noted, because of the nature of the society and government, *campesinos* are far removed from the central government and seldom feel the effect of changes initiated so far from them by groups toward which they are either suspicious or indifferent.

7

Undoubtedly the most successful foreign program of the United States is the Peace Corps, which is well represented in Panama, with more than 150 volunteers. In Veraguas alone there were in 1967 some thirty-six Peace Corps volunteers working directly with the *campesinos* in community development and cooperative projects and with government agencies. Several worked closely with CEPAS.

The Peace Corps has been effective in the development of rural areas, unlike both AID and the Panamanian agencies. From its inception it has wisely proceeded cautiously, its volunteers assuming minimal responsibility for action and change, concentrating rather on working with and through viable, existing governmental structures or directly with *campesinos*, providing almost individual assistance to them. Increasingly, however, enormous opportunities for Peace Corps volunteers to help in the achievement of structural change are becoming apparent. For example, in Veraguas a more explicit and clear assignment of volunteers directly to CEPAS and its associated groups might be beneficial.*

One of the first techniques used by CEPAS to organize the *campesinos* and to train them in new agricultural methods was the "precooperative." This term was chosen because the *campesino* did not have the minimum training, experience, or land needed to form a legal cooperative. The term "precooperative" was selected because it suggested the goals toward which the organization was striving.

Precooperatives were usually established by inviting a CEPAS

* Currently, the Peace Corps volunteers in Veraguas are officially assigned to MACI.

field worker to call an evening meeting in a *campesino* community, stressing the goal of greater agricultural production or easier credit. In a typical community, almost 100 per cent of the men and women turn out for the initial meeting. The leader explains to them the meaning of a cooperative, and the benefits which may be derived from joining it. He underscores the *campesino's* needs for credit, land, seed, fertilizer, and so on, and tries to make the individuals understand that if they band together they may be able to realize a better way of life. In other words, he agitates the *campesino* in order to motivate him.

If a few comprehend the basic concept of a cooperative and agree to hold another meeting, the first meeting is considered a success. If at least 20 to 30 per cent of the men are still interested after two or three more meetings and show signs of recognizing what steps must be taken, a leader is chosen. Usually eight to ten workers form the nucleus, with ten or twelve others going along. As each precooperative is formed, a president and secretary are elected and the names of all members are recorded. If possible, officers should be able to write and read, and to command the respect of the group.

In two communities CEPAS has started housing projects with money raised locally, one for seventeen houses, the other for twenty. These projects are aimed at those who cannot afford the relatively expensive government low-cost housing program. Several local businessmen assisted, signing a $4,000 bank loan for the housing.

In 1966 Osvaldo Rodríguez, a twenty-six-year-old native of Veraguas who was at that time the director of CEPAS, organized a group into a multiservice cooperative which split amicably from CEPAS. Named Juan XXIII, after the late pope, it is completely independent of the Church. One of the first moves of Juan XXIII was to buy a tractor on the installment plan, and there have been no defaults in payments. Although used extensively, the tractor was not profitable during its first year, largely because of the inexperience of the *campesinos*. Land was not ready on time; drivers were untrained. But the tractor was not important because it was efficient or because it was profitable. It was important as a symbol that represented a vision of a new and better life, and thus was profoundly significant in political terms, although relatively unimportant economically. By 1968 the first tractor had become profitable and a second one was purchased.* Furthermore, as farmers came to have faith in these new machines, they began to farm larger communal plots, as well as their own land.

Juan XXIII is now making plans to build and operate its own rice mill and storage bins. This would produce income for the cooperative to use for financing educational and training programs and for general expansion. These facilities will permit the agricultural cooperatives to store their rice after harvesting, mill it themselves, and sell it when the price is best.

In 1966 Juan XXIII opened a cooperative store in Santiago, selling fertilizer, seed, weed-killer, and fish from a fishing cooperative which had been originally started by an enterprising Peace Corps volunteer in 1964 but had languished since for lack of a market. Used refrigerators from the Canal Zone were repaired at the CEPAS vocational school and employed to preserve the fish. The store is now the largest in Santiago; it is making a good profit, and has opened branches in four smaller communities. Its success is well understood. For the first time the *campesino* from the countryside has a sense of ownership and of personal access to things of the city. Also, prices at the cooperative stores are lower than elsewhere in town, and the *campesino* is beginning to see a simple and direct way to a better life.

Not the least of CEPAS's achievements has been its ability to organize various international and governmental agencies so that their services are actually extended to the peasants. For example, it has utilized the services of several technical assistants from the British government and the United Nations. To integrate all these various activities, Bishop McGrath stimulated a wide-ranging socio-economic study of Veraguas, recruiting some of the best talent in Panama for the job. This study surveys the province's resources, assesses priorities, and lays out a long-term development plan. The budget for CEPAS–Juan XXIII has been roughly $30,000 a year. The money has been obtained

* Juan XXIII rents out its tractor for $3.50 per hour. The commercial rate is $4.50.

largely from the German Catholic Church. AID has contributed
small matching grants and two $10,000 loans for the organiza-
tion's loan fund.

Since 1967 CEPAS and Juan XXIII have begun more precooperatives, increased the number of peasants in the existing
ones, and stressed new economic activities besides the growing
of rice. The two organizations will continue to train new precooperative members and leaders; to advise the cooperatives and
provide marketing assistance; to seek agrarian-reform action to
secure land titles; and to introduce new crops and improve old
ones, hopefully securing the assistance of DAP and MACI.
They will also encourage new community action such as the construction of community centers.

CEPAS and Juan XXIII face many problems. Most of the
land under use by cooperative members is not owned by them.
It is borrowed, rented, or used by permission of the government.
Harvests have not reached the size they should have; and enlist-
ment of new members has been slow. The organizations see their
problems as being lack of leaders—especially ones with administrative and managerial capability—lack of expert advice on agricultural problems, and lack of financial resources to expand
their operations.

Why has CEPAS been successful? First and foremost, because it has been completely staffed by local leaders. Its principal
architects come from Veraguas but were trained first for six
months to a year in outside institutions. They have shown a
dedication to their work and an ability to communicate with the
campesino that few foreigners, or even leaders from another
province, could equal.

CEPAS has also moved slowly in introducing the *campesino*
to changes. It is easy to minimize the rapidity and scope of
"change" in an environment such as Veraguas. Choosing a one-
hectare experimental plot and having it worked communally by
ten men using a few new agricultural techniques seems a small
venture to us, but it is a gigantic and revolutionary step in the
eyes of the *campesino*. Time is necessary to digest and build
further upon such change.

CEPAS deals directly with the *campesino*, with no intermediaries. Its thrust has been toward working directly in the communities with the people; its bureaucracy in Santiago serves that end exclusively. By harnessing the young potential leaders of Veraguas this drive has been maintained. Working constantly with the *campesinos* has enabled CEPAS to gain their confidence. This, in turn, makes it possible to introduce more changes. Experimental plots, worked on in the villages themselves by local groups, provide the *campesino* with firsthand evidence and experience concerning the means of change and success and a degree of confidence which could never be derived from, for example, a demonstration plot at an experimental farm.

Nor is it accidental that CEPAS was able to succeed as a movement once it focused upon increasing rice production, waiting to work toward savings, credit, and other functions until a measure of motivation and organization had been achieved. While many things are needed in the countryside, improving the basic economic position of the *campesino* is the one most apparent to him. The appeal of improving rice production over building latrines or schoolhouses or small bridges is obvious. Focusing on and about an important need of the people makes CEPAS a serious and persuasive movement to its members.

CEPAS and Juan XXIII are multifunctional organizations in several senses. Allied, but mutually independent, they are involved in all stages of rice production: selecting the land, making it available, preparing it by tractor, securing financing for the *campesinos*, assisting and advising concerning seeding, weeding, harvesting, milling, and, finally, selling. The problems of rice production alone are not isolated as part agricultural, part marketing, and so forth. An integrated organization is needed to handle them. Moreover, CEPAS also extends "horizontally," not just "vertically." Through its educational and training activities it is encouraging the use of other crops, stressing the importance of individual saving, teaching the value and strength of working with a group. In short, it does not isolate a single problem in the countryside, but treats a series of problems together. Thus, CEPAS and Juan XXIII are at once providing technical advice, giving moral backing, forming groups, training and developing leaders among the *campesinos,* providing cooperative tractors and a store, and reaching into a variety of agricultural activities. Intelligent direction to focus on the problems and to pull them together into a system without scattering efforts appears to be a prerequisite to developmental success in the countryside. CEPAS is able to fill in the structural void between the *campesino* and the rest of society, performing perhaps most importantly a vital function of socio-political organization.

In conclusion, the following thoughts of Bishop McGrath are relevant:

> It is obvious that the achievements of CEPAS so far are moderate in scope. It is always possible that a social effort of this nature for any of various possible reasons might lose its thrust and gradually subside. However, if this movement can continue in solid growth, it could mean a genuine breakthrough into the development of democratic structures in which our marginal farmers who make up the bulk of our rural population could rise into a position of productive contribution and conscious citizenship.
>
> The various government agencies have consistently contributed their services to the cooperative groups. There is always the danger of paternalism in all this assistance, whether on the part of the Church or the state. We feel that the Church's role has been to create the *initial* confidence and help in the development of leaders who are gradually taking over their own movement. The government's services, which are logically far broader than those which the Church or any other private institution can provide, will be successful in promoting the development of productive and democratic structures among the poor farmers to the extent that they are effective services which carefully *refrain* from taking over the direction of the movement. Such a take-over would be a new form of paternalism in the face of which the *campesinos* would revert to the passive acceptance of favors.

6

A DOCTRINE ABOUT CHANGE
AND THE ENVIRONMENT

> *Those who profess to favor freedom and yet de-*
> *preciate agitation are men who want crops without*
> *plowing up the ground, they want rain without*
> *thunder and lightning. . . . Power concedes nothing*
> *without a demand. It never did and it never will.*
>
> Frederick Douglass

The problems, pressures, and characteristics discussed so far suggest several conclusions concerning the Latin American environment. With these in mind we can begin to perceive some of the prerequisites for change or development. Assuming change is what is wanted,* we then can set out the specifications for an effective engine of change and its probable sequence of action. This in turn will allow an assessment of the various engines of change at work today in the region and their relevance to the government and the corporations of the United States. All of these together will make what perhaps pretentiously we shall call a doctrine.

I

The first conclusion is that the problems of Latin America are interrelated, self-supporting parts of a whole, and they are

---

* An idealistic student of mine once told me that he wanted to devote his life to "development." I asked him why and he replied that he felt morally bound to help the poor, the sick, and the ignorant. "In what way do you want to change them?" I asked. "Oh, I don't want to change them," he answered, "I just want to help them." Barbara Ward discusses this matter in "We May Be Rich, but They Are Happy" (*The New York Times Magazine*, May 5, 1963, p. 121).

deeply rooted in the economic, social, and political structures of the region. Development is indeed a total process.[1] We have seen, explicitly in the example of Veraguas, the intricate connections between living standards, agricultural production, market and credit structures, land-tenure patterns, the political system, allocation of power, the social structure, education, health, values, and culture. It is fruitless to attempt to isolate one of these problems artificially for the application of expertise. An effective change engine, therefore, is sensitive to the entire problem circle and is capable of dealing with several problems, as appropriate, more or less simultaneously. It must be able to move in many directions at once and work in the political and social sphere as well as the economic sphere. It must, furthermore, be inherently capable of making natural computations concerning the manner in which actions in one sphere, related to one order of problem, can provide useful leverage and support for action in another sphere affecting other problems. A successful change engine, for example, recognizes the extent to which increased access to land and improved production methods can be used to force more useful market and credit structures; and the extent to which this change will in turn produce more advantageous political influence, which will help to insure, over time, more beneficial governmental attention.

2

The second conclusion which we can draw concerning these problems is that they can be seen as deriving from two general inadequacies. The first has to do with motivation. It reveals itself in a lack of purpose, hope, confidence, and identity; and in problems of direction and values, which are moral, spiritual, and ideological. The second inadequacy has to do with organization, and reveals itself in problems of power, access, communication, bargaining, and negotiation; of institutions, leadership, authority, and elites. In these two categories lie the obstacles to change which frustrate the formation of nations and communities.

Material and technical injections into areas which are characterized by motivational and organizational vacuums accomplish no purpose. In fact, such injections can be positively harmful in several ways.

Matter is of no value unless its recipients are clear regarding its purpose. Unless there is a receptacle for matter which can provide it with purpose, the matter is wasted. Such a receptacle, however, must also be an engine with a sense of direction, capable of using material and technical injections for the achievement of structural change and growth. This requires an ideology and a doctrine.

The introduction of an administrative bureaucracy without local roots, unattached to local needs and unrepresentative of local interests, is apt to bring corruption. This is particularly true when the administrative bureaucracy is called upon and expected to perform tasks which, given the nature of the system as a whole, it cannot perform.

To the extent that matter and technique are provided from "the outside," unrelated to local initiative or action, the people are reinforced in their conviction that they have little or no control over their own destinies and are further discouraged from organizing to help themselves.

3

This leads to the third and most fundamental conclusion. For change or development to be real and permanent in the environment as we have described it, material and technical inputs must be preceded or at least accompanied by the creation of certain socio-political institutions or organizations. These organizations are, in effect, receptacles for matter and technique; but they are more than receptacles because they must have the capacity to convert the matter and the technique into fuel and, like an engine, burn it for a purpose. The receptacles, therefore, must at the same time be engines.

Furthermore, to be effective, given what we have said so far, they must be engines able to motivate and organize, and able to approach the problem circle in an integrative, coordinated, multifaceted fashion.

Mexico's revolutionary leadership, Castro in the Sierra Maestra, the Peasant League of Northeast Brazil, Bishop McGrath and CEPAS, the food-processing enterprise, the commercial farm, the factory, the university, the labor union—these and more we shall examine as examples of engines of change.*

Economic factors, therefore, which by definition are material and technical, affect change or development only to the extent that they constitute fuel for one or another engine of change. Their effect otherwise is purely haphazard. Economic development, then, is clearly dependent upon the prior or simultaneous formation of political structures (engines). Economic need in this context assumes importance not so much for itself or its fulfillment but as a means to and reason for motivation and organization.

It has been observed for centuries that economic, material, or technical factors may not at all be the most significant motivation of man toward development. It is almost a truism that the motivations which cause change or development go well beyond the economic self-interest with which Karl Marx was so concerned. In fact, Marx's hypnotic power and the frailty of his rivals are dramatically evident in the extent to which development thinking has been mistakenly cast in economic terms—even by the most capitalistic of us. Everett E. Hagen, in a fascinating study of ninety-two innovators in Britain during the seventeenth and eighteenth centuries, for example, clearly demonstrates that they were motivated by inquisitiveness, curiosity about their environment, lack of inhibitions against change, and an unrelenting drive to achieve. They were generally men of adequate means, for whom economic motives were plainly not paramount.[2]

On a different plane we can point to the motivation of the peasant leaders of the Mexican Revolution—Zapata, Villa, Amaro—and to others who likewise were poor and had little ambition to be rich—Obregon, Calles, Cardena, Mujica, and many others. In an awkward, chaotic, disorganized, wasteful,

* In his account of European reconstruction after World War II, James A. Perkins wrote (*Foreign Affairs,* July 1966) that success did not lie in "concrete and steel" but in "modern men working both in industry and the civil service . . . Europe did not have to be invented; it only had to be remembered." In other words, the structures were there; the engines of change in place and running.

and agonizing sequence of action between 1910 and 1940 in Mexico, a million lives were lost, a ruling elite destroyed, the transition from an agricultural to an industrial society was begun, and, most important, a people were awakened, a nation was born. As Dr. Frank Tannenbaum writes: "The significance of the story lies more in the moral and spiritual changes that have occurred than in the striking economic or even the political spheres . . . self-awakening is the real fruit of their bitter, cruel and bloody revolution. . . . They have for the first time in four hundred years identified themselves with their ancient history, and one can see the results in the work of their great artists, architects, and more recently in their music, poetry and fiction. The Mexicans, like the ancient Greeks, now look upon all people beyond their own borders as barbarians." [3]

This is not to suggest that economic gain or profit is not an important motivator of human action. It can be a very effective motivating device for the construction of a change engine, as we have seen in the success of CEPAS, which gained its foothold by increasing the *campesinos'* return on production. But in itself, as an economic fact it has no necessary relationship to change. The pursuit of profit can lead to change or to the maintenance of the status quo, and it has done both in Latin America. [4]

Economic development is therefore dependent upon the prior or simultaneous formation of motivational-organizational political structures which we can regard as engines of change. Material or technical injections produce planned, orderly, or creative change only to the extent that they fuel such engines. Plainly, the laws of chance make it conceivable for injections outside the engines to produce change, but the odds are heavily against such change being permanent.

Samuel Huntington has developed an interesting and important corollary of this principle. Distinguishing between economic development and political stability, Huntington points out that economic development—reducing poverty, disease, and ignorance—has no relevance to political stability or development. "Indeed, there is much evidence to suggest that it is not poverty but rapid improvement in standards of living, not disease but the spread of modern health practices, not illiteracy but the expansion of education and mass communications which encourage political instability and the decay of political institutions." *

4

Veraguas and the experience of the CEPAS movement suggest the sequence of action that a successful engine of change appears to follow, granted that in practice one step may merge with or overlap another. Although I shall describe the sequence in terms of rural Veraguas, its application may not necessarily be limited to rural areas and their *campesino* inhabitants. Given the problems and circumstances of Latin America today, however, such areas are where the doctrine will be most important, relevant, and useful.

First comes agitation. The *campesino* must be made clearly aware of a need which is more compelling than his fears, his doubts, and his conditioned hopelessness and indifference. If you ask a Veraguas *campesino* about his needs, he may give you a list including money, a tin roof for his hut, a bottle of liquor, or a new woman. For development purposes these needs, as such, are useless. Their satisfaction has no necessary relation to the task of development. Agitation, in the sense in which we are using the word, means the isolation, analysis, and dramatization of *one* need, the fulfillment of which is reasonably manageable and around which successful motivation and organization can take place. In Veraguas we have seen that the needs for greater rice production and access to credit were two useful needs about which CEPAS successfully agitated.**

---

* A recent study by the Rand Corporation of the effects of land reform in South Viet Nam, for example, reveals that the most secure provinces in Viet Nam—that is, the most politically stable—are generally those that have large estates and where there has been a minimum redistribution of land by the government. Such a revelation emphasizes the importance of precise objectives. Why do we want development and change? Plainly, political stability, at least in the short run, cannot be the answer, for the way to stability—albeit the stability of the tomb—is surely not through change. (See Edward J. Mitchell, "The Significance of Land Tenure in the Vietnamese Insurgency," *Asian Survey*, August, 1967, Vol. III, No. 8, pp. 577 ff.)

** Dr. Donald R. Schon has some relevant thoughts: "You talk to people and

The passivity of the *campesino* having been shaken, he begins to envision the possibility of change and the achievement of a new and more attractive relation to his environment. He begins to have aspirations. So the second step can be defined as **motivation.** He is ready to move to fulfill the need about which he has become agitated. He is thus prepared to acquire the necessary new skills and competence. Their acquisition in turn provides him with the confidence in himself and his abilities which is necessary for him to fulfill his needs. His motivation and his competence thus are closely interrelated and self-supporting.

Having greater understanding of his needs and confidence in his competence to deal with them, the *campesino* becomes willing to join with—and trust—others in order to achieve the power necessary to reach his newfound objective. Thus, the third step in the sequence is **organization,** to allow him to move more forcibly into the surrounding political, social, and economic environment in a continuing and institutional way. The organization then becomes a useful receptacle for material and technical inputs, the purpose of which is to strengthen it and provide it with the means for growth and expansion into new areas of need and change. As the organization grows, it has increased capacity to agitate and motivate its members, thus strengthening itself.

Finally, the *campesino* achieves **commitment** to whatever group or individual (engine) has brought him successfully through the first three steps of the sequence. He develops a sense of loyalty, a sense of identity and belonging, a sense of community. He has the beginnings of an ideology.

The principal criterion for the selection of the need around which to agitate is the degree to which it is useful for motiva-

---

say, 'What do you need?' and they are incapable of telling you what they need. They can tell you what they have and they can tell you what they do not have, that somebody else has. They can tell you what irritates them about what they have. They can tell you all that by their behavior. They can also tell you certain other things, but not in words. It is very difficult to talk about a pre-existing need. The issue of whether there is a need or not is partly an after-the-fact idea. . . . A need gets to be seen as a kind of a gap or a hole. If you can find the right plug for the hole, you have met the need. You go around looking for holes." (Remarks in a seminar, *The Institute for Marketing Communications Bulletin,* mimeographed, July 19, 1967.)

tional and organizational purposes. That is, the need must be perceived with reasonable facility; it must be manageable; it must be big enough and broad enough to be meaningful; and it must provide the basis for a continuing effort, not a one-shot undertaking. It may not, however, be the need which would have been selected if other criteria, say those of an economist or agricultural technician, were applied.

5

So much for the action sequence which a successful change engine follows. What does it need to have or provide in order to succeed?

The process of change is filled with risks and dangers, for in any society there are always forces present whose interests are threatened by change. A movement for change, therefore, needs the protection and guidance of authoritative forces. It also needs the capacity to communicate up the hierarchical ladder in order to explain itself. Communication is generally difficult in a developing society. In Latin America relatively few people can talk to the *campesino* and be understood, believed, and trusted. He likewise can talk to few in authority. He needs help in building the communication "bridges" as well as the political, social, and economic links which will make him part of the national system. The process requires material, technical, and managerial assistance—all carefully applied so as to serve an organizational or institutional end.

Looking again at Veraguas and the movement associated with Bishop McGrath and CEPAS, it appears that a successful change engine or agent must have the following characteristics:

Authority. The agent of change must be listened to and believed in by the *campesino.*

Communication and access to power. He must be able to communicate with the most remote *campesino,* and at the same time have access to the power structure, so that, for example, he can obtain funds, material, and technical help as necessary.

Competence and the ability to import it. He must be able to understand and deal with, more or less simultaneously, a broad spectrum of rural needs, and to bring appropriate technological innovations to bear.

Protection. He must have the sustained will and capacity to protect the newly developing organization against the forces of the status quo and other predatory elements in the environment.

Sustained purpose and will. Some groups and organizations have all the qualifications necessary to produce change but fail because change is not their purpose; or if it is, it has a low priority and will be sacrificed to other purposes considered more important. The military falls in this category, as do some traditional urban trade unions and some business enterprises.

A variety of groups and individuals—Bishop McGrath in Veraguas, for example—can provide these characteristics. Oddly enough, it seems that frequently foreigners are able to. In the *barrio* outside Guayaquil, where the inhabitants lived on top of raw garbage, a young Peace Corps couple who had been working to organize this slum complained one day to the local military authorities about the failure of the army to produce the promised sand to cover the putrid streets. They found out where the local commander lived and, clad in their smelly dungarees, trudged up the hill to visit him. He was out, but they told his wife about the situation. She became interested, and after viewing the conditions herself shared the indignation of the young people. She had the capacity to make her husband's life miserable until he delivered some fill, at least to the neighborhood where the Peace Corps couple were working.

The Peace Corps volunteers had authority and access to power. Their action furthermore demonstrated competence to those whom they were seeking to change, and as the organization of the slum grew and began to threaten the lords of the local status quo the volunteers were able to prove their capacity to protect the infant engine.

6

Change as here described tends to be radical, structural, and permanent. It is, therefore, revolutionary and disruptive. It undermines or subverts existing power structures and arrangements.

It is not surprising that the governments of Latin America and the power groups which sustain them are not only ineffective engines of change, but are generally positive obstacles. Actually, what passes for development planning on the part of Latin American governments and their United States assistants often amounts to a scheme for the peaceful maintenance of the system, a procedure by which adjustments are made within the existing order in the hope that pressures will be relieved and tensions altered, avoiding change as much as possible. This is especially true when our aid substantially strengthens the one institution best equipped to resist change: the military establishment.

Furthermore, if we were to presume that a particular government was determined to initiate basic change, as, for example, the administration of Eduardo Frei Montalva in Chile, or of Carlos Lleras Restrepo in Colombia, the nature of the political process is such that its capacity to do so is severely limited. Governmental incompetence in this direction is particularly acute in the rural areas where the government's reach and identity have been traditionally feeble.

It may well be, however, that the forces for change which are at work in Latin America essentially outside the political process will persevere and eventually be successful. Given the rigidities of the existing system, a continuing encounter of drastic change on the one hand, and rigid resistance to change on the other, is likely. But no change at all would seem to be an idle dream and inconsistent with the experience of the world in general and of Mexico, Cuba, and Bolivia in particular. So we are left to consider how, given the peculiar condition of the Latin American environment, the inevitable processes of change will work. What will be its nature and dimensions? Who has the power and the will to produce it? What means will they employ? How will change work itself through the convoluted, resistant channels of the system? How will its chilling characteristics be ameliorated? Can it be peaceful, or must it be bloody? It would be foolish to pretend to be able to answer all these questions, but we can make a start on some of them, and perhaps draw some conclusions which will be useful.

A variety of groups and organizations in Latin America seem

to have the characteristics necessary to be successful engines of change and to be capable of the sequence of action mentioned above. It is a strange collection: the radical social-action wing of the Roman Catholic Church; community and cooperative groups and organizations which the radical Church inspires, supports and protects; peasant leagues and federations; plantation workers' organizations and other labor unions; students; subversive organizations, some supported from foreign bases and some not; certain sectors of government, political parties, and the military; new local managers and entrepreneurs; and foreign managers and entrepreneurs, in particular those in the large, modern, integrated industries producing and processing food.

7

APPLYING THE DOCTRINE: Mexico, Venezuela and Brazil

It would be pretentious to suppose that the doctrine of change just set forth is capable of precise proof. Nor do I contend that the characteristics and the sequence of action which I assign to the successful engine of change can be viewed as absolute and universal. But one test of the validity of this theory is to measure the extent to which the doctrine that grew from experience with a church-sponsored organization in Veraguas can apply in other circumstances.

Three test cases will suit the purpose: agriculture in Mexico, land reform in Venezuela, and development in Northeast Brazil.

I

Mexico's overall agricultural production during the last twenty-five years has broken all Latin American and most world records, growing at an annual rate of almost 5 per cent between 1940 and 1962 and at a somewhat higher rate in 1962 and 1963. Despite a drop in growth to 1.6 per cent in 1966, agriculture has been a major contributor to Mexico's rising economic vitality.[1]

At the same time, agricultural productivity (average output per worker) is mediocre. Per-capita productivity in 1966 was only slightly ahead of what it had been in 1960, and substantially less than that of several other Latin American countries. Crop output per hectare today is only about $100, and output

per agricultural worker is $420, which is less than the output in
Argentina, Venezuela, Colombia, or Chile.[2]

These figures tell the story of the two distinct and in many
ways divergent sectors of Mexican agriculture: the subsistent
and the commercial. About 80 per cent of Mexico's economically
active rural population continue to live at a subsistence level of
poverty and isolation not too different from that in Veraguas.
These include some three million landless peasants, squatters,
and seasonal workers, about two and a half million *ejidatarios*
(members of an *ejido**), and about a million private land-holders
with five hectares or less.[3] Thus, there are some six million Mexican peasants whose condition of life is in some ways no better
than it was before the revolution in 1910. They are essentially
outside the nation's market and credit systems, with little political power or participation, and little control over their environment. On the other hand, the large and medium-sized commercial farms and plantations of the northwest and Pacific areas,
although employing a small percentage of agricultural workers,
have been phenomenally productive. Looking at these two sectors in terms of change, one reflects substantial change and
the other an entrenched status quo which has effectively restricted change.

Let us look at the historical phases of land tenure in Mexico.[4]

The period from 1860 to 1910 saw the consolidation of the
hacienda system in Mexico. Indian communal lands and the
small holdings of *mestizo* farmers were confiscated by the ruling
oligarchy and given or sold to a relative handful of landowners.
Peasants were reduced to little more than slaves, without rights
or protection. Ninety-five per cent of the rural population owned
no land at all. Protest and sporadic violence became increasingly
intense, particularly in the densely populated central sections of
Mexico. Lands were seized, *hacendados* murdered and their
great houses burned; the revolution was ignited.

* The term *"ejido"* refers to all types of land and water resources, the title to
which is vested in villages as a whole (or, in reality, the government), and
which are exploited in common or individually by the members of the
village. It originally referred to communal lands outside (at the "exit" of) the
medieval Spanish village.

The revolution of 1910 thus grew from the discontented rural proletariat of central Mexico; it was not born in the cities or the mining areas. So it was that agrarian reform and radical shifts in land-tenure patterns became its primary demand and its first promise. Deeply imbedded in the spirit of the revolution was the claim of the Indian for the return of his traditional village lands, which had been so brutally taken away. Successive revolutionary governments felt keenly the urgent necessity of speedily breaking up the large *haciendas* and distributing them to the peasant masses.

"The promise of land was the crucial commitment that enabled political leaders to gain and hold power," writes Wolf Ladejinsky.[5] In many instances, the peasants were ahead of the government, having taken the land by force. Governments were thus understandably little concerned with the niceties of agricultural planning or with dividing the land so as to make it most productive. Their principal concern was to mollify the often savage peasant demands. This led to breaking up the land into pitifully small parcels and returning it in the form of *ejidos* to the communities from which it had been taken.

A network of these rural land-reform communities was established which today embraces 45 per cent of all crop land in Mexico and 54 per cent of all land-holders. But this network is responsible for only 30 per cent of the value of crop and livestock production.[6] The nature and causes of its creation have meant that the *ejidos* are largely located in the more heavily populated rural areas, where the old *haciendas* had once been. They are most common in Mexico's central provinces, where more than 40 per cent of the rural population lives.

The *ejidos* have been closely watched by successive governments in Mexico City. The *ejidatarios*, unable to own their lands outright, have grown up to become in most cases what Ladejinsky calls "indigent wards of the state." They quickly came to be used as political organizations by the ruling PRI to maintain control, and their leadership has suffered from political patronage. Becoming "the kept children of the PRI,"[7] they have been unable to generate political influence upward to the centers of power. Thus, since 1940 they have received decreasing attention from the government, which felt the need of concentrating its economic and technical aid on the far more profitable nonejidal private sector. Because the *ejidatarios* cannot own land, they are unable to obtain credit from normal credit sources and must rely on the government credit institution, Banco Ejidal. The bank is woefully inadequate and inefficient, and labors under an ever-mounting debt.[8]

This brings us to the phase of Mexican land-tenure development which began in 1940, when the government realized that the economic needs of the nation for agricultural production were not going to be met by the *ejido* system. It therefore shifted its emphasis to the promotion of medium- and large-sized private holdings, producing cash crops, aided by massive investments for irrigation, fertilizer and seed, price supports, marketing assistance, and crop loans. While the revolutionary statutes provided for private land, they limited the amount any individual could hold to 100 hectares for irrigated land, 200 hectares for unirrigated land, 150 hectares for land in cotton and under irrigation, and so on. These restrictions have come to be honored more in the breach than in the observance, with the growth of large commercial cotton, wheat, and vegetable farms in the north and on the Pacific coast, areas which at the time of the revolution were largely uncultivated and underpopulated.

Between 1930 and 1960, for example, the northwest provinces of Sonora and Sinaloa showed a production increase of 555 per cent, compared to about 200 per cent nationally.[9] The following table depicts graphically the manner in which private commercial agriculture has outstripped ejidal production.

The remarkable agricultural production of the north and coastal regions is, of course, partly due to the fact that they have received the greatest public investment for irrigation. But what is more important is that the farms and farmers of these regions were able to obtain and effectively utilize these public injections of matter and technology because they qualified as engines of motivation and organization within our definition. Likewise, the *ejidos* have failed to the extent that they have not so qualified, regardless of whatever material they have or have not received.

The Mexican government thus has pursued a relatively suc-

TABLE 4

Rank Ordering of Regions with Highest
Growth of Agricultural Productivity
Compared with Regions Having Highest
Share of Ejidal Land

	Ranking of Growth of Agric. Output per Rural Dweller (1930–60)	Ranking of Share of Ejidal Acreage in Total Cultivated Acreage (1950)
South Pacific	1	5
North	2	3
North Pacific	3	4
Center	4	2
Gulf	5	1

(Highest = 1; Lowest = 5)

Source: Clark W. Reynolds, "Land Reform and Its Implications for Mexican Agricultural Development," mimeographed, p. 5.

cessful dual agricultural policy. First, it expropriated and redistributed the less fertile, older lands in the densely populated regions, converting them into essentially subsistence *ejidos*. Secondly, it made the most of the entrepreneurial spirit released by the revolution itself to encourage the development of large-scale commercial agriculture in previously sparsely populated regions which, with water and enterprise, have bloomed. As Clark Reynolds has pointed out: "The first policy satisfied political stability . . . the second satisfied growth criteria." [10]

But all is not rosy in Mexico's countryside. The principal worry of the government and the ruling PRI party is that the promises of the revolution have soured for the majority of Mexican *campesinos*. Increasingly, the *ejidatarios*, the small landholders, and the landless are said to be "eyeing the broad acres of the large owners enviously and hungrily." [11] As the population gallops ahead at a rate of 3.6 per cent a year, rural poverty and underemployment swell. Cultivable land becomes scarcer, the large modern and efficient farms expand and prosper, and the

vast majority of farmers are stuck with pitifully small, unirrigated, unfertilized, and unimproved plots.

The figures are striking. Some 50 million hectares are distributed among some 22,000 *ejidos*. While some *ejidos*, particularly in the north, are farmed cooperatively and take advantage
of modern technology, the vast majority are little more than
subsistence plots. Privately owned land totals about 125 million
hectares, divided among 1,346,000 holdings. Seventy-four per
cent of these private holdings are of ten hectares or less and
account for only 1.6 per cent of the total area. At the other end
of the scale, .3 per cent of the holdings are over 5,000 hectares
and comprise almost 57 per cent of all the land privately held.
There are 4,000 such holdings in Mexico. Some of this land, of
course, is not planted or used for pasturage because of lack of
water, but a somewhat similar spread can be seen in the figures
for crop land.[12] The violation of the revolutionary norms, intended to prohibit such disparity, are obvious. Efficient and economically profitable as the large commercial farms may be, the
six million who benefit little from them are vulnerable to agitators. And it is a perverse irony that one of the most active sources
of such peasant agitation is the Roman Catholic Church, which
the revolution violently oppressed and banished for its oligarchical attachments and commitments. Today, in many a rural pulpit
the priest is calling the peasant's attention to the inequities of his
environment.

The questions are obvious. Why is roughly 20 per cent of
Mexican agriculture booming while 80 per cent languishes?
Why do 3 per cent of the farmers, few of whom are within the
revolutionary *ejidos*, produce more than 50 per cent of crop
sales? [13] Why have the *ejidos* been such disappointing engines
of change, of motivation and organization, and why have the
entrepreneurial commercial farmers of the north and west been
so successful in this regard?

There can be no denying or underestimating the great effects
of the Mexican Revolution and the fundamental realignment
of power which it caused. There had been the agitation, the
motivation, and the organization; and there was a new and real

commitment. Mexico emerged from this revolution a nation as well as a state, a more unified political community, conscious of its traditions, imbued with an unprecedented purpose and pride in all things Mexican. Class distinctions were reduced and political participation was broadened, albeit within the structures of the single revolutionary party, the PRI. It seems plain that the spirit and the fact of the revolution released and kindled the motivations and entrepreneurial zeal of thousands of the ablest and most energetic Mexicans. With new lands to cultivate and new resources to exploit, these men had the confidence, hope, and vision necessary to initiate radical and lasting change. While at first the government paid slight attention to these pioneering groups, in the 1940's it became apparent that the future of Mexican growth lay with them. They had become engines of change; it only remained to fuel and support them. This the government did abundantly. In 1940 government investments in fertilizer, for example, were 8.1 thousand tons; in 1960 they were 171 thousand tons, and in 1964 they were 270 thousand tons. Public investment in water and irrigation systems in 1950 produced a distribution of 6.5 billion cubic meters of water. Five years later the figure had doubled, and in 1960, 17.3 billion cubic meters were made available for crop-land irrigation, 70 per cent of the cost being subsidized by the Mexican government. But it should be emphasized that this and other public investment were heavily concentrated in the private commercial land areas of the north and west.

Technology also arrived in abundance, much of it from the United States. Seeds, insecticides, and technical assistance were dispatched from the Rockefeller Foundation; farm equipment and other help from AID; and a wide variety of managerial, market, and technological access and strengthening came from such American companies as Anderson Clayton. Furthermore, that all-important commodity, credit, was supplied abundantly by newly formed Mexican banks, most recently the Banco Agropecuario, and by foreign investment. This was credit extended on a commercial basis, investment in the profitable, far different from the inadequate and unprofitable credit of the Banco Ejidal.

These new entrepreneurial engines were able to acquire the

characteristics vital for their preservation and growth. They quickly gained authority and political access to the power groups in Mexico City. Proof of this would seem to lie clearly in the extent to which they have been able to stretch liberally the revolutionary land-tenure restrictions and obtain for themselves the principal share of public investment in agriculture. They were also able to form and command market and credit systems and to gain the competence necessary to employ modern technology.

Now, what of the *ejidos?* They were formed largely in the early fires of the revolution out of urgent political necessity. There was no time for planning or calculation. They were a revolutionary necessity, and as such their importance was only partly economic. Their purpose was as much, if not more, to restore and invigorate the dignity of the Indian, to return to him his ancestral and traditional lands, to give him a sense of participation in the great movement of his country.

Some years ago an astute observer recorded the effects of the *ejidos* on the previously oppressed Indians:

> Everywhere they reported that they are enjoying personal freedom that was nonexistent previously. They might be living in the same shacks, subsisting on the same type of diet (with, perhaps, some improvement in quantity), wearing the same types of clothes, and drinking the same polluted water; but at least they are not abused by the landlord or kept in perpetual debt slavery, or hunted down by the *rurales* if they try to escape. They are not required to purchase their food and clothing through the *tienda de raya* (*hacienda* store). There is now no fear of arbitrary arrest and punishment without trial; *ley fuga* is no longer the dreaded fate of those who incur the displeasure of government officials.[14]

It appears, however, that in haste and by force of circumstances, a new though certainly more benevolent form of paternalism was substituted for the old. The Indian, unprepared for change, found himself a ward of the state. His leader came to be the local *cacique* or boss of the party, who sought more than anything else his vote, his support, his docility. It is not surprising that the leaders of the *ejidos* did not see themselves as agitators, motivators, and organizers of local power, but as supporters of the PRI.

This marginal existence makes the *ejiditarios* understandably wary of new ways and procedures. What material injections they do receive, such as credit, are generally misused. I am unfamiliar with any studies on the effect of the substantial public investment which has been made in the *ejido* areas of central Mexico in roads, schools, and electrification, but if our doctrine holds, these will have had only a marginal impact. One would speculate, for example, that schooling is marred by low attendance, numerous dropouts, and general lack of student motivation.

2

In contrast to Mexico is Venezuela, where the most extensive nonviolent land-reform program in Latin America has been carried out. Perhaps Venezuela is really not comparable to other Latin American countries because of its enormous petroleum deposits, which contribute almost 30 per cent of its gross domestic product and give it the highest per-capita wealth in Latin America ($735 in 1966).[15] With this kind of income, some say, the Venezuelan government can afford to buy revolutionary change without any real violence. Perhaps, but even so, it is useful to consider how such a feat is accomplished. It hasn't happened often in world history.

Since 1960 Venezuelan agriculture has grown at a somewhat faster annual rate than Mexico's—5.7 per cent compared to 4.7 per cent. It has been among the few Latin American countries which have managed to keep food production significantly ahead of population growth in the last decade. At the same time, since 1958 some three million hectares of land have been distributed to about 200,000 Venezuelan farm families.*

* It is important to note that in spite of undoubted progress, close to one fourth of Venezuela's one million agricultural workers fall into the category of renter, sharecropper, day laborer, or squatter, who by and large are impoverished, landless, isolated, and vulnerable. (John D. Powell, *The Politics of Agrarian Reform in Venezuela*, Ph.D. thesis, Univ. of Wisconsin, 1966, updated to 1967, p. 183.)

The purpose of Venezuela's land-reform program is to create a new class of small, family farmers out of some 250,000 subsistence farm families. This is being achieved through a network of cooperative settlements called *asentamientos,* an arrangement quite distinct from the *ejidos* but similar to the Israeli *moshav,* in which the farmer owns his land but has the benefits of a cooperative arrangement with respect to credit, marketing, equipment, and the like.

One of the best studies of the Venezuelan experience has been made by Dr. John D. Powell. He points out that in 1937 practically 90 per cent of all the cultivated land in Venezuela was included in 5 per cent of the farm holdings, a condition not unlike that of many other Latin American countries today. About three quarters of those active in agriculture (700,000) were landless and impoverished.[16] During the early 1930's there were sporadic outbreaks of peasant violence and attempts at concerted action which were ruthlessly put down by one of Latin America's most savage dictators, Juan Vicente Gómez, who ruled Venezuela from 1908 to 1935.

Conditions in the countryside and the government's response to those conditions had two effects. Many fled rural poverty for the urban slums. Government, as is so often the case, did not perceive the migration as a rural problem so much as an urban one. And the basis was laid for the growth of peasant organizations to give those who remained in the countryside the land they needed and the power to use and benefit from it.

These peasant groups, together with urban industrial worker organizations, provided the political foundations for a new revolutionary party which emerged during the thirties, Acción Democrática. Its young, revolutionary leaders, chief among whom was Rómulo Betancourt, were frequently forced to hide in the countryside, when they were not in exile or in jail. The AD party thus grew almost organically from the peasants' huts where its early plans were laid.

In 1945 the liberal but inept president, Isaías Medina Angarita, responded to the increasing pressure from the peasants and AD groups by promulgating an agrarian reform law, the principal purpose of which was to offer for sale to peasants at a low price some 80,000 hectares of farmland held by the agricultural bank. It also empowered the state to negotiate the purchase of private lands which were not productive and to distribute these lands in small parcels to farmers.

The signing of the reform law aroused the oligarchs, who prepared to seize the government. Then a remarkable political event took place. Betancourt and the AD joined with a group of young military officers known as the Patriotic Military Union (PMU), who were chafing under the domination of the army by the old families of wealth and influence. To preserve the reform gains made and to pursue them further, AD, with PMU power, overthrew the Medina government in October 1945 and substituted a revolutionary junta with Betancourt in charge.[17]

With AD in control of the government, its rural organizations had new power and access. Composed of some five hundred peasant unions or syndicates with perhaps 100,000 members, the Venezuelan Campesino Federation (FCV) became an integral part of the country's revolutionary process. FCV leadership, tested in twenty years of rural struggle, was also a critical part of the leadership of Acción Democrática. FCV was in a position to help formulate the nature and application of land-reform programs, and to insure their appropriate adjustment to the needs of the farmers; to provide, for example, that farmers have the right to own land, and to stipulate the sort of services and assistance which were necessary. Furthermore, there was a field organization in existence, a network of socio-political institutions, ready to react and move with the new government to guarantee effective reform. The *campesino* unions were also able to take the peasant from the elementary stage of land tenure through the increasingly complex environmental maze with its myriad hazards, distortions, and obstacles. Unlike the Mexican *ejidos,* the Venezuelan peasant unions preceded or accompanied the AD party. They were not its children so much as they were its parents. They were an integral part of the revolutionary machinery. Their leaders were thus in a position to form the entire process in an integrated way, shaping the policies of government to the needs of the *campesinos,* and at the same time forming engines of motivation and organization in the countryside which could serve as useful receptacles for government inputs.

Venezuelan land reform started slowly. Between 1945 and 1948 only 125,000 hectares were distributed to 73,000 peasants, but the program's political effect was profound and widespread.[18] Initially, the government was able to use state lands, acquired partly through defaults on credit payments to the state's agricultural bank. It sold these to individual farmers in small parcels at a low price. But in 1947 it became apparent that a new and more radical approach would have to be taken, aimed at the large landowners whose properties were unproductive. Betancourt signed a law in March of that year establishing regional agrarian commissions with broad powers. The law was seen as an additional threat by the landowners, who were already feeling the political heat of the peasant unions. It was not long until AD was out of power, but the organization which it built in the three critical years, 1945 to 1948, survived the subsequent "decade of persecution."

In the elections of December 1947, Rómulo Gallegos became the first freely elected president of Venezuela under the new election laws promulgated by the AD, which gave everyone over the age of eighteen the right to vote. But the counterrevolutionary pressures were too great; the AD's political base was still too frail. Colonel Marcos Pérez Jiménez seized the government, with the backing of the oligarchs, and declared that he had come to save Venezuela from the "communistic" Acción Democrática. Once again, jail, exile, hiding, and torture befell Betancourt and his men. The entire Venezuelan Confederation of Labor, including the 515 peasant unions which had banded together to form it, was dissolved and declared illegal. For a decade the leaders of AD were hunted men, its organization clandestine. The land-reform program came to an abrupt halt, with widespread eviction of peasants from their newly acquired lands.

Once again, however, the organizational genius and perseverance of Rómulo Betancourt combined with military might to force Pérez Jiménez to flee to the Dominican Republic early on the morning of January 24, 1958.

The FCV quickly reorganized itself, its leaders returning from exile and jail. A new agrarian reform law was enacted, designed to establish a network of land-reform settlements, the previously mentioned *asentamientos,* to provide integrated services to a surrounding community of small farmers. The number of FCV unions climbed from 130 in 1958 to 3,476 in 1965, and membership rose from 4,586 to 171,299.[19] It has increased considerably since then. Released from the oppression of Pérez Jiménez, Venezuelan farmers reacted violently in many instances, invading lands, burning fields, and exerting intense pressure for prompt governmental action. Many government decisions during the early sixties, therefore, necessarily constituted after-the-fact acceptance of the actions of local peasant organizations. But the original integration of the FCV with the AD political party insured that in all events and at all levels the peasants had unusual and continuing access to political power and decision. They were, in effect, guaranteed continuing governmental attention in a more or less appropriate and useful form. The FCV had thus become a "broker for the *campesinos*" and a political engine "organizing electoral support for the government in return for influence in shaping and directing the program of agrarian reform." To continue in Powell's words: "The FCV . . . was born of the marriage between masses of *campesinos* seeking help in improving their conditions of life and democratic political parties seeking bases of mass electoral support. The peasant union movement was the instrument in which these two forces joined in common purpose." [20]

But the FCV was neither a creature of the AD nor a tool of the government. The FCV and its unions, unlike the Mexican *ejidos* in general, have a strong and independent life of their own. They have their own powers of representation within the *asentamientos,* the party, and the government. Increasingly, the Christian Democratic opposition to AD, COPEI, which is now in power in Venezuela, has been gaining allegiance within the FCV. The Federation has within it, therefore, the invigoration of political competition which the *ejidos* lack.

Of course, it is by no means certain that Venezuelan agricultural development will continue along its present path. There are still several hundred thousand impoverished, landless *campesinos* who have not felt the benefits of land reform. And there are still many unproductive *latifundias*. The need for continuing and increasing food production is real. It does seem certain, however, that whatever the course of events, the FCV will continue to play a central and significant role in initiating, guiding, and effecting rural change in Venezuela. One can be as sure about this as one can that commercial agricultural entrepreneurs in Mexico will continue to expand that country's rural capacity, politically as well as economically. And the reason for this certainty in both cases lies in our analysis of the capabilities which an engine of change must have in Latin America.

The significance of the FCV in Venezuelan land reform becomes particularly dramatic if we look at the lack of similar change in Colombia. In spite of the fact that Colombia has had an agrarian reform law on the books for a number of years and has recently put considerable effort and funds into its implementation, the results have been meager.[21] The reason is plain. Able and dedicated government servants are involved in the work. President Carlos Lleras Restrepo is one of the most forward-looking statesmen of the hemisphere. But the inertia of the status quo is profound. Lacking a similarly organized and powerful force on the other side, change is slow and inconsequential. The peasants are as disorganized, remote, and isolated as before. Their power over their environment is hardly greater; their connection with their government no more meaningful. There is a struggling national agrarian federation known as FANAL (Federación Agraria Nacional) which may offer promise for the future, and there are an increasing number of commercial enterprises, such as W. R. Grace and Company, which may bring essential ingredients for change.

3

Northeast Brazil is in a sense a gigantic version of Veraguas Province. Since 1877 its development has been a political issue for Brazil and, more recently, for the United States.[22] The region is inhabited by twenty-five million of the hemisphere's poorest people, the vast majority of whom have an annual income of between $50 and $100.* Almost 70 per cent of the school-age population are unable to read or write.[23] Brazil has a literacy test for voting; consequently, the majority of *nordestinos* are denied participation in the political process.

The Northeast is dominated economically and politically by large plantations of sugar, cotton, and manioc, and by extensive cattle ranches. These employ the majority of the region's people, maintaining them in a condition which is best described as semifeudal, subsistence serfdom. Close to 90 per cent of the population in agriculture do not own the land they work on; mortality rates are abnormally high; disease is widespread, social mobility virtually nonexistent. In spite of much fertile land now underutilized, the Northeast today imports from elsewhere in Brazil large quantities of food, particularly beef, rice, and dairy products. Transport difficulties being what they are, this is an extremely expensive importation. These characteristics are, of course, not abnormal for Latin America. What makes Brazil's Northeast distinctive is that periodically but unpredictably it has been seized by appalling droughts. Between 1877 and 1879 half of the one million inhabitants of the state of Ceará perished because of drought. "In the interior many died of hunger and thirst," Hirschman records, "or because they took to eating poisonous roots. Even larger numbers who reached the cities perished there as smallpox, yellow fever and typhoid swept the improvised encampments. Banditry and crime were rife and several instances of cannibalism were reported." [24]

Gradually dams, reservoirs, and irrigation systems have been completed, their construction and operation being accompanied by a substantial wash of scandal, corruption, and inefficiency. In completion, however, these extensive public works produced little basic change, but tended to strengthen and solidify the

* In this discussion of Northeast Brazil I have relied in part on Stefan Robock's excellent study, *Brazil's Developing Northeast: A Study of Regional Planning & Foreign Aid* (The Brookings Institution, Washington, D.C., 1963). He reports that per-capita income in the Northeast was $140 in 1960, compared to $410 in the south and an average of $280 for all of Brazil. There are no measurements, however, for distribution of income. It is known, however, that a small proportion of the population receives a major share of the income and, therefore, my estimate seems justified.

status quo. The dams and reservoirs watered the land of the cattlemen and the large landowners; the roads enabled them and their produce to reach the cities more smoothly and quickly.

At the end of 1966, the government of the state of Pernambuco proudly announced that 34 per cent of the people were served by electricity. The state, however, did not say who these 34 per cent were or whether electricity had meant change in or sustenance for the status quo.

Celso Furtado, the Brazilian economist who was for a time a leader in Northeast development, has said that these material injections in fact made matters worse, because as the large farms prospered, peasants were attracted to remain in or to come to the region for seasonal work, thus increasing the problem when droughts came.[25] In Furtado's view, the droughts were a "smoke-screen" hiding the real and much larger problem of change and development in the Northeast. The primary problem, he said, had to do with the political, economic, and social structure of the region, the pattern of land ownership, the allocation of and participation in power. It became apparent that little change could occur as long as the region was controlled by a handful of powerful men who were able effectively to isolate the peasant from any countervailing power and regulate his economic and political relationship with the environment. As long as this small group could command and channel government intervention, economic and technical injections by government were likely to have the effect of solidifying rather than altering the existing structure.[26]

Peasant revolutionary activity has flared periodically in Northeast Brazil,[27] and priests of the region were engaging in it as early as 1817. But, generally, in the past it has been quickly extinguished by the landowners and their police, backed by government force for law and order. In the last decade, however, movements for widespread institutional and structural change have arisen which, even today, have not been entirely extinguished and are perhaps among the harbingers of the first real and continuing change in the region.

In the mid-fifties, during the presidency of Juscelino Kubitschek, peasant uprisings became increasingly frequent. Great houses were burned, agitators and suspects were shot by police, bombings occurred in the cities, and fear spread that the peasants of the Northeast were organizing a movement similar to that which Fidel Castro was leading at the time in the mountains of Cuba.

The peasants sought and received leadership from several quarters. Sharecroppers in a small town near Recife organized a cooperative for the protection of their interests and needed a lawyer who could help and defend them.[28] They appealed to Francisco Julião, a Socialist deputy to the state legislature, who was to become a self-styled communist in the manner of Castro. He showed marked qualities of leadership and soon had formed the Ligas Campesinas, or Peasant Leagues, with 30,000 members in the Pernambuco area alone and more in the north and northwest.

At about the same time Dom Helder Pessoa Camara, archbishop of Olinda and Recife, was organizing his forces for the agitation and organization of the peasants for revolutionary action. In addition to the organization of Fathers de Melo and Crespo discussed earlier (SORPE), Dom Eugénio Salas, the bishop of Natal, formed groups which competed with Julião's Peasant Leagues. It is estimated that by 1963 close to 300,000 peasants were participating in one organization or another. The number is undoubtedly greater today, in spite of government opposition.

During this same period, and in response to the same conditions, Celso Furtado returned from the University of Cambridge to become director of the National Bank for Economic Development. Furtado, a native of the Northeast, had already given much thought to its problems. In 1958 he began a careful and extensive study of the region which was submitted to President Kubitschek in 1959.[29] Furtado proposed an integrated, comprehensive, and coordinated development scheme for the Northeast, all under the direction of a supercentralized Superintendency for the Development of the Northeast (SUDENE). It came into existence in 1960 with Furtado as its chief, and was hailed by economists from Washington to Buenos Aires as the answer to the problems of development and a model of economic planning and reform. Its powers were sweeping, its resources substantial. Stimulated by the threat of Julião and the political pressure of Helder Camara, both the Brazilian government and the new administration of President Kennedy vastly increased the material assistance to the Northeast. In 1961 United States aid to the region was about $250,000 a year. In 1962 it jumped to $65 million a year. (Before Julião, Brazilians, according to Robock, "were frank to complain that they did not have enough communists to warrant U.S. attention." [30])

Although Furtado was undoubtedly able, and SUDENE was formed with promises of revolutionary change, it failed to achieve its objectives. During the presidential regimes of Jânio Quadros, and even of communist-inclined João Goulart, the political system of Brazil, and especially entrenched power in the Northeast, effectively prevented change. SUDENE, like so many of its predecessors, became merely a more efficient public works agency, concentrating virtually all of its enormous resources on highways, electric power, water supply, and industrialization, with little attention as to how these material and technical injections were going to alter the status quo or produce the political ingredients and prerequisites for development. Furtado himself made frequent speeches declaring himself to be "a man of the left," working for a "controlled" social transformation.[31] But the fury of his enemies, combined with the ineptness of the regime, was too strong. In 1969 SUDENE was attempting to "colonize" peasants in the northern states on unused government land in the untouched interior. These programs, modeled after Israel's cooperative communities, are showing some promise, but they do not compare in impact with the efforts of the radical Church. Indeed, SUDENE's impact on the rural population of the Brazilian Northeast has been negligible.

In 1964 Goulart was overthrown by Marshal Mastelo Branco. Julião was imprisoned and later moved to Mexico, where he now lives. Furtado was purged and went to teach at the Sorbonne.[32] The Peasant Leagues were dissolved, but the work of the Church and its organizations continued. Indeed, the indomitable Dom Helder and those around him today represent the most secure hope for change in Northeast Brazil. More than once, the archbishop has stood between the peasants and the army, protecting the only political organizations in the region which can insure development.

In 1966 Dom Helder refused to celebrate a mass for the second anniversary of the Castelo Branco coup and Catholic students supporting him were thrown in jail. But incidents such as this were ineffective in curbing the archbishop. By 1968 he and his priests had organized rural union leaders, giving them technical assistance as well as political instruction, on the proviso that the unions would adopt nonviolent ways to achieve basic reforms. Although Pessoa Camara's chief target is Brazilian status quo leadership, he also criticizes the United States for being more interested in having Latin America "calm" than in realizing the reforms which Americans claim to support.

It seems unlikely that Pessoa Camara will be stopped. Conceivably, his program will eventually provide the basis for effective structural reformation in the region, which is at the heart of the problem. As Brazilian geographer Hilgard O'Reilly Sternberg has noted, Brazil needs more than a mere redistribution of land or letters of marque for indiscriminate invasion of property. It needs a land reform which will permit the greatest possible number of people to own, manage, and work their piece of ground. But the reform has to do more than assure the farmer clear title to the land. He must have water rights, credit, technical assistance, cooperative organizations, and the possibility of developing rural industries, among other things.[33]

If the Church and its peasant organizations represent one type of change engine, producing motivation, organization, and commitment in Northeast Brazil, another is exemplified by the increasing numbers of small manufacturing enterprises which have sprung up in the region's cities and towns. These include food-processing plants, engineering firms, and factories making sewing machines, electrical appliances, leather goods, and the like. The government has encouraged industrialization of the Northeast through a package of tax and other incentives. In 1958 there were 4,000 manufacturing firms with five or more employees and a total of 200,000 employed in manufacturing. As of 1967, 285 new plants had been constructed with the help of government incentive programs, of which 110 were in production. In addition, 205 old operations had been expanded. This in a region half the size of the United States is perhaps a small achievement, but it is not insignificant.

It seems possible to speculate that development or change in Northeast Brazil will result from two socio-political components which follow the sequence of our engine of change and which have its characteristics. The first, the peasant organizations, was created by radical political forces and the Church and is sustained and protected by the Church. It exists in opposition to the government and in spite of hostile action by the government. The second, the business enterprise, was created by entrepreneurial forces, some of which were relatively radical, and is sustained by governmental elements and special government tax benefits. It is clear that the peasant organizations in Northeast Brazil were formed using the same general sequence of action as in Veraguas. It may not be so clear that business enterprises came into being using a similar sequence. At this point, we can only speculate that the formation of such an enterprise in a region like the Northeast requires a strong injection of agitation, motivation, and organization. In both cases, the resulting engine is of importance principally as a socio-political institution, capable of receiving, using, and directing economic and technical inputs for the purpose of reallocating power, redistributing wealth, and reforming structures.

AN ASSESSMENT OF
VARIOUS ENGINES
OF CHANGE

8

THE MILITARY

The soldier and the priest have played such a powerful and pervasive role in the history of Latin America that it seems appropriate to start our consideration of the engines of change at work in the region with them. On the basis of past performance the military in general can hardly be classed as such an engine, as I define it, but it surely cannot be neglected.

Since the start of the Alliance for Progress in 1961, the military establishments of Latin America have overthrown thirteen governments:

1962	Dominican Republic	1964	Brazil
	Argentina		Bolivia
	Peru	1965	Dominican Republic
1963	Guatemala	1966	Argentina
	Ecuador	1968	Peru
	Dominican Republic		Panama
	Honduras		

Nine of these governments had been led by civilian presidents elected according to constitutional form.[1] Four countries, which include most of the people and land of South America, are now ruled by military regimes that clearly intend to maintain control indefinitely: Argentina, Brazil, Peru, and Paraguay. So is Panama under its constabulary-like Guardia Nacional. The generals who rule Bolivia, Nicaragua, Honduras, and Paraguay mask military control under constitutional forms. In five other countries the military is in a position to take control at any time: Venezuela, Ecuador, Guatemala, El Salvador, and the Dominican Republic. (It is only in the most ruthless of all current Latin dictatorships that the military is not the central source of power: Haiti is a *police* state.) Only four Latin American countries have not had at least one military *golpe de estado* since World War II: Mexico, Chile, Uruguay, and the Somoza family's Nicaragua. Even in Mexico increasing tension between the forces of the status quo and those committed to radical change may result in a move by the military.

Yet the enduring strength and pervasiveness of military institutions in Latin America almost defy useful, accurate analysis. It says much that between 1930 and 1957 some fifty-six military men held presidential office in the twenty republics for as long as a year,[2] and that the political importance of military institutions has been taking on new and changing aspects since then. But both the opponents and proponents of a strong military role in the political development of Latin America bog down in polemical debating points. One side draws sweeping conclusions from the history of Trujillo, Somoza, Batista, Perón, Pérez Jiménez, Rojas Pinilla, etc., etc., and argues that even the least repressive military dictator is inimical to the true interests of the Latin American people. The other side argues that the old brutal *caudillos* have given way to a generation of military men whose control of governments is based on a strong moral and social conscience; they cite Odría, Castello Branco, Costa e Silva, Onganía, and Velasco, and emphasize the corruption or ineptitude of the civilian governments they replaced.

With a careful selection of examples you can show that the armed forces have been implacable obstacles to change or formidable protective adjuncts of the engines of change. In recent years they have used their modern skills to retard the formation of political, social, and economic structures, and they have been agents of modernization, introducing and encouraging technological, administrative, and industrial innovation and efficiency. They have plundered their countries* and enriched them; they have been corrupt and profligate, honest and efficient. When we finally come to understand the role of the military in twentieth-century Latin America our view is likely to be much more subtle and complex than the generalizations we now project from our various North American biases.

Meanwhile both extremes of the argument, and many gradations between, are passionately propounded in Washington— in the Pentagon and the Department of State, before committees of the Senate, all over. The conflict produces one painful ambivalence after another: to recognize or not to recognize each new military government, to grant or withhold military aid, to modernize the Latin American military forces or to penalize them for modernizing, and so on. In the absence of a clear answer to these questions, we go on providing grants, sales, and training for military purposes at a rate close to $100 million a year; United States military advisers and training groups are active throughout the hemisphere. But year by year we seem to be buying less and less influence or good will with our money and arms and training.

The really basic conflict in our thinking I shall discuss later: the conflict between wanting Latin America to become stable and wanting it to change. First, however, we must recognize that the work and purpose of the armed forces—whether army, navy, air force, national guard, or police—are essentially political in the largest and most pervasive sense of the word. The least of their professional functions is the protection of the homeland from foreign enemies. The largest is the suppression of civil disorder, the control of internal subversion, and the maintenance of the threat of force for use in the political gaming process.

The military in Latin America is not a cause of political instability: it is a manifestation and result of it. Political generals

---

* It is estimated that between 1954 and 1959 Latin American military dictators carried out more than a billion dollars. (Source: Edwin Lieuwen, in J. J. Johnson, ed., *The Role of the Military in Underdeveloped Countries*, pp. 159–60.)

are a product of the absence or ineffectualness of civilian institutions and of the inclination of those civilians with power to use the armed forces for their own purposes.

I

Glorification of the soldier lies deep in Latin America's colonial heritage. That heritage fixed the soldier's role as enforcer of the king's rule, controller of unrest among the masses, and first and foremost as the symbol of nationality and sovereignty.[3] This primary role is particularly significant, the search for nationality being as important as it is in Latin America, and it accounts for the unexpectedly high prestige of the military. John J. Johnson of Stanford University concluded after an extensive investigation of public attitudes toward the military in Brazil, for example, that it is widely respected among virtually every social group, including intellectuals.[4] A plebiscite in Latin America would not, it seems, produce many votes for curtailment of the military. Latin American military leaders have thus come to be a privileged and powerful group.

They are regarded and accepted by most of the people as keepers of order, regulators of politicians, and protectors of the state against democratic surprises. They have enjoyed a unique position in the political process, preventing extremist swings and moderating conflicts between otherwise irreconcilable forces. In this they have used more the threat of force than force itself.

Increasingly Latin America's armed forces, now totaling 720,-000 men, are becoming an important ladder of social mobility, a way up for the able sons of the poor and middle classes. The military provides good education and training for its members, much of it paid for by the United States. Some see these factors and the greater national and international awareness they cause as harbingers of that progressive military professionalism known as "Nasserism." Lyle McAlister, for example, predicts that some day the political concern of the military "will no longer be the maintenance of narrow corporate and class privileges but rather a desire to participate in and accelerate change."[5] He argues the necessity of making a sharp distinction between military protection of the status quo against reform, and the protection of the state against Maoist-Castro type insurgencies.

The ability to make such a distinction, like the preoccupation it shows with insurgency, is a product of the 1960's. Most of the old-fashioned military rulers of earlier days had simpler, more old-fashioned motives. Some, like Batista, were outright tools of the oligarchs and defenders of the status quo. Others, like Trujillo and Somoza, ruthlessly displaced the oligarchs and filled their seats with family and friends.[6]

One is tempted to regard such men and their organizations as engines of change, but upon inspection of their work it is clear that they merely substituted one oligarchy for another. The system remained quite intact in their hands.

Other generals, such as Perón in Argentina and Rojas Pinilla in Colombia, came to power as charismatic spokesmen for the poor, promising reform and social justice, only to be corrupted either by themselves or by those around them. Their support among the workers and the poor was and still remains strong and pervasive. Although their achievements are perhaps outweighed by their failures, the dictators of the left have aroused considerable popular enthusiasm. In 1957 Vernon Fluharty wrote that Rojas Pinilla had turned the clock forward on social achievement for the masses of Colombia, and had given them status and a sense of their importance, if only because his government had emphasized their welfare. Fluharty observed that they would never forget that lesson, and that nothing less would be acceptable from other governments to come. As he saw it, military dictatorships have made a necessary and lasting contribution, and nothing will be quite the same after they have come, spoken to and for the masses, and gone their way. Whether they were sincere in their solicitude for the people or merely self-seeking, the masses will never forget they had at last been recognized.[7]

Even after fourteen years in exile, Perón's support in Argentina continues, and while Rojas Pinilla in hindsight does not look quite so good as he did to Fluharty in 1957, there can be no doubt that he is dear to the heart of the poor people of Colombia. That either dictator wrought basic or permanent change seems highly doubtful. Neither the lives, expectations, confidence, or hope of the people were appreciably altered.

Another type of military power is quite different. It can be regarded as revolutionary in the fundamental sense and as a genuine force for change. In this category falls the Patriotic Military Union of young officers who put Betancourt and his Acción Democrática into power in 1945 in Venezuela; the dissident naval and air force officers who returned him to power in 1958, throwing out General Pérez Jiménez; the Mexican armed forces that were an essential element in the Revolution, willingly accepting a subservient role to radical peasant and worker leaders; and the Chilean military that has stood quietly by watching the forces of labor and the political left grow increasingly.[8]

More recently the military rulers of Latin America are gathering around them young, well-educated technocrats. They are asserting their prowess in appearing to bring the fruits of modernization to their people. Without question this generation of military rulers—Onganía in Argentina, Costa e Silva in Brazil, Anastasio Somoza, Jr., in Nicaragua—seems different from the old-timers. They are better educated, more sophisticated, and conscious of the fact that they are in a real sense caretakers, that their days are numbered, that like Scrooge they are making for themselves while in office the chain they must wear afterward. It is too early to judge the extent to which they have been the constructors and drivers of genuine change engines. Certainly Onganía has brought a degree of economic modernization to Argentina, and under Somoza Nicaragua has had perhaps the fastest growth rate in Latin America. Whether their political institutions will match their economic pace and provide the foundation for effective change remains to be seen.

General Juan Velasco Alvarado has announced a program of radical change in Peru. It is too early to know whether he will be able to persist against almost certain opposition from the Peruvian oligarchy. His agrarian reform law surely stands as the most revolutionary in Latin America outside of Cuba.

In line with their new role, military contingents throughout most of Latin America are constructing churches, schools, and houses, conducting literacy and elementary education programs, and effecting reforestation and disease control.[9] Authorized duties of military police units in Guatemala, for example, include giving aid in emergencies to the owners or administrators of farms, plantations, forests, and all types of rural property. They are also supposed to report all activities that are upsetting the peasants or rural populations, and to help in areas where accidents, floods, or anything sinister occurs.

But "civic action" is not always obviously beneficial: it is often a pretext for defending the status quo. Giving aid to landowners inevitably identifies the military police units with those who have traditionally oppressed the peasants. This order has become, in effect, a blank check authorizing the military police to pursue anyone whom the landowner identifies as troublesome. If the culprit is thought guilty, there will be at most a "killed in action" report made to headquarters.

Honduran *campesinos,* for example, are reliably reported to live in constant fear that they will be chastised if not punished by the military authorities in their villages when they return home from *campesino* organization meetings, because the large landholders and the army officers who support them are convinced that all attempts by the peasants to organize are communist-inspired. Efrain Díaz, the democratically elected leader of the noncommunist Honduran Independent Campesino Organization, was shot in the face four times in 1966. Although the assailant was officially "unknown," reliable sources reported that it was an army officer from a nearby military headquarters who had warned Díaz to stop his organizing activities.

Other sorts of "civic action" programs are equally questionable. In southwest Colombia, in the region around Cali, for example, the local civic action battalion built a school. Upon its completion it was evident that no funds were available with which to operate the school, no provision for books, teachers, even students, since parents in the region felt that they were too poor to buy the necessary shoes and clothes with which to send their children to school. The problems inherent in this and other similar "social projects" are beyond the army's competence.

In Peru there have been numerous reports of Civil Guard

personnel abusing and mistreating peasants. In Ecuador a United States university research team reported that two peasant girls were accidentally suffocated on November 8, 1965, while returning to their village after having been forced to work on a civic action building project for Ecuadorean army engineers at Chimborazo. The project was the construction of a battalion headquarters building, and 128 *campesinos*, men, women, and children, were forced to work on it under penalty of "heavy fines." For the trip home they were herded into the rear of an army truck and because of the faulty exhaust system the two young girls perished. The report stated that the only indemnity given to the grief-stricken parents was a barrel of *chicha* (an alcoholic beverage). The local police commissioner ordered an autopsy. Angered when the parents said they had no money to pay for one, he had the craniums of the two corpses sawn in half while the family waited nearby.

There is reason to believe that such callousness on the part of military personnel toward civilians is not confined to Ecuador. Numerous reports show it to be widespread, bearing particularly heavily on the *campesinos*.

Even where "civic action" may be beneficial, it seems unlikely that it can be any real or permanent substitute for more traditional military action. There is good reason to doubt that the truly *macho* (gutsy, masculine) Latin American soldier who has learned to fight with the latest U.S. weapons in U.S. Army and Special Forces training programs will be satisfied with only good works. It is quite probable that he will respond much more enthusiastically to fighting guerrillas and revolutionaries wherever they may be.

General Robert W. Porter, former head of the U.S. Southern Command, has said that Latin America threatens to become another Vietnam unless the U.S. helps the armed forces provide a shield against insurgency while the governments build a stable society.[10] This is the kind of persuasive talk that underlies U.S. military aid to Latin America (grants and sales) of about $98 million a year; the assignment by the Department of Defense of about seven hundred officers and men throughout the hemisphere (not counting the forces in the Panama Canal Zone and at

Guantanamo); and U.S. training of some 3,500 Latin American officers and men annually.[11] There is thus a substantial "shield against insurgency" actually ready, which presumably will seek and expect insurgents against which to exercise itself.

2

But who is an "insurgent"? In Guatemala in recent years the question has presented itself dramatically. Guatemala's population is at least fifty-five per cent Indian. Living in remote and isolated communities in the mountainous interior, the Indian has little or no sense of nationality or community. In his midst here and there in 1965 small guerrilla bands were formed. As with Castro in the Sierra Maestra in 1959, the intention of these bands was to overthrow the regime and to change radically the nature of power allocation in Guatemala. The guerrillas received aid and support from Cuba, and perhaps from Moscow and even Peking. They terrorized the countryside and kidnapped wealthy landowners and industrialists, holding them for fat ransoms. Although it was probably not their intention, they also undoubtedly contributed to the Guatemalan powerholders' acceptance of the results of the 1966 presidential election, in which Julio César Méndez Montenegro, an outspoken reformer, defeated two colonels who had been sponsored by the military. As with Che Guevara in Bolivia, however, the Guatemalan guerrillas have been conspicuously unsuccessful in rallying to their cause any appreciable number of Indians, whose fear, apathy, and isolation are notably impermeable.* The Guatemalan army, itself composed largely of illiterate Indians, was also singularly unsuccessful in rooting out the guerrillas. So an enterprising colonel, Carlos Arana Osorio, in Zacapa Province, east of Guatemala City, struck upon the idea of arming the ladino (mestizo) farmers of that region and forming them into vigilante bands.

* Guatemala did once produce a guerrilla movement that attracted hordes of Indians, captured Guatemala City, and broke up the United Provinces of Central America; but that was in 1838, and their battle cry was "Long live religion and death to the foreigners." Their leader, an illiterate Indian religious fanatic, Rafael Carrera, went on to rule Guatemala until he died in 1865 (Herring, pp. 470–3). By contrast, the principal insurgent today—Sosa—is known as "Chino" ("Chinaman").

Incidentally, the farmers of Zacapa are known traditionally as a relatively bellicose lot prone to feuding and violent displays not unlike the hill people of Kentucky and Arkansas. Under Col. Arana they made rather quick work of the local guerrillas. Having tasted power, the colonel was reluctant to disband his forces. Powerful landowners and pillars of the status quo urged him to continue his "counter-insurgent" activities and lent him substantial assistance to do so, even encouraging him to consider overthrowing the liberal Méndez government.* They felt it would be handy to have such an effective force around in case of trouble.

To the landowners, of course, anyone carrying on activities which threatened them was a "Communist" and an "insurgent." In 1967 two priests came to be threats because of their success in organizing Indian labor groups, cooperatives, and community development efforts. Landowners called in the army; the priests fought back and were subsequently evicted from Guatemala. There is no doubt that the guns of the army, the police, and the vigilantes are used to shoot anyone the landowners feel is a threat. Terrorism has resulted, and since U.S. arms and training have long sustained the Guatemalan military, it perhaps was not surprising that two officers of the U.S. military mission and Ambassador John Gordon Mein were assassinated in Guatemala City in 1968.

Once the army, with the support of conservative oligarchs, was successful in handling the guerrillas and other troublesome elements, they turned their attention to curbing the social and economic reform programs of the Méndez Montenegro government. A wave of kidnappings and assassinations of party officials loyal to the government ensued. The result was that in 1968 the government felt obliged to slow down and in some cases abandon its development programs in order to insure its survival against the combined action of the police and right-wing groups.[12]

It is quite probable that agents of Castro are still at work in Guatemala, but this only complicates the question: what is an insurgent?

---

* In 1966, eleven of Méndez's party leaders in Zacapa were shot by the vigilantes.

The case for the opposition to U.S. military policy in Latin America is put well by Salvador Allende, losing candidate for president of Chile in 1964 and leader of the Socialist-Communist coalition in Chile. Commenting on the pledge at Punta del Este in 1967 on the part of all governments to limit "unnecessary" armaments, he said: "What could necessary armaments be? Only those maintained to suppress the movements of popular protest. In other words, arms for the 'special forces' trained by the Pentagon to suppress the *campesino* peasants who demand better wages and to annihilate the peoples that aspire to win their independence. There will be arms enough for these special forces but none for the armies that fulfill the mission for which they were created since the dawn of history: the defense of national sovereignty. . . ." [13]

Closely related is the question: what is "the government" General Porter speaks of shielding? We know that governments of Latin America are quite different from those of Europe and the United States. Few could be described as democratic. Their reach, identity, and control are extremely limited. They exist invariably as long as they serve the interests of an oligarchy, which, while tolerant, is also powerful and resilient.

As is evident in Veraguas and Northeast Brazil, it is sometimes difficult to perceive any real government at all. Power emanates from whoever may have it or get it: the owner of a sugar mill, a landowner, the bishop, the army. The government is hardly a meaningful entity. It is an established fact that the failure of the United States and the South Vietnamese to control Viet Cong insurgent activities in the countryside was not a military failure so much as it was a governmental one. We constantly fooled ourselves into believing that in rural South Viet Nam there was something resembling government that we could shield. The most secure areas in South Viet Nam have not been so because of government. They have been where large estates had been organized under the firm authority of landlords or where the militant religious sect, Hoa Hao, held sway. In other words, the landlord and the priest are in many rural areas more government than government. [14]

Then, too, there is the problem of the quality and characteristics of that which calls itself government. There was no doubt that Rafael Trujillo governed the Dominican Republic for thirty-one years. Reading the history of his times shows conclusively that the U.S. armed forces, as agents of U.S. policies, had a good deal to do with establishing him in power. Indeed, for many years before Trujillo, the U.S. government, through its military components, particularly the Marines, had been trying to establish an honest, efficient, effective, apolitical national security force in the Dominican Republic. To this end it created, trained, and supplied the Dominican Constabulary, put Trujillo in charge, and then in 1924 withdrew from the island. It seems quite clear that Trujillo was not what we meant to grow in that fertile garden, but within six years he was in full control. Somoza followed a similar way to power in Nicaragua.

General Porter's dictum raises a third question: what is the most effective way to cope with insurgency? There seems little doubt, for example, that Betancourt defeated Castro's attempts at insurgency in Venezuela in the mid-sixties as much by effective organization of the peasants and industrial workers as by the army. As Victor Alba says of the events: "It was political action that isolated the guerrillas and the terrorists, not the army or the police." [15]

3

It is clear that the armed forces of Latin America have some of the characteristics required of an engine of change—authority, ability to communicate, access to power, the ability to protect, and competence. They have the capacity to follow or at least to support and assist the sequence of action necessary for change. In Mexico, Bolivia, and Venezuela they have done so. In more countries, however, they have lacked the will or direction to do so.

The military as such, therefore, cannot be said to be an engine of change.* It has only become so as factions within it ally themselves with, and accept direction from, other power contenders who are themselves change engines. These may be organizations of workers or peasants, political parties, or student groups. It is

---

* The Peruvian military may be the first exception to this rule.

primarily a question of purpose, because the military plainly has power to do what it will. Thus far its initiative has generally been to thwart change, even though occasionally it has accepted leadership in the other direction. Professor Edwin Lieuwen, one of the foremost U.S. authorities on the subject, agrees. In a U.S. Senate report he concluded: "The social effect of the Latin American military's political stance has been to stall or slow down the process of reform. . . . There is not a single military establishment in Latin America today that advocates rapid social reform. The military are not opposed to all social reform, but they insist that it be restricted to a pace which they consider consistent with the preservation of public order." [16]

Considering the future, one must take into account the singular importance of the United States and particularly the U.S. military. For in no sector of Latin American political power does the United States have more direct and effective influence. Latin American and U.S. officers have gone to school together and have shared campsites and hardships. The armies of Latin America depend largely on the United States for training, technology, and equipment. In short, the United States has an unusual ability to influence the design and direction of Latin America's military component. This is not necessarily an attractive capability either for the United States or for Latin America, but it cannot be obscured by pretense. We can avoid exercising our influence or we can continue to employ it. If we do the latter, we must resolve some difficult questions of purpose.

9

THE RADICAL CHURCH

> . . . the judgment of God and the wrath
> of the poor. . . .
>
> > Pope Paul VI,
> > *Populorum Progressio*

The military has had the power to be an engine of change, but has lacked the will and the purpose. The Roman Catholic Church has long had the power and recently has acquired the will and the purpose.

After centuries of support of the status quo, the Church, together with a complex of socio-political forces and organizations centered upon it, is becoming the most formidable engine of change in Latin America. This is not to underestimate the power still held by conservatives within the Church in a number of countries. It is to recognize, however, that at least in Brazil, Chile, Uruguay, Bolivia, and the Dominican Republic, the power of the Church is moving inevitably into the hands of the radicals. Furthermore, it is fair to predict that this progression will follow in Argentina, Peru, Central America, and even in traditionally conservative Colombia.

There are two reasons for this prediction: Older prelates are dying off and are being replaced by young radical priests for whom revolution is a moral necessity; and for the first time in history the Vatican has placed itself squarely in support of those working for radical change in economic, political, and social structures. This move by the Vatican was embodied in the encyclicals of Pope John XXIII and most particularly in *Populorum Progressio (On the Development of Peoples)* of Pope

Paul VI. While there are those who felt that Pope Paul applied the brakes to the Church reform movement in August 1968, when he warned against violence during his visit to Colombia, the Church's commitment to basic change in Latin America seems likely to stick and to grow deeper.*

One Church leader estimates that today Latin American bishops can be divided into three roughly equal groups. The first sees radical structural change as necessary for the achievement of social justice and thus an essential objective of Christianity. The second believes that radical social action is not the Church's business; and the third is indifferent on the issue. It appears certain that the first group will increase and become unquestionably dominant before long.

It is this new Church leadership which has made the related Christian forces the most pervasive force for change in Latin America. These Christian forces are impressive when added up: some 40,000 priests and many more laymen trained in religious service, a substantial number of whom come from Europe, Canada, and the United States; associated but separate and nonconfessional Christian Democratic parties; organizations of Catholic youth and university students; Christian-oriented labor movements; Catholic associations of businessmen; and even Catholic organizations within the military itself. These groups are closely related to, if not part of, international organizations with headquarters in Europe.

In the words of a worried Communist leader of Latin America: "The Church is working persistently to penetrate all the pores of public life. At present there is not a single important sociopolitical sphere without its institutions studying the corresponding problems." [1] In Brazil, Argentina, the Dominican Republic, and many other countries, the radical Church and its allied groups are the most significant forces for change—invariably in opposition to the government in power. That the Church clearly recognizes its role is evident from Pope Paul's *Populorum Progressio* of March 28, 1967, in which he calls for concerted action

---

* It is important to distinguish Vatican resistance to those seeking *doctrinal* change from its position regarding social and political change in Latin America, which has been consistent since *Populorum Progressio* in 1967.

against "glaring inequalities," based on a clear vision of all economic, social, cultural, and spiritual aspects.[2]

Among the conditions which the pope labels as "less human" are "oppressive social structures, whether due to the abuse of ownership or to the abuse of power, to the exploitation of workers or to unjust transactions." He then goes on to consider the matter of private property: "To quote St. Ambrose: 'You are not making a gift of your possessions to the poor person. You are handing over to him what is his. For what has been given in common for the use of all, you have arrogated to yourself. The world is given to all and not only to the rich.' That is, private property does not constitute for anyone an absolute and unconditional right. No one is justified in keeping for his exclusive use what he does not need, when others lack necessities." It is not surprising that a number of power contenders in Latin America regard this statement as not only profoundly political but fundamentally revolutionary, particularly when it was followed and made explicit by the statement: "If certain landed estates impede the general prosperity because they are extensive, unused or poorly used, or because they bring hardships to peoples or are detrimental to the interests of the country, the common good sometimes demands their expropriation."

Pope Paul speaks of the necessity for haste, and adds: "We want to be clearly understood: the present situation must be faced with courage, and the injustices linked with it must be fought against and overcome. Development [which elsewhere he defines as the "new word for peace"] demands bold transformation, innovations that go deep. Urgent reforms should be undertaken without delay."

A few weeks after the encyclical was promulgated, a bishop from rural Colombia, where the hierarchy is not noted for its liberality, was blinking before Bogotá television cameras announcing: "The encyclical *Populorum Progressio* states that 'private property is not an absolute right. Social justice demands that everyone, but especially the Church, use their possessions for the good of all men.'" So saying, the Most Reverend Giulio Franco Arango gave eight hundred acres of his land to the government of Colombia for distribution to the peasants.[3]

A year earlier, Camilo Torres, a young Colombian priest from one of the country's oldest families, was ambushed by government troops and shot down, while fighting with the guerrilla Army of National Liberation (ELN). Between the mildly progressive Bishop Franco Arango and the militantly revolutionary Father Torres there are great differences within the liberal wing of Latin American Catholicism, differences of method, tactics, judgment, and timing. Between these extremes are, for example, the small band of Jesuits organizing peasants in the Dominican Republic; Archbishop Dom Helder Camara in Northeast Brazil; Bishop Marcos McGrath in Veraguas; and Father Blase Bonpane and the Melville brothers, who were expelled from Guatemala for guerrilla activity.

In Brazil Bishop Jorge Marcos de Oliveira of Santo Andre declared that he "would accept a popular armed revolution" and that he thought Pope Paul would also support an armed revolt.[4] In the summer of 1967 the Brazilian government arrested but later released twelve Benedictine priests for allowing the illegal National Students Union to hold a meeting in Vinherdo Convent, São Paulo. In April 1968 a group of priests shielded students from mounted policemen in Rio de Janeiro, asserting that the Brazilian government had failed to bring the changes it had promised.[5] And by far the most radical movement in Brazil at this writing is the Catholic student organization, Acción Popular (AP), whose leaders were imprisoned by the government in the summer of 1968.

In Bolivia, where in 1967 government troops attacked the miners union and closed its headquarters, a group of priests from the mining region, under the leadership of Cardinal José Clemente Maurer, asked for and received the president's attention to the plight of the miners. The priests eventually negotiated a new contract for the workers in Bolivia's nationalized mines.[6]

Early in 1969, thirty priests in the diocese of Rosario, Argentina, one of the most populous in the country, rebelled against their bishop, Guillermo Bolatti, and submitted their resignation en masse. The bishop had attempted to remove some of the priests from their positions in worker districts where they had apparently been a source of agitation and the priests charged him with lacking "social sensitivity."[7]

Priestly rebellion against existing political, social, and economic structure is even affecting traditionally anti-clerical Uruguay, where in April of 1969 ten thousand Christians gathered "to see, to judge and to take action." Previously several priests had resigned under attack for guerrilla activities.[8]

The progressives and the extremists differ more concerning the means and the speed of change than on the objectives of such change. The extremists are advocating the destruction of the entire structure, by bloody revolution if necessary. The progressives, on the other hand, are more confident that adequate and timely change can be induced within the system without violence. The major practical disagreement between the two factions arises from their attitude toward guerrilla militancy, Marxism, and communism. The extremists advocate cooperation with such groups where their ends are the same. The progressives maintain that any kind of collaboration with Communists requires a violation of fundamental Christian doctrine. They argue further that cooperation leads inevitably to Communist control and subsequent defeat of their objectives of change.

Both groups are firmly united in their determination to make the Church a forceful instrument for substantially recasting all the vital systems of Latin American life. Thus, both must be regarded as comprising a fundamentally radical force for change. They understand, furthermore, that their battle is of the greatest importance to world Catholicism and indeed to Christianity. Nowhere has the Church held more power than in Latin America; nowhere is its ability to change itself and the communities it serves, according to its most solemn declarations, undergoing a more critical test. The significance of the Church's struggle in Latin America is doubly plain when one realizes that more than a third of the world's Catholics live in the region.[9] It is estimated that within thirty years one out of every two Catholics will be Latin American. This is a region in which 93 per cent of the population profess Catholicism. A smaller number practice it, of course, but loyalty to the Church is generally held to be of great importance, particularly in rural areas.*

* In a study for the Center for Rural Development in Colombia, John D. Powell found that 62 per cent of the *campesinos* interviewed felt that their most important loyalty was to the Church. Only 13 per cent ranked loyalty

It is no wonder, then, that the Vatican and the European and North American Church regard Latin America with special attention. There are approximately 1,700 Canadian priests in the region, with many thousands more lay Canadians engaged in religious work. From Spain have come more than a thousand priests and some 15,000 others who are engaged in religious activities. There are several hundred Belgian priests, as well as many from West Germany, Ireland, Portugal, and France. In addition, there are probably 10,000 to 15,000 United States clergy, monks, and sisters in the region. In Bolivia, for example, only six of the twenty bishops and 200 of the 800 priests are Bolivians. In Brazil, where 80 million profess Catholicism, 41 per cent of the priests come from abroad.[10] Among the most important in Latin America are 5,000 Jesuit priests and religious, many of whom direct the region's Catholic universities. The intellectual thrust for the radical Jesuits has been coming partly from CIDOC (Center for Intercultural Documentation) in Cuernavaca, Mexico, founded in 1961 by Monsignor Ivan Illich of Fordham University and placed out of bounds for Catholic priests and nuns by the Vatican early in 1969.*

I

The role of the Church in the political life of Latin America was assured by Pope Alexander VI in 1493 when he gave to the king of Spain both temporal and spiritual power over the Church in the New World. The Church became the organizer and justifier of political power, first for the king, then for his colonial lieutenants, and later for those men of wealth and land who succeeded to the royal power. But the Church in Latin America has also always had its rebels, seeking to upset the comfortable relations between the clergy and the oligarchs, to alter the ways

---

to country first; 10 per cent put family first. (John D. Powell, *Organizing Colombian Peasants*, Mimeographed, Center for Rural Development, Cambridge, Mass., Nov. 1968, p. 38.)

* This ban was announced by Franjo Cardinal Seper, who is charged with defending Church doctrine. The reason for his action remains obscure. He wrote that "the center has pernicious effects on clerics because it encourages independent thinking." (The Washington *Post*, June 24, 1969; p. A16.)

of the state, to subvert to a greater or lesser extent the existing political order.

The crucial time of change for the Church started in 1955 with the formation of CELAM (Consejo Episcopal Latinoamericano), the Latin American Bishops' Council. The council set itself the task of designing and implementing the new role of the Church in the region through its various commissions. Within its structures, the radicals have argued against the conservatives. Currently, CELAM is in the hands of strongly progressive bishops, for example: Dom Avelar Brandão Vilela, president; Dom Eugénio de Araujo Salas, director of CELAM's important social action department; and Dom Cándido Padín, head of educational activities. These three men are Brazilians and firmly in the tradition of their more fiery colleague, Helder Camara.[11]

CELAM's thirteen departments, each headed by a bishop, have effected substantial changes in many phases of the social, economic, and, inevitably, the political life of Latin America. Under CELAM's general direction Catholic student and youth groups have been formed throughout Latin America, and activities have been organized among Catholic workers and peasants. Church-sponsored courses have been conducted for businessmen, and cooperative research efforts undertaken with the region's association of sociologists through a Secretariat of Information, Documentation and Technical Studies (SIDEAC).

The council has probably been most effective in initiating change within Latin America's Catholic universities, which are the best of the region's institutions of higher learning. In 1967 it issued a report which indicted the universities in Latin America, and especially the Catholic universities, for not being sufficiently aware of the social changes in the continent. The council declared that the universities should understand that this lack of commitment, this "inertia before the social reality," alienates them from any constructive role in the development of the people of the Latin American continent.

This document became the basis for student rebellions at the two principal Catholic universities in Chile, at Santiago and at Valparaiso, leading to substantial reforms at both. The Chilean cardinal, Raúl Silva Henríquez, in accepting the student's point of view, pointed to the CELAM document as the Church's position on university reform.

2

The Church's single most powerful resource for social and economic change in Latin America generally is DESAL (Centro para el Desarrollo Económico y Social de América Latina), the Center for the Economic and Social Development of Latin America. Founded in Santiago, Chile, in 1960 by its current director, the brilliant and charismatic Belgian sociologist, Father Roger Vekemans, S.J., DESAL has an active presence in almost every Latin American country. Some estimates have placed its total annual expenditures as high as $100 million.

DESAL describes itself as a private autonomous foundation of international scope, whose aim is to help integrate the grassroots sectors into the social and economic development of Latin America.[12] Father Vekemans deplores the marginal existence of more than half of Latin America. The answer to the problem, he says, is "promocion Popular," human development at the local level, through the systematic fostering of organization—trade unions, cooperatives, community groups, peasant associations— with the aim of training of new leaders and offering basic services.

DESAL claims to have established more than a thousand organizational projects throughout Latin America. An outstanding example is DESEC (Centro Desarrollo Social y Económico), the Center for Social and Economic Development, in Bolivia (see pp. 49–50). I met DESEC's founder, Jean de Meure, in La Paz in 1966, three years after the organization was begun, and was impressed by the intensity of his views. He told me that 80 or 90 per cent of the people of Bolivia were almost completely cut off from society, with no possibility of active participation in the decisions of their country. He scoffed at the "democratic" elections held every four years, which he recognized as a mere formality. The real problem was that the people were unorganized; that without pressure groups there could be no real democracy. De Meure said DESEC's program found spiritual inspiration in the social teachings of the Church and its doctrine of the complete development of man.

De Meure and others like him are critical of many activities of United States Catholics in Latin America. They see the Americans helping the poor in a charitable but "atomistic" way, teaching them, feeding them, studying them, but not changing or organizing them. The radical wing of the Latin American Church, influenced as it is substantially by Europeans, on the other hand is concerned primarily with structural changes in the basic systems of the community. It is seeking essential political reformation. This runs deeply counter to the conventional precept of the United States, separating the roles of Church and state, and prohibiting the entrance of religion into political matters. The issue is most clearly drawn in the thought of the French philosopher Jacques Maritain, whose early works in particular have become the intellectual guide of many Latin American Catholic reformers, but who appears to be rejected by many Catholics in the United States. Maritain argues explicitly for the synthesis of Christian values and political practice, for the active introduction of Christian principles into the total life of the community.

Let us look at the DESAL-Maritain doctrine at work in several instances and it will become apparent how alien it is to United States Church practice.

In Veraguas the Church has played a central role in creating the framework of power and understanding by which change can take place and be accepted as legitimate.[13] The peasant in general is deeply ingrained with fear and suspicion of those who seek to introduce. Those who hold power are equally resistant. The Latin American Church today is unique and peculiar in its ability to legitimize change for both of these groups, the rich and the poor, the powerful and the weak.

3

In the Dominican Republic, the role of the Church in supporting and protecting FEDELAC (Federación Dominicana de Ligas Agrarias Cristianas), the Federation of Peasant Leagues, demonstrates its capacity to make change legitimate. FEDELAC was

conceived in 1961 as the rural arm of the newly organized Social
Christian Party.* By the spring of 1967 it was composed of more
than a hundred active leagues and affected the lives of many
thousands of Dominican peasants. It had become a major contender for political power in the country.

To understand the sequence of events and their significance
we must look at the background. During his thirty-one-year rule
of the Dominican Republic, from 1930 until he was shot in
1961, Rafael Trujillo introduced two important changes: First,
he destroyed the traditional oligarchs and concentrated political
power in his own centralized military bureaucracy; and secondly,
he brought about the rapid expansion of the country's economy.
For all his ruthless cruelty, Trujillo possessed considerable political ability and succeeded in building a reasonably efficient and
unusually active governmental administration; but beneath it he
would allow no political organization to occur.

In 1962 and 1963 Juan Bosch ineffectively sought to reorganize the country for change and was replaced by a triumvirate
which lasted until the insurrection of 1965, when United States
armed forces intervened. Since his election as president in 1966,
Joachim Balaguer, with the massive assistance of the United
States government, has sought to extend governmental programs
into every part of the Dominican Republic. As in Veraguas,
however, no matter how massive the injections, money, matter,
and technique are not able to cause change until the structures of
motivation and organization are already in place. And the rootless
character of Trujillo's vast administrative network has become
increasingly obvious in recent years, as the Balaguer govern-

---

* I am indebted to Robert Charles Hart for information on the organization and
activities of FEDELAC. A student of mine in his junior year, Hart spent
the summer before his senior year, under a grant from the Center for Rural
Development, attending a FEDELAC leader-training course and working with
the organization's leadership in several rural areas of the Dominican Republic.
His honors thesis, "Political Participation and Public Administration: The
Overseer Role as a Basis and Function of Peasant Organization," is a valuable
and original examination of the relationship between the Church and peasant
organizations. Recent reports from the Dominican Republic indicate that both
FEDELAC and the radical Church have been curbed as a result of governmental and other pressures.

ment has searched for political organization upon which to build support.

Trujillo, having destroyed all structures but his own, left little behind him but chaos. The Dominican Church, free of any local entanglements, was particularly independent because three quarters of its clergy were foreign born. In 1961, therefore, it was in a good position to move quickly into the political vacuum. One might say that the Church was ready to move with "the winds of change" if it were not more accurate to suggest that it was in large part responsible for the winds themselves.

Within a few weeks of Trujillo's assassination, FEDELAC was formed, with Church assistance, to organize Dominican peasants. Its first objective was to gather peasant votes for the Social Christian candidate for president in the election of 1962. In this effort it failed completely.

A new policy was designed in 1963 by two priests, Father Francisco Guzmán and Father Luis Quín, and fixed leadership training as its first priority. It was decided not to attempt to increase the number of leagues belonging to the federation, but to improve those few which existed. It was also decided to concentrate all efforts in two areas, La Vega and Padre Las Casas. Guzmán supervised the training and recruitment of leaders in La Vega; Quín did the same in Las Casas. In October 1964 FEDELAC's congress brought to Santiago more than three hundred delegates from forty-five well-organized leagues.

Campesino leadership was elected, but Fathers Guzmán and Quín, as well as several priests from Cuba and Canada, were active behind the scenes, particularly in the selection and training of leaders for the local leagues. Father Cipriando Cavero took control and expanded the range of a radio station, Radio Santa Maria, which included in its programing a daily message from FEDELAC. Mobile education programs were also formed by the priests, teaching cooperative and agricultural technique as well as promoting FEDELAC. In 1966, FEDELAC submitted demands to government, calling for laws giving leagues legal recognition, *campesino* representation on the government's agrarian institute, and liberalization of loan terms by the agrarian bank. By the end of the year FEDELAC had more than one hundred active leagues, clustered in groups of five to ten, each cluster having its priest adviser.

The time was ready for a more active effort. On Saturday morning, April 15, 1967, FEDELAC Secretary-General Luis Estrella sent the following telegram to President Balaguer: "The situation between Ortega [a land owner] and his renters in San Francisco de Macoris is worsening. Twenty-four *campesinos* are now in jail for not accepting the conditions of a criminal contract. Other *campesinos* are ready to go to battle Monday, April 17 at 9 in the morning." [14] On Monday 353 *campesinos* were arrested for invading the property of Luis Basilio Ortega, 5,000 *tareas** of extremely fertile land in the village of Indios de Cenovi near San Francisco. The FEDELAC league in Cenovi had been formed and heavily influenced by three of the priests already mentioned. The contract in question, which had been presented in February 1967 by Ortega, stipulated that the *campesinos* were to pay all costs of agricultural production and were to give Ortega 50 per cent of the produce. The FEDELAC members, acting on advice from national headquarters, refused to sign, arguing that the rent demanded was higher than that set forth in Law No. 89 for the Cenovi area. This law, passed by the Balaguer government in 1966, fixed a rent figure for each of the various areas in the country. Until then, however, the law had been generally disregarded by the landowners and was unknown to most *campesinos*.

The day before the telegram Ortega had taken steps to expel Esteban Durán, the twenty-four-year-old leader of the Cenovi league, who had been trained by Father Guzmán. When Durán refused to comply with an eviction notice, the police came to arrest him on Friday, April 14. Eleven members of the Cenovi league blocked the way to Durán's house. All were arrested and put in jail in San Francisco. Immediately, FEDELAC went into action. Radio Santa Maria broadcast that members should prepare for a confrontation on the coming Monday. During the weekend broadcast, calls for unity and solidarity were issued. Thirteen more *campesinos* were arrested for protesting the arrest of Durán

* One *tarea* equals 0.1554 acre.

and the others. These arrests prompted the telegram from Estrella to Balaguer.

Ortega then went to La Vega to see Bishop Juan Flores. He said that Father Cavero was a Communist and was using the radio station to foment a peasant uprising. But the bishop disagreed, so that Sunday, Ortega drove to the capital to consult with the minister of police and the attorney-general. As he returned to San Francisco early Monday morning, Ortega saw several truckloads of *campesinos* which he thought were headed for Cenovi. He drove immediately to the *fortaleza* (jail) and ordered the minister of police to send police and government troops to meet the peasants. By eleven in the morning, 353 peasants had been arrested and taken to the *fortaleza*, among them Luis Estrella and four other high FEDELAC officials.[15]

Bishop Flores drove to San Francisco that afternoon, and in a stirring speech praised the jailed peasants for their fortitude and solidarity. Most of the *campesinos* were released that night, largely because of his efforts. The Church's position was thus made clear to Ortega and to the government.

On Tuesday the Secretary of Agriculture received a telegram from his representative in San Francisco, reporting that the *campesinos* had "invaded the property" of Ortega and were "intent upon disregarding all laws of private property." [16] It so happened that on that same morning Father Francisco Dorta-Duque, a Cuban Jesuit and director of the Office of Planning in the Ministry of Agriculture, had just returned from a visit to India.* The Secretary of Agriculture requested Dorta-Duque to proceed immediately to San Francisco to investigate the situation. Before he left, the president asked him to head a commission to settle the dispute.

On Thursday, April 20, Father Dorta-Duque reported to the president that the eviction had been "quite irregular in that Ortega had neither complied with Law No. 89 nor with Law No. 5933 in drawing up his contract with the peasants." He also

---

* Dorta-Duque, educated in agricultural economics in the United States, has often been referred to as the Roger Vekemans of the Dominican Republic. He has been a major influence in extending the programs of DESAL into the Dominican countryside.

said that there had been no Communist influence in the invasion
or in the preparations leading to it. This was contrary to the
opinion which had formed in the capital that the land invasion
was a Communist-inspired attempt to overthrow the existing
system of private property.[17]

Dorta-Duque's settlement gave the *campesinos* a six-month
period of farming on Ortega's land without paying rent and
stipulated that they would then be moved to new land nearby to
be provided by the government's land-reform institute, Instituto
Agrario Dominicano (IAD). All costs were to be borne by the
government. This in itself was something of a breakthrough,
since the distribution of land by IAD had consistently encountered strong opposition from landowners and military elements.

The impact of the Cenovi incident can perhaps best be measured by the fact that on April 19, four days after the trouble
began, President Balaguer announced the transfer of 40,000
tareas to the IAD, and on April 20 the state reported the purchase of 80,000 *tareas* from Julio Peynado, the largest landowner
in the Dominican Republic, for distribution to *campesinos*. In
other words, laws which had been long on the books were being
enforced as the result of the pressure of FEDELAC and the
force of the Church. Without the Church it is quite clear that
the peasants would have been "fined and forgotten," to use
Hart's phrase.

The incident gave new vitality to FEDELAC. It learned
where to focus its power and how to use it; and realized that
through the intelligent use of direct action and propaganda it
could force the government to enforce the laws over the objection of those who had previously opposed both these laws and
their application. FEDELAC learned, in short, how to put the
government to work for its own interests. In June 1967, for
example, it began a campaign to secure more farm-to-market
roads, making specific requests to government and setting forth
peasant priorities. In July FEDELAC staged another confrontation similar to that at Cenovi, with much the same result, except
this time the leaders were invited to Balaguer's office to settle
the dispute.

In September 1967, the full Dominican Church hierarchy

gave official recognition and approval to FEDELAC and to the members of the clergy who had been assisting it. The Church also pledged to continue to support it in keeping with the papal encyclicals, particularly *Populorum Progressio,* and the conclusions of the Second Vatican Council.

It must be repeated that the formula designed by FEDELAC and its religious supporters may well have been successful in the Dominican Republic because of some very special circumstances: Trujillo's weakening of the oligarchy and strengthening of the institutions of central government; the lack of ties between the Church and those concerned with maintaining the status quo; and probably considerable pressure from the United States over the years not only to enact land reform legislation but to enforce it. Nevertheless, the purpose and actions of the Church in this case cannot be regarded as exceptional in Latin America. It may not always be so successful; it generally does not meet with such a hospitable response from government; and the Church itself is often not so unified. But the fact remains that thousands of priests throughout the region are similarly engaged in battling for change.

4

There is little doubt that today's radical Church was born, nourished, and intellectually formed in Chile.* There have been two branches to the Chilean Christian movement.

The first is the hierarchy itself, best represented by the late Bishop Manuel Larrain, the first president of CELAM.

The second branch is the group of brilliant, militant, and

---

* We should note here, however, that Professor Frederick B. Pike of the University of Pennsylvania, after a year's research in Chile and Peru, reports: "On the whole churchmen are as much in the vanguard of change and modernization in Peru as in Chile. If their pronouncements tend sometimes to be less bold than those of Chilean clergymen, if the vanguard has advanced less far in Peru than in Chile, it is because the de facto backwardness at the present moment—according to Western criteria at least—of the Indians who constitute approximately 40 per cent of Peru's populace, and the glaring lack of technically trained specialists, makes social change more complex and difficult to achieve than in the more racially integrated and better educated republic to the south." [18]

politically capable Jesuits, scholars, social scientists, and organizers who revolve around a remarkable organization called Centro Bellarmino. Created through the merger of Father Vekemans's Center of Research and Social Action (CIAS) and *Mensaje* (*Message*), a magazine founded many years earlier by Father Alberto Hurtado, the Centro has become an intellectual laboratory and training center for church workers as well as for the Christian Democratic political movement. While Eduardo Frei continually and accurately asserts the independence of Christian Democracy from the Church and Centro Bellarmino, reminding his people that the party is "nonconfessional," there can be no doubt about the intimate relationship between the two. Both have come from the same root.

Now the Church and its political allies are engaged in a crucial battle, testing whether Christian Democratic idealism and reform in Chile can stand up against the combined attack of a coalition of far left Socialists and Communists and the oligarchical right. Chile is unique among Latin American nations in the extent of organization and power of its Communists and Socialists. They are allied in a front movement called FRAP (Popular Action Front). It is quite possible that a new but similar popular front, which might include some radical Christian Democrats, will win the 1970 presidential election. The issue already is clear: the speed of change. Since this is the issue also in most of Latin America, the rest of the hemisphere is watching Chile.

5

It is significant that the two Maryknoll priests and a nun who were expelled from Guatemala have put the moral issues of violence and change most dramatically to the American people and government.

On December 21, 1967, Father Thomas R. Melville and his brother, Father Arthur Melville were stripped of their priestly faculties and ordered to leave Guatemala after ten years of work among the poor Indians in the countryside. Sister Marian Peter Bradford, who had been assisting the priests, was also recalled. They were charged with conspiring with Communists and inciting the Indians to revolution against the government of the country. The full facts about the events leading up to Father Melville's suspension as a priest and his eviction from Guatemala remain obscure, but the story seems briefly to be as follows.

Father Melville, his brother, and other priests had been working for some years among the impoverished Indians in the highland area around Quezaltenango, Huehuetenango, and La Libertad, an area in which guerrilla bands, some supported from Havana, had also been operating for several years. The objective of the guerrillas was to overthrow the government of Guatemala and the power structure behind it, much as Castro had done in Cuba. The priests were concerned with organizing the peasants into various forms of cooperative groups, much like CEPAS in Veraguas, so as to improve their life and give them some limited control over their environment.

The guerrillas flourished. The Guatemalan army was unable to control their forays and terrorism. Colonel Arana Osorio in Zacapa Province organized a civilian vigilante battalion. Armed with United States antiguerrilla weapons, and trained according to the proven methods of the Special Forces, the vigilantes were singularly successful. Other army officers followed Colonel Arana's example, recognizing in his exploits a quick route to political power and influence. Conservative oligarchs who had been wary of President Méndez Montenegro's liberal program for change and reform became interested. They lent financial support and assistance to the anti-Communist bands, which had acquired the name Mano Blanca (White Hand). They saw the Mano Blanca not only as a means to destroy the Communists but as a way to curb the social programs of the government and any other movements which offended them. Chaotic civil strife ensued, in which probably one thousand were killed in 1967.[19]

As a result, the peasant organizations which Father Melville and his fellow priests were organizing in the highlands came under attack. The wealthy sugar planters saw these unions as dangerous threats to their well-being and acted to destroy them, calling on the Mano Blanco. Father Melville asserts that organizers were shot, the president of one of the cooperatives killed, and threats made against the lives of the others. He reacted by arming the Indians with what have been called Communist arms.

In a remarkable manifesto Father Thomas Melville offers the basis for his action in these circumstances:

> Having come to the conclusion that the actual state of violence, composed of the malnutrition, ignorance, sickness and hunger of the vast majority of the Guatemalan population, is the direct result of a capitalist system that makes the defenseless Indian compete against the powerful and well-armed landowner, my brother and myself decided not to be silent accomplices of the mass murder that this system generates.
>
> We began teaching the Indians that no one will defend their rights, if they do not defend them themselves. If the government and oligarchy are using arms to maintain them in their position of misery, then they have the obligation to take up arms and defend their God-given right to be men.
>
> We were accused of being Communist along with the people who listened to us, and were asked to leave the country by our religious superiors and the U.S. ambassador. We did so.
>
> But I say here that I am a Communist only if Christ was a communist. I did what I did and will continue to do so because of the teachings of Christ and not because of Marx or Lenin. And I say here too, that we are many more than the hierarchy and the U.S. government think.
>
> When the fight breaks out more in the open, let the world know that we do it not for Russia, not for China, nor for any other country but for Guatemala. Our response to the present situation is not because we have read either Marx or Lenin, but because we have read the New Testament.[20]

In 1968, under continued right-wing pressure, the government was forced to rescind its new tax measures, which were designed to raise an additional $10 million needed to finance the Méndez reform program. The government's defeat was regarded as a major victory for the landowning and business groups. But

Guatemala is not likely to stay quiet. In spite of relatively generous United States aid assistance over the years, 75 per cent of
the population have no access to modern civilization and culture,
80 per cent of the children get virtually no schooling, and the
population is eating one third of what it should. Furthermore,
the gap between rich and poor is increasing every day. These
figures are taken from a report of the Guatemalan Economic
Planning Council.[21]

6

It is important to recognize the peculiarly critical role of the
Church and religion to the process of change and development
in Latin America. We in the United States may have difficulty
understanding this.

It is certainly true that religious systems had an important
effect upon secular developments of the United States and industrial Europe. However, it is perhaps even more true that
these developments—whether they were social or economic or
political—profoundly affected the nature of religion. R. H.
Tawney, for example, has documented the effects of early
capitalism on Christianity.[22] We are quite familiar with the
convenient merging of virtue and profit which Protestantism
came to provide for the great entrepreneurs of America. And
Northrop has described the distinctive shaping of Catholicism in
the United States as a result of the impact upon it of the prevailing Protestantism.[23] Essentially, during the three hundred
years of the industrial development of Europe and North America, religious systems have adjusted to the process of political
and economic change. They have not been primarily responsible
for that change. Indeed, religion has positively shunned such
responsibility in the United States as being beyond its proper
jurisdiction. It can even be said that a principal characteristic
of a developed society is that change has become regular, accepted, institutionalized, and in most ways self-propelled. As
long as change is otherwise comfortably absorbed and assured,
the Church's role tends to be relatively more conservative and
less ideological in a total sense. When, however, change is not
provided for within the system and is forcefully demanded, the

Church may play a more primary and critical ideological, or, in the largest sense, political or purpose-giving role. Thus, priests in the United States today are found burning draft cards and leading Black Power militants. These acts are significant because of their historical rarity in the United States, but they provide a vivid example of what is moving the leaders of the Church in Latin America.

Whereas in the United States only perhaps 20 per cent of the population have been without the capacity to change or influence their environment, in Latin America the proportion is 80 per cent or more. In Latin America, as we have seen, change is by no means regular, accepted, or part of the traditional way of life. Change is, in fact, a monumental negation of that way of life. The present in Latin America is not the point where the past and the future join in any kind of smooth and articulate fashion. Rather, it is a place of torment and agony; the point where, as Dr. Ricardo Arias Calderón has said, the past and the future are most dramatically disjoined.

Under these circumstances change in Latin America, unlike change in the developed countries, requires the construction of a past-to-future joint which does not now exist. Such a joint in turn requires a fundamental conversion which is both personal and social, a reinterpretation of the meaning of life. For not only are the procedures for change in Latin America unsure and weak; even the direction and object of change have yet to be adopted. This is a spiritual or ideological task with, of course, vital political implications. Without an adequate ideology, change lacks consistent purpose. So the role of religion in Latin America becomes transcendent, the political task of the Church being essential and primary rather than a by-product of the process of change.

We have seen that Rostow's stages of economic growth follow his predictive sequence well in the developed world—North America, including Mexico; Europe; the Soviet Union; Japan; Taiwan, and probably China. They do not work so well, however, for Argentina, nor for other countries in Latin America which have for some time shown signs of take-off but which do not quite seem to be able to make it. The stages of growth are

not so automatic or so economically determined as he—or Marx
—implied. The problem is basically ideological. The stages follow one another only to the extent that society has laid out a
determined course for itself, upon which power-holders have
broad agreement. Where there is no course or where the course
is retrogressive, the theory falters.

This indispensable need for ideology or purpose as a prerequisite for change—for movement from past to future—has
been strangely neglected by development planners. It is, however, the mainspring for the new movement of the Latin American Church and its secular branches. It is also the root of serious misunderstanding and even antagonism between that movement and the United States, which has had a long and positive
aversion to making explicit its ideology for itself or for others.
The United States has found it virtually impossible to perceive
the ideological or transcendental needs of Latin America. Jacques
Maritain has told us: "You are advancing in the night bearing
torches toward which mankind would be glad to turn but you
leave them enveloped in the fog of a merely experimental approach and mere practical conceptualization with no universal
idea to communicate. For lack of an adequate ideology your
lights cannot be seen." [24] We find it hard to understand, and
somewhat preposterous, that Latin Americans find us ideologically unsatisfying. We cannot quite accept that we are not
superior in all things. This unfortunate but deeply rooted trait
is the source of increasing tension as Latin America feels the impact of the new Christian movement. For many of its intellectual
and political leaders today truly believe—and perhaps rightly—
that they are the bearers of a new humanity, a new vision, which
surpasses anything which we can offer. These leaders are chilled
and offended that we who are willing to give so much are disposed to receive so little.[25]

The role of religion in Latin America is thus central and
causal to the very existence of change. Latin America is unique
in the extent to which its social order, and thus to a large extent
its political and economic order, is based on the Catholic
Church.[26] Even anticlerical Mexico has been described as being

basically motivated by religiosity.[27] Latin American scholars are repeatedly finding that the depth and force of religion in Latin American history and modern development have been almost uniformly underestimated. In the midst of the extraordinary and baffling chaos, poverty, misery, disillusionment, and hopelessness, Latin America finds in Christianity its only sense of history, consistency of endeavor, and "convincing eschatology." In spite of the sins of the Church itself, which are as flagrant and abominable in Latin America as anywhere, it continues to shine as a thing of singular beauty, striving to form a modern crusade.

Latin America's culture and social order must be linked to the Church as an organization. The reasons for this are important. Only the Church has survived, essentially unchallenged, the four and a half centuries of modern Latin American history. It is, as Ivan Vallier points out, "the only formal organization and value-transmitting agency that supersedes national boundaries." [28] And for this purpose, as we have seen, it is becoming increasingly well organized in CELAM.

The Church is one of the very few organizations which can communicate with the poor and at the same time maintain access to power at the top of the structure. This is of crucial importance in Veraguas, the Dominican Republic, and other places. For this reason it has peculiar powers of initiating and protecting change, of levering reform and lending its assistance and authority to other groups to do so. These powers are, of course, limited by a severe shortage of priests, particularly of native priests.

All this the Church and the Catholic system can do in the community around it. The danger, the challenge, the temptation, are bound to the question: Can the Church continue to maintain its freedom from the particular strategies of political groups with whom its cause may be or may seem to be common? Involved as it unquestionably is in the business of politics, can it maintain a safe distance from the bruising combat of the political power groups themselves? In Chile the Church has come perilously close to overt participation in the fortunes of the Christian Democratic Party. In recent years, it has wisely backed away from this position. Its purposes would not be served if a defeat of Christian Democracy at the polls could be interpreted as an electoral repudiation of itself and Christianity.*

Looking ahead, the issue of political involvement comes perhaps most dramatically with respect to the attitude of Catholic entities and agencies toward Communist or Marxist groups, that is to say, groups who are in some way supported by or loyal to Moscow, Peking, or Havana, and who are ideologically committed to Marxist-Leninist materialism. Merely putting the question is a somewhat shocking sign of the times and an indicator of the speed and distance of recent change. A related issue is the morality of violence; the justification for bloody revolution and the Church's participation in it.

As the Latin American Church moves with increasing militancy to mobilize a collective consciousness of poverty in Latin America, it is not surprising that it finds itself in common cause with those who call themselves Communists. That the final objectives and ultimate values of the Catholic and the Communist may be quite different does not mean that along the way collaboration may not be tempting. The Melvilles in Guatemala and Camilo Torres in Colombia are but two of many examples.

The temptation to collaborate becomes all the stronger to the extent that the United States is, or appears to be, unsympathetic to radical change. It is clear that the radical Church is becoming more and more anti-American, asserting that the United States, its aid programs, its business investments, and its military missions are the most important source of strength for the status quo.

The Communists are understandably gleeful at this turn of events. In an extraordinary article entitled "Catholics and Communists in Latin America," Roque Dalton, a Latin American Communist leader, praises the social action of the Church and what he calls its "flexible pragmatism," and calls for increased "dialogue between Catholics and Marxists to achieve common action." Dalton's prescription for Latin America is interestingly

---

* As this is being written, the progressive leaders of the Peruvian Church are supporting the reform actions of Peru's regime, even though the Church has been generally opposed to military governments in principle.

echoed in Europe, where there is increasing talk of a "Christian-Marxist dialogue."[29]

The Vatican, however, referring to similar notions in Italy, has left no doubt about its position. Speaking through *L'Osservatore Romano* on March 8, 1968, it completely rejected the notion that Catholics could ever directly or indirectly adhere to the doctrine of communism, and added that indeed even the thought on the part of Catholics that they might work with Communists shows how necessary it is to maintain moral and doctrinal vigilance.

To the thoughtful and intelligent Latin American Catholic an alliance with the Communists is plainly folly. In the first place, it would involve flagrant doctrinal disloyalty from which it is doubtful that even the Church could recover. It would also be tactically ill-advised since the Communist movements of Latin America, with the exception of Chile, are singularly decrepit and unsuccessful. None of them has been responsible for anything approaching revolution, and most of them have repeatedly been corrupted by the oligarchs whenever the need arose.

Nevertheless, the fact that Christian-Communist cooperation is being contemplated by both Catholics and Marxists demonstrates the urgency of the situation. The Latin American Church increasingly is sensing its essential role as an initiator and leader of necessary radical change. It is encountering obstacles sustained at least in part by the arms and money of the United States. The United States is seen as the symbol of anticommunism, its actions in Latin America are thus seen largely in this context. Unless we transform our outlook, our policies, and our programs, we shall be tending to force even the Church into the most uneasy and unwholesome alliances.[30]

Pope Paul IV wrote in *Populorum Progressio* that violent revolution only produces new injustices, except when clear-cut and long-standing tyranny seriously threatens the fundamental rights of persons and the common good of the nation.[31] Many Christians, in spite of recent cautionary advice from the Vatican, will describe conditions in many Latin American nations as those fitting the exception. The question then left is: What kind of revolutionary can a Christian be? And where does the answer leave the corporations and the government of the United States?

The local Church's answers are forthright. While preferring the ways of peace, the 1968 Bishops' Conference in Colombia recognized that those who place their hopes in violence often do so with "noble impulses toward justice and solidarity." The harshest words were reserved for those in power who "oppose the profound changes which are needed." "If they hold firmly to their privileges," the bishops warned, "and, above all, if they themselves use violent means to defend them, they become responsible to history for provoking explosive revolutions of desperation." [32]

Brazil's Dom Helder Camara, meeting with Harvard students early in 1969, was asked if violence was not necessary in Latin America to break the hold of the oligarchy. His answer, according to my notes of the meeting, was as follows: "If there were such violence, it would be war and it would be a war of liberation. Such a war, however, would not be consistent with political realism. The United States would not allow it. In any case, those who have nothing to live for have nothing to fight for."

10

GOVERNMENT, POLITICAL PARTIES, AND STUDENT MOVEMENTS

We have seen fairly consistently in this discussion that governments are relatively inefficient engines of change. Now we shall make this conclusion explicit, consider some apparent exceptions, and go on to examine several political movements which have been directed toward radical change, particularly Christian Democracy in Chile and elsewhere.

I

Governments and political systems survive so long as they are sustained by an assembly of leadership and organization which provides for an acceptable balance between power and responsiveness.[1] Acceptability depends upon the values of the citizenry and its will and capacity to exert influence to promote those values. That is, the theocratic state of ancient Egypt or the Stalinist regime of the Soviet Union rested upon a combination of ideological responsiveness and power control. When these were altered the system changed.

In democratic or republican communities where the values, ideology, or needs of the citizenry require its participation in government, the effectiveness of government depends upon citizens having the ability to act and to influence the course of events.

In all societies there are those who govern; a political elite.

In successful political communities, whether authoritarian or elected, citizens for one reason or another are willing to allow these elites to exert power over them. In democratic societies citizens have enough confidence in their capacity to enforce their will on the elite to trust an elite to rule.

In general, then, governments remain useful as long as there is a workable or enforceable balance between governmental power and governmental responsiveness.

In the United States the power base upon which government rests is exceptionally broad. A vast, complex, and continually conflicting set of nongovernmental interest and pressure groups has been organized to insure that the political elite remains responsive. Our political system is, however, being questioned today on at least two counts: a substantial number of poor Americans, many of whom are black, have been unable to join or form an effective interest group, and the system has become so large and cumbersome that increasing numbers of the remaining feel unable or are unwilling to make the effort required to initiate change or to achieve governmental response. The first problem is exemplified on the one hand by the singular inability of government, particularly at the local level, to subvert itself by encouraging—or even allowing—structural change in the black community, and on the other by black-power organizations aimed at doing so. The second problem is seen in the tendency, particularly on the part of the young, toward varieties of anarchism and political disorder. The ability of the system, or more precisely, of the political leadership and the administrative bureaucracy which are supposed to serve it, to respond to these two problems will determine government's future form in the United States.

In Latin America government and politics have a somewhat different nature. The power base upon which the system rests is exceptionally narrow. In general, governments are only democratic in the sense that they tend to reflect the will of the small and limited organized groups which we have called the Tolerant Oligarchy. Otherwise, they tend to be authoritarian, operating under rules which have been sufficiently flexible and artful so as to make the political system remarkably resilient, as well as effective at absorbing demands for and stifling the introduction of change. Like all governments, those of Latin America are unable to initiate change which is unacceptable to the groups and organizations which control effective power. They are, therefore, notably ineffective engines of change. Where radical structural change has taken place, in Mexico, Cuba, and Bolivia, the governments and the political systems upon which they rested were destroyed.

Some exceptions to this rule, suggested earlier, must be noted.

A variety of Latin American political systems have been forced into radical change and have not been destroyed in the process. Venezuela, for example, has undergone structural shifts in land-holding patterns. These, however, depended upon the existence of nongovernmental organizations such as the Venezuelan Campesino Federation (FCV), which had organic ties to the ruling Acción Democrática political party and thus to the government. A somewhat similar enforcement and overseer role was played, as we saw, by the Church in the Dominican Republic. The Peasant Leagues and the radical Christian movement in Northeast Brazil are other examples of nongovernmental groups forcing political change.

Also, in Northeast Brazil there is at work what might be loosely called surreptitious radical change, which is being aided by government. By offering generous tax and other incentives the government has encouraged domestic and foreign business entrepreneurs to enter the region. It is doubtful that government and the powers which control it are fully aware that these entrepreneurial forces will have at least as radical effect upon existing structures in Northeast Brazil as the more inflammatory peasant organizations. Here we see purveyors of radical change, wrapped in a safe economic cover, receiving positive encouragement which might well be denied if their political effects were fully comprehended.

Other sorts of government activity also capable of surreptitious change are the special agencies endowed with exceptional leadership and presidential interest. INCORA, Colombia's Agrarian Reform Institute, is a case in point. Started in 1961, INCORA languished until the inauguration of President Carlos Lleras Restrepo in 1966 and his appointment of Enrique Peñalosa

Camargo as its director. In 1967 it provided supervised credit and technical help to almost 25,000 farmers. Peñalosa expected to have 50,000 farms under his credit program by 1970. The division and redistribution of Colombia's huge land-holdings, however, has gone appreciably slower. This is not the sort of innovation that can be easily sneaked past the watchful eyes of the oligarchy.[2]

Chile's land-reform program also should be mentioned. Here too, however, major advances have been held up both by the recalcitrance of the right and by the opposition of the Communist-Socialist FRAP alliance, which wants no credit for change to go to the Christian Democrats.

But there is no doubt that radical land changes in both Colombia and Chile, as in Venezuela, may well depend upon the mobilization of nongovernmental engines of change. In Colombia, for example, Peñalosa has great hopes for the Atlántico project near Barranquilla, which involves the settling of landless peasants on some 50,000 acres to produce tomatoes. Critical to this venture is the W. R. Grace Company, which will buy the tomatoes and manufacture them into paste and catsup for domestic sales as well as export. In both Colombia and Chile, strong peasant federations will also undoubtedly prove to be essential to real rural change.*

Here are three varieties of change engines with somewhat different objectives but similar effects, having different relations with government. The peasant organizations of Northeast Brazil and the Dominican Republic have gained strength in combat with the established order, but have been allowed by that order to exist. New business enterprises in Northeast Brazil and elsewhere have emerged independent of government but with positive assistance from it. The large, integrated, United States-based food-processing company, which can provide an expanding market as well as credit and technology, also exists independent of government but at its discretion. It is significant that governmental agencies in Latin America, even under capable and forceful leadership, find it difficult to introduce radical transformation

---

* This suggests that in Peru, for example, General Velasco's agrarian reform will fail unless engines of change are created to organize and press it.

without some form of partnership with motive forces such as these.

The Alliance for Progress and the United States government also have had a mild change effect on Latin American governments. Particularly important is the financial assistance which the United States supplies to and through governmental agencies such as INCORA. There is a serious question, however, whether the policy and programs of the United States in Latin America have not been more of a promise of change than its reality. Some Latin Americans who are friendly to the United States have reluctantly concluded that our programs since 1960 have consisted mainly of injecting economic and technical resources into governments and their satellite organizations, and thus into the existing political system, sustaining its capacity to resist modification. They point out that although laws are passed and agencies established to pursue reform, little actually happens; and that many things that pass for change or development are merely inadequate and superficial symbols such as schoolhouses, roads, and housing projects.

Whatever may be the phrases and forms, the promises or intentions, governments in Latin America—or anywhere else—can only initiate and achieve what those who control them will allow. Professions of democracy cannot alter this fact. Again we can see that certain conventional notions about "development" become misleading.

A number of economists, Latin American and North American, have tended to suppose that government expenditures would bring about change. The assumption behind such a belief was that a responsive government would allocate funds to meet the needs of the people as a whole. The question unasked and unanswered by these developers was, of course: To whom was the government responsive? The Somozas of Nicaragua, the landowners of Guatemala, the sugar planters of Northeast Brazil, the ranchers of Argentina, the armies of Panama and Peru, or the peasants and slum dwellers?

The answer to this question should not be the subject of praise or blame. It lies in the nature of things that political systems move according to the allocation, direction, and force of power. It is not surprising that those who have power do not easily or freely give it up; it must be bargained from them. The importance of this is not that power is either good or bad, but rather that it is part of the way things are; and if change is an objective, under these circumstances government can rarely be relied upon to initiate or execute it.

Secondly, much that has been written about development implies that one can measure stable and successful political and governmental organization by social and economic indicators.[3] During the last ten years Panama has had one of the fastest moving GNP's in Latin America, rising at an annual per-capita rate of 4.5 per cent, with other indicators keeping pace. The military overthrow of President Arnulfo Arias in the fall of 1968 served to remind us, however, that Panama has neither political stability nor democracy. Furthermore, if stability means concentration of power in the sure hands of a few, as is particularly the case in rural Latin America, then it is an actual cause of national impoverishment. In several countries municipalities are expected to use their own tax revenue to build and maintain roads, schools, hospitals, public utilities, and market facilities. But these communities have very limited power to assess and collect taxes and to select their own local officials. As a result, a limbo exists in which no unit acts to obtain the social overhead capital needed and those who own most of the resources contribute little tax revenue. In this case political stability solidifies poverty.[4]

2

In general, the political parties of Latin America have been fragile and ineffective, reflecting the unorganized condition of the people as a whole. Rarely are they conscious of any particular constituency or directed at mobilizing support for policies and programs. They are, rather, superimposed as the personal political vehicle for one or another charismatic leader. A good example is the career of José Maria Velasco Ibarra, who was re-elected president of Ecuador in 1968 after a stormy career during which he was in and out of exile quite regularly. Ibarra's basic support comes from the traditional poor, and particularly from the parish priests. "The little people light candles to him,"

an Ecuadorian friend told me. "He has captured their imagina-
tions." He buys nothing but radio time and reaches the people
through their transistors. An Ecuadorian opponent of his once
lamented: "I was violently opposed to his policies and uniformly
voted against them. One day, however, President Velasco Ibarra
came to Congress to deliver personally a message urging passage
of one of his projects. . . . Never before had I heard such a
speech! When it was finished, the president and Congress were
unashamedly in tears, and we stood up and voted unanimously
for his bill. . . . On my way home, I scolded myself many
times, for I had been a fool, such a fool, to vote for his insane
measure!" [5]

In some Latin American countries political parties have played
a much more substantial institutional and less personal role.
Mexico's Party of Institutionalized Revolution (Partido Revolucionario Institucional or PRI), as its name implies, did indeed
organize the results of the Mexican Revolution, and it has served
for some thirty years as the political base upon which the Mexican
government rests and through which it executes its will. As
change becomes increasingly necessary, however, particularly in
rural Mexico, the PRI is showing signs of strain. Competition is
emerging; nongovernmental forces are mobilizing.

The National Revolutionary Movement (Movimiento Nacional Revolucionario, or MNR) of Bolivia has also sought to
organize the deep structural changes of revolution. Splintered
and in the political opposition, it seems hardly equipped today,
however, to continue ordering the change process or to give
adequate access to power to many of the groups which are
demanding it.

In other countries, where violent revolution has not destroyed
the old order, political parties have had an important effect in
modifying structures, defining leadership, and setting some new
directions.

The Aprista movement of Víctor Raúl Haya de la Torre
in Peru has had a profound and continuing influence upon the
political leadership of that country. In particular, it has prompted
greater recognition of Peru's large Indian population, giving to
the Indians a greater sense of participation in the nation as a

whole. It has failed, however, to change the basic political, economic, and social structures of Peru. For more than thirty years Peru's army has stood between Haya and national power. The nearest he came to such power was in coalition with the followers of President Fernando Belaúnde Terry, whose overthrow by the military in October 1968 seems to have been due to the strong Aprista showing in the municipal elections of 1967 and the likely candidacy of Haya de la Torre for president in 1969.

The Acción Democrática Party, founded by Rómulo Betancourt in Venezuela, has had a more profoundly revolutionary effect. Indeed, it may well have started that country on a unique transition toward peaceful radical change. But with its defeat by the Christian Democrats in 1969 the party itself seems to be faltering, lacking the ideological force which is so essential to the change process in Latin America. Its vision of the new community it seeks may well be insufficient to hold together the conflicting elements within it. AD's most lasting contribution to the revolutionary development of Venezuela may in fact be the nongovernmental organizations, the Campesino Federation and trade unions which have grown with it and will live after it.

The National Liberation Movement (Partido de Liberación Nacional) of José Figueres in Costa Rica gave that republic a secure base from which real and far-reaching political democracy can come. It is hardly, however, an engine of change in Costa Rican life today.[6]

These parties and others like them all started with substantial revolutionary zeal. Many of their leaders were Marxists in their youth. Much of their intellectual energy was spent in discovering that Marxism did not apply to the Latin American scene. Later, they tended reluctantly to turn to the United States where, by and large, they were received hospitably with offers of much needed assistance. Over the years it has become apparent that while the United States could and did give them money and technical assistance, it was really no better than the Marxists at giving them a useful ideology for the transformation of their countries. And so the revolutionaries of the last two decades resigned themselves to making do as best they could, pragmatically altering things where the opportunity occurred, taking advantage of the Alliance for Progress and United States help to do so, but basically altering very little.

Then in the early 1960's a new political movement emerged, Christian Democracy. It was unique in one important respect. It looked for its political vision within Latin America rather than in Moscow, Peking, New York, or Washington. It sought in Latin America's own history the traditions and the forms upon which to build a political system. It has evoked the Christian tradition of Latin America and infused it with the militancy of the papal encyclicals and the writings of philosophers like Maritain. It has thus begun the formation of a revolutionary ideology, rooted in Latin America and drawn from Christian principles of social justice and individual dignity. Although Christian Democracy was victorious in Venezuela in 1968 with the election of Caldera, it is sorely challenged in Chile, where it began, by a formidable coalition of Marxists and oligarchs. This, incidentally, is not an unusual combination in Latin America. It demonstrates the tolerance of the oligarchy, and, in Chile, their confident expectation that once the Christian Democrats have been defeated, the leftist front can be diverted and distorted into playing by the rules of the old game.

Christian Democracy offers the best opportunity for a philosophical regeneration in Latin America. Together with the radical Church, with which it is closely allied, it presents answers to the questions of purpose which have plagued Latin Americans.

In the words of its principal founder, Eduardo Frei Montalva, President of Chile: "The central tenet of Christian Democracy is the belief that we are witnesses to the crisis of a world exhausted, to the death of paternalism, and to the birth of a civilization of work and solidarity with man as its center, rather than the pursuit of monetary gain that had pervaded the bourgeois society. And its inspiration is that this new era in history and the new social condition will be based on Christian values and concepts of Christianity." [7]

It implies a breaking with the established order, with prevailing structures. "The achievement of power no longer means for us," says Frei, "as it does for the people of the United States, simply slight variations in political structures, but rather a change in the entire social structure, requiring new orientations for family, education, state, and man." [8] He emphasizes that though Christian in philosophy, the movement is not devised by Catholics for Catholics.[9]

The Christian Democrat rarely speaks against communism, and occasionally criticizes the United States for seemingly supporting the status quo with what appears to him to be a policy which is both pragmatic and materialistic. For this reason he is frequently branded as "anti-American."

It is important, therefore, to understand President Frei on this matter, recognizing that he is surely no Communist, that indeed his most vituperative political foes in Chile are Communists, and that on many occasions he has shown profound regard for the United States. Frei thinks that many people feel the Communist system clarifies their roles as workers and their place in the class structure. He goes on to say that those who answer the Communist challenge by peaceful attempts to maintain "order" or by force manifested in military coups are doomed. The masses, and especially youth, find these reactions completely unsympathetic. He believes it is equally fruitless to ground all policy on the concept of free enterprise, which "does not satisfy anyone's soul or intelligence." And finally, glowing words about freedom and democracy are meaningless to people who have no land, housing, schools, or opportunities.[10]

Although they attack the United States and what they interpret as capitalism, Christian Democrats have always been more militant in their denunciation of communism for its antireligious and antidemocratic practices, as well as for its subservience to the Soviet Union. The Christian Democrats in Chile ran Frei as their first candidate for president in 1958. His opponents were Jorge Alessandri, supported by the liberals and conservatives, and Salvador Allende, who represented the Socialist-Communist FRAP alliance. Frei received only 20 per cent of the vote, but the party was launched, and at the 1964 election, in which Frei's only opponent was Allende, the Christian Democrats won 56 per cent of the vote, gaining strong support from all groups in the country.

Frei sent a collection of radical programs to Congress, including a call for "Chileanization" of the United States-owned copper mines. He proposed that the Chilean government buy a part interest in the mines, which was to vary from 51 per cent of Kennecott's Braden Copper Company to 25 per cent of Anaconda's new Exotica mines. The companies were to agree to use the Chilean government's money to build new facilities in order to expand production by one million tons by 1970, and they were also given certain tax and import concessions. Frei also proposed an extensive agrarian reform bill, expansion of education, the nationalization of the electricity and telephone companies, the establishment of a state bank, and later, legislation designed to promote the organization of labor.[11]

Congress failed to act on these proposals, and Frei appealed to the country, winning a dramatic victory in the congressional elections of 1965. In the 147-member Chamber of Deputies, Christian Democratic seats increased from 23 to 82. In the Senate, party representation rose from 4 to 13 seats out of a total of 45.

Despite these victories, however, Frei has had continual difficulty getting his program adopted. The most intense opposition came on his copper proposals. FRAP (Frente de Acción Popular, or Popular Action front), which is composed of old-line, Moscow-oriented Communists and the far more radical Havana-tending Socialists,[12] argued for outright nationalization. The conservatives joined FRAP for political reasons, hoping to obtain FRAP support in their battles against Christian-Democratic reform.

Antagonism on this issue became particularly heated in late 1965 and early 1966 when FRAP-dominated copper unions staged a series of illegal strikes in protest against the legislation. The government sent troops to maintain order, and the Ministry of Labor discharged a number of the leaders responsible for the strikes. The government was incensed when one of the companies involved reportedly hired FRAP leaders back after the soldiers had gone. The copper bill was finally passed in March

1966, but the problem of the unions and FRAP control remained as perhaps the government's major difficulty with the companies. In 1966 the National Board of the Confederation of Copper Workers was composed of ten Socialists, two Communists, and one Christian Democrat. This has enormous political significance. A job in the mines is highly prized, since wages there are the highest in the country, and over the years the companies have adopted the practice of hiring at least partly through the unions. The result is that it is often difficult for a Christian Democrat to obtain mine work. Those who do are subject to threats and intimidation, and sometimes are even physically harmed.[13]

The problem between United States copper companies and the Chilean government has not been so much on the issue of Chileanization, in which the companies have cooperated, as on the question of jobs in the mines.* FRAP derives great political strength from the Mineworkers Union and intends to keep control of it; the Christian Democrats continue to covet that control.

Since 1966 President Frei has had continuing difficulties getting his programs through the combined opposition of the conservatives and the leftists. In January 1967 he was embarrassed by his opponents successfully voting to prevent him from making a planned visit to the United States. He has also lost ground in congressional and municipal elections, and his own party is deeply divided. In spite of unquestionable accomplishments in many areas, his program has been slow to take shape, and the country is suffering from soaring inflation. Efforts to control inflation are never popular or easy, and Frei's vacillation on austerity caused Chile's most respected statesman, Raúl Saez, to resign in 1968 as Minister of Finance and Economics. This was a serious blow to the already shaken Christian Democrat government, and means that a FRAP victory in the presi-

* The Anaconda Copper Company agreed in June 1969 to sell 51 per cent of its holdings to the Chilean government and to make other concessions toward a "negotiated and progressive" nationalization of the company's huge interests in Chile. (Benjamin Welles, *The New York Times*, June 29, 1969; p. 1)

dential elections of 1970 has become a real possibility. If this happens, it will be the first Communist take-over through a free and democratic national election. Christian Democracy, therefore, faces an obviously critical test, the outcome of which will be of immense significance to Latin America and the United States.

There can be no doubt that the Christian Democratic Party has contributed a substantial and badly needed moral vision to Chileans and indeed to other Latin Americans. In this it is being assiduously assisted by the radical Church. In Chile, however, it has yet to translate this vision into sure administrative practice. It has tried to bolt tradition before the organization necessary to do so was firmly in place. This is especially obvious in the attempts of the Frei government to introduce the principles of "communitarianism," designed to give to the peasants and urban workers control of their own communities and factories. In the words of Eduardo Frei, communitarianism "is a social structure in which the community formed by those who work in the same industrial or agrarian enterprise is of basic importance. This implies the ending of the profound class conflict inherent in our present social organization, in which a fairly small group possesses the power, the resources, and the authority that go with control over property, whereas the vast majority are wage earners. The communitarian ideal thus demands an order of things in which capital and labor are no longer divorced and therefore do not come into conflict, no longer belong to different groups but are united in the same hands." [14]

The Christian Democrat sees communitarianism as being in opposition to the traditional conceptions of liberalism, capitalism, and individualism. It seeks to identify and maintain its roots in Latin America's own past, thereby constructing a spiritual or philosophical basis for modernization. Historically, in Latin America the municipality, the Church, and communal lands were of great importance. The Christian Democrat wants to draw on this importance and awaken community structures, avoiding what it sees as Anglo-Saxon individualism. This requires close collaboration between the Church and political institutions to design and promulgate communitary values and implies greater emphasis on levels of values than on levels of technology.

Conscious of the frailty of these notions, the Christian Democrat is anxious about receiving help from the United States. He knows the need of his country for our material and technical assistance, but he fears that in accepting it he will somehow be corrupted and tempted to abandon his own search for valid, historically based purposes and methods. It is not that we North Americans are thought of as malevolent, but rather that we are so massive that we are apt to crush inadvertently the delicate flowers beginning to bloom from local roots.

But the Christian Democrat does not envisage the "communitarian way" being imposed from above as a "hard and rigid mechanism." The idea of a communitarian society is appealing and has been philosophically useful for the Christian Democrats in designing their program. It may even have clear parallels in the development of both United States and European societies. The modern American corporation, for example, can be said to be moving toward a more communitary form, "an order of things in which capital and labor . . . no longer belong to different groups but are united in the same hands," ownership becoming widespread and anonymous, workers increasing their voice in decisions that once were exclusively management's.[15]

In developed countries, however, "communitary" forms have emerged from the complex of nongovernmental organizations and interest groups upon which society rests. It was not imposed from on high. Frei wants this to happen in Chile. The difficulty is that his country lacks the essential institutions from which it can be expected to grow. And appealing as the principle is theoretically, communitarianism runs directly counter to deeply set Chilean traditions of paternalism and centralized governmental authority. To expect that a fragile governmental bureaucracy can somehow infiltrate communitarianism into an alien society without militant and strenuous support from nongovernmental organizations committed to Christian Democracy is unrealistic. And the plain fact is that such organizations do not exist.

In the Chilean Trade Union Confederation (CUTCH), for example, as of 1967, nine members of the twelve-man executive board were Socialists (more extreme in Chile than Communists). Among the locals in which Christian Democrats have strength, it is unlikely that its leaders put communitarianism as high on their list of priorities as wage increases. Perhaps the strongest Christian Democratic rural labor group is the CNC, the National Campesino Confederation, which is headed by a remarkably effective organizer, Hector Alarcón. While Alarcón undoubtedly believes in communitarianism, he is beset by numerous day-to-day difficulties, including the militant opposing efforts of FRAP to organize peasants, and bureaucratic problems with the government itself, particularly CORA, the Agrarian Reform Corporation.

An American ambassador to Chile, who was a staunch friend of Frei and his government, put the problem succinctly when he said: "The trouble with the Christian Democrats is that they spend so much time on first principles that they have no time left for second and third principles."

The ironies of Chile are many; its dilemmas demonstrate the structural characteristics of Latin American politics already discussed and offer a particular challenge to United States policies. Our country, particularly the Kennedy Administration, has been warm and generous in its support of Eduardo Frei and all he sought to achieve. Our AID program in Chile has been regularly among the largest per capita in the world, and is much the largest in Latin America. Between 1961 and 1966 Chile received $696,300,000 in United States economic assistance, $79 per capita. This compares with an overall Latin American average during the same period of $20 per capita. The bulk of this was grants and loans made by AID to the Chilean government for such purposes as transport, schools, agricultural and industrial development, health facilities, airport construction, and housing. The assumption was that these injections of money and technology would somehow promote the change which the Christian

Democrats had promised and which we believed to be salutary and in keeping with the principles of the Alliance for Progress.

By anybody's yardstick the change has not been what we expected. The government of Frei was seen as having the magical ability to promote revolution and keep the country safe from communism. It is perhaps too early to speak of failure, but there seems cause to wonder whether our policies and programs were right. Although our embrace has not yet been fatal, there has been something about it of the kiss of death.

Oversimplifying, we could sketch the sequence like this: the embassy is warm and cordial to Frei, furnishing large amounts of money to the Chilean government bureaucracy. The assumptions are: that Frei controls the bureaucracy; that the bureaucracy has the will and capacity to introduce expected change; and that money and technology are the essential ingredients to make it happen. Frei starts out with a set of bold proposals, backed by the United States. The conservative right and the radical left—for quite different reasons—unite in their anger, alienation, and resentment toward both the proposals and United States backing. Congress slowly adopts the proposals in watered-down form. Then, however, the three critical assumptions come into question. The landowners scurry to make their land more productive to escape expropriation. That reform which does take place thus tends to be either on relatively poor private land or on government property. The oligarchs organize themselves in opposition. FRAP steps up its activities in the countryside, cities, and mines. The Christian Democratic nongovernmental groups—trade unions, peasant federations, and the like—seek to increase their strength, but frequently run afoul of Christian Democratic governmental machinery as they do so. The end result is that our political friends are weakened and embarrassed and our own interests seem to have suffered. So we have one more example of the impracticality of expecting radical change from government before substantial and appropriate nongovernmental engines of change are in place. Even though the Christian Democratic Party may be such an instrument, once it also becomes "the government" its capacity to change society becomes seriously restricted.

This example is particularly poignant because of the excellence of Chilean political leadership and the admirable quality of its moral vision. We have implied that the Chilean governmental bureaucracy was at least among the villains in this drama. In reality, it is not villainous or even malicious, but merely a part of the unintegrated and politically baseless political system which pervades Latin America, even a country so advanced as Chile.

Robert E. Scott, professor of political science at the University of Illinois, has put the case well.[16] The first consideration is that while throughout Latin America there are able and energetic young men like Enrique Peñalosa of Colombia's INCORA serving government and eager for change, the bulk of the administrative class perceives the preservation of law and order as the central task of government.[17] Even though a great many young men such as Peñalosa enter the bureaucracy, the dominance of the status quo effectively hampers them.

In a sense, the difficulty goes back to the problem of values and purpose. Those which are strongest continue to emanate from the Tolerant Oligarchy. The lack of an integrated national motivation, to the contrary, makes it hard for the bureaucrat to stand the heat of change.

The bureaucrat in a regime like Chile's is being asked to do what for him is an impossible task: to reconcile the conflicting demands of transition. In Chile he is, of course, assisted and guided by the Christian Democratic Party, but this party still has limited reach within the controlling sectors of society, particularly among the landowners and the mines. There is insufficient organization in the country to force and focus demand, aggregate incompatible groups, and support movements for change. The frail administration of government is therefore left to do battle virtually alone. As Scott says: ". . . the units which might act as buffers between the masses and the public servants simply do not perform this function."

Another problem is that the political elite may support new and modern administrative forms for the sole purpose of controlling rather than promoting change. That is, a land-reform law is often easily endorsed and an agency to administer it set up. But when the agency confronts the unorganized countryside, its capacity to change existing patterns is severely limited.

Again we come back to the central and primary institutions, the "integrative mechanisms" which are the prerequisites to the construction of a nation. Until these institutions and pressure groups exist, the administrators of government are bound to abort the plans of those who theoretically lead them. Perón filled the ranks of the Argentine government with *peronista* bureaucrats, but when his programs began to run counter to the values of the traditional administrative class the bureaucrats "first sabotaged their implementation and later cooperated with other conservative interests to cause his downfall." [18]

That the Christian Democrats in Chile have neglected or failed to give sufficient emphasis to this primary organizational task may be in part due to the impatience, enthusiasm, and influence of the United States. We tend to seek quick solutions and to underestimate the difficulties involved in—or indeed ignore the necessity of—building structures of motivation and organization. We cannot help assuming that they are present, since we have always had them in our country to a remarkable degree, as have our European peers to varying degrees. Offering governments large sums of money to leap immediately into action cannot help but distract and dissuade them from insuring that the preliminary receptacles are in place before dispersing that money. This leaves us with the obvious question: If these non-governmental structures or engines are so important, is there not a way in which the United States can speed their mobilization?

3

One of the unique characteristics of Christian Democracy among Latin American political movements is its regionality. There is a Christian Democratic Party, or something closely resembling it, in all but three countries of Latin America—Honduras, and of course Haiti and Cuba. For more than a decade the Christian Democrats have been firmly committed to the integration of Latin America, economically, culturally, and eventually polit-ically. Although the overall Latin American organization ODCA (Organización Democrática Cristiana de América) is small and for the time being inconsequential, the fact that it exists at all is worth noting. The Christian Democratic youth organization, JUDCA (Union Internacional de Juvientad Democratas Cristianos de America), on the other hand, appears to be having a substantial impact in a number of Latin American universities.

Second only to Chile's in importance is the Christian Democratic movement of Venezuela. There the party is called Social Christian and has the initials COPEI. Its founder and leader, Dr. Rafael Caldera, was elected president in December 1968 by a slim margin over the Democratic Action candidate, Dr. Gonzalo Barrios. Caldera was credited with an unusually good campaign organization that was relatively well financed by funds from Christian Democratic parties in Chile, West Germany, and Italy. Caldera is a fifty-two-year-old lawyer, university professor, and sociologist whose philosophy is similar to that of Frei. "The imminence of a revolution is palpable," he wrote. "Either we carry out a peaceful, constructive and Christian revolution, or our people will be dragged to their own misfortune into a violent, materialistic and destructive one. This is true of all the different countries [in Latin America], for despite their adversity, there exists a fundamental unity." [19]

Although small in terms of number of votes polled, the Christian Democratic movement of Peru played a decisive role in the election of Belaúnde as president in 1963. Its membership includes some of the most talented leaders in the country, three of whom served in Belaúnde's cabinet. The mayor of Lima, Luis Bedoya Reyes, is also a Christian Democrat and before the military seizure was considered a leading contender for the presidency in 1969.

In Bolivia, where the military regime of General Barrientos sees itself as the architect of revolutionary reconstruction, his party is called the Popular Christian Movement (MCP). It has replaced the old MNR as the dominant political formation and is closely allied with, if not indistinguishable from, the official Christian Democratic Party (PDC).

In recent years the party's strength in the Dominican Republic has increased substantially. In the 1968 municipal election it polled 12 per cent of the vote generally and 21 per cent in Santo Domingo. There are also Christian Democratic parties in each of the Central American countries, combined loosely into UDCCA (Unión Democrática Cristiana de Centroamérica).

In Panama its percentage of the vote in the 1968 elections was only 3 per cent in the official tally, but the party has exceptionally able leadership and played a significant role in the various bizarre confrontations between President Arnulfo Arias, his predecessor, Marco Robles, and his opponent, David Samudio. Its candidate for president was the much-respected surgeon, Dr. Antonio González Revilla, and its vice-presidential candidate was Dr. Ricardo Arias Colderón, one of the leading Christian Democratic thinkers in the hemisphere. More will undoubtedly be heard from the Christian Democrats in Panama.

It will be particularly interesting to watch the fortunes of Christian Democracy in El Salvador, where it is perhaps the only engine of change in a relatively unchanging country. The party was founded in 1958 when a small group of prominent lawyers and doctors met regularly with some young priests to study the papal encyclicals. Among them was Dr. Abrahán Rodríguez, who at the age of thirty-eight ran for president in 1967 and received 22 per cent of the vote. Another was José Napoleón Duarte, a young graduate of Notre Dame University, who in 1964 was elected mayor of San Salvador. He became recognized as one of the best municipal administrators in Latin America and was overwhelmingly re-elected in 1966.[20]

Formed as a party in 1960, Christian Democracy in El Salvador had a most remarkable experience in 1961 when two army officers, Colonel Aníbal Portillo and Lieutenant Colonel Julio Rivera, who had just led the overthrow of a leftist junta, offered the Christian Democrats the opportunity to become the new "official" party, promising to hold elections and endorse the Christian Democrats as the group most qualified to form a civilian government. They attached one qualification, however: that the selection of the presidential candidate would be left to Portillo and Rivera.[21] The party rejected the offer for three reasons: To come to power so quickly in this manner would smother the idealism of many party members and would impair the ability of the party to advocate social reform; the terms of the offer were vague and implausible in the context of the times; the party would become little more than an appendage to an essentially military regime.[22]

Colonel Rivera thereupon decided to take over the government himself, and the Christian Democrats on their own, voicing continual protest against the military regime, were able not only to elect Napoleón Duarte mayor but poll 32 per cent of the vote in the elections for the legislative assembly in 1966. In 1968 the party polled 42 per cent of the vote in these elections.

There are several interesting sidelights on this situation. In spite of the fact that Napoleón Duarte was recognized by all as an exceptionally competent city administrator, the United States ambassador, at least for a time, carefully avoided assisting him in any way lest it interfere with his own good relations with Colonel Rivera. In 1966, therefore, there was no AID assistance to the municipality of San Salvador. It is not surprising that Salvadoran Christian Democrats have little confidence in the United States.

The future of Christian Democracy in Latin America is in doubt as this is being written. The outcome of the 1970 presidential elections in Chile will plainly be of great importance. As we have said, the movement's unique significance is the strength of its ideology, the morality of its purpose and conduct, and the grandeur of its vision. Whether the party continues to develop successfully depends on how effectively it can organize the underpinnings upon which its vision must rest. There are three important groups to whom the Christian Democrats can look for assistance: the radical Church and the organizations associated with it; organizations of university students; and new forms of labor organizations, particularly peasant unions such as FEDELAC in the Dominican Republic and the CEPAS organizations in Panama. The vitality of Christian Democracy may well depend upon the extent to which these three types of movements extend their organization and influence.

4

Consideration of student movements and organizations appropriately follows that of Christian Democracy, because no political party in recent years has more appealed to the imagination of Latin American youth. Latin American university students, like our own of late, must be counted as among the region's engines of change. Many of the great political leaders of Latin America began as student leaders, Haya de la Torre, Eduardo Frei, Rómulo Betancourt, among others.

In nearly every Latin American country the political parties have their extensions in the university. In many instances these are organizationally their most important part. When the Christian Democrats defeated the FRAP in the Chilean election of 1964, university students were important elements of both parties. Students have played a leading role in the various revolutionary movements in Guatemala in 1944, 1954, and more recently. In that country, as in many others, students in the 1940's and 1950's sought to pursue change through democratic institutions, rallying to the post-World War II idealism of the Atlantic Charter and similar pronouncements. More recently, however, they realized the weakness and incapacity of democratic forms and saw no alternative to the Communist Party as a means to radical change in the status quo. With few exceptions the leadership of the Guatemalan Communist Party has come from young middle-class intellectuals in or just graduated from the university. That these Guatemalans became Communists is significant because for them there was little choice. It can hardly be regarded as a reflection of loyalty to Moscow or Peking, or even to Havana, for that matter. The label "Communist," connoting as it does the conservative ways of the Moscow traditionalists as well as foreign domination is less and less satisfactory for those students in Guatemala and elsewhere who demand quick change now. In Brazil, as we have noted, the radical student organization, AP, is quite independent of communism.

Examples of student activity throughout Latin America are plentiful and need only be listed here. In Argentina, students and professors alike have been continually at odds, often militantly, with the government of General Juan Carlos Onganía. Since August 1966, leading professors from the University of Buenos Aires have been leaving the country, while students have joined workers in repeated displays of violence and protest. To secure their objectives, the students at Cordoba launched an indefinite strike and occupied the professors' quarters. The struggle still continues today.

A student strike in Chile in 1967 cost 4,500 students at the University of Concepcion a full year of education. The University was closed down when students struck in protest against Peace Corps teachers and "imperialist" intervention financed by a Ford Foundation teacher-training team from the University of Minnesota. Concepcion had received about $2.2 million from Ford and the United Nations to finance a model academic reform. The rector refused to seek police help in dislodging the sit-ins because it would have been against "Chile's university tradition." [23]

In Brazil, student action, aimed at the United States, the government in power, and the oligarchs, is commonplace. In 1966 the prime target was a set of agreements signed by Brazil's Ministry of Education and Culture with AID. Again the students were protesting what they saw as a United States attempt at "cultural imperialism." The United States said it was just trying to improve the system of higher education.[24] At the same time, students in Recife took to the streets in a political challenge to the regime of President Humberto Castelo Branco, protesting: "The Government says peace but we don't want this peace of the tomb. We want freedom and the right to be heard." [25]

In August 1968 the government called more than 1,500 infantrymen and state policemen to Rio de Janeiro to control student demonstrations against the military regime of President Arthur da Costa e Silva and its imprisonment of a twenty-three-year-old student leader, Vladimir Palmeira. Earlier in Rio, priests in their vestments had formed a line to protect the students against Brazilian cavalry.[26]

In the same month, 4,800 Guatemalan university students refused to attend classes in protest against a General Studies school. The school, which all students were required to attend for the first two years at the National University, was established in 1964 under the guidance of AID, and Michigan State University. The government was forced to abolish the school.[27]

The year 1968 also marked unprecedented student revolt in Mexico, aimed principally at the authoritarianism of the ruling PRI regime and the inadequacy of budget allocations for education.

Underlying the student movements of Latin America are many of the same concerns of some of the older generation: a longing for a sense of national purpose, a vision of the future, a sense of legitimacy and independence, liberation from what is seen as the heavy hand of United States materialism, honesty in politics. It is for this reason that Catholic Action groups and the Christian Democratic Party in many countries have had particular success in organizing student movements. In most large universities of Latin America these represent the allegiance of some of the most vigorous student organizations. Others include: right-wing activist groups and neofascists; anarchists; Marxists, undefined leftists and Fidelistas; Soviet Communists; Peking Communists. In most countries student organizations are overwhelmingly antigovernment. This is true in Central America, Panama, Venezuela, Brazil, Argentina, Peru, Colombia, Ecuador, and Bolivia.

The Latin American student mistrusts his government and is bitterly in conflict with what it represents. A university assistance program which has the blessing of the local government will be successful only if that approval can be somehow overcome by the excellence of the program. As a matter of fact, the traditional affinity of U.S. scholars and students toward their government may also be a thing of the past. If so, we will at least better understand Latin American university-government relations. Certainly the phenomenon of the students and Eugene McCarthy in the election campaign of 1968 had a strongly Latin American tinge to it. In fact, one Latin American commented that Senator McCarthy reminded him of a Christian Democrat. The same was said of John and Robert Kennedy.

Student movements are tending to polarize between those who favor Christian Democracy and its relatively peaceful methods and those who want radical change, with speed, blood, and violence. It is significant that both the United States and the Soviet Union are becoming further and further removed from either side.

Some will argue that for all their bluster and militancy Latin American student organizations have grave weaknesses. Recalling the characteristics of an engine of change, they are notably lacking in access to power and in the capacity to protect themselves. But where student movements do possess these characteristics—for example, when they combine with the Christian Democrats in Chile or with the mineworkers union in Bolivia, as happened when Víctor Paz Estenssoro was overthrown in 1963 —they are formidable. In this connection it will be interesting to see the effect of Peru's new university law, which formally recognizes that the purpose of the university is to promote "a just society" through "the transformation of socio-economic structures" and guarantees free expression of opinion concerning this transformation.

The third and perhaps most subtle lack of these groups might be labeled "competence," or the operating skills with which the Latin American student is equipped in his university. This derives from the fact that the Latin American university continues to be very much of a European overlay, theoretical and dogmatic, focused on a different culture than that which lies around it. It thus finds itself alien, its purposes unclear, its connections with the environment uncertain.[28] With some brilliant exceptions it abjures from rigorous research of its own community and is thus incapable of responding to the needs of that community or preparing its students to affect that community. It lives in cultural suspension at a time when its cultural product is sorely needed to cope with the urgent problems of renovation around it.

In this regard, I should mention the work of Harvard in Central America. In 1963 the Harvard Business School was asked by President Kennedy to help start an institution in Central America and Panama which could train managers. The university recognized from the beginning that neither Harvard nor Latin American professors could begin to teach usefully in this field until substantial research had been conducted into what the problems of managers were in the region. Several years and substantial money were invested in such research before thought was given to starting the institution. Casewriters went far and wide into the factories, offices, and fields of almost two hundred Central American enterprises. Teaching material was prepared, and with this material courses for forty young men began in January 1968 at the Central American Institute of Business Education (INCAE) in Managua, Nicaragua. For the first time these students were able to analyze objectively the real problems of real enterprises of their communities, guided and prodded by Harvard-trained Central American professors and several temporary professors from Cambridge. It is hard to describe the excitement of these students at grasping and wrestling with the real, complex, and manifold problems around them. They were being trained not as specialists or technicians, but as generalists, capable of understanding that the problems of management—or change —require simultaneous responses to many different environmental characteristics at once. Production, finance, marketing, human relations, politics, all merge in the managerial process as they do in the conduct of any successful engine of change. It is not too much to suggest that from the graduates of INCAE and other institutions like it may well come the most effective and constructive revolutionaries of Latin America.*

Politics is obviously not merely a game in Latin American universities. Student leaders are playing for high stakes, confident that they are an important force for change in an environment where those forces are seriously limited. They see themselves as beginning careers devoted to changing the societies around them. That they invariably become absorbed by those very societies and instead of changing them are themselves changed is but further evidence of the enormous obstacles yet to be overcome before the processes of development are assured.

* This work has been carried out under a contract between Harvard and AID.

11

COMMUNISTS AND REVOLUTIONARIES

Contrary to popular mythology, Communists in Latin America are not, generally speaking, revolutionaries. And the most extreme revolutionaries are becoming more and more anti-Communist.

That is to say, the Communist parties which have attached themselves to the political system of virtually every Latin American country for the last forty years or more are not engines of change. Communism should not be confused with the extreme revolutionary nationalism of Fidel Castro and Che Guevara which, in Cuba at least, has caused unquestioned changes. The issues between the two are ones of purpose and loyalty as well as timing and strategy. They are in part the same issues that separate the Soviet Union and China.

Chile is a special case. There, as we have seen, Communism and revolutionary nationalism are combined in an uneasy alliance for the purpose of electoral victory in 1970.

I

Latin America's Communist apparatus, among the oldest in the world, has been singularly lacking in revolutionary fervor. It can claim only one major attempt to seize power by force. This was the 1935 military coup in Brazil led by Luis Carlos Prestes, who had been a celebrated guerrilla leader before he joined the Party. The coup failed when expected civilian support did not materialize, and Prestes promptly became a determined advocate of peaceful change. For example, in 1961 he denounced Francisco Julião and his Peasant Leagues as "ultra-leftist adventurists." [1]

Somehow, the totalitarianism of the Latin American Communist parties has not given them the ruthless determination to seize power. In the words of Ernst Halperin: "They are content to play the normal game of Latin American politics, cooperating both with dictators and with democrats in return for small benefits." Sometimes, as in Venezuela during the Pérez Jiménez dictatorship, they split into two parties with opposite policies, one going underground with the democratic opposition and the other staying in the open, hoping to celebrate victory with whoever won. They also have a long record of unwholesome alliances with such dictators as Trujillo, Somoza, and Batista. "Thus," says Halperin, "most of the Latin American Communist parties have degenerated into small machines run by professional politicians who hire out their services to dictators and democrats alike in return for petty concessions." [2]

We should, however, understand the plight of Latin American Communist parties before ridiculing their failure. Stuck with an alien and essentially urban doctrine of change, far from headquarters and assistance, low on Moscow's list of priorities, and confronted by an ingenious political system which is both flexible and concentrated, powerful and tolerant, it is a wonder they have survived at all. They undoubtedly would have succumbed long ago had it not been that the ruling groups found them tactically useful in controlling power.

This was the case until Castro. After years of humiliation and discouragement, Latin American Communists felt that at last they were to have a place in the sun. The climax came with the location of Soviet missiles on Cuba in 1962. Moscow was finally backing its words and ideology with strength against the all-powerful United States. And then, ignominiously, the missiles were withdrawn, and Communists throughout the hemisphere saw what their enemies had been telling them: In the clinch their Russian friends were of little value.

This event marked the serious beginning of the anti-Party revolutionary movement in Latin America. Unwilling to take orders from Moscow—or Peking—although prepared to accept money and guns, the revolutionaries have no time for the old-fashioned Marxist-Leninists; no patience for the argument that conditions are not yet ripe for revolution, that "the masses" have not been aroused. They are even less interested in playing a role in Soviet foreign policy, which for the time being calls for peaceful competition and coexistence with the United States.

The Castroites want an immediate and violent revolution, warfare in the countryside, strikes in the cities, sabotage and terrorism everywhere, "Viet Nams" in Latin America. That it is sometimes convenient for these militant nationalists to call themselves Communists and to receive guns and bullets under that label does not lessen their differences with traditional Moscow Communists.

The position of Castroite groups coincides with that of the Chinese Communists on three important issues: both reject Soviet peaceful coexistence and a lessening of tensions with the United States; both favor aggressive promotion of revolution everywhere; and both regard the Soviets' "peaceful road to socialism" as a path to nowhere. But as Halperin points out, Castroite groups are not therefore Maoists, or in any way inspired by Peking. The coincidence results from common interests: Both want revolution now, whether this bothers the Soviet Union or not, and both are trying to prevent a detente between the Soviet Union and the United States.[3] The position of the militant nationalists, the Castroites, is thus strictly Latin American. They are not the agents of either China or the Soviet Union; they are not part of any international Communist movement. The extent to which China and the Soviet Union are prepared to render assistance to these undisciplined and disobedient Latin American revolutionaries is an important but very definitely unanswered question.

2

It is misleading and imprecise to regard Fidel Castro as first and foremost a Communist. The sequence of Castro's rise to power is by now familiar: the gathering of a small group of followers in the early 1950's, of whom none were Communists but all were

loyal to him personally; the flight to the Sierra Maestra mountains in Oriente in 1956; the final disintegration and internal
collapse of the Batista regime; and the rise of Castro to full power
in January 1959.

During and before this period, the Communist Party of Cuba
had been a weak and corrupt ally of Batista. There is no evidence
to show and no reason to suppose that Castro should have had
any serious contact with it or with Moscow. Intellectually, it
seems that Ernest Hemingway and *For Whom the Bell Tolls*
had as much influence on Castro as Marx and Lenin.[4]

The unalterable fact seems to be that Cuba in 1959 was
long overdue for a change. Castro's extraordinary leadership
awoke the nation and rallied to his side the Cuban people,
including highly placed men of power and means. It was soon
clear that he had decided upon a total social revolution in Cuba
and throughout the hemisphere. To inspire such a movement
Castro needed an archenemy. It was not difficult for him to vent
his natural emotions and to use the United States for this purpose.
Our traditional policy of help and comfort to dictators and oligarchs was cut to fit admirably into his lengthy harangues, which
echoed year after year throughout Latin America. His decision
must have been further confirmed in June 1959 when the
United States refused to sell him arms and brought pressure on
Europeans to follow suit. Relations between the two countries
deteriorated rapidly, culminating in the return of Ambassador
Philip Bonsal in January 1960.

Meanwhile, Castro had turned to the Soviet Union for help.
After some hesitation, in February the Russians made a grant of
$100 million in credits and agreed to purchase 425,000 tons of
sugar. Russian oil began arriving in April; arms came in June
and July. At this point Castro must have felt that he could
proceed along his revolutionary road with success assured. He
had the support of a major world power. He could vilify the
United States with impunity, becoming the hero and the leader
of all the millions of Latin Americans who he supposed were
ready to rise up in war against "Yankee imperialism" and their
own oligarchies. So on July 26, 1960, Castro shouted to the

world that he would "convert the Andes mountain range into the Sierra Maestra of all Latin America."

The expropriation of American companies followed, as well as the progressive nationalization of all Cuban private business. The United States decreed a trade embargo and on January 2, 1961, President Eisenhower severed all diplomatic relations.

It was not until April 16, 1961, the day after the air attacks which preceded the Bay of Pigs invasion, that Castro declared his resolve to be "socialist." It was only then that he sought entry into the Soviet camp. By all appearances this offering of Cuba as a member of the socialist bloc came as a surprise to the Soviets and must have caused considerable consternation. The matter was allowed to lie unnoticed for more than a year. In fact, it was not until May of 1963 that Cuba was formally admitted to the Communist bloc.*

Whether the Kremlin ideologists have given him a clean bill of health must be a matter of some doubt. It surely was plain even then that Fidel's marks were going to be consistently low with respect to Party discipline and obedience. Even as he professed his commitment to Marx and Lenin, old-line Communist heads were rolling in Cuba. As recently as January 1968, veteran Party leader Aníbal Escalante and eight others were tried as "traitors" and imprisoned for fifteen years for passing information about the Cuban economy to a Russian diplomat.

The arrival of the missiles and the ensuing crisis of October 1962 are well known. The results, however, have been generally underestimated. When the Soviet Union backed down in the face of United States power, not only was Castro humiliated, but his revolutionary standing in Latin America was badly shaken. Conversely, the standing of the United States, and particularly that of President Kennedy, soared. The inspiring promise of the Alliance for Progress had kindled hope of change

---

* Castro signed the joint Russian-Cuban declaration on May 23, 1963, during his first trip to Moscow. He acted as Prime Minister of Cuba and Secretary General of the United Party of the Socialist Revolution (PURS), a new party which he had formed a few months earlier expressly for the purpose of his mission.

and the United States had used its power artfully and successfully against a dangerous foreign invader.

Today Castro is in serious disagreement with the Soviet Union on several counts, principally concerned with getting along with the United States and nonviolent gradualism on the part of Communist parties in Latin America. The disagreements have reverberated through Latin America, the Communists roundly denouncing Castro, and the Castroites just as roundly denouncing the Communists. At the same time, Castro has suffered continuing setbacks. His attempts to upset Venezuela, in the elections of December 1963 and since, have failed. The Goulart regime in Brazil, with which he was building close relationships, collapsed in March 1964. The Chilean election of 1964 was another disappointment.

A further serious blow came with the Soviet repudiation of the conference of the Organization of Latin American Solidarity (OLAS) which Castro called in Havana in August 1967 to condemn United States "imperialism." Perhaps the most significant event of the conference was *Pravda*'s denunciation of it before it even began. This came in the form of a demand by Luis Corvalan, Communist leader of Chile and chief Soviet spokesman in Latin America, that Castro stop meddling in the revolutionary affairs of other nations.[5] He accused Castro of seeking to destroy other Communist parties and thus provide a "gift to imperialism." * After a fierce debate OLAS responded by condemning Soviet economic and technical policy in the Western Hemisphere.**

* A few days earlier, oddly enough, Chile's Christian Democratic National Council had endorsed guerrilla warfare as a legitimate method of achieving social revolution and invited OLAS to Chile. (*The New York Times*, July 16, 1967, p. 17.)

** This referred in part to the determined efforts of the Soviet Union to increase trade relations with all Latin American countries, regardless of their political bias. In 1957 their trade was only $200 million a year. By 1960 it had doubled; at the same time, the United States proportion of Latin American trade was slipping. In 1967, however, apart from an estimated $1 billion of trade with Cuba, Russian trade with Latin America amounted to only about $100 million. An indicator of the unwillingness of the Soviet Union to allow ideological considerations to interfere with their economic ties is the following quip by Viktor Volski, head of a Soviet trade delegation to

Scarcely four months after Corvalan's warning, Ernesto Che Guevara, blood brother of Fidel Castro and designer of the Castro brand of guerrilla warfare, lay dead and defeated in the remote jungles of La Higuera, Bolivia. In his remarkable introduction to Che Guevara's diary, Castro revealed that he had been directly involved in the planning of Guevara's revolt. What is more, he charged that the Bolivian Communist Party was a principal cause of the revolt's failure. He accused Mario Monje, the party's chief, of sabotaging "the movement, intercepting well-trained Communist militants in La Paz who were going to join the guerrillas." The diaries reveal that another reason for the guerrillas' defeat was the lack of an urban support organization, which presumably was to have been the responsibility of the Communist Party in La Paz.[6] A further interesting revelation of the diaries is that Guevara clearly chose the wrong country for his undertaking. Bolivia had had a full revolution in 1952, followed by substantial chaos which has frustrated its promise, but the structures in Bolivia are not so much in need of destruction as of ordering. This, together with a natural apathy and distrust of foreigners, accounts for the unwillingness of Bolivia's peasants to join Guevara and explains the repeated betrayal of guerrilla positions and activities to the local military by *campesino* informers.

Castro and Moscow have now stretched their relationship toward the breaking-point. Banking on the huge economic and political investment which the Soviet Union already has in Cuba, Castro is evidently confident that he can go his own way with impunity.*

Venezuela in 1965: "We shall not discriminate in our trade agreements. Just like we do it with Cuba—absolute equality, mutual respect and fraternal collaboration." At the same time the use of trade as a political weapon was clearly demonstrated when Russia opened trade with Peru in February 1969, during the International Petroleum Company crisis. (Walter La Feber, *America, Russia and the Cold War, 1945–1966,* New York, John Wiley and Sons, 1967, p. 207; Carlos Conde, "Latest Gambit by Soviets," Boston *Globe,* April 10, 1965. See also "Insurgency in Latin America," *Survey of the Alliance for Progress,* a study for the Subcommittee on American Republic Affairs of the Committee on Foreign Relations, U.S. Senate, January 15, 1968, p. 11.)

* In a study for the Senate Foreign Affairs Committee in January 1968,

Castro's independence today is in sharp contrast to what many Europeans and North Americans predicted. It is quite consistent, however, with Latin American political history, in which dictators, *caudillos,* and even democratic politicians have used the Communists for their purposes without being in the least made captive.[7]

Whatever the Cuban revolution may be and whatever it may foreshadow, it is misleading and superficial to call it Communist. The revolution is intensely nationalistic and militantly independent, even though it has international pretensions. The marriage with Moscow is a tactical ploy, not an ideological commitment or a promise of allegiance. It is, therefore, not Communist in any precise sense, though indeed totalitarian.

Castroism has its own bible, Che Guevara's *Guerrilla Warfare,* and its own revision of this bible, the even more remarkable, and anti-Communist, *Revolution Within the Revolution?* by Jules-Régis Debray, a French author and associate of Che Guevara who was imprisoned in Bolivia when Che was killed. Most important, the revolution has fired the imagination of millions of Latin American youth. While it has changed nothing, except in Cuba, its fires are unlikely to die.

One must recognize, however, exactly what this fire is. It is not kindled by Marx or Lenin or Stalin or Khrushchev or Kosygin, but by Castro, Mao, Guevara, and the Viet Cong. The latter are seen, rightly or wrongly, as radical and effective agents of change, as proponents of social justice and independence from domestic oligarchs and foreign powers. The fire is also pride at having discovered and perfected a new kind of war in which a handful of barefoot peasants can harass and embarrass a fully equipped modern army division. It is David and Goliath;

Professor David D. Burks reports: ". . . in the United States and Latin America the tendency has been to exaggerate the monetary value of Cuban aid [to Latin American insurgents]. In part this arises from the unfounded assumption that the Soviets have provided a blank check for Cuban subversive activities. Though the Soviets may have given some aid for this purpose, circumstantial evidence suggests that they prefer to disburse funds directly or through agents more amenable to their commands. The Soviet use of the Italian party in 1965 to ship $300,000 to the Venezuelan Communist Party is an example of the bypassing of the Cubans."

it is heroism in lands without heroes, glory in an inglorious time, idealism in a setting where ideals have long been a sham. Before Castro the fire could perhaps have been accurately associated with communism because, partly as a result of United States blindness and ineptitude, it was by default in many instances identified with Communists, that is, with the international, Moscow-centered Communist Party apparatus. But time plays funny tricks. The fire has outflanked Moscow too. It is foolish to suppose that Moscow can control the Castroite movements of Latin America when all the evidence is that it cannot.

Luis Turcios, the twenty-four-year-old guerrilla leader of Guatemala, who was killed in an auto accident in 1967, had the fire deep within him. He was twelve years old when U.S.-made Thunderbolt bombers roared over Guatemala City, heralding the overthrow of the government of Jacobo Arbenz. The United States engineered the coup because Arbenz was a tool of the Soviet Union and it was unacceptable to have a Soviet base on our southern doorstep. Arbenz, however, was also a reformer, and had threatened to take considerable land from large owners and distribute it to the poor peasants of Guatemala. He had also pledged rigorous tax increases and other measures unpopular with the oligarchy.

The United States then helped to install a dictator, Castillo Armas, who immediately undid the reforms which Arbenz had begun. During this period Turcios was growing up, receiving as good an education as Guatemala could provide. He graduated as a second lieutenant from the Polytechnical School in 1959 and received Ranger training at Fort Benning, Georgia.

In 1960 he gave up a promising career and went into the hills with a small group of followers. He may have received some money and arms from the Soviet Union, but if he did it was inconsequential. He told an interviewer: "I saw the misery of our peasants, the misery of our Indians, the exploitation—and behind each one of these I saw North American imperialism. We cannot advance any reforms except through a war against reactionary forces, against the army of Guatemala and probably against the United States Marines." [8] When asked how he would

describe himself, he said: "I am a Communist without a party."
This, of course, is a contradiction in terms. What he meant was
that he was a "Communist" in the sense that in Guatemala, as
far as he knew, everything that was related to change, reform,
and the objectives he believed in was associated with "Communists." But he was not a "Communist" in the sense that he
was obedient to a foreign power. In fact, it must be presumed
that he was an ardent nationalist.

Furthermore, it is significant that there is little or no evidence
that the Guatemalan guerrillas have received substantial assistance from Cuba. A United States Senate study reports that
no Cubans are known to have fought with them and "very little
of either arms or money has been supplied by Castro. . . .
Castro has supplied training for a few of the guerrillas and, of
course, propaganda support." The report goes on to state that
"events in Guatemala have their origins in the thwarted revolution of 1954 much more than in Castro's Cuba.[9] There is, however, considerable evidence of Cuban support and direction for
similar movements in Venezuela, Colombia, Nicaragua and, of
course, for Che Guevara in Bolivia.

3

There is one Communist movement in Latin America which has
been relatively successful, although even its success derives from
its willingness to be ideologically adulterated.

The Chilean Communist Party, under the leadership of Luis
Corvalan, is thoroughly responsive to Moscow. The best organized and most powerful Communist unit in Latin America, it
polled about 15 per cent of the vote in the municipal elections
of 1967. The Chilean Party has a traditional Marxist-Leninist
urban orientation, as do other Communist parties in Latin America. Unlike others, however, Corvalan's followers have been successful in gaining substantial influence among the trade unions
of the cities.* Also unlike others, they have ventured into the

* The trade union movement of Uruguay is dominated by Communists but
the Party is insignificant politically. It is also governed by a conservative
Moscow-directed policy.

rural areas, using cadres of schoolteachers to instruct the youth in Marx as well as mathematics.

Without question, however, a good deal of the Chilean Communist Party's vitality derives from its uneasy alliance since 1956 (in FRAP) with the Socialist Party, which has been notoriously unstable ideologically. Halperin points out that within the space of only thirty years the Chilean Socialists have been militant anti-Communists, members of a Communist-sponsored popular front, admirers of the Argentinian fascist regime of Juan Perón, Titoists, and finally enthusiastic pro-Cubans. Lately, its left wing has begun to lean toward Peking.[10] Two traits have remained constant, however; militant nationalism and a profound distrust of the Communists, with whom their alliance in FRAP has been strictly a matter of expediency. The Socialist presidential candidate, Salvador Allende, with Communist help, polled almost 40 per cent of the vote against Eduardo Frei in the 1964 election.

Today the Chilean Socialists find themselves in an odd situation. Their leader, Allende, is an urbane and dignified gentleman who lives in considerable luxury. He speaks of the necessity of "armed struggle" throughout Latin America, but not in Chile. There, he believes, the constitutional process is too strong, and the best chance of victory lies in the electoral processes. For this purpose he has allied his party with the Communists.

It is no secret that the Soviet Union regards a victory in 1970 dominated by Chilean Communists as being of primary importance, and it is doing what it can to bring this about.

4

We see, then, two quite distinct movements in Latin America: Communism and Castroite revolution. The first is the traditional handmaiden of the Soviet Union, nurtured on the teachings of Marx and Lenin. The second is an indigenous revolutionary force, whose ideology as set forth by Debray is in large part revolution itself, violent seizure of power for its own sake. Only in Chile are the two in any way combined. The position of the Soviet Union with respect to these two movements is equivocal, to say the least. Obligated to support the first, Moscow appears antagonistic toward the second, which it may, however, be forced to acknowledge. Peking for the moment is too far away and too engrossed in its own difficulties to be a real factor.

Traditional Communism appears to be failing fast, if indeed it ever can be judged to have prospered in Latin America. It has suffered from a lack of revolutionary zeal among urban workers, who as fast as they have organized have moved into the Tolerant Oligarchy. It has made little headway even in the urban slums, where surprisingly enough newcomers find life considerably better than it was in the countryside. European influence, thought, and experience have dominated the Party's leadership, and the Party has been seriously weakened by the ineffectiveness of its alliance with the Soviet Union. Perhaps most important, its fundamental Marxian tenets have been repeatedly proven invalid in Latin America.[11] The Party today is under continuing attack from its own left and from new Castroite groups who understand that communism has neither a doctrine nor an apparatus which is useful for revolution; that its loyalty and dependence upon the Soviet Union disqualify it as a legitimate, indigenous movement; and that a corrupt and immoral record make it less than inspiring for the region's youth.

Some suggest that communism may be saved by an alliance with the Castroite revolutionary left, but the trend seems to be all in the other direction. A radical shift in the policy and program of the Soviet Union in the direction of violent aggressive revolution could conceivably breathe life into the Party, but that too seems an unlikely happening. Therefore, we must conclude that communism in Latin America has not been an engine of change and is not likely to become one.

The doctrine for the second movement, Castroite revolution, which is diametrically opposed to that of the Communist parties, was set forth originally by Che Guevara. Its three basic principles are: that guerrilla bands in league with the people can defeat a regular army; that "it is not necessary to wait until all conditions for making revolution exist—the insurrection can create them; and that the countryside not the cities is the basic area for armed fighting."[12]

A major attempt to implement this strategy was made in

Venezuela, where Cuban groups joined with disenchanted local Communists who had left the Soviet fold. This was defeated in 1963, essentially by the Venezuelan people, when they participated overwhelmingly in a national election which had been condemned and boycotted by the leftists. Guevara's efforts in Bolivia to organize a peasant uprising were similarly unsuccessful, defeated by a well-trained and effective regular army. Attempts in Colombia, Peru, Brazil, the Dominican Republic, Argentina, and Guatemala were also crushed. The failure of these forays seems to be due to two principal factors. The armies of Latin America, with United States assistance and training, are becoming increasingly efficient. And the Castroites—like many others—have seriously underestimated the difficulties of agitating, motivating, and organizing Latin American peasants. They have also lacked funds and material.

But as we have said, the fire is by no means dead. The guerrilla revolutionary movement first designed for Latin American purposes by Fidel Castro, in spite of its current difficulties, seems likely to qualify as an engine of change in the years to come. Therefore, it behooves us to study it in more detail.

With Guevara's death, Régis Debray has become the movement's most articulate strategist. In his remarkable and at times eloquent pamphlet, *Revolution Within the Revolution?*, Debray makes two major points. He declares that successful revolutions in Latin America will result mainly from effective military actions, and not from political parties or programs; and he is impatient with both Marxist-Leninist parties and what he calls "pro-Chinese" parties, who "have done nothing except delay the beginning of a decisive struggle of the masses." [13]

Debray is a pragmatist, singularly lacking in ideology. He says it was "a fortuitous event that Fidel was unfamiliar with the military works of Mao Tse-tung before landing ashore in Oriente Province." [14] He attributes the success of the Cuban revolution in large part to the fact that it was pragmatic and experiential, designed to fit the particular situation. In this connection, he takes to task several doctrinaire approaches to revolution, including that of Marx, Lenin, and Trotsky. [15] But he is a great believer in guerrilla warfare and draws on Guevara for the three golden rules of this kind of combat: "constant vigilance, constant mistrust, constant mobility." [16] His approach to propaganda and the motivation of the peasants is aggressive and violent. "To destroy the age-old concept[s], this fear of and humbleness toward the owners, the police, the rural guards, which is centuries old, there is nothing better than combat . . . the destruction of a troop transport truck or the public execution of a police torturer is more effective propaganda for the . . . population . . . than 200 speeches." [17]

Debray sees the cities as "graveyards for revolutionaries;" [18] "great Yankee suburbs" which corrupt leaders, soften the combatants, and betray the movement. They and their organizations are to be avoided at all costs. In discussing the relationship between the guerrilla units and the political party, he admits to a Marxist-Leninist heresy in his belief that the people's army is its own political authority.[19] He acknowledges that this differs from the Chinese and North Viet Namese doctrines, but frankly blames the decrepit state of Latin American communism.[20] Then he speaks of the inadequacy of old, urban-oriented leadership, which cannot possibly expect to direct the young guerrilla fighters. Indeed, the Party, with its "plethora of commissions, secretariats, congresses, conferences, mass gatherings, plenary sessions, meetings and assemblies on all levels . . . is a hindrance in the best of cases, and catastrophic in the worst." [21]

Most eloquent is the letter quoted by Debray from Castro to his friend Frank País, in Mexico, written in the Sierra Maestra on July 21, 1957:

> The spirit of renovation, the eagerness for collective excellence and the awareness of a higher destiny are at their highest point and could carry us immeasurably further ahead. We had frequently heard about such things which had the taste of abstractions, and suspected their beautiful meaning. Now, however, we are living all these, we are feeling it in all its aspects, and this is really something unique. We have seen it develop in an incredible way in this Sierra which is our small world. The word "people" which had been mentioned so many times as a vague and confused

meaning is converted here into a reality which is live, marvelous and dazzling. Now I do know what the meaning of "people" is; I can see it in this invincible force which surrounds us from everywhere, I see it in the columns of 30 or 40 men who, under the light of torches, go down muddy slopes, at 2 or 3 A.M., carrying a 60-pound load on their shoulders, bringing us supplies. Who has organized them so marvelously? Where have they found such skill, such cunning, valor and abnegation? No one knows! It is almost a mystery! They organize by themselves; spontaneously! When the animals get tired and fall on the ground, unable to carry on, men show up from somewhere and bring the goods. They cannot be stopped by any force. They would have to be killed, all, to the last peasant, which is impossible, which the tyrannical regime cannot do; the people realize this and are becoming more and more aware, with every passing day, of their immense force.[22]

One cannot help but wonder whether the general and critical weakness of the Castro revolutionary movement in Latin America, like that of its Communist ancestor, is not an ideological one. It is clear from Debray, Guevara, and Castro himself that the objective is to destroy the existing order of things and to substantially reallocate power. But the terms and criteria of reallocation are left unstated. There is no mention of the new society and renovated community which they presumably propose to establish. There is no vision, only a very short-run purpose. It should not be surprising if this revolutionary movement, like the Communists, were to seek to establish a relationship with priests and laymen of the radical Church, whose vision it badly needs. As we saw with the brothers Melville in Guatemala, the Church may also need some of the things the revolutionaries have to offer.

12

ORGANIZATIONS OF WORKERS

In measuring the effectiveness of worker organizations as engines of change, we come across great variety and diversity of effect.

We are dealing with two general groups of institutions, which are related at once to social and political as well as to economic structures. One is the old, traditional, generally urban trade unions in industries such as railroads, mines, textiles, communications, banks, and government services. The other includes a wide variety of peasant leagues, unions, cooperatives, and community organizations, which represent the newest and most radical form of worker organizations in Latin America.

Organizations in the first group are distinct from those in the second on several counts. They represent more or less discrete and homogeneous bodies of workers who are engaged in particular activities for a particular employer. Their operation is often governed and circumscribed by some sort of collective contract or agreement with an employer and by an elaborate and long-standing body of law, which may or may not be enforced. They are in this way tied to the structure and order of things, and over the years they have generally worked out a *modus vivendi* with the oligarchy in government and business. Membership figures are unreliable and of questionable meaning, but there are, roughly speaking, twenty-five million Latin Americans who count themselves members of such organizations.* Of these, it is doubtful that more than 10 to 15 per cent have a status comparable to the trade union member in the United States.¹ While unions are without doubt increasing in strength and importance, their growth is slow and in many instances seems contingent upon their compliance with the rules of the status quo.

Organizations in the second group, on the other hand, are more heterogeneous, performing many different functions for a wide variety of rural people. Their members may or may not receive a salary; thus, they may or may not have a relationship with an employer. The functions of these organizations may include representation of peasants with the landowner, the plantation manager, the government, or the army. They may provide broad services involving education, housing, credit, the market, land tenure, and access to political and economic power. Remote from government, they are generally unresponsive to its machinery and left relatively untouched by its laws. These organizations are for the most part radical influences within their environment, since they are aimed more at multistructural change than at negotiating a position within the structure. It is difficult to estimate the number of members in such organizations. A United States government estimate concludes that there are 105 million peasant farmers and farm workers in Latin America. In Northeast Brazil, in the region around Pernambuco alone, there are peasant organizations which claim 200,000 members.² FEDELAC, in the Dominican Republic, has perhaps 14,000 members. If we extend these figures to Chile, Peru, Bolivia, Central America, and elsewhere, it is perhaps reasonable to estimate that as many as five million country people are in one way or another attached to an organization of some sort.

This number is indeed small, but of the two types of worker organizations, the peasant movements, with all their acknowledged weaknesses, today rank higher as change engines. Both types have the capacity, indeed the basic function, to agitate,

* This estimate is updated from one made in 1964 by Frank Bonilla in *Continuity and Change in Latin America*, John J. Johnson, ed., Stanford Univ. Press, Stanford, Calif., p. 199.

motivate, organize, and commit (see the discussion of doctrine in Chapter 7). The leaders of both groups to varying degrees exert authority over their membership; have the capacity to communicate with those whom they seek to organize; are capable of providing them with protection; have a certain access to power, political or economic; have that competence essential to organization; and are by their nature endowed with focus, purpose, and direction. They all, therefore, qualify, at least theoretically, as potential engines of change. The rub comes in that, despite their historic protestations to the contrary, the bulk of the older trade union organizations in type one have been satisfied with relatively little change. In short, the very fact that they exist and function in a restricted and limited way has been sufficient to satisfy their conception of their purpose. (This, incidentally, runs contrary to a prediction I made in an earlier book that these organizations were in truth a continuing revolutionary force.)[3] They seem today to be quite prepared to work and prosper within the confines of the environment as it is, within the rules of the game to which they have been admitted by the Tolerant Oligarchy. It was not, of course, always so, and is not completely so today. Furthermore, the changes wrought by these organizations over the years have been significant and in some cases profound and permanent.

The peasant organizations of the second type have no choice. Their purpose requires an absolute commitment to radical structural change of the most profound sort. In spite of their weakness and frailty, they are among the most potent engines of change on the continent and are destined to become more so.

Let us look briefly at the historical development of worker organizations in Latin America, noting how the first group were genuine engines of change until about the last decade and how the second seems now to have taken over from them this revolutionary role.

I

In general, the historical purposes of worker organizations in Latin America have far transcended the economic welfare of their members; or more precisely, they have understood that economic change must be preceded by, or at least connected to, radical transformation of political, social, and economic systems. They have in this sense been revolutionary in their intention. Their greatest importance and achievement have been political: They have been integrators where there was little integration, communicators where there was little communication, motivators where there was little motivation, and organizers where there was confusion and chaos. They are, at least theoretically, the institutions in many ways best suited to ease the painful transition from traditional rural agricultural life to urban industrialism. It is also within their capacity, if not their natural function, to identify ever-increasing areas of mutuality of interest between management and labor, between the employer and the employee, and to break down the destructive myth that there is an irreconcilable conflict between the various groups and classes in society. Perhaps most important, they are a means of giving power to those who have never had it. In this sense, they build the capacity of the citizen to participate in the life of his community and the formation of his nation. They are thus of rare importance to the political development of Latin America, where institutions of this nature are scarce.

Historically, organized labor in Latin America has had revolutionary objectives. It has not sought a fairer distribution of the pie but an entirely new pie, a radically different social, political, and economic structure. In Mexico and Bolivia organized labor was a principal factor in causing such structural change. In Venezuela it has been the organizational backbone of Acción Democrática and thus in many ways responsible for the change which has occurred in that country. Elsewhere its revolutionary achievements have been less dramatic.

As with so much of Latin America's socio-political structure, the central problem of labor has been and remains ideological— its will and its purpose. The region's trade union movement, which dates back to 1853 when the printing trades were organized in Buenos Aires, was superimposed on an essentially docile, rural mass by reformers, intellectuals, and politicians of all sorts. It was by no means a result of the initiative of a congested mass of factory workers, as was true in the United States and

Europe. The early leaders were for the most part immigrants, imbued with European ideologies of the time, particularly Marxism and anarchosyndicalism. They were thus committed to the notion of class warfare and tended to regard any agreement with an employer as collaboration with the enemy. They looked to politicians, political parties, and the state as the means of achieving their vision of society. Thus, the trade union movement generally became the tool of political interests, ranging from dictators like Perón and Vargas to reformers like Betancourt, rising and falling with the fortunes of those interests.

The orientation of its ideology also directed labor's primary attention to securing social and labor legislation similar to that being enacted in industrial Europe and North America. Again we see an alien mode being superimposed on the unready Latin American environment. Both the Latin American state and the elites behind it found it simple and appealing to enact an ultramodern labor code. It was convenient lip service to forestall radical change; it produced worker votes at the polls; it enhanced national prestige in the community of nations; and the general inapplicability of the laws to Latin America's industrial and economic situation meant that they couldn't, or at least didn't have to, be enforced. Furthermore, the paucity of manufacturing, factories, and factory workers deprived labor unions of the militant base which in the industrialized world tended to compel enforcement. In France and the United States, for example, manufacturing employees are more than 25 per cent of the work force; in the United Kingdom, 40 per cent. In Latin America, however, only Argentina has as many as 25 per cent of its work force in manufacturing. In Chile the figure is only about 17 per cent; in Venezuela and Colombia, about 11 or 12 per cent.[4]

The labor movement suffered triple damages as a result of the course it followed. First, its birth was forced prematurely, before there was an adequate base from which it could derive strength for an independent life. Secondly, it sought the means of change from the state, thereby placing itself in the unyielding hands of the controlling political elite, who were unwilling to award power to labor. Provided by legislation with the forms of progress, the movement denied itself the opportunity to organize its own power to achieve the substance. Thirdly, these two circumstances have combined to make the social and labor laws for which the labor movement successfully fought little more than hollow promises—at most, somewhat tarnished objectives. And the very existence of these laws has served to limit and crimp the scope and effectiveness of collective bargaining.

Thus impeded, the labor movement has in many instances been forced to depend for life on its opponents. Given the radical nature of its initial ideology, this has entailed a corruption of purpose, leading to a profound ideological crisis. Like the Apristas and so many other of the old Marxist-oriented reformers and revolutionaries, labor has for the most part realized that the European ideology with which it was born is invalid and useless. Like so many institutions of Latin America it too is in search of purpose.

2

A brief nation-by-nation rundown of the role of some of the trade union movements will document my theoretical analysis of their nature. In Argentina, when Juan Perón became Minister of Labor and Social Welfare in November 1943, following a military coup, he found the oldest labor movement in Latin America in a state of division and factional dispute and he used his governmental power to unify the warring factions. With the support of labor and the army Perón took control of the government in June 1946 and ruled Argentina for ten years. During this period the labor movement, purged of all opposition under the watchful eye of his wife, Evita, was a faithful handmaiden to his regime.[5] This alliance of labor with dictators is by no means unusual in Latin America. Since Perón's exile, succeeding presidents have continued to use labor groups as a main political support, not hesitating to crack down on them if they threatened to get out of control.[6] By March 1967 the General Confederation of Labor had about two million members, half of its strength under Perón.[7] More recently, further splintering of the movement has undoubtedly reduced its members further.

The story of labor in Brazil is somewhat similar. In 1937 Getúlio Vargas seized the labor movement, sent many of its leaders into exile, and placed the reorganized remains under strict government control. Trade unions became, in effect, arms of the government and were used to build Vargas's popularity among urban workers.

During the Kubitschek regime, from 1956 to 1961, the labor movement enjoyed unequaled freedom, and Communist leadership made considerable headway, with the encouragement of Vice-President João Goulart. Goulart took over the government after the short presidency of Jânio Quadros in 1961 and the labor movement continued to prosper, particularly the Communists. On March 31, 1964, Goulart was overthrown by the armed forces; the labor movement was plunged into a state of confusion; many of its militant leaders were jailed, even those associated with Catholic trade unions; and the movement returned to a state of governmentally imposed somnolence.[8]

In Bolivia the mineworkers played a more direct role in politics. They were prime makers of the revolution of 1952 under the leadership of Juan Lechín. In fact, so clearly recognized was their role that Lechín became Minister of Mines and Petroleum in the new regime headed by President Víctor Paz Estenssoro. His union increasingly became his political machine in a succession of disputes with President Paz, who in turn looked for support to peasant syndicates, the organization of which he had encouraged. The conflict between Lechín and his miners on the one hand and Paz Estenssoro and the peasants on the other came to a head in 1963 over the issue of reorganizing the mining industry on a more efficient basis. The miners embarked on a general strike, which failed, but in December 1964 the miners, joined by students, were a key element in undermining the Paz regime. The government's peasant organizations failed to produce adequate support and the military, richly equipped by the United States, finally delivered the *coup de grâce* to both President Paz and the MNR.[9]

In Venezuela and Mexico, as in Bolivia, urban and rural worker organizations formed an important political base for substantial change. This was institutionalized in Venezuela first through Betancourt's Acción Democrática and later by a coalition of parties; and in Mexico by the PRI, the single party of the revolution. In both countries the labor movement, in collaboration with the army and other elements, has been an engine of change, but it has not sustained itself in this role. It has either become a component of the new elite or it has become subservient to that elite. In Mexico the trade unions are basically arms of the government. They perform the usual union functions, but in many ways their most important activity is keeping the membership actively loyal to the government and its objectives.[10]

The abstract design and purpose of the Latin American trade union, as well as its periodic, short-term achievements, compel its consideration as an engine of change. On the other hand, experience has shown it to be gravely limited in this regard and has led most current observers to conclude that at the moment it is more conservative than revolutionary.[11]

The labor movement has undoubtedly been an integrating force in urban society, as well as in the countryside, in those few instances where it has succeeded in organizing salaried plantation workers. It has provided access to power to many without it, thus broadening the political base and constituting a pressure to which the power-holders have had to respond. In this way it has improved the standard of living of its employed members. Labor has also eased the transition of rural peasants into urban workers, contributing to the general politicization of urbanization.[12] In short, in societies marked by a scarcity of organization of any kind, the traditional labor union, for all its weakness and frailty, has been of singular political significance. In this sense, it has from time to time been a revolutionary force and a formidable change engine.

However, the labor movement has not been a continuing force for structural change. In the Cuban Revolution, in which it was quickly swallowed by Castro, it was a negligible factor. It has tended to become the creature of political leaders, parties and governments, particularly ministries of labor, submitting to their regulation and serving their needs. It has in many places clearly become part of the elite. In Argentina, for example, the light and power workers operate three luxury hotels, and their sports club swimming pool in Buenos Aires has an electrically operated elevator to the top of the diving board.

In spite of its Marxist leanings and predilections, Latin American labor has been consistently anti-Communist for the most part, its less extreme elements exercising controlling leadership. (Chile and Uruguay are exceptions.) Most Latin American labor leaders today see their function as being predominantly within the existing order; their attitudes toward employers, for example, is by no means generally hostile. They do not feel themselves alienated from the existing political system, nor do they advocate drastic or immediate change. Most astonishingly, studies by Alex Inkeles and Henry Landsberger, and interviews by the author have revealed that Latin American workers are not generally in the least antagonistic to foreign enterprises.[13] In fact, I have had labor leaders reported to be Communists complain to me that there were too few American companies in their countries. When I asked why they wanted the presence of those whom they regarded as "Yanqui imperialists," they replied in so many words that this line was all very well for the politicians, but as far as they were concerned, American companies were the easiest to organize, the best to deal with, and the most generous in wages and benefits. This point should not, however, be overstated. These same men will also advocate radical change in speeches and might well support such change if others initiated it.

These conflicts in ideology, purpose, and practice, have caused widespread problems of corruption and will: misuse of strike, building, and welfare funds to blackmail employers; kickbacks for "soft" contracts; acceptance of bribes; and the use of governmental machinery to suppress rivals.[14] The labor movement has suffered confusion and self-doubt because so much of its European-based ideology and purpose are invalid in Latin America. Attempts by the United States to introduce its labor relations philosophy and practice have not provided an entirely adequate replacement, although there is no question that the strengthening practice of collective bargaining is growing as industrialization provides increasing opportunities for it.

This brings up the relation of Latin American labor organizations to the AFL-CIO and to international labor in general. There are three general world federations of labor unions. The World Federation of Trade Unions (WFTU) is composed of Communist trade unions, with more than 90 per cent of its membership in the Soviet Union or Eastern European countries. The International Confederation of Free Trade Unions (ICFTU) was formed in 1949 in the chill of the Cold War when free labor broke from the WFTU. It claims some sixty million workers through its affiliated unions in more than one hundred countries. The third is the International Federation of Christian Trade Unions (CISC) with some 2.5 million members. The CISC emanated from the European union movements related to Christian Democratic parties. Its initial international focus was on trade unions in the former French and Belgian colonies in Africa and Asia. The Latin American regional arm of the Christian federation is CLASC (Confederación Latinoamericana de Sindicatos Cristianos), which has been gaining strength and notoriety in recent years as an adjunct of the radical Christian movement. The Latin American branch of the ICFTU is ORIT (Organización Regional Interamericana de Trabajadores), formed in 1951 with substantial assistance and guidance from the American labor movement for the purpose of strengthening democratic trade unions and fighting Communist attempts to gain control of Latin American labor. During the fifties and early sixties, these attempts were militant and continuous, although largely unsuccessful. The WFTU has no real Latin American affiliate. Communism's failure was due in part to the energetic and courageous efforts of American labor, directed and led by Serafino Romualdi, inter-American representatives of the American Federation of Labor and later of the merged AFL-CIO. Most of the large and well-established trade unions of Latin America became affiliated with ORIT, receiving from it funds and assistance.[15]

In 1962 still another group, the American Institute for Free Labor Development (AIFLD) was formed and Romualdi was appointed its first executive director.[16] Its purpose was to augment the capacity of the AFL-CIO to strengthen worker organ-

izations in Latin America by making AID financing available
for that purpose. In its first years AIFLD spent some $16 million
assisting trade unions in nearly every Latin American country.[17]
Ninety per cent of its funds come from AID, the remainder from
United States business and labor. Its activities include education,
training in collective bargaining, workers' housing, credit unions,
banks, cooperatives, and community services. The ideological
commitment of the institute is plain in the fact that George
Meany is its president and J. Peter Grace is chairman of the
board. Meany stated it as follows:

> We believe in the capitalist system, and we are members
> of the capitalist society. We are dedicated to the preserva-
> tion of this system, which rewards the workers, which is one
> in which management also has such a great stake. The in-
> vestors of risk capital also must be rewarded. It is, perhaps,
> not a perfect device, but it is the best that the world has
> ever produced and it operates effectively in a free society.[18]

The institute's objectives go beyond that of strengthening
democratic trade unionism in Latin America. It wants to make
possible direct worker participation in the Alliance for Progress.
It hopes also to create conditions which will allow unions to
become self-reliant and independent, thereby making trade unionism a powerful force for democratic development and social
change in Latin America.[19]

The AIFLD has quite naturally centered its attention on
ORIT-affiliated unions with which its first director, Romualdi,
and its current administrator, William G. Doherty, Jr., had
strong personal attachments in the days when "fighting Communism" was a major United States preoccupation. Today, although it is clear that the Communists are no longer the threat
that they were, the old attachments have tended to stick, causing
resentment on the part of non-ORIT organizations, particularly
those associated with CLASC, and an increasing restiveness on
the part of ORIT itself, as well as others, at the overwhelming
role of the AFL-CIO in Latin American labor affairs.*

---

* AIFLD's orientation toward ORIT, its identification with the United States
labor movement, and its particular prejudices and beliefs have caused it special

3

Unionism has played a less strong but potentially more important role in the countryside. Most of the world's people are peasant farmers and landless farmworkers. In Latin America there are well over 100 million in these categories.

Before we consider peasant organizations in general as engines of change we should look briefly at the Federación Campesina de Venezuela (FCV), the peasant union movement of Venezuela.* It is undoubtedly one of the most important organizations of its kind in Latin America, and differs from the other peasant groups which we have discussed in its political dimensions and the absence of the Church from its origins. FCV was formed as an integral part of the political process which has brought an unprecedented measure of democracy to Venezuela. In this sense it resembles the peasant (*ejido*) movement of Mexico, but it differs sharply from the Mexican pattern in that Venezuela has become a multiparty political system and the FCV an organization with multiparty loyalties. It, therefore, has retained a certain degree of independence within government and from any single party.

The FCV has played a critical role in Venezuelan land reform, and has also contributed significantly to the integration of Venezuela into a coherent nation.

In the early 1930's the Venezuelan countryside was beset by severe poverty, unrest and violence. World markets for the traditional crops of sugar, coffee, and cacao were tight and prices were low. The development of the country's petroleum resources drew

problems in Chile, where as of 1968 it was virtually *persona non grata.* "We would like to take help from AIFLD," said a highly placed Chilean friend of mine, "but they just don't understand the Chilean labor scene. They also refuse to understand that our doctrine, which is not capitalism, may have some merit in it." (Interview with Guillermo Videla, former Director of Labor, Chilean Ministry of Labor.)

* In this discussion of the FCV I have relied heavily on the findings of Dr. John D. Powell. See particularly: John D. Powell, *The Peasant Union Movement in Venezuela,* School of International Relations, Univ. of S. Calif. Los Angeles, November 1966, mimeographed; and *The Role of the Federación Campesina in the Venezuelan Agrarian Reform Process,* mimeographed research paper, Land Tenure Center, Univ. of Wis., Madison, 1967.

credit, investment, entrepreneurial talent, and governmental attention away from agriculture; and the nation's two million peasants, as well as their impecunious landlords, were the losers. In 1936 agitators and organizers began to move into the rural areas to build peasant support for political change. Their work resulted in the formation in 1941 of Acción Democrática (AD), the Democratic Action Party of Rómulo Betancourt and Rául Leoni.

Betancourt's revolutionary strategy in the early years depended heavily upon the organization of mass political support through the labor movement, particularly through peasant organizations.[20] It was with this political base that Betancourt and AD were able to secure admission to power following the military *coup d'état* which overthrew the dictatorship in October 1945. Immediately, both rural and urban unions received the governmental endorsement and recognition which they had been previously denied. By 1948 the peasant movement could claim 100,-000 members. Many peasant leaders were brought to serve in the new government and elected to Congress.

With this kind of representation in the seats of power, peasant leaders in the field were able to move forcefully and effectively to petition for land for their followers. The government also assisted the peasants to form local credit organizations, directed in part by peasant union leaders. Within a short time the peasant union and its leadership thus acquired considerable political and economic power, the greatest of which was access to land. In 1947 this power was increased by a governmental decree requiring all owners of private lands not actively under cultivation to rent them to government agencies or directly to a peasant union.[21] In addition, the same decree placed all government land under the control of the Land Commission and its local bodies, in the direction of which the local peasant union also participated. Here again, considerable new power was shifted to local leaders and their organizations.

On November 24, 1948, the Acción Democrática revolutionary regime was overthrown by Colonel Pérez Jiménez, who immediately dissolved all urban and rural unions and established his own labor movement, placing a Communist at its head.[22]

The AD unions and political leaders went underground or into exile. The dictatorship halted the land-reform program of 1945 to 1948, forcing 96 per cent of the peasants who had benefited from it off private as well as public lands.[23] Many of the latter were transferred to friends of the regime.

In spite of considerable hardship, torture, and assassination, the FCV and the rest of the Venezuelan labor movement emerged from the dictatorship in 1958 very much intact, united and inspired by their common struggle. In that year Betancourt, head of the AD party, was elected president, and he wasted little time reinstituting massive rural change. By 1966, 700 agrarian-reform settlements had been established, furnishing more than 5 million acres of land to more than 100,000 *campesino* families. As in the period from 1945 to 1948, the FCV played a key role in the organization and conduct of this program, its membership growing in 1967 to 650,000 members in more than 4,000 local unions.

The motto of the FCV describes its largest goal: "The Social and Economic Emancipation of the Peasantry." Its organizers have sought to build a system of local unions, designed to attack a variety of peasant problems, more or less simultaneously. These include land, credit, production, agricultural technique, marketing, and bargaining with both government and private employers. The FCV has helped the peasant gain control over his environment in innumerable ways, which range all the way from providing him with access to international credit, technology, and markets to helping him obtain the use of the neighboring landlord's water supply for his thirsty cattle.

It is remarkable that the FCV was able to achieve such rapid and profound change in deeply rooted rural structures without appreciable violence. The reason is important. Immediately following the overthrow of Pérez Jiménez, the FCV initiated widespread land invasions to recover the land which the dictatorship had taken from the peasants. Much of it the FCV had gained initially in the 1945 to 1948 period.[24] Violence was, therefore, incipient. By 1961, however, the Betancourt government, with FCV help, had reopened sufficient channels of power to the peasants and established adequate means for orderly change with the temporary landowners so that violence was not necessary. Peasant leaders, at least for the time being, were able to achieve their objectives within the system, using their representational capacities.

Of special interest, particularly for the purpose of our doctrine, is the complex of income-producing *campesino* service enterprises which the FCV began to establish in 1965 and which today are given high priority. The first was SUCAM (Suministros Campesinos), a privately managed firm in which the FCV is principal stockholder. It imports agricultural and farm machinery for sale to FCV organizations and members. Its control of and access to a large, dependable, and expanding market allows SUCAM to buy from United States and European manufacturers in some quantity, to sell at minimum prices, and to provide servicing and spare parts efficiently and at low cost. *Campesinos* have been able to buy tractors, for example, through SUCAM for as much as 25 per cent below the general commercial price.[25] FCV has contracted with its foreign equipment suppliers to establish a second enterprise, SERVICAM (Servicios Campesinos), which trains *campesinos* in mechanics and maintenance. SERVICAM plans to operate a network of repair and maintenance stations throughout rural Venezuela. This activity was partly forced on the FCV because of the unwillingness or inability of local farm machinery franchise-holders to repair or service farm equipment.[26]

The federation has also established a rice-processing plant as part of a large, irrigated agrarian-reform project at Calabozo. Known as INDUCAM (Industrias Campesinas), it sells its high-quality rice to a nationwide supermarket chain, CADA (Compania Anónima Distribuidora de Alimentaciones). CADA is one of a number of supermarket operations in Latin America undertaken by IBEC (International Basic Economy Corporation), a Rockefeller enterprise. The market chain is of vital importance to INDUCAM. Without the solid, dependable, and continuing market for its rice which CADA provides, INDUCAM and the farmers who supply it would be thrown back on the cluttered and distorted traditional market system.

The FCV has made other important and innovative forays

against the manifold market problems confronting its membership. In 1963, for example, a bumper harvest of tomatoes at the agrarian-reform settlement of La Julia was lost due to the refusal of the local tomato processors to deal with FCV representatives who were trying to sell the crop. The national leadership thereupon arranged in 1965 for the export of La Julia's crop and that of other nearby farms through United States food companies. In 1967 the federation started the first of what it hopes will be a nationwide chain of urban farmers' markets (MERCAM) to assist the *campesino* in overcoming the barriers which impede the flow of his crop to the consumer and seriously reduce his return.[27]

In its bargaining activities the FCV faces three fronts: the state, the landowners, and employers. Its confrontation with the state occurs with the Agricultural Bank (BAP), the Land Reform Institute (IAN), the Ministry of Agriculture (MAC), and other agencies having to do with land, land titles, credit and technical assistance, and public works such as roads, schools, health facilities, and the like. In these dealings its political influence is of primary importance.

In some areas the federation's major problems are with landowners. In these confrontations it uses its organizational power locally, as well as its political and governmental influence to protect and promote the rights of tenant farmers and sharecroppers.

In other areas where commercial farming is prevalent, the problems of its members are those of salaried workers with an employer. In such cases, the FCV functions in much the same manner as a conventional trade union, bargaining within the framework of an agreement or a contract for wages, hours, and working conditions.

The 650,000 members of the FCV come from a total of some two million rural workers. Their incomes average about $150 a year; 62 per cent of them are illiterate; and they suffer high rates of disease. FCV leadership has tended to be relatively young and well educated. In the early days, leadership generally came from outside the *campesino* community. Today, however, 85 per cent of local leadership comes from among the *campesinos* themselves.

At the national level, however, only 47 per cent come from this background; 22 per cent are the sons of laborers; 18 per cent the sons of professional men; 9 per cent from a business background, and 4 per cent have fathers whom they characterized as large landowners.[28] The biggest problem of the federation is the scarcity of well-trained leaders and administrators.

Perhaps the most important aspect of the FCV structure is its relationship with the Venezuelan political system and the political parties, with FCV leaders holding important positions in the three major parties.[29] The effects of the FCV on Venezuela generally have been substantial. Besides the benefits it has brought the peasants, it has provided an important base of votes for the major parties. Moreover, this base has tended to be more stable and dependable than that in the cities. It is estimated, for example, that in the 1958 and 1963 elections, peasant movements produced more than half the votes for AD and one third of the votes for the other major parties. In addition, since 1958 the FCV, in its political as well as its operating capacity, has played a significant role in assisting and allowing the government to introduce substantial and radical agrarian change, thus benefiting the population in general and not just FCV members.

The flexible relationships and interchanges between the peasant union movement and government seem to promise a continuing basis for orderly change and growth of the Venezuelan nation. Furthermore, the FCV itself appears to have produced significant changes in the motivation and personal characteristics of its leaders and members. When questioned, for example, about their desire to migrate from the countryside to the cities, almost 90 per cent of FCV local leaders indicated satisfaction with what they were doing. Other interviews revealed that members and leaders of the FCV were far more investment-oriented, innovative, and convinced of the value of hard work than most Latin American peasants.[30]

It may be argued that FCV's political ties will be debilitating, as has been the case in several countries, most notably Mexico. There is, however, a crucial difference. In Venezuela, FCV is not tied to a single party. The federation and its component parts can shop around; political parties must compete for its support. This would seem to give it a guarantee of life as an engine of change as long as a reasonably democratic system prevails in the country and its objectives are unattained.

4

At this stage in the development of rural Latin America, peasant organizations appear in general to be in essence revolutionary. In Panama, the Dominican Republic, Northeast Brazil, Chile, Venezuela, Guatemala, and elsewhere, their goals and purposes, indeed their very being, involve a radical change in fundamental structures of land ownership and political power, a realignment of credit and wealth, a reconstruction of the ruling elite. This does not mean that such radical change is generally either understood or intended by peasant leaders. Their objectives are frequently concrete and immediate piecemeal adjustments. Within the context of the environment, however, these seemingly minor adjustments erode traditional and rigid structures and upon accumulation become revolutionary. Theoretically, at least, peasant organizations have the will and the capacity to follow the necessary sequence of change action—agitation, motivation, organization, and commitment—by bringing to bear the essential characteristics—authority, access to power, communication, the capacity to protest, competence, and sustained will.

Exceptions to this rule are Mexico, Bolivia, and Cuba, which have had substantial and real revolutions and where the peasant movements have become more or less the creatures of the ruling revolutionary elite, thus losing their mandate and will for change. This is the familiar sequence at work, in which the children of the revolution become to a certain extent its captives. The once-radical revolutionary forces become institutionalized, creating their own power system and their own bureaucracy to sustain it—what Djilas in Yugoslavia has called the New Class. So the *ejidos* in Mexico and the peasant unions in Bolivia are not so much revolutionary agents as they are institutionalizers of the revolution which has already occurred. In Cuba it is unclear what sort of peasant organization Castro has allowed, but it is quite reasonable to assume that it is not a revolutionary force.

Whether or not these revolutionary movements create or use

violence seems to depend on their objectives, the speed with which they seek fulfillment of those objectives, the nature of the obstacles in the path to fulfillment, and the alternatives which they perceive. In Venezuela in 1958 peasants were prepared to risk violence to regain the land which the dictatorship had taken from them. The government, however, was quick enough in opening up new channels and the structure of the FCV was penetrating enough to take advantage of those channels so that change came without violence. In Guatemala, on the other hand, the structure of government and the weakness of peasant organization and leadership make sporadic violence virtually inevitable.

The chaos of *La Violencia* in Colombia is another example of violence—ten years of it—arising out of aimlessness and disorganization on the side of both peasants and government. "The violence" started in 1948 as a Conservative-Liberal political civil war, but was continued in the countryside as a form of "sociopolitical banditry," the peasants turning their kindled wrath in a rather chaotic fashion against the power of the landowners.[31] A third phase was a form of revolutionary guerrilla warfare, aided and abetted by a variety of political forces, some from outside Colombia. Thus, a breakdown in the political structure caused a civil war, which continued in chaotic violence because there was insufficient organization either to clarify objectives or to plan their fulfillment. Lacking organization and access to power, the Colombian peasantry drifted in a limbo of aimless violence. This chaos might have been avoided if the Colombian peasant organization, FANAL, had had something of the capacity and opportunity of Venezuela's *campesino* federation and the political system some of the characteristics of Venezuela's.*

In any case, whether or not peasant movements cultivate

* As in Venezuela, Landsberger and Hewitt explain the absence of violence on the part of the peasant organization in Taretán, Michoacán, Mexico, as being due to a "reasonably high expectation on the part of peasant leaders that working through legitimate channels will eventually get the desired result." (Henry A. Landsberger and Cynthia Hewitt, *Preliminary Report on a Case Study of Mexican Peasant Organization*, Cornell Univ. Press, Ithaca, N.Y., p. 60.

violence seems to depend on what their alternatives are, whether they are able to perceive and effect peaceful solutions to urgent problems, whether there is a habit of violence, and whether the authorities are able and willing to curtail it. The effectiveness of violence in general, as Huntington points out, seems to lie not so much in its "inherent character" as it does in "the shock and novelty involved. It is the demonstrated willingness of a social group to go beyond the accepted patterns of action which gives impetus to its demands." In 1963, for example, the self-immolation of the Buddhist monks in South Viet Nam and the race riots in the United States "helped to produce significant changes in governmental policy and political leadership. Three years later similar events failed to produce similar consequences."[32]

As might be expected, peasant organizations seem to rise and prosper where and when traditional power-holders have lost ground. This loss may be due to a variety of factors. Trujillo destroyed the landed aristocracy of the Dominican Republic, and paved the way for FEDELAC. Declining prices and restriction of world markets weakened the hold of the sugar planters on Northeast Brazil, and opened the way for the peasant leagues. Neglect and general impoverishment have weakened the power of the traditional elites of Veraguas, encouraging if not inspiring CEPAS.[33]

The goals of peasant organizations tend to be broad, covering wide sweeps of the political, social, and economic environment. The organizations themselves are aimed in several directions at once, seeking to alter the peasant's relationships with his environment on a wide front. This organizational direction has arisen because of the practical requirements of the movement and not out of theory. The organizations, therefore, are designed and directed to fit the problems which the peasant confronts. In Latin America they are exceptionally indigenous and legitimate, that is, they are not European, Marxist, or North American transplants. They are homegrown in every sense of the word.

The range of operations of peasant organizations include everything from the provision of credit to bargaining and running profit-making enterprises. Such enterprises seem to be particularly essential to the continued vitality of peasant organizations. They provide badly needed income which cannot as a rule be acquired through dues; they provide a means for short-circuiting middlemen, thus offering goods and services to the *campesinos* at a lower price and at the same time providing him with access to a more profitable market.

Although the working objectives and practices of peasant organizations have been nonviolent, their ideology—their vision of the new community which they hope will emerge—is apt to be radical. At least, it is frequently couched in language which to a North American has a radical ring. The ideology of peasant movements in general tends to be militant, revolutionary, and oriented toward a kind of Christian activism which is consciously distinct from existing systems of economics and politics. Again, we see that these movements are striving for an indigenous spiritual validity, the lack of which is at the root of so much of Latin America's agony and confusion.

Allies outside the peasant community are essential for the success of a *campesino* movement, though the movement must be basically indigenous. These allies perform multiple roles. They provide initial leadership and inspiration, access to power, protection from the status quo, and competence. They are necessary bridges both within the divided peasant world and between that world and the rest of the nation. Allies include the radical Church, political leaders, exceptional bureaucrats and, in a sense, food-processing enterprises.

In Chile, the leader of the Molina Vineyard Workers was Emilio Lorenzini, "a graduate of Chile's best schools and universities," the son of "well-to-do immigrants." [34] Francisco Julião, initiator of the peasant leagues in Brazil, was a landowning lawyer, and the organizers of rival unions were priests, Fathers Crespo and de Melo. Hugo Blanco of La Convención Valley fame in Peru was "an outside intellectual," and he was joined by lawyers and tradesmen from the neighborhood. [35]

At the same time, outside leadership is frequently quick to tire, and peasant organizations generally fail if they do not swiftly generate their own leaders internally. In Veraguas Bishop

McGrath was acutely aware of the importance of identifying, training, and promoting local organizers for CEPAS and the cooperative Juan XXIII. He saw the life of the movement depending upon the speed with which he could transfer his authority and leadership to local lay leaders. These of necessity tend to be young, intelligent, relatively well educated, and energetic.

A final conclusion is that peasant organization is essential to increased agricultural production. Here we confront some interesting ideological byplay. Productive farming requires efficient management, optimal use of land and technology, a satisfied and well-motivated work force, standardized quality and quantity, facilities for processing the products and distributing and marketing them, and access to capital and credit.

These factors may be provided, theoretically, by a variety of organizations, for example:

a) The traditional *hacienda* or plantation, such as the sugar plantations of Northeast Brazil or the coffee farms of Peru and Guatemala.

b) The modern, commercial farm, such as the banana plantations of Central America or the cotton or vegetable farms of northwestern Mexico.

c) The modern peasant farms managed within varying cooperative structures, such as those of the FCV.

d) Combinations of these, such as the FCV farms which sell to IBEC's supermarket chain, the Colombian agrarian reform settlements which sell tomatoes to Grace for processing, and so on.

Again theoretically, each of these forms for the management of agricultural production organizes the peasants to a degree, although in different ways and for different purposes. In some instances, the economic and even the political effects of these different forms are surprisingly similar. The FCV in Venezuela, FEDELAC in the Dominican Republic, and CEPAS in Panama increase agricultural production, increase peasant income, and improve his standard of living. They also increase the *campesino's* political awareness and his capacity to affect his political environment. The same effect can be seen, however, as a result of commercial farm organizations in Mexico. These also have introduced widespread economic change and changed the peasants' political orientation. As we saw earlier, the principal opposition to the ruling PRI is in the commercial farming areas of northern Mexico.

Similarly, United Fruit Company's plantation in Honduras has brought substantial economic and social improvements to workers in incomes, housing, health, and education. It has at the same time been at least a factor in greatly increasing the power of the banana workers in the political environment of Honduras, a power which derives from their organization into what is the strongest union in Central America, SITRATERCO (Union of Workers and Employees of the Tela Railroad Company).

On the other hand, the traditional *hacienda* or plantation form of peasant organization is characterized by low agricultural production and inefficiency. Its management is rarely efficient; its use of land and technology is not optimal; its work force is generally far from satisfied or motivated; its paternal, semifeudal social structure and employer-employee relationships are no longer valid, and so on. Thus, efficiency of production may vary directly with the degree and appropriateness of peasant organization.

As to the future, it seems likely that peasant organizations will continue to grow and to be the cutting edge of revolutionary change in Latin America, especially in alliance with other forces. These may be Castroite guerrilla bands, components of the radical Church, political parties, or various kinds of entrepreneurial organizations. The *campesino* organizations have snatched the revolutionary gauntlet from the older, urban-based trade unions, and it seems unlikely that the traditional unions will either join or compete with peasant organizations as change engines. They have become too firmly attached to the status quo.

5

As most of the important, traditional, urban-oriented trade unions of Latin America are associated internationally with ORIT, so peasant organizations are feeling an increasing affinity with

CLASC, or with what CLASC symbolizes. This does not mean that these organizations are formally connected to CLASC. In many instances—the FCV, for example—they are not. But this is not necessarily significant. Spiritually, emotionally, and ideologically, CLASC is coming to speak for peasant movements, and substantively it is giving them assistance, especially in the Dominican Republic. A broad cleavage has thus developed between the well-established, United States-oriented, ORIT-affiliated, conventional unions, on the one hand, and the newer, unorthodox, and revolutionary movements of the countryside.

CLASC, founded in 1954, has a small meaningful affiliated membership, perhaps less than a million. (It claims a total of five million members, of whom no more than 300,000 pay dues.) CLASC is highly ideological in outlook, believing in fundamental social and economic revolution based on Christian principles. Although it praised John F. Kennedy, it has become increasingly hostile to the United States. CLASC advocates Latin Americanism (as opposed to Pan Americanism) as a militant force against what it sees as the imperialism of United States power, rejecting notions of inter-American labor solidarity, an issue which has been such a strong factor in ORIT's development; and it is openly hostile to the AIFLD. It sees itself as standing between the Communist labor organization in Latin America, the Unified Center of Latin American Workers (CUTAL), and "capitalist" labor (ORIT). It thus rejects Washington, Moscow, and Havana, although many believe it is moving perceptibly closer to the latter two.

Emilio Maspero has been general secretary of CLASC since 1963 and is its leading voice. Ebullient and antagonistic, Maspero has a strong appeal for young idealists. "In Latin America," he writes, "trade unionism constantly comes face to face with the greed for power of Communism, with the utilitarian ambitions of capitalism, and with the programs of various dictators and political parties. . . . The only feasible goal for labor in Latin America is to organize the working forces in a decisive manner as an instrument for effecting social revolution." [36]

For many years CLASC was regarded by American labor and government as an inconsequential upstart, mouthing impractical,

unreal, and unfriendly spiritualisms. Its lack of pragmatism made
it almost inevitable that Americans would regard it with disdain. More important for all concerned, however, CLASC was
until recently systematically excluded from all United States
assistance programs—the Alliance for Progress, AID, and the
AIFLD. This has been bitterly resented. In some countries efforts
have been made lately to woo back CLASC groups. These have
been disappointing, the organization apparently feeling that it
can get more mileage out of flaunting its refusal to accept United
States help and money. It also is able to get considerable financial
help from European sources.

Numerically, CLASC is small, but it speaks for many more
than are affiliated with it. It is representative of a revolutionary
force which is bound to be of importance in the hemisphere.
A Latin American friend who is a leading Christian Democratic
thinker described ORIT and CLASC as follows:

> ORIT is composed of old labor unions, propped up by
> U.S. money. These unions have been historical misfits,
> guided by two alien ideologies: Marxism and capitalism.
> Without indigenous militancy they have become the kept
> creatures of the status quo—Latin American and North
> American. Tainted by corruption, their leadership old and
> tired, they are frightened of the revolutionary forces which
> are on the move particularly in the countryside.
>
> CLASC is to be sure weak, small and poor. But it has
> the fire of conviction and the energy of youth. Its ideology
> increasingly comes directly from the Latin American peas-
> ant; its purposes are the fulfillment of his needs; its pro-
> grams are fitted to those purposes. It is indigenous, not
> alien. It needs money, but friends in Europe will provide.
> It is the wave of the future.

Arturo Jauregui, the capable and forceful general secretary
of ORIT, answers these criticisms by labeling as "worn-out
gibberish" the contention that ORIT is an instrument of the
United States and countering that in effect CLASC is a bag
of hot air without support among workers. "The persistent and
deceitful campaign carried on by CLASC against the inter-

American free trade union movement forces us to describe it as a mixing bowl of unqualified persons, whose respective past histories identify them as ex-Perónists [Maspero is an Argentine], as ex-Communists, ex-Democrats or ex-leaders of democratic confederations, who for understandable reasons were removed from their ranks." Juaregui also accused CLASC leaders of coming "tamely" to both the United States government and labor seeking money as well as using "high ecclesiastical authorities" for the same purpose.[37]

But the disagreement is more than superficial. It goes to the heart of many misunderstandings and imprecisions which confuse both Americans and Latin Americans about the processes of change and revolution in the hemisphere.

13

BUSINESS AND ENTREPRENEURS:
National and International

Given the characteristics of the Latin American environment, the business enterprise ideally has within its nature the attributes necessary to change that environment.

That the business enterprise theoretically qualifies as an engine of change can be accepted without much argument. Also, the successful enterprise generally possesses the characteristics which we have identified as necessary to produce change in the Latin American environment: authority, communication and access to power, competence, capacity to protect, and continuing will and purpose. As with other theoretical or potential engines of change we have discussed, however, the will and purpose of the enterprise and its leaders may limit its capacity to effect change. The corporation may—and, of course, often does—decide that its best interests lie with the status quo, but the fact remains that it has an innate capacity to cause change.

When the successful enterprise seeks environmental change, it follows the sequence of action which we prescribed for a successful change engine: agitation, motivation, and organization, from which its work force derives a measure of commitment. The degree or nature of agitation which a business practices varies widely, depending on a broad variety of factors: the amount of change it is seeking to cause, the weight it gives to other environmental factors which may be affected by either the agitation itself or by its resulting change, and the extent to which it is associated with other organizations, such as a trade union, upon which it can count not only to agitate (or prepare) its work force but also to motivate and organize that force for change.

In fact, abstractly, the enterprise is perhaps the most ideal engine of change of those which we have discussed, because it is fundamentally designed to sustain itself financially. Organizations for socio-economic and political change, such as CEPAS and the Venezuelan Campesino Federation, often find it necessary to acquire profitable enterprises in order to improve their ability to confront a broader environmental arc as well as to provide income for the benefit of the organization and its membership. But since their income-producing elements are frail, these organizations frequently find themselves dependent on financial injections from outside sources, such as government, political parties, or Christian charity. The efficient business enterprise, on the other hand, is modeled to be self-sufficient; deep within its very design is the means for satisfying the market upon which it depends. Its managers are theoretically trained in the skills of production of goods or services; it is built to have access to necessary sources of credit and finance; it is organized to reach the markets for its product in the most direct and profitable fashion. These integrative characteristics of the business, besides making it prosperous and self-sufficient, also enhance directly its abilities as a change engine, providing it with unusual capacities to bridge the gaps, and fill the vacuums which impede change in the Latin American environment.

So much for theoretical speculation.

In practice, there are wide differences between enterprises when they are measured according to change produced. Two general categories of entrepreneurial activity suggest themselves.[1]

The first includes that which is relatively traditional, routine, and well established. The techniques of production are well known, the markets clearly defined, the return on investment relatively secure, immediate, and generous. The level of risk is low, the degree of enterprise required minimal. Without drawing too fine a line, activities in this category tend to be urban-oriented and include ordinary import substitution—the production of consumer items, and building materials, for example—retail trade, commerce and banking, traditional transportation, power and utilities. Those rural enterprises which fall within category one include plantation agriculture and mining, undertaken in the traditional way. Except for mining, such enterprises are largely owned and managed by nationals. In some cases they may have been initiated by foreigners, but as they become routine and traditional the pressure increases for nationals to take them over. Electric power companies are a case in point. Requiring substantial risk, capital, innovation, and technological proficiency to start, these companies have tended to be in foreign hands until they became sufficiently well established to be taken over locally. Railroads have followed a similar sequence.

The second category includes entrepreneurial activities which are likely to be innovative, risky, and capital intensive. The techniques of production are new and complex and the markets tend to be large—even global—but relatively undefined, disorganized, or distant. The return on investment is initially often small; and requirements for research, development, and planning are high. It is in category two that foreign investment, management, and technology are most welcome and prevalent. This category includes such industries as new chemicals and plastics, advanced electronics and manufacturing, and, most important—for the purposes of our argument—enterprises engaged in large-scale integrated commercial food production, processing, and distribution.[2]

It would be most inaccurate, of course, to suggest that all national enterprises are in category one and all foreign firms in category two, but it is reasonable to suggest this as a generality. Many border-line cases are in transition from the second to the first—electric power and mining companies, for example. Historically, foreign technology, management, market access, and capital were essential to the success of a new large-scale mining enterprise. Over time, this dependence on foreigners has diminished, as the technical competence of nationals and the confidence and power of their governments have increased. It is now an uphill battle for the foreign mining companies to protect their interests in Latin America from nationalist incursions. One device used to do so is exemplified by the oil companies in Venezuela. Besides paying something like 60 per cent of their profits to government, they also have invested substantially in petrochemicals and other development-oriented industries requiring sophisticated research and technology. Much as many Latin Americans would like to own and control the wealth in their mountains and beneath their soil, the fact remains that whether it is oil in Venezuela, zinc in Bolivia, or manganese in the Amazonian wilderness of Brazil,* at this stage foreign capital, technology, and management are necessary to unearth, process, and market it. Mining, then, like electric power, is an example of an entrepreneurial activity which starts in category two— innovative, capital intensive, and risky—but which inexorably moves into category one. And just as it is difficult for a foreign-owned company to survive in a category one activity, so it is unusual for a domestic entrepreneur to move into category two without some form of foreign partnership or assistance.

Since category two undertakings are most essentially involved with change, they are apt to qualify more often than category one enterprises as engines of change. It follows, then, that foreign firms and their local partners are more often engines of change than those which are purely domestic, which accounts for their indispensability in the change or development process. Likewise, this fact explains many of the difficulties which the foreign company encounters in Latin America. Carrying with him the means and the threat of radical change, the foreign manager—a conservative perhaps at home—frequently fails to recognize how revolutionary he appears to local power holders. This phenomenon among others shows the importance and urgency of increasing to the utmost the managerial capacity of Latin

---

* Bethlehem Steel's ICOMI (Industria e Comercio de Minerías, S.A.) manganese mines are located in Serra do Navio in the jungles of Amopa, two hundred kilometers north of the Amazon River. The deposit was discovered in 1946 when Mario Cruz, a local trader, dug a piece of black rock from the banks of the Amopore River to use as ballast for his canoe. That rock was found to be high-grade manganese ore.

Americans, and consequently their ability to move themselves with force and confidence into more category two activities.

I

Before turning to the more extreme entrepreneurial engines of change which are now generally in the hands of giant multinational firms, let us consider where domestic entrepreneurs and their organizations register on the change scale.

As with so much already written, an apology and a caution concerning generalization must be noted. I have been closely involved with Latin American businessmen off and on during the past half dozen years. There is among them fully as wide a range of intelligence, capacity, talent, and vision as among any business community anywhere. And yet, like the rest of us, they are to an extent creatures of their environment, formed by its standards, moved by its values, and governed by its traditions. They live and work and utilize their power within the economic, political, and social framework which has been delineated earlier. Culturally, they are perhaps more affected by the United States than any other single group, but beneath the surface lie the values, the priorities, and the agony of Latin American culture.

Latin American entrepreneurs can be arranged in order of their will and capacity to initiate change. Most protective of the status quo and confident of its maintenance is the hard core of the Tolerant Oligarchy, the *latifundista* with his vast and inefficient land-holdings, his exploited workers, and the surrounding community of neglect and despair. Around him in the seats of power sits a varied array of men of commerce and industry, generally old men with antiquated, inherited businesses, *patrones* in the true sense of the word. They tend to be authoritarian, inflexible, aristocratic, regarding their workers as dependent children, treating them as they deem fair. For these men, change appears as a monstrous danger, a threat to all they cherish, the devilish plot of the Communist or of United States materialists. They see society as closed and hierarchical, and are resentful of the modernity which makes it open and flexible. The *latifundistas* deplore the technology, the science, and the knowledge which they cannot understand or control.

What worries their more perceptive colleagues and their sons, who comprise a second group, is what it will take to shake their hold. This second group is composed of industrialists, entrepreneurs, and businessmen in general, perhaps younger than the first, more technically educated—often in the United States or Europe—who see the inevitability of radical structural change; who acknowledge its necessity theoretically; but who are unable or unwilling to accept it in reality. Unable to see their path in the labyrinth of revolution and fearful of its awful consequences, they seek solace and protection in the status quo.

The third group are the new managers and entrepreneurs of Latin America who understand the necessity of radical change, are prepared to accept its risks, and are working to guide and direct their activities in ways which are harmonious and complementary to it. It is this new elite which is most critical to the construction of the organizations through which the vast changes demanded by Latin America must take place. The importance of the new managers derives not from their numbers, since they are few, but from the fact that they have a unique combination of power, knowledge, competence, and vision. The question is whether they have enough time before they are overtaken by the massive change which may well submerge them.

Many of these new entrepreneurs are the sons of professional men, but many are self-made. Some are the children of recent immigrants. They are found in virtually every country of the hemisphere. Quite a few of these entrepreneurs have felt the pressure of the radical Church and have been inspired and stimulated by its call to social action. They belong to Christian Democratic groups or to church organizations such as the European-centered UNIAPAC (the International Christian Union of Business Executives, or l'Union Internationale Chrétienne des Dirigéants d'Entreprise).

Their companies and factories are growing and prospering, frequently in some form of partnership with foreign companies. Increasingly, they are abandoning the paternal ways of their predecessors and are accepting, if not encouraging, the organization of their employees into bargaining units through which their workers may for the first time achieve a sense of power and confidence. They are developing the skills and capacities for effective business and government planning to secure efficient and cooperative development. Indeed, a number of them are accepting temporary assignments in government.

It is these new managers who are pressing most urgently for improved education in Latin America, particularly for education focused on the real problems of the community. These are the men who in Central America have banded together to contribute time, money, and prestige to the establishment of a new regional graduate school of management (INCAE). This institute is now graduating about fifty young Central Americans a year from a two-year, full-time master's program. Similar advanced educational efforts have been started in Monterrey (in 1943), Cali, Lima, São Paulo, and elsewhere.

As leaders for change, the new managers are the target of opposition from both the right and the left. What is perhaps more insidious, however, is that they, like so many committed to change before them, are being sorely tempted to enroll in the old oligarchy, to agree to play by its rules, and to conform to its tempo. It will take unusual strength, capacity, and vision for them to resist the temptation to abdicate leadership to those who have always held it.

Rufo López Fresquet, the Cuban economist and historian who assisted Castro in the Sierra Maestra later to flee his tyranny, holds to the persuasive theory that the root cause of Castro in Cuba today was the abdication of leadership by progressive Cuban business leaders in the early 1940's. By relinquishing their control and obligations they provided the basis for Batista's corrosive dictatorship and thus for Castro himself.

There are, however, compelling forces pulling Latin America's new managers from such a course and driving them and their enterprises in the direction of radical and deep change. Foremost among these are their own self-interest and the welfare of their companies. Consider, for example, the hypothetical case of Aire Libre S.A., a sugar mill and plantation which is very typical of many in Latin America. Since we already know the province of Veraguas in Panama, we shall asume that it is located there.

Owned by one of the country's leading families, Aire Libre is managed by Señor Váldez, a well-educated Cuban emigrant with considerable experience in sugar production in Cuba before Castro forced his exile. In 1965 Aire Libre had total sales of $3.5 million, producing 410,000 *quintales* of sugar. One third was produced from cane raised on its own fields and two thirds from the cane of *colonos,* small peasant farmers who grow cane to sell to the mill in addition to subsistence crops of rice and corn.

Señor Váldez has a number of problems.

He wants to produce more cane so he can sell more to the United States, since his country's sugar quota is frequently unfilled. But he does not want to increase the amount of land planted in cane; it is already difficult and costly to carry cane by truck from the fields within the twenty-mile radius now serving the mill, and property is not readily available to add to the mill's own land. He is, therefore, faced with the problem of somehow prevailing upon the *colonos* to increase their yield of cane per hectare (which is now very low—40 tons per year compared to 100 tons on the mill's lands and 160 tons on the best Cuban land).

Mindful of what befell his homeland, Señor Váldez is also concerned about signs of unrest among the *campesinos.* He fears "Communists and agitators," who in recent years he feels have become more prevalent. Several years earlier, the National Federation of Sugar Workers had organized the workers in the mill itself and they had struck for higher wages. The company refused their demands, arguing that they were already receiving well above the government minimum. There was sporadic violence, and Aire Libre's union members joined with workers from other mills and marched on the capital city to demand government intervention. Newspapers at the time reported that the strike and the march were led by Communists. "I see more dangers in this country than I did in Cuba a few years ago," Señor Váldez said. "This country is more backward.

"We want to have better producers in the broadest sense," he went on, "ones who are more prosperous, better prepared, better educated, better equipped. From this flows our policy of attempting to introduce tractors, fertilizer, and insecticides among the *colonos.*" The mill has four inspectors, who are supposed

to keep in touch with its one thousand *colonos* to insure that
their land is properly prepared for seeding, to encourage the
use of fertilizers, to approve mill loans, and to answer their
questions.

In spite of the mill's efforts, however, *colono* productivity
is actually decreasing. "The *campesino* does not trust anyone,"
explains Váldez. "He lacks confidence; he is apathetic."

But the world, of course, looks different to the *campesino*
than it does to Señor Váldez. The *campesino* lives in an environment over which he has no control. Apart from the $75
or so which he may receive each year for his cane, he has little.
He depends for food on the rice and corn which he generally
grows among his cane, a practice which decreases the yield of
all three crops and is unsuccessfully discouraged by the mill. He
does not understand the complicated formula by which the mill
pays him for his cane; he resents what he conceives to be
exorbitant charges by the truckers for transporting the harvest;
he is reluctant to accept credit from the mill for equipment,
fertilizer, and insecticides because he does not want to increase
his burden of debt. When he does obtain credit, he is more
than likely to use it for drink to drown his troubles.

He is impervious to the "demonstration effect" which the
mill's own efficiently cultivated land is supposed to have on
him. He is unwilling to learn from the United-States-financed
agricultural school nearby. A *colono* from Veraguas attended a
one-week program at this school on the use of fertilizers. He did
not practice what he had learned, nor did he communicate any
of it to his fellow *campesinos*. When asked why, he replied
with the same litany of hopelessness and fatalism with which he
accepts his unchanging lot.

Things are changing in Veraguas, however. Last year one
of the CEPAS cooperative groups undertook to organize its
own cane production. The group obtained the use of the cooperative's tractor, bought fertilizer and insecticide from the
cooperative's store, and were regular attendants at the CEPAS
agricultural programs. They planted and cultivated a larger
field of cane than ever before and grew their rice and corn
separately. Their yields were as high or higher than that of

Aire Libre itself on its own land. They are negotiating now to purchase a truck for the cooperative so as to liberate themselves from high trucking charges, and they are beginning to think about challenging the formula on the basis of which they are paid by the mill.

Señor Váldez is thus in a position to associate Aire Libre with an important engine of change in Veraguas. In a modest way the mill has already been such an engine itself; its future depends upon its being more so. By encouraging and assisting the organization of his *colonos* he can increase their confidence, their hope, their trust, their power; he can thus increase their motivation. In this way he can achieve his first objective.

But Señor Váldez is uncertain about such a course. The Veraguas cooperative organization is rumored to be "a hotbed of Christian Democracy" in a country in which such a label is considered dangerously radical. He is concerned that an independent organization of *colonos* may bring with it the unsettling problems of the union: agitators, strikes, and continuing protest. He wonders whether the mill cannot maintain its old control, increasing the number of inspectors, organizing the *colonos* under the mill's direction, continuing the traditional paternal structure, maintaining the *campesino* in his traditional environmental relationship.

As of this writing, Señor Váldez has not made his decision. In the case of the group of *colonos* who have taken the initiative within the CEPAS movement, his decision was made for him. It seems plain that if he chooses to continue the old paternalistic way, he may succeed in advancing the motivation of the cane growers to increase their productivity and thus mill profits. He may increase the bargaining power of the *colonos* with the truckers, and conceivably even with the mill. He may thus make the mill into a more effective engine of change in Veraguas.

On the other hand, if he were to choose a course of collaboration with CEPAS, taking advantage of the movement's leadership and proven effectiveness in agitating, motivating, and obtaining the organization and the commitment of the *campesino*, he could become an integral part of a far more extensive and substantial change engine. In this case, the Church's role and influence being what it is, the risk of "Communist" subversion would appear negligible and the opportunity for Aire Libre to achieve its primary objective would seem substantial. If Señor Váldez were to choose the more radical course, it would hasten the time when the mill itself has to make a more extensive commitment to the refabrication of many elements in the environment. The mill would be in the midst of the political effort upon which economic change depends—for itself as well as in general.

Such a decision is understandably difficult for Señor Váldez and the owners of Aire Libre. It would represent a radical departure from deeply held notions. Profitable as it might be in terms of increased productivity of cane, it also carries risks. The test is whether or not Latin American entrepreneurs will make engines of change of their organizations.

Farming operations need not necessarily be attached to cooperatives in order for change to take place. Certainly, the large private commercial farms of Mexico are formidable engines of change, much more so indeed than the impoverished ejidal cooperatives. Yields of the most flourishing Mexican agriculture are even surpassing those across the border in the United States. But it must be remembered that managers and workers of these farms are children of a profound revolution. The traditional environmental structures were overturned and shattered. The way was clear for entrepreneurs to build anew with maximum efficiency. But for nearly all of rural Latin America there has been no revolution. In a sense, therefore, it is up to managers like Señor Váldez and organizations like CEPAS to effect revolution as part of their commercial pursuits. It seems increasingly clear that they cannot have one without the other.

2

There are other ways in which the domestic enterprise functions as an engine of change than those which we have described at Aire Libre. Many scholars, most notably Alex Inkeles, have noted the strong effect of the factory in motivating and organizing rural men for participation in a larger world than that from which they came. Not only does the factory cast men together for cooperative action, but it seems to have a profound influence on their values and on their conception of life. It emphasizes rationality over mystical fatalism, performance and skill over hierarchical status, and innovation and invention over the existing order. Further, the factory tends to teach the necessity of organization and planning, the value of education and training, the possibility of dominance over one's environment, confidence in and respect for science and technology. Since it brings men together who previously may have lived in extremely atomistic communities, the factory also teaches awareness of others and, in a surprising way, the dignity of the individual. Although perhaps the factory threatens that dignity, the numerous human encounters in the factory day after day in the normal course of work also make men aware of their own dignity and of that of others. In these ways, the factory is surely an engine of change, following very much our prescribed sequence of action.

Also, the factory tends to raise incomes so that workers have enough to eat, as well as both the energy and the time to participate more in the life of their community—the more so since the factory has organized them, whether through a union or not. There is good reason to speculate that the more a man earns, the more he is moved to participate in the political process. Few really poor people are radicals. There is considerable evidence to suggest that in Latin America, as well as in the United States, radicalism rises with income.[3]

Finally, the enterprise becomes an engine of change at those critical occasions when it coalesces and galvanizes many events and circumstances by its injection of one relatively small factor. I am unable to find as good an example of such a happening in Latin America as that of the large-scale introduction of tube wells for irrigation in Pakistan.

During the 1950's growth in agricultural output in Pakistan was roughly 1 per cent a year, well below the rate of population increase, despite the fact that agriculture employed nearly three quarters of the labor force.[4] Between 1960 and 1965, however, agricultural output increased at the rate of 3.5 per cent, and it has been nearly 4 per cent in recent years. One of the major causes for this jump was the increased availability of irrigation, fertilizer, seed, and farm equipment, chief among these being irrigation. Between 1960 and 1965 an additional eleven million acre feet of irrigation were applied. Although many factors were responsible for this increase, including government policies, changes in the motivation of the farmers, technical assistance, and the like, the critical factor seems to have been the unplanned and unexpected introduction of tube wells. This alone accounted for five million additional acre feet of irrigation and for fully half the increase in agricultural output.[5]

In 1960 there were 1,350 tube wells in West Pakistan; by July 1965, there were 31,500. For approximately thirty years the government had been sinking small numbers of tube wells and helping to spread the idea of irrigation. But the astounding increase in tube wells between 1960 and 1965 was due to their private manufacture and installation. Entrepreneurs thus were essential catalysts of this change; and, incidentally, the wells were extraordinarily profitable. Some 20 per cent of the installations were made by investors in the towns that had little or no land.[6] A substantial machine-tool industry to manufacture pumps and engines accompanied increased use of the wells, and the government encouraged their development by incentives, reduction in taxes, and the lifting of various controls.

It might seem that the change effect of tube wells in Pakistan, if applied to Latin America, would violate our earlier conclusion that economic and technical injections are secondary producers of change. But on a closer look it is plain that the tube-well business did not take off until the countryside had undergone substantial political preparation. The large, commercial farmers followed the lead of government demonstrators and gave effect to their efforts. As in Mexico, these relatively modern and politicized entrepreneurs had all the characteristics necessary to receive and utilize technical and material inputs.

3

It is important to assess the influence of foreign entrepreneurial activity in Latin America. United States assets and investment total something more than $20 billion, about one half of which is in direct private investment: some six billion of this is more or less equally divided between manufacturing and petroleum, 1.2 billion is in mining and smelting, a little over half a billion in utilities, and something over a billion in trade. The remainder, about a billion, is invested in "other" fields (see Tables 5 and 6). If we look at net capital outflows from the United States to manufacturing affiliates in Latin America, we find that chemicals and allied products are the largest and fastest-growing sector. This follows the principle set out earlier that foreign investment is most welcome and useful in entrepreneurial activity in which the foreigner brings something which is both unique and essential: technology, invention, innovation, management, and market access. Of special interest to us are food products, where capital outflows have been sporadic but substantial.[7]

It seems reasonable to predict that in the normal course of events United States entrepreneurial activity will increase and prosper in those fields of endeavor to which it brings these unique and essential services. When the enterprise's services cease to meet this standard, it becomes naturally vulnerable to national forces which say: "We can do as well or better ourselves." The enforcement of this principle is likely to become increasingly strict and pervasive as Latin American states pursue, as they must, policies aimed at nationalizing their historically nonnationalized jurisdictions. That they have the bargaining power versus foreign investors to pursue such policies seems evident for several reasons.

First, the state can point to strong internal pressures to which it must respond. Not the least of these is the radical Church and its allies in politics, labor, and the universities. The vociferous pronouncements and demonstrations of Acão Popular, the left-wing Catholic students' organization in Brazil, demonstrates the sort of anti-United States business sentiment with which the Brazilian government must reckon. In Brazil, as elsewhere, there is also an invigorated anti-American alliance between the Communist Party and Brazilian businessmen, who fear United States competition and resent what is seen as special favors from government to foreign business.* Particularly rankling to Brazilians was

---

* Peru's nationalization program has shown that the military also may constitute a strong pressure for the curtailment of certain types of foreign business control.

TABLE 5

Type of Investment	Total			Western Europe	
	*1965*r	*1966*r	*1967*p	*1966*r	*1967*p
U.S. Assets and Investments Abroad (Total)	106,270	111,840	122,292	32,039	35,378
Private Investments	81,147	86,321	93,287	23,342	25,279
Long-term	70,994	75,715	81,442	20,723	22,569
Direct	49,424	54,711	59,267	16,209	17,882

r Revised   p Preliminary
Source: *Survey of Current Business*, October 1968, p. 20.

pressure from our government, backed by United States business, to prevent soluble coffee manufactured in Brazil from entering the United States market. Brazilian entrepreneurs felt let down by their own government on this issue and were vocal in protest. The United States pressured the Brazilian government to tax exports of soluble coffee sufficiently to eliminate the cost advantage over United States producers in North American markets. Also, Brazilian businessmen feel that their government has ruined many companies by raising the cost of credit, while business in the United States has flourished with easy access to cheaper credit. A distinguished Brazilian newspaper editor sees the issue as involving a form of collusion between the ruling Brazilian elite and United States interests, government, and business. "Should the solution be left to elites that have shown no ability to solve problems or do we believe that the people should have more say?" he asks.[8] There seems little doubt that pressures on Latin American governments will increasingly give them power in bargaining with foreign entrepreneurs, whether they like it or not.

International Investment Position of the United States at Year-end
(Millions of Dollars)

Canada		Latin American Republics		Other Foreign Countries		International Organizations and Unallocated	
1966ʳ	*1967ᵖ*	*1966ʳ*	*1967ᵖ*	*1966ʳ*	*1967ᵖ*	*1966ʳ*	*1967ᵖ*
27,705	29,368	19,287	20,748	28,249	31,691	4,560	5,107
27,693	29,330	15,102	16,172	17,045	19,028	3,139	3,478
26,565	28,103	12,294	13,083	12,994	14,209	3,139	3,478
16,999	18,069	9,826	10,213	9,661	10,782	2,016²	2,321²

² Represents the estimated investment in shipping companies registered primarily in Panama and Liberia.

Closely related is a second reason why Latin America's governments have found their bargaining power increased: In almost every country there has been a dramatic increase in local entrepreneurship, both public and private. Much of this has been spawned by United States business itself, but there can be little doubt that these new managers want to get out from under this domination as quickly as they can.

Thirdly, the change in the nature of the conflict between the United States and the Soviet Union, combined with the increasing realization by the United States of the limitations on its power, have tended to diminish the responsiveness of the United States government to the cries for protection against nationalism of United States companies abroad. American business is realizing that Washington and its embassies are of questionable value in a Latin American scuffle.*

* Raymond Vernon suggests some additional and complementary reasons for the increased bargaining power of host governments over foreign oil companies: "the proliferation of crude oil sources; the growing availability of packaged

TABLE 6

Line	Area and Country	Total	1966ʳ Mining and Smelt- ing	Petro- leum	Man- ufac- tur- ing	Pub- lic Utili- ties
1	All Areas (Total)	54,711	4,315	16,205	22,058	2,284
2	Canada	16,999	2,089	3,608	7,675	495
3	Latin American Republics (Total)	9,826	1,148	2,897	3,081	624
4	Mexico	1,248	108	42	802	29
5	Panama	792	19	153	28	44
6	Other Central America and West Indies	683	35	162	82	154
7	Argentina	1,035	(*)	(*)	656	(*)
8	Brazil	1,247	58	69	846	38
9	Chile	844	494	(*)	51	(*)
10	Colombia	571	(*)	277	190	29
11	Peru	548	291	29	93	22
12	Venezuela	2,615	(*)	1,862	291	19
13	Other Countries	242	12	96	44	25
14	Other Western Hemisphere	1,622	367	578	236	48
15	Europe (Total)	16,209	54	3,981	8,876	67

ʳ Revised   ᵖ Preliminary
* Combined in "Other" industries

It seems unlikely that any administration will send the marines
in to protect a United States company. Even the Hickenlooper
Amendment to the Foreign Assistance Act is outdated and im-

refineries purchasable on a turnkey basis; and the greater ease with which such
operations can be financed, due to the appearance of new financial sources
such as the World Bank institutions and the regional banks." "Conflict and
Resolution Between Foreign and Direct Investors and Less Developed Countries," *Public Policy*, Vol. XVII, Fall 1968, John F. Kennedy School of
Public Administration, Harvard University, Cambridge, Mass., p. 344.

Value of Direct Investments Abroad by Selected Countries and Industries at Year-end
(Millions of Dollars)

| | | 1967ᵖ | | | | | | |
Trade	Other	Total	Mining and Smelting	Petroleum	Manufacturing	Public Utilities	Trade	Other
4,716	5,133	59,267	4,810	17,410	24,124	2,387	4,995	5,541
996	2,137	18,069	2,337	3,819	8,083	506	1,032	2,292
1,159	917	10,213	1,218	2,917	3,301	614	1,207	956
152	114	1,342	100	43	890	27	166	115
317	231	804	19	158	33	44	326	223
38	213	756	34	184	104	155	43	237
44	335	1,080	(*)	(*)	677	(*)	53	350
183	53	1,326	68	79	891	32	195	62
32	268	878	517	(*)	61	(*)	37	263
54	21	610	(*)	309	192	28	56	26
63	51	605	340	38	98	22	54	53
253	190	2,553	(*)	1,789	310	19	255	180
22	42	257	16	100	44	27	21	48
87	306	1,708	431	585	271	51	92	278
1,933	1,297	17,882	61	4,404	9,781	78	2,055	1,504

Source: *Survey of Current Business*, October 1968, p. 24.

practical, if not downright damaging to our country's interests. In 1962 the governor of a Brazilian state seized a United States-owned telephone company, and the federal government of Brazil hesitated to resolve the consequent dispute. Nettled by the failure of the State Department to act forcefully, Congress passed an amendment introduced by Senator Bourke B. Hickenlooper of Iowa. Immune from Presidential waiver, it required that United States aid be cut off if United States property was seized without swift and just compensation. Shortly before the deadline a solution to the dispute in Brazil was worked out.

This seizure by a state government, however, triggered the Brazilian federal government to take over several other utilities owned by American and Foreign Power, a United States company. A settlement was finally made calling for payment by the Brazilian government of $135 million in compensation: $10 million as a down payment and $125 million to be paid over a twenty-two-year period. Seventy-five per cent of the compensation was to be reinvested in nonutility enterprises in Brazil. After this agreement was reached in 1963 the Goulart administration delayed its implementation. In November 1964, after the military take-over, American and Foreign Power began carrying out the terms of the agreement with the new government.[9] Whether or not the Hickenlooper Amendment worked for the benefit of United States enterprise in Brazil, its effectiveness and use elsewhere seem most questionable, given the antagonism its passage caused among Latin American nationalists. The idea of using foreign assistance as a club to coerce foreign governments to behave according to United States interests is highly repugnant to local nationalists; and the takeover of the International Petroleum Company by the military government of Peru has put the issue in its darkest terms yet.

Late in 1968 General Juan Velasco Alvarado's regime seized the $200 million oil fields and refineries belonging to I.P.C., a subsidiary of the Standard Oil Company of New Jersey, against a claimed indebtedness of $690 million. It is now quite apparent that the Hickenlooper Amendment has been of little help in obtaining compensation from the Peruvian Government; in fact, it has been a dreadful embarrassment requiring the U. S. Government to indulge in tortuous legalisms to avoid its application. Under the terms of the Amendment, if full and fair settlement of the controversy was not reached by April 1969 the United States was bound not only to halt all assistance to Peru but, more importantly, to refuse to purchase its regular quota of some forty million dollars' worth of Peruvian sugar. When the April date came it was extended to August and then was extended again. It is reported that the U.S.S.R. stands ready to purchase Peru's sugar if we choose not to. Negotiations under such a ceiling cannot help but be suffocating.

Other forms of U.S. government coercion seem similarly doubtful. In April 1965 the Venezuelan Senate considered legislation requiring that 51 per cent of the shares of all insurance companies in the country be owned by Venezuelans. The bill had already been passed by the Chamber of Deputies over the strenuous opposition of the local United States insurance industry. On April 21, Senator Wayne Morse condemned the Venezuelan bill. He went on to advocate that the Securities and Exchange Commission, which at the time was considering the sale of Venezuelan government bonds in the United States, withhold clearance "until we find out what the Venezuelan Congress is going to do about this form of expropriation of American investments."

One United States insurance company manager in Venezuela wrote to Senator Morse expressing his appreciation, saying that he and his colleagues had repeatedly asked the State Department for help, but had been told only that the department could not interfere in the internal affairs of another country. Unfortunately for the American insurance men, Senator Morse's speech galvanized Venezuelan support for the bill, which passed by an overwhelming majority in June and was signed by President Leoni on July 2.[10]

These experiences are teaching United States companies that their survival and prosperity in the changing environment of Latin America depend very much on themselves, the way they use their substantial power, and the intelligence and imagination with which they direct their activities.* The ability of their government to help them is becoming increasingly restricted; and indeed most company officials with whom I have spoken do not want it otherwise. Their biggest complaint, in fact, is that their government unduly restricts the companies' activities by, for example, limiting their capacity to invest abroad in what

* For a cogent review of Latin American attitudes toward United States companies, see Miguel S. Wionczek, "A Latin American View," in *How Latin America Views the U.S. Investor,* Raymond Vernon, ed., Frederick A. Praeger, New York, 1966.

many feel is a short-sighted approach to our balance of payments problem.* If a company needs to call on the power of the United States government to protect it against the economic and political forces which are plainly and visibly at work, it has somehow failed to manage itself and its interests properly. United States entrepreneurs are more than ever alert to the subtle differences between the traditional companies, which are under national pressures, and innovative firms, where the principal challenge and opportunity exist for them. They are also becoming adept at detecting when their operations slide from the second to the first category.

No longer, for example, does the thought of intervention by local governments strike terror. In fact, as we saw in Chile, Kennecott Copper willingly sold 51 per cent of its huge El Teniente mine to the Chilean government (Anaconda later followed suit) and then proceeded to lend the new company $93 million to help finance a $230-million five-year program to raise copper production by 60 per cent. In spite of the fact that Kennecott now has but a minority interest in the mine, Chilean tax rates have been cut so drastically that its share in El Teniente's earnings rose from 19 per cent in 1966 to 27 per cent in 1968.[11] **

United States entrepreneurs in Latin America thus tend to be in the forefront of change. A good many of their difficulties arise from this fact. Their new technology and methods, as well as their financial and marketing strength, make them formidable competitors. The political and social tradition which they bring with

* Another example of a United States company being adversely affected by its government's policies was the rebuff in July 1968 by the Argentine military regime of an attempt by the United States Steel Corporation to buy a one-third interest in Argentina's largest private steel company. The military, which controls such things, reportedly was vexed at United States government efforts to curb Latin American arms purchases and wanted, therefore, to open up more connections with Europe. (*Business Week,* July 13, 1968.)
** British international companies have long been adept at such sailing with the winds of change, none more so than Booker McConnell, one of the last survivors of the great British trading companies. Its deputy chairman in Zambia gave up his British citizenship to become a Zambian at the same time that the local government became a 51 per cent partner. A similar arrangement was made in Malawi. Withal, the company's after-tax profits between 1947 and 1967 rose from $564,000 to $4.8 million.[12]

them constitutes an equally formidable threat to the status quo. American companies, for example, are with some exceptions well prepared to deal with labor unions in a fair and effective fashion. Latin American businessmen, on the other hand, who in many cases are still caught up in the traditions of paternalism, regard labor organizations as somewhat subversive. They do not thank the North Americans for strengthening their influence.

One segment of American industry bears special analysis, the large international company for production, processing, and distributing food. While constituting a most efficient engine of change in the Latin American countryside, it has also been unusually successful in adjusting itself to the local environment. It has perceived that the revolution under way in Latin America is like a river, falling swiftly sometimes over dangerous rapids, in other places meandering almost imperceptibly; but always moving, and only strengthened by obstruction. It also has seen that large American enterprise is too big and powerful to sit on the bank of this river and watch, reporting the river's progress to headquarters. It is in the river, in a relatively frail craft. The decisions it has to make involve whether it will glide easily with the current, angle across it, or attempt to move directly upstream. The enterprise is also—and here the metaphor falters—a part of the river itself, affecting its strength and direction.

The success of the American food-processing enterprise derives from several important factors which are inherent in the business. It is strongly rooted in the countryside and is designed to increase badly needed food supplies. Even though much of its processing and distribution system may be urban-centered, it is generally not caught up in the competition of the turbulent city, and it is engaged in work which virtually all domestic groups regard as important to the country's development. As one official of W. R. Grace and Company put it: "Can you imagine a senator getting up in the Congress and calling for the nationalization of a manufacturer of baby foods in a country where malnutrition is a continuing problem? It's just not a popular stand." Also, the foreign food company has few local competitors, since the typical Latin American entrepreneurs tend to be urban-oriented. Apart from traditional export staples such as coffee, sugar, cotton, and the like, the risks of commercial agriculture are too high and the profits too long in coming. The entrepreneur tends to be unconvinced of the opportunities which exist for the efficient production, manufacture, and marketing of food for domestic consumption. He knows little about his own countryside, and is understandably apprehensive about venturing into it. Furthermore, his attitude is often one of "Why bother, when I can make high profits in manufacture for import substitution in the big city?" Both indigenous managers and their governments, therefore, are often happy to have foreigners establish food-processing systems in their countries.* The United States company in this field conforms easily to the development plans of the nation.[13]

Without question, the food-processing enterprise simultaneously agitates, motivates, and organizes. For example, Carnation Company's international division, General Milk Company, buys the raw material for its powdered milk operation in Arequipa from some five thousand *campesinos* in southern Peru. To secure quality standards and regularity of supply all three of these actions were necessary. The same can be said for many similar companies. It is not surprising that in the province next to Veraguas, the Nestlé Company has had an effect on the peasants living there similar to that of the CEPAS movement in Veraguas, and much the same procedures were followed.

Another and more dramatic example is that of W. R. Grace and Company in Guatemala, where the company is providing a steady market for a group of Guatemalan farmers who for the first time have entered the cash economy of their country and are tilling their land for profit rather than subsistence. The relationship started in 1966 when Grace acquired Alimentos Kern,

---

* While this statement holds as a generality, there are a number of significant exceptions to it. Anderson Clayton's cotton-seed oil undertaking in Mexico has been the target of continued harassment by local entrepreneurs and the government. General Mills's flour operations in Panama will undoubtedly sustain similar difficulties from competitors who have influence with the local government. Pressures on the foreigner in the food as in other industries increase as his enterprise becomes safer, less innovative, and more traditional; in other words, as it moves toward category one. The recent nationalization of Grace's sugar plantations in Peru is another case in point.

a Guatemalan producer of nectars, juices, and tomato products. In so doing, Grace inherited ties with a group of small farmers in Zacapa, 170 kilometers northeast of the capital, a province which has been notorious for its guerrilla bands. These farmers formed a small cooperative to grow and sell tomatoes. Grace's needs for tomatoes have more than doubled since then, and the farmers' organization has prospered accordingly. The change for the Zacapa *campesino* has been substantial. Apart from a rise in his standard of living, he has found through organization that he can exert influence within his environment. He has access which is wider and deeper than he had ever dreamed possible. He has new power, new confidence, and new dignity.

In Colombia, Grace is following a similar policy of working through a farmers' cooperative. Here again it inherited a going relationship by acquiring a local tomato-processing company, Conservas California, located in Barranquilla. Conservas buys its tomatoes from a group of several hundred families farming a narrow strip of land on the bank of the Magdalena River, between Barranquilla and Calamar. For three months a year, during the rainy season, the land is under water, and when the river recedes it leaves a new deposit of rich soil that is ideal for growing tomatoes. Each year Conservas grows seedlings on its own land, and then ships the young plants upriver to the farmers for transplanting. "We hand out the seedlings," a Grace official explained, "and these guys take off their shoes and walk around ankle-deep in the mud and just put them in the ground—it's that simple. It's too soft for a plow or tractor and you don't even need to dig a hole."

Although an informal cooperative organization has existed among the farmers for more than a decade, only in the last three or four years has it produced significantly greater yields. Working through the cooperative leaders, Grace was able to achieve crop standardization so that adjoining family plots were all planted with tomatoes. This made it possible for the company to spray the entire area from the air with insecticides and fungicides; it also facilitated the inspection of the tomato plants by the company's agronomists.

The company encountered a problem of assuring a regular

supply for the processing plant. Prices in town for fresh tomatoes ran higher than prices paid by canning companies, and when the differential was great enough farmers would bypass the plant and truck their produce to market. To insure a regular supply, the company decided to pay the cooperative a premium for each box of raw tomatoes: the higher the total volume, the higher the premium. The cooperative then took the money and used it for communal projects, such as constructing paths between plots and houses, and experimenting with new seeds and crops.

A Grace official explained that he makes it a practice to maintain contact with the leader of the cooperative. "I try to explain to him what the company is doing. I tell him about our advertising and marketing in the rest of the country, and bring along any new labels or packages we may be using. It's sort of like reporting to a board of directors. He appreciates this, and now identifies with the company to a considerable degree."

Conservas has also set up a business relationship with INCORA, the Colombian land-reform agency. Noting the rapid expansion in the market for tomatoes, INCORA acquired two thousand acres of land in the Barranquilla region for the resettlement of landless peasants and the commercial growing of tomatoes and other crops. The agency then signed a contract with Conservas to supply tomatoes at a fixed price. The agreement provides for no technical or financial assistance on the part of Grace, though an official noted that it was easy to work out informal contacts between the company's agronomists and the directors of INCORA. The general manager of Conservas is himself an agronomist, with close contacts in the land-reform agency.

Drawing on its experience in Guatemala and Colombia, Grace emphasizes the importance of some kind of farmers' organization if a food-processing plant is to succeed in rural areas. "You have to have organization," an official said. "You can't go in and deal with farmers individually and get a truckload of tomatoes today and another in a week and the next no one knows when. You can't run a plant that way."

Grace and other United States food companies have moved

away from the old landlord-tenant relationship and have disarmed the political time bomb of being a large foreign landholder. The Colombian example also demonstrates how effective it can be to work with government land-reform organizations, which can protect the United States company against charges of exploitation. Such a relationship also helps land-reform programs to be efficient, scotching the criticism that land reform means low production. For this reason it should not be surprising if the enemies of Grace in Colombia are the large landowners. For them Grace is a revolutionary.

A distinction must be made between the early operations of Grace, and more especially, those of the United Fruit Company, and the contemporary activities of both these companies and of others like them. When United Fruit began its banana operations, it became the owner of large tracts of land; it built and owned the region's railroads, communication system, and many of its port facilities. It constructed and operated large company towns. It acquired vast economic and political power in small, weak countries. This power was not always used wisely. Until the 1950's United Fruit resisted the organization of its workers into unions. It was a giant in dwarf countries, convinced that its paternalism was beneficent, pointing to its enormous contribution to the local economy and its relatively high wages. But in reality, United Fruit had become an extractive industry. It had brought formidable technical and managerial skills to bear in order to harvest bananas for sale in the markets of the world. It maintained strict distance from surrounding communities, building its plantations into classic models of the foreign enclave.[14]

United Fruit was vulnerable to criticism not because it was exploitative but because of its failure to perceive or to use itself as an engine of change. The company felt it could sit on the banks of the revolutionary river and mind its own business.

The sixties brought great transformations to United Fruit, however, and these are increasing as the seventies approach. Today in Honduras the company is dealing with the strongest labor union in Central America, SITRATERCO (the Tela Railroad workers' union). Under the leadership of an extraordinary Honduran, Oscar Gale, SITRATERCO has taken over

many of the responsibilities of the company in housing and community services. It has given the workers a new sense of participation in the life of Honduras, new political and economic
power, new confidence and dignity. The company has divested
itself of much of its land and most of its nonagricultural properties. More important, it is joining the Central American development community. It is using its unique experience and capacity
to introduce new crops to the area. It is joining with local
partners and employing local managers not only to diversify the
region's agricultural exports but to build internal food supplies
and markets. Realizing that tax payments are not enough to keep
it in an innovative status, United Fruit is applying itself as an
integrated whole to the problems of the region, bringing technology, motivation, organization, processing, packaging, distribution, and marketing to bear inside Central America as well as in
the markets of the world. It has moved into the production of
edible oils, fish products, rice, nuts, and other crops, and it has
done so as part of the local community instead of apart from
it.

Perhaps the most innovative of all United States agricultural
operations in Latin America is IBEC (The International Basic
Economy Corporation), which for more than twenty years has
been pioneering the expansion of production, processing, and
marketing of food in Venezuela, Brazil, Argentina, Colombia,
Peru, and Central America.[15] Backed by the Rockefeller family,
which still holds 70 per cent of the company's equity, IBEC has
concentrated on relatively high-risk ventures with local partners
wherever they are willing to participate. Its objective is both to
promote economic development and to make a profit. So far, it
has established 200 separate IBEC companies in 33 countries, of
which 119 have survived and prospered.[16]

IBEC's greatest contribution has been in showing the way to
the integrated development of systems for food production, processing, distribution, and marketing. In Venezuela, for example,
it started companies to produce, among other things, vegetables,
fish, poultry, and milk. At the same time, it organized a chain
of supermarkets (CADA) to bring these and other food products
to the consumer at the lowest possible cost. In the process it

streamlined all the channels between the field and the consumer, and brought fundamental changes to the agriculture of the country. Among its greatest difficulties has been finding and keeping local partners who are prepared to take risks and wait for profits. In many instances, it has found that a 50–50 division of ownership works best for this purpose. Another of its difficulties is in motivating and organizing the peasants and fishermen with whom it deals. To the extent it has succeeded in doing so IBEC has conformed well to our model of an engine of change. One of IBEC's most important findings is that size is critical to the success of any high-risk, multipurpose, urban-rural venture. Tempted to "start small," IBEC sometimes denied itself the leverage it needed to have a sustained impact on the old and rigid systems which it was trying to change. This requirement of size emphasizes how important the United States food industry—its capital, knowledge and resources—will be in effecting change in rural Latin America.[17]

Many other United States companies in these sorts of activities could be listed: Van Camp in the fishing industry in Ecuador and elsewhere; Corn Products in seven countries; Quaker Oats, particularly its innovative production of Incaparina, a low-cost, high-protein cereal developed by a United Nations task force; Campbell Soup in Mexico and in other countries; The Borden Company, and many others.[18] We have, however, laid sufficient groundwork for a concluding generalization.

There is no doubt that the large, integrated food company can have an extraordinary impact on the *campesino*. He realizes that by providing food of standard quality in regular quantities he can have a consistent market, a greater return on his effort, access to reasonable credit, and continuing supplies of fertilizer, farm equipment, and technical assistance. The *campesino* can also see that he has a protector and a communicator to represent him in the confusing hierarchy of which he has never been a part. Furthermore, he understands that all this comes as part of a continuing institutional process; it is not a one-shot deal offered by a transient technician who is here today and gone tomorrow, or by a government bureaucrat in whom he historically has never been able to have much trust. He can, in short, become inte-

grated into the national structure of his country, politically, socially, and economically.

Food-processing by its nature is often a decentralized industry;
it is frequently better located where food is grown than in cities.
The industry, therefore, helps to bridge the rural-urban gap,
both in providing a source of employment to surplus rural labor
and in slowing the flow of population to the cities. By increasing
the number of wage-earners, it increases consumer buying power
in the countryside and thus provides markets for industries serving rural needs. Moreover, by virtue of its power and importance
relative to what is around it, the food-processing enterprise can
have a profoundly beneficial effect on the total organization of
the community in which it locates. This is by no means limited
to the more efficient production of larger quantities of higher
quality food. The effect can extend as well to the administration of local government, the judicial system, education, skill-
training, the removal of distortions in the credit and market systems, and the introduction of efficient, low-cost transport.

Similarly, the rural-based food-processing plant can have an
important effect on the large central cities where the principal
markets for its product are located. By preserving and processing
food, and by organizing its efficient transport and distribution,
the enterprise can assure the urban consumer of more and higher
quality foods at lower prices. Distribution deserves particular
emphasis. If existing food supplies were evenly distributed, there
would be little shortage.

In sum, the food-processing industry can be an important and
highly constructive agent or revolution in the developing world
—causing radical institutional change, and contributing simultaneously to the solution of virtually every problem on the broad
spectrum of development. Most significantly, however, it can
help to knit together what has been fractured: it can build a
community, connect that community to the nation, and even
connect the nation to the world. Above all it synthesizes and
integrates at a time when integration and synthesis are perhaps
the primary requirements for the orderly and peaceful development of mankind.

4

Partly because of its effectiveness as an engine of change, the foreign firm is bound to be increasingly controversial. Total foreign investment in the Latin American economy is actually modest.[19] But foreign power, real and imaginary, outstrips its size. Nationalist elites, on the one hand, are apprehensive about an outside threat to their country's political and economic independence; and on the other, traditionalists and members of the ruling groups fear the competition and socio-political disruption foreign power brings. Both groups, however, may be cowed by the pronouncements of the economists that in order to reach the per-capita income increase of 2.5 per cent set by the Alliance for Progress an annual injection of foreign private investment of about $550 million is required.[20]

Other factors govern the acceptability of business as an engine of change. They are complicated, often contradictory, emotional, and sometimes irrational, but it is useful to unravel them. First, private business in Latin America is widely held to be fundamentally immoral. Capitalism and private enterprise are for many synonymous with exorbitant profits, exploitation of the poor, tax evasion, and the like. Alberto Lleras Camargo, former President of Colombia, has put it well: "Under the umbrella of capitalism and free enterprise, the United States has grown in power and justice. But in Latin America, the very same system not infrequently has led to odious and infamous concentrations of capital and of means of production. This type of capitalism owns vast land areas—certainly the best land; it scarcely pays any taxes; it controls agricultural and industrial credit; and there is no law or power in the state that can stand against its monolithic advance." [21]

Secondly, this fundamental moral suspicion is exacerbated when it comes to large foreign private enterprises because they are seen as bringing not only size, weight, and power, but outside domination as well. This feeling is one of the strongest forces behind the push for regional integration and cooperation. Many of the new leaders of Latin America are determined to substitute regional interdependence for dependence on foreigners, Latin Americanism for Pan Americanism.[22]

Thirdly, there is the concern that foreign entrepreneurial activities are not harmonious with the requirements of development, and that even if they are, the foreigners will run off with an unfair amount of profits. This presents an interesting dilemma for the foreign corporation. If a United States company repatriates its earnings made in a Latin American country, as Washington has asked, having in mind our balance of payments problems, the company is accused of draining the country's resources. If, on the other hand, it reinvests, it may be accused of seeking increased control over the local country and often of aggravating the host country's balance of payments position.[23]

There are unquestionably variations on these themes, but this is enough to allow us to group the factors impeding the mobilization of foreign entrepreneurial engines of change in Latin America. There is first the issue of sovereignty. Both Latin American states and the United States have historic sovereign interests which they seek to promote and protect in changing but still more or less traditional ways. But even in its evolutionary youth the nation-state is becoming something of an antique. There are many things it cannot do. It cannot coordinate international production, distribution, and marketing; it cannot run an international tele-communication network or an international transport system.[24] The efforts of the various states of the world to build international systems of any kind have been sadly disappointing. Another system of sovereignty is emerging, young, energetic, ill-defined, but growing fast. It is composed of the world corporations which are supranational, multinational, and international. Widely owned, by citizens of many countries, these corporate bodies have more of a public—although nonstatist—than of a private nature, more a global than a national one. They are increasing in number and power, and they will continue to do so as long as their markets are served, because unlike older national sovereigns they do not depend on taxes for survival, but rather on their inherent ability to provide a service in response to a need. The management of these giant organizations comes from many

places and can be thought of as world citizens rather than nationals of a country. Their competence is what counts. Their
function, their markets, their commitment, are international.

These world companies must be regarded as multiservice organizations that perform their integrated global function for a
fee.[25] Their purpose being international, their political and economic interests are only secondarily national; their national interests by the nature of things must be subservient to their international interests.

This, of course, is not the way the sovereignty issue is seen
today in Latin America, or indeed in the United States. Latin
Americans consider the world corporations which are domiciled
in the United States as being in some way agents or creatures
of the United States, and there have been occasions when the
United States too has regarded the word "corporation" with mis-
givings, if not suspicion. The issue has become dramatic with
respect to such legislation as the Trading with the Enemy Act,
under which the United States has placed an embargo on exports to Communist China, North Korea, North Viet Nam, and
Cuba. The French subsidiary of an American company would
be violating United States law if it sold goods to a French firm
which in turn sold the goods to one of these countries, in spite
of the fact that France has no such embargo. We have already
mentioned the difficulties which our balance of payments restraints have caused for United States-based world corporations.
As Raymond Vernon puts it: "the advanced world, carried ebul-
liently on the crest of a technological revolution in transportation and communication, has absentmindedly set up a virile system of international institutions and relationships that sit alongside the system of nation-states." [26] Sometimes the two systems
are complementary; sometimes they are at odds.

In the future natural pressures and interests will doubtless
force the creation of an international framework within which
the multinational corporations can be domiciled. An International Companies law has already been suggested for this purpose by former Ambassador George Ball and Herbert C. Cor-
nuelle, president of the United Fruit Company. If this comes to
pass, the issue of sovereignty as it now impedes the work of

international corporations in Latin America and elsewhere should be somewhat blunted. But the nation-states will not relinquish their hold easily.

A second issue is that of purpose and control. In days gone by, the large international corporation had very much of a free hand. Latin American governments granted liberal concessions to all comers. Standards and criteria of entrepreneurial activity were few. However, the bargaining power of the Latin American state and pressures upon it to use that power have grown substantially. There remains uncertainty about the objectives to be served by the use of state control over foreign corporations. If an international framework were designed within which international companies would be domiciled, Latin American governments would presumably be represented and would exert a measure of control. But the recurring priority still remains for the Latin American state and nation to clarify its own ends and means, its own ideology and political doctrine.* The issue of control will remain obscure and chaotic until that happens. It can, of course, be mitigated by the inclusion of Latin Americans in the ownership and management of the foreign corporation. But this is by no means a perfect answer because the question remains *which* Latin Americans—oligarch and traditionalists, or the "new managers" or government bureaucrats?

Here is where new formulas for participation and ownership by the international food companies have special import. Let us project present experience into the immediate future and compose a theoretical case. The vast and undeveloped state of Maranhão, in Brazil's mid-north, borders on the sea. It is about the size of New Mexico and has a population of three million people. Located between the arid Northeast and the dense Amazon basin, Maranhão's sparsely populated interior contains large areas of fertile land. But there are few roads, and except for some babassu nut pickers, most of the land remains virgin. The babassu trees, which grow wild in great abundance, are the region's principal money producer. The oil which is extracted from the nuts is valuable for cooking and soap-making. In spite

* Mexico is most advanced in this regard and consequently has the most dependable investment climate.

of its fertility, Maranhão, and Northeast Brazil as well, import close to two thirds of their food. The waters off the port of São Luis are notably abundant in fish, but there is little fishing. The governor of Maranhão, José Sarney Costa, is an energetic man in his late thirties who came to office as a progressive reformer. He is regarded as an exceptional leader and is often compared to the late John F. Kennedy. A strong nationalist, he is somewhat leftwing and mildly anti-United States. In his student days he was arrested as a radical, protesting against the dictatorship of Getúlio Vargas. But he is eager to develop his state.

SUDENE, the federal government's Northeast development agency, has been organizing colonization programs in the interior of Maranhão, and Catholic priests have several working corporatives in the interior. It is clear, however, that if radical change is going to be introduced into the state, it will not be through government, either state or federal, or through the Church alone.

Brazil's development-incentive laws make it easy and attractive for companies to acquire land and to invest in the underdeveloped interior of Maranhão. It is probable that a concession of 50,000 hectares of fertile land could be had with little difficulty. This land would be good for the cultivation of a wide variety of food crops, beef cattle, and cotton. It also would contain substantial numbers of babassu trees. But the project would require the construction of many miles of road and considerable housing and other facilities in the wilderness. Preliminary estimates, however, indicate that there would be a generous return on an investment in babassu oil, food crops, and cotton. In addition, a lucrative fishing enterprise could be launched from São Luis and some 240 varieties of commercial drug plants are known to grow in Maranhão.

What would be the design of such a venture, given all these circumstances? One possibility is as follows.

Form a Maranhão development corporation, with 30 per cent of the shares to be owned by one or several international food companies. In cooperation with SUDENE and the Catholic priests, organize five hundred carefully selected families to settle a 50,000-hectare agricultural site, providing each family immediately with twenty hectares of land for themselves and an equity

in larger tracts of land which would be reserved for cooperative commercial farming. The cooperative would eventually own
20 per cent of the equity in the corporation. The remaining 50
per cent would be for sale to Brazilian entrepreneurs and to the
Brazilian management of the enterprise. The management
would probably be recruited locally, perhaps from among young,
well-educated SUDENE officials, who have become increasingly
frustrated by the red tape and administrative lags which government development efforts inevitably involve. After the first few
years, more families would be moved in and made part of the
cooperative organization. Eventually, the entire land area would
be owned privately and cooperatively by the people who were
working it. They would also own a share in the development
corporation itself, and in its related enterprises, which would
include a modern fishing, processing, and exporting business.
The success of this venture would, of course, require much from
the international partners: capital, technology, training, organization, production management, processing, and most important
of all, access and distribution to Brazilian and world-wide
markets.

This is not meant to be a precise or complete project description but merely an indicator of one method of building in assur-
ances regarding local control and direction so as to give this
essentially profitable undertaking a guarantee of stability and satisfaction.[27]

The third and final issue is essentially a moral one, in the
sense that it has to do with what makes a good community, as
opposed to a bad one. The moral or community purpose of the
corporation in the United States has long been troublesome.
Quantities of words have been spoken and written about the
"social responsibility" of business. Invariably, these boil down
to business doing what it must in society in order to maximize,
or, as some businessmen prefer, "optimize" profits. Until recently
in the United States there was little difficulty perceived with this
definition; business was moral if it paid its taxes, gave its share
to philanthropy, and obeyed both the letter and the spirit of
the law. This conception of business morality rested on the pre-

sumption that democratic government—the product of our political system—had the wisdom and the capacity to form the good community. In recent years, we have been routinely shocked by the revelation that even our government may not have either the wisdom or the capacity to design and maintain the good community. Today increasing numbers of businessmen and companies, together with many other private organizations, are seeing the formation of the good community as part of their inherent purpose. To be sure, the reason for this new view of morality may still arise from a concern for survival and prosperity, but that does not diminish its difference from the older conception.

Similarly, in Latin America paying taxes, giving money to the poor, and obeying the law do little to introduce the changes which many think justice and morality require. It therefore has become the position of the Church that all who have power and property have an obligation to direct and use it so as to form the good community as moral authorities define it. This is the unusual significance of *Populorum Progressio,* and it is the reason why its implications are so revolutionary.

The bishops of Latin America in 1968 condemned both what they called "the liberal capitalist system" and Marxism. "Both systems violate the dignity of the human individual, because one is based on the primacy of capital, its power and its discriminatory use for the making of profits. The other, although ideologically it seeks to promote humanism, is focused rather on collective man and in practice is translated into totalitarian concentration of power in the state." The bishops went on to issue "an urgent appeal to businessmen . . . for a drastic modification of . . . goals, organization and functioning of business enterprises . . . along lines set forth by the social scholars of the Church . . ." [28]

Business, both national and international, in Latin America confronts this new moral issue. It is challenged to ask itself: What is the nature of the community which our power is sustaining? Is it a just community? If not, in what ways can that power be used to introduce changes in order to make it so?

These questions are no longer abstract or confined to the vaults of religion. They are at the heart of the revolution in Latin America, and new generations are demanding answers which the old fear to hear.

UNITED STATES
INTERESTS, POLICIES,
AND PROGRAMS

14

THE INTERESTS OF THE UNITED STATES

The future of our hemisphere can be seen as an extension of time within which these engines of change will compete with one another and with the status quo. Some will combine, others remain single; some will unify, some will divide; some will gain and others will lose; some will live, some will die. As the competition proceeds, the winning combinations at any given moment will determine the course of events; they will set the purposes and priorities which govern the activities of their communities in Latin America.

Radical structural change and reallocation of power are virtually inevitable. These have been delayed by the peculiar tolerance and resiliency of the oligarchy. The longer they are delayed, the more pressure and force they are apt to amass beneath them.

Change may well come as the product of a deepening and prolonged anarchy, the result of a chaotic but continuing obliteration of the social and political structures, eventually culminating in a completely new order. If this is the course that revolution follows, it will almost certainly be violent and bloody. It will also constitute a serious threat to world peace by inviting the aggressive intervention of world powers who see in chaos a way to power, those whom Walt Rostow graphically called "the scavengers of the modernization process."

On the other hand, change could come as a radical transformation, more or less consciously directed by some combination of the winning change engines. The end result would also be a new social and political order, but the need for violence might be minimized; the level and dimension of conflict better controlled. It is difficult to find in history incidents of radical change unattended by violence and sacrifice. Bloodshed almost seems to be required to produce the necessary heroes, symbols, myths, and legends. The Mexican Revolution took close to a million lives, and yet today Mexico is regarded as a development model. If mankind were realistic and clever about the workings of change engines, perhaps we could devise revolution without such pain and waste.

The alternative confronting the United States is not between the status quo and revolution. It is between revolution which is hostile to United States interests and revolution which is less so. A principal United States interest in Latin America must be the protection of United States security and that of other nations with which it is associated by treaty. The primary immediate threat to this interest is from foreign predators who have shown aggressive will and capacity, most especially Cuba, the Soviet Union, and China. Cuba's ambitions have been made clear in word and deed. The Soviet Union believes its interest can be best promoted by peaceful operations in Latin America, but it may at any time consider it useful to take a more aggressive stance because of events and its world interests. China is still far away from Latin America and is preoccupied with itself and its neighbors, but it must be regarded as a potential threat. All three countries have identified themselves with revolution, its instigation and support.

An immediate and primary objective of the United States, therefore, is to protect the independence of the inevitable revolution from the control of these powers which have proffered it support, both moral and material.* To the extent that we

* Soviet support of a revolution does not, of course, guarantee that the outcome will necessarily be consistent with Soviet interests and contrary to those of the United States. It is, however, a possibility sufficiently serious to deserve attention.

fail in this objective we are forced into either a sacrifice of vital interests or military action committing us to war against the revolution. And that kind of war cannot be won. This is the lesson of Viet Nam. Furthermore, such a war would be immoral since we have already recognized in the Alliance for Progress and elsewhere that radical change of revolutionary proportions is both good and necessary. In addition, it is quite possible that the expenses of such a war would be inconsistent with the urgent demand for our own domestic change and the general needs of our economy.

The United States thus finds itself in competition with Cuba, the Soviet Union, and to a lesser degree with China in establishing a constructive relationship with the forces of radical change. The opponents of change—the status quo, the oligarchy—in this event become as much the enemies of the United States as they are of the revolution itself.

We are sadly behind in this competition. Long bemused by the misconception that the conspiratorial activities of communism lay at the base of the revolution, we have lumped both together, clumsily attacking both at once. Were the Soviet threat to disappear tomorrow, we would continue to be confronted by the inevitability of revolution in Latin America; and, as things stand now, it will be an anti-American revolution. This is an enormous tragedy, given the fact that no government has tried harder than the United States to promote the development of poor countries. The tragedy is double-faced: Not only have we cast ourselves in an adverse political posture but we have also failed to achieve even our economic goals. In Latin America generally, gross national product has grown by a smaller percentage in each five-year period from 1950 to 1967.* It seems certain that in spite of the Alliance for Progress the decade of the 1950's will prove to have been economically better for Latin America than the 1960's. It is a tragedy which can be cut short of disaster, however, if we can but understand that what we bless as "development" requires fundamental change—revolu-

* Latin American economics growth average: 5% per year, 1951–1955; 4.8%, 1956–1960; 4.6%, 1961–1967.

tion—to implement. Present policies and procedures profoundly threaten the moral, political, and economic interests of the United States.

I

If present trends in Latin America continue, there will probably emerge in the near future (five to twenty years) two general combinations of engines of change which will have the best opportunity of saving the revolution from the route of chaos.

The first combination is composed of radical Christian, nationalist, revolutionary groups plus their numerous allies. In this combination belong the increasingly militant priests and bishops committed to social action and change; Christian Democratic parties; new, radical labor organizations, particularly those in rural areas; and nationalist revolutionary student groups. It is quite possible in some countries that these elements will be associated, indirectly or directly, in secret or in public, with armed bands in the countryside. The principal strengths which this combination represents are its purpose and vision; its ideology and the motivation which it brings; its sense of legitimacy and pride; its consciousness of independence and dignity. To succeed, this combination of forces will need to infiltrate, influence, and gain the support of (or at least cope with the hostility of) the military, government bureaucracies, and the new managerial group in business. In this way the Christian-nationalists may become gradually pervasive and capable of producing radical transformation in a relatively controlled and peaceful fashion.

The second combination most likely to succeed is composed of and related to large, integrated, multinational food production, processing, and distribution enterprises, foreign or domestic, organized for profit or nonprofit, cooperative or otherwise. This combination is strong where the first is weak and weak where the first is strong. The economic contributions of these undertakings—and their associated worker organizations—will appeal to some in government and business as well as to employees and consumers; their organizing and stabilizing effects will generally be seen as consistent with internal political objectives. Problems may arise in persuading the first combination of forces that the purposes of the second group are consistent with theirs.

If our predictions are correct, and if the chaotic way to change can be avoided, the future of Latin America can be seen in terms of continuing conflict at several different levels. There will be tension within the two giant combined change engines themselves over questions of power, leadership, methods, purpose, and priorities. There will also be conflict between them on these matters. Then there will be the most fundamental and serious cleavage between the two engines and the forces of the status quo itself.

It is doubtful that the United States government can substantially affect the final outcome of this revolutionary process; it certainly cannot stop the tide. Any effort to do so would only increase the already strong urge on the part of Latin Americans to break free from what are seen as humiliating relationships of the past. Any real or suspected opposition to change on the part of the United States would only serve as the external pressure against which internal action, unity, and strength can be organized and developed. It would also be the surest way to force engines of change to look to Cuba and the Soviet Union, even though in many instances they would prefer not to do so. Although the ability of the United States to alter the revolution's ultimate outcome is strictly limited, we can help to maintain its independence and to make manifest at every stage the right of the people of Latin America to self-determination. In so doing we can hope at the same time to protect United States interests to the extent that those interests are consistent with those of the revolution. Our ability to do this depends very much on our conception of our interests and our objectives. We have already stated a principal interest in preventing hostile incursions by Cuba, the Soviet Union, or China. It is doubtful, however, whether this interest by itself is a sufficient objective of the United States in Latin America. Neither Cuba's efforts nor those of the Soviet Union have been so extensive or successful as to justify their being the sole pinion of the foreign policy and program of the United States. Indeed, it would seem likely that if this were our only interest, we would fail even in its achievement.

2

The task of identifying interests has become particularly difficult because of the decline of communism in Latin America. Communist Party organizations have little power except in Chile; they are no longer—if they ever were—engines of change, and they are not likely to become such. Furthermore, while the Soviet Union certainly has the power to force its way into the hemisphere, it is no longer the warlike threat which it was before it withdrew its missiles from Cuba in 1962. The decline or absence of our old enemy in the hemisphere has left us strangely and suddenly bereft. We are up against the stark necessity of defining anew for ourselves and others what our purposes and priorities really are; we are faced with the disconcerting requirement to formulate our ideology, our vision of the good community and a just world.

Some will say that we have done this *ad nauseam*. They will point to the litany which has proceeded from every hemispheric meeting for a hundred years defining our objectives as freedom, democracy, and self-determination. But what have these words meant? How seriously can they be taken? The United States minister to Guatemala in 1920 described Washington's policy —as have, I am sure, many other United States representatives before and since—as being "to encourage constitutional government and free elections in Central America." [1] When one looks at the record of words and action, one cannot be surprised if either our sincerity, our effectiveness, or our understanding and use of the English language is called into question. Since 1945 we have been able to linger with inexplicit or insincere goals because all concerned in the United States and Latin America understood our real objective to be protecting ourselves and our neighbors from Soviet power and control—from the menace of communism. No matter how frequently we repeated that aid was necessary whether or not there were Communists, no one really believed it; and it is probably not surprising that the decline of communism has been followed by a curtailment of foreign aid.

Not only was anticommunism understood as our objective; it was generally regarded as quite an acceptable one from several points of view. Communism has never been widely popular in Latin America, identified as it has been with dictators and corruption as much as with social change. The neocolonialism implicit in Castro's attempt to subvert Venezuela, Guevara's efforts in Bolivia, and the Soviet Union's in Chile are inconsistent with national independence. But more important, as long as anticommunism was plainly the United States objective its aid and assistance could be taken not as charitable gifts offered often with angelic condescension, but rather as intimately connected to the self-interest of the United States. Our confusing and ambiguous moralizing was excused because the truth behind it was evident, understandable, and acceptable. We did not want communism in Latin America any more than did most Latin Americans.

Within the United States anticommunism has been a very useful objective; it was relatively simple and easy to accept. There was a broad public consensus that communism was fundamentally evil and dangerous. Politicians could campaign against it and Congress could with impunity vote large amounts to protect the "free world" from its grasp. In fact, it has been so satisfactory as a target of effort that we have never had to be too precise about it, nor have we had to concern ourselves with the fact that it means quite different things to different people.

In its purest form communism means nonproprietary communal living. We have no real objection to that, although we do not want to practice it ourselves. In this sense, however, it has a strong basis in religious teaching and a lingering ideological appeal. To some communism is seen as a variety of socialism, a system in which a strong and authoritarian government acts, sometimes ruthlessly, for the benefit of the poor people. Many Latin Americans, for example, who are anticommunist in an organizational or political sense are not unsympathetic with it ideologically. For them communism is simply the opposite of capitalism, not the opposite of democracy or liberty or freedom. Therefore, when we say we are anticommunist many understand us to be saying in effect that we are procapitalist. This causes difficulty and confusion, because for the vast majority of Latin Americans capitalism means exploitation, imperialism, and abuse; absentee landlords, monopolies, exorbitant return on investment, and worse. Capitalism means, in short, nearly the opposite of the economic system in the United States, which while non-statist is extremely responsive to the public consensus.[2]

To Americans communism has meant an international conspiracy emanating from Moscow and Peking which destroys the independence of nations and the liberty and dignity of the individual. But this position becomes distorted when viewed from Latin America, as the following comment from a non-communist leader of the revolutionary left explains:

> In the United States, communism is seen as a physical menace to the established way of life and the institutions that have brought a considerable degree of well-being to the vast majority of citizens. . . . In Latin America, however, communism is seen as a means of change, as a possible solution to an unsatisfactory way of life. . . . Negative anti-communism, often associated with blind opposition to change, is habitually fostered by American foreign policy . . . [and that has] often worked to the advantage of communism.
>
> Democracy has many times been confused with capitalism, as if the capitalist system were essential to democracy. The fact is that the majority of the governments on our continent, wrongly called democratic, have always been in the hands of financial oligarchs that have practiced exploitation through capitalism. This democracy has nothing to do with capitalism as it now exists in Latin America.[3]

Our difficulty with respect to words and concepts such as communism, capitalism, and democracy has had an odd effect on our image. To some extent the struggle in Latin America is one between materialism and ideology. As a result of a series of misunderstandings, imprecisions, commitments to meaningless jargon, and ideological naïveté, we find ourselves strangely identified with materialism, while Cuba, China, the Soviet Union, and their supporters are associated with spiritual ideology.

At the same time we seem to be unwittingly driving the ideologists—the radical Church, Christian Democrats, radicals in general, Socialists, Marxists, Communists, and revolutionary nationalists—to unite, although of course they have very little on which to be united.[4]

Now that communism—that is, the Communist Party organization—is declining as a real and present danger in Latin America, we ought to realize the confusion caused by the word and appreciate the fact that to at least some extent we are the ones breathing air into its collapsing lungs. We should stop using the word entirely, and call instances of Cuban or Soviet subversion or aggression exactly that rather than shroud these actions in an ambiguous cover-all which has an appealing ring to many who have no use for the imperialistic ambitions of either Moscow or Havana. But if we are to drop communism from our ideological rhetoric, then we must obviously drop anticommunism too. That will come hard, because we will be forced to face the fundamental contradiction in our objectives which the good, old call to anticommunism allowed us to avoid. This is the contradiction between change and stability.

In the past we have been able to advocate a wide variety of radical change, while at the same time contributing a good deal to sustaining the structure which has thwarted change. This we have done, arguing the necessity of stability, the result of instability being presumably a Communist take-over. We have preached freedom, democracy, and self-determination, asserting that both change and stability were preconditions to the fulfillment of these political ideals. We have in effect said we are in favor of change to the extent that it does not de-stabilize the existing structure of power. This is an absurdity, unless it is seen as a ruse for maintaining the status quo in the face of Communist attacks. Because of communism we were able to avoid facing the hard reality that in much of Latin America democracy is a euphemism and will remain so until there is the widespread political organization upon which democracy must rest. Because of communism we were able, when speaking of self-determination, to skirt the issue of who is "determining" what for whom. And because of communism we have been conducting a policy which has paid lip service to radical structural change but has in fact sustained the status quo.

3

Without anticommunism, we are left with the unveiled question of where we stand on the radical change or revolution which is inevitable in Latin America. The answer again requires a precise identification of our moral, political, and economic interests and a profound ideological commitment to their fulfillment. With these well in hand, it becomes possible for us to use our power and resources to promote our interests.

The purpose of our policy is just exactly that—to promote our own interests. An insidious presumption has lurked behind many of our past pronouncements which seems to imply that we have devised our policy for the good of the world or for some other nation or community. This is not only demeaning in the extreme to those whose good we are theoretically self-ordained to insure; it is an approach which is doomed to failure. Neither the corporations nor the government of the United States are philanthropies; they have no special hot line to God; they will not know what is best for anyone outside their lawful and legitimate jurisdictions. It must be made plain and clear that the foreign objectives, policies, and programs of the United States are designed purely and simply to promote the self-interest of the American people. This is their sole justification. Any other view rests on intolerable arrogance and pretentiousness, or on self-deception. We must leave it to the United Nations and other multinational agencies (to which we give our strong support) to design objectives, policies, and programs to serve world interests.

It is important to emphasize this point, because anyone who has pondered the matter of change and development inevitably runs up against difficult questions: Why change? For what purpose? By what right do we Americans set out to change Latin America? I do not believe that the answer can be: We are trying to change Latin America for the good of the Latin American people. I for one am not sure what that good is. The peasant in Veraguas is by some standards happier than some of my neighbors. He doesn't live as long; he is diseased and hungry; but I am not prepared to say unalterably that he would be better off in my neighbor's shoes.

4

There are three sides to our self-interest in causing change in Veraguas and places like it: moral, political, and economic. Our moral interest lies first in the compulsion of justice, which requires the rich man to give to the poor, not for the benefit of the poor man's body, but for the benefit of the rich man's soul. This is the morality of St. Vincent de Paul, who ordered his disciples to deport themselves so that the poor "will forgive you the bread you give them." [5] It is the morality of the Buddhist who says "Thank you" to the beggar who receives his offering, the beggar replying: "God bless you." We are helping the poor of this world for our own moral health as a nation.

Secondly, our moral interest is tied to our vision of the good community. This we laid down emphatically in what is our one and only statement of national ideology, which says that all men—not some, but all—have certain rights, including life, liberty, and the pursuit of happiness; that governments are instituted to "secure these rights"; and that "whenever any Form of Government becomes destructive of these ends, it is the Right of the People to alter or abolish it, and to institute new Government . . ." We have thus said to all people everywhere that in our view they have certain essentially revolutionary rights. We have further implied that we will help them to secure those rights. It is also implicit, however, in this declaration that other communities must define for themselves the meaning of those crucial words: life, liberty, and the pursuit of happiness. We cannot presume to do that. But once defined, if these rights are in jeopardy, so are our interests. If these rights are being violated and if we are asked to help, we are bound, according to our most solemn founding assertion, to comply as best we can. This we are committed to do out of self-interest, since a threat anywhere to the fundamental values upon which we rest as a nation is a threat to the nation. Needless to say, the questions of balance and judgment which the implementation or fulfillment of this interest entails would try Solomon. But at this point we are simply laying out the foundation of interest upon which implementation must rest.

In terms of political interests, the chief concern of the United States must be the survival of its citizens; it is thus a chief interest to avoid wars which today more than ever threaten that survival. We, therefore, have an interest of the highest priority in the control of conflict which tends to lead to such wars.

Careful distinctions, however, need to be made between conflict which is legal and that which is illegal, between conflict which is justified, moral, and right and that which is not. There are many examples of conflicts which we have regarded as consistent with the highest human values: our own Revolution and Civil War, the Mexican Revolution and, indeed, the Cuban Revolution until it betrayed itself to Soviet domination. These conflicts and others like them all had something in common: they arose from the efforts of a particular community to resolve for itself long-standing problems of justice and power. They were in this sense a necessary part of the process by which nations have been formed the world over. They were not the result of aggression by a foreign power. They were thus conflicts totally different and distinct from those, for example, which were initiated by Napoleon, Hitler, or Stalin. Although it may be hoped that less bloody and wasteful methods of forming nations may be devised, it seems intolerable to rule out this sort of internal and historically noble conflict. To do so might retard the change which is necessary for development and in the long run might produce even higher and more dangerous levels of violence.[6]

But nowadays the pure internal form of such conflict is rare. We must face the possibility that a predatory foreigner is somewhere off the beach or across the border, seeking to use the conflict to promote his own ends. Since this is a form of aggression which could lead to a direct challenge to the safety and security of the American people, it is in the interest of the United States to insulate and protect internal conflicts from such predators. This protection will be neither acceptable nor

effective, however, unless the position of the United States
toward the parties in the conflict is clear and consistent with
our moral values or ideology as they apply in the situation.

Let us assume, for example, that an internal revolutionary
struggle breaks out in Guatemala. The revolutionaries are composed of small guerrilla bands and students led by ardent nationalists. Although some of the leaders have been trained in
Cuba, they insist that their purpose is a just Guatemalan community and that they are not Cuban-controlled. The army over-
throws the constitutional government in the name of restoring
order. Right-wing elements in the army and in Guatemalan
business take control of the government. Civil war ensues. In
this instance it is difficult to contend that one party is more
legitimate than the other, given our promise in the Declaration
of Independence. And yet, plainly one side has received considerable United States assistance. Our objective in this case
would seem clear: to protect the conflict from Cuban domination, particularly from Soviet domination through Cuba. We are
handicapped in the pursuit of this policy because of past assistance to the armed forces which tends to force, and to make
legitimate, Cuban aid to the revolutionaries. On the other hand,
some past assistance to the Guatemalan army can be justified
since the state, under whatever government, required police
forces to protect the population from another form of conflict,
namely, that of the criminal and the bandit. With the overthrow of the constitutional government, however, United States
military assistance becomes not only illegitimate but against our
interests.

This brief rationale woven around a crude crisis scenario
leaves many questions unanswered:

Doesn't the army have a head start because of our help and,
therefore, aren't the revolutionaries justified in seeking comparable outside help?

On the other hand, doesn't the army retain some of the
legitimacy which it derived while it served a "constitutional
regime"?

But then, is "constitutional government" and what is called

"democracy" in states like Guatemala different from rule by oligarchy through the power of the army? What is form and what is substance?

We must leave these questions hanging because they are out of our main focus. Nevertheless, they are perhaps helpful in identifying further political interests in those countries which have not yet had their revolution or which are in its inevitable throes.

It is in our interest to minimize and restrict political, economic, or military support and commitment to the status quo. When even the forms of constitutionality are discarded and a condition of active revolution occurs, then all such commitments and support should be stopped and commitments minimized.

Likewise, we should develop and maintain contact with revolutionary groups, seeking to use our resources and influence to promote those which are most consistent with our other moral, political, and economic interests. While it is in our general interest to minimize conflict, its necessity at times must be recognized. We must, in short, qualify ourselves as eligible to protect the independence of the revolution.

It thus becomes our interest to identify and actively to assist those engines of change which are moving in a direction consistent with our larger interests which are embraced by what we have defined as the two winning combinations. To a great extent these engines are today alienated from us; they feel abandoned by our power and condemned by our ideology. Much as they fear and resent foreign predators, they are in no mood to be protected by us.

It follows then that our interests call for the strict limitation of United States military power and influence to preventing the infiltration of predatory arms and force into Latin America. Working through the Organization of American States or some other regional body, the objective of the military should be to seal off and protect the process of change within each community without discouraging the process. Utopian as this may appear today, it is the goal to be pursued.

In order to avoid the difficulty and danger inherent in unilaterally distinguishing between internal lawlessness, legitimate revolution, and foreign aggression, military and police training and assistance should be provided to individual states only through regional groupings such as OAS.

Lastly, avenues of communication should be open and clear between the United States and the Soviet Union and Cuba, so that each may understand to the fullest extent the purposes of the other. This is particularly important with respect to Cuba. In the long run, in spite of Castro's vitriol, it seems inevitable that the mutuality of interests between Cuba and the United States will—or should—far outweigh the conflicts of interest.

Apart from crisis situations such as the one I have hypothetically suggested in Guatemala, the United States would seem to have a general interest in promoting the development of true communities in Latin America. This is especially important in the unorganized and highly vulnerable rural sectors. But it is also true on the national and regional level. It is in our interest to help to form communities, whether they be villages, provinces, or nations, to form and organize in such a way that these communities can govern themselves, determine their values and goals, and build the institutions and organizations necessary for a vigorous, responsive, and lasting political system. This says only that a community is better than a non-community. A lone *caboclo* in the Amazonian bush, an isolated *campesino* in the mountains of Veraguas, is powerless to exercise his will, enjoy freedom, or achieve dignity unless he is part of a community within which he has influence. A sense of purpose is necessary to form communities, and it follows that it is in the interest of the United States in particular to promote purpose-making institutions, not in any sense with the objective of directing or even influencing their selection of purposes, but only with the objective of helping them to achieve the confidence and the competence to develop their own purposes. We have seen repeatedly that the matter of purpose—and legitimacy—is at the heart of Latin America's difficulties.

Lastly, our economic interests are substantial in Latin America. It receives one fifth of our exports and accounts for one third of our income from foreign investments. We are dependent strategically upon the region for oil, copper, bauxite, and other minerals, as well as for a wide variety of agricultural commodities. United States companies have more than $10 billion invested in Latin America. Their prosperity is important to the millions of Americans who own stock in these companies. Their survival is of interest to the United States government, which must be concerned for the economic health of the nation, the strategic needs of the economy, and the rights of United States citizens.

United States economic interests in Latin America are also of the utmost importance to the success of the revolutionary process in the hemisphere. Here, however, we strike an important ambiguity. United States enterprise brings a long and familiar list of useful resources, products, and techniques to Latin America. It pays big tax bills, employs millions of Latin Americans, invests large amounts of capital, pays good wages, provides relatively good working conditions, introduces needed training and technology, builds local markets and gains access to world markets, expands and diversifies local production, lowers imports and raises exports. In an economic sense we have played both a good and a bad role: good in that there obviously have been direct benefits derived from our activities; bad in that our enterprise has perhaps hampered the development of Latin American economic intiative and independent organization. In a political sense the effect of United States enterprise is equivocal and increasingly subject to question.

North American companies for the most part have tended to enrich the oligarchs and solidify the status quo. They have used their power to build a place for themselves within the existing power structure. The United States company looking for local partners, investors, or assistance quite naturally looks to those who are in or near the seats of power, conforming to the environment as one finds it. This also, of course, means contributing to the maintenance of that environment. When United States companies depart from the conventional ways, as when they encourage the growth of labor unions or when they are able through efficiency or greater resources to lower prices for the consumer, they are invariably chastised by the status quo. The oligarchs seek to punish them and even to exclude them. When the United States firm threatens the existing structures, it encounters strong opposition, in the face of which it is apt to compromise. Anti-United States business attitudes, therefore, in the past have not emanated so much from the revolutionaries as from the oligarchs, in company with their kept "revolutionaries."

But this is changing. The strong and mutually sustaining link between United States companies and Latin American oligarchs is becoming a target for those who would change present allocations of power. Earlier we drew special attention to those United States enterprises which are entering more fully into the revolutionary stream, either in remote rural areas where the oligarchs are less watchful or in company with the "new managers" who are themselves aware of the necessity of radical change. The protection of United States economic interests in Latin America depends upon accentuation of this movement so that such enterprise becomes increasingly allied with effective and efficient local engines of change.

The question of control is another factor in determining whether or not the economic benefits which United States companies bring is also regarded as political benefit. It is becoming increasingly unacceptable to Latin Americans generally that large elements in a national economy should be controlled by outsiders. United States companies realize this and are moving as quickly as they can to acquire local partners. But this often is not so simple. IBEC has had continuing difficulty obtaining Latin American partners who will stay with an investment during the lean years; they can make more money quicker doing other things. Furthermore, many United States companies have acquired oligarchs for local partners; they return to the vulnerability cited above. If majority ownership in a joint venture rests with the Americans, the issue of control remains substantially unresolved.

The matter is further complicated by the fact that many Latin American governments are so eager to bring foreign investors to their countries that they will offer a wide variety of incentives without any very clear or explicit criteria about which forms of foreign investment are in their own national interest.

Obviously, there are priorities, but these are often blurred, sometimes in the interest of local power-holders. Even in Mexico, where there are rules against foreign ownership of businesses, it is not unusual to find such ownership in fact existing. It is hard to expect the United States investor to resist the attractive offerings of Latin American governments, to turn down a good deal with a local oligarch, to understand that dealing "normally" with the status quo is only effective as long as the status quo exists.

If the revolution is inevitable, then the protection of United States economic interests requires that United States companies perceive their revolutionary role in all its aspects. They should explore new formulas for sharing control, new ways of allocating their power, and new criteria for appraising their activities, all of which must be consistent with the revolutionary process itself. They cannot wait for governments to tell them what to do. The governments of Latin America are not the governments of France, England, Japan, or the United States. "Getting along with government" is not good enough. The revolution in most cases is going on outside of and in spite of government; it is certainly not a governmental process. Therefore, the protection of American economic interests depends upon the effectiveness with which American enterprise can move within the revolutionary circuit; the speed with which it can create new designs and procedures for becoming a part of the winning combination of engines of change.

The alternative to United States enterprise devising these new forms for itself is not, in most cases, letting present Latin American governments do it for them. It is rather the introduction of hostile governments, probably of a totalitarian variety, which will introduce dictatorial systems of controls within which there is little room for private enterprise or initiative. The Soviet Union and China have shown that within the space of one generation a backward, unstable, and poor nation can develop unsuspected technical and productive capacities and achieve a radical social and cultural transformation. Can United States enterprise, in its own interest and in consort with Latin American managers, achieve a comparable transformation? I believe so, but not unless it conceives of itself as being first and foremost an engine of change of revolutionary proportions. What is more important, it can do so with more justice, economy, and efficiency than the totalitarian models.

It is not arrogant to describe our interests so broadly. To do less is to underestimate the extent of the power and resources of the United States; to minimize our concern for peace and to overlook our unequaled capacity to promote it. We might wish to withdraw and concentrate on rebuilding our somewhat dilapidated homeland, but this is not in the cards. This would only invite further deterioration.

In implementing our interests we should not expect or desire thanks. We are not engaged in a popularity contest and should not be disheartened if we are not loved. The rich man on the hill, however benign and beneficent, is rarely loved: He has to find his security in himself. Frequently, indeed, anti-Americanism has been a useful device for the construction of useful movements and organizations. The Mexican nation is one example. The FEDELAC *campesino* federation in the Dominican Republic is another. We can, however, hope that anti-Americanism, when it occurs, serves a larger and more useful purpose than the smashing of an embassy window or the assassination of a United States official.

15

A COMMITMENT TO CHANGE

> Revolution is a mettlesome horse. One must either
> ride it or be trampled to death by it. The Hapsburg
> Monarchy and the Czardom have both been
> trampled to death within the last half century. But
> how did a revolutionary-minded Russian acrobat man-
> age subsequently to vault into the saddle? He
> found the saddle vacant; so, by the date at which
> the present Russian rider lodged himself there,
> the original American rider must have dismounted.
> Can the United States recapture her revolutionary
> birthright? President Kennedy has proclaimed
> that as his ambition for her. Is the United States
> going to take the leap, or is she going to stall? Her
> destiny hangs on her choice; for to linger dis-
> mounted in the arena is to court death—especially
> in our day, when the world arena is rapidly
> contracting, so that the trampling horse is thundering
> round it in ever-narrowing circles.
>
> Arnold Toynbee[1]

Those who saw it will never forget it. The fresh snow
shone bright in the Capitol plaza. The January skies were clear
and blue. The new President stood without coat or hat, his
voice ringing in the frosty air: "Let the word go forth from this
time and place, to friend and foe alike, that the torch has been
passed to a new generation of Americans—born in this century,
tempered by war, disciplined by a hard and bitter peace, proud
of our ancient heritage." The word of John F. Kennedy did
indeed go forth, and it was heard by millions in Latin America

who saw in this man a commitment to change and who believed. "To our sister republics south of our border," the President said, "we offer a special pledge—to convert our good words into good deeds—in a new alliance for progress to assist free men and free governments in casting off the chains of poverty."

A month later on February 16, 1961, Adolf A. Berle, whom Kennedy had appointed to lead a Latin American task force, defined the United States interest as the development of policies and programs which would channel the revolution now going on in Latin America in the proper direction and prevent it from being taken over by the Sino-Soviet bloc.[2] Richard Goodwin, the President's special adviser on Latin America, called together representatives from all the agencies concerned with Latin America as well as distinguished Latin Americans who were in Washington, and sought their advice. His memorandum to the President began: "Latin America is in a state of crisis. Deep-running currents are bringing about great changes in the economic and social structure. These changes cannot and should not be stopped for they stem from needs which, in the present situation of Latin America, permit no delay." The memorandum recognized that the responsibility for change was up to Latin Americans, but that the United States could help to bring it about. It also acknowledged that "vigorous state action" was necessary to "overcome the resistance of private groups."[3]

So it was that on March 13 the Latin American diplomatic corps assembled in the East Room of the White House to hear the young leader of a seemingly awakened United States call "on all the people of the hemisphere to join in a new Alliance for Progress—Alianza para Progreso—a vast cooperative effort, unparalleled in magnitude and nobility of purpose, to satisfy the basic needs of the American people for homes, work and land, health and schools—*techo, trabajo y tierra, salud y escuela*.

"If the countries of Latin America are ready to do their part . . . then I believe the United States, for its part, should help provide resources of a scope and magnitude sufficient to make this bold development plan a success."

The room was alive with excitement as the President concluded: "Let us once again transform the American continent into a vast crucible of revolutionary ideas and efforts—a tribute to the power of the creative energies of free men and women— an example to all the world that liberty and progress walk hand in hand." [4]

The euphoria was palpable. But within a month bombers of Cuban-exile Brigade Number 2506 were striking Havana and Santiago and the landings had begun at the Bay of Pigs. A few days later Castro proclaimed his greatest victory; the United States was humiliated; and the Alliance sullied by the suspicion that its existence depended upon the threat of Castro.

The gleam soon returned, however, largely because of President Kennedy's forthright admission of error. On August 5, 1961, at the request of the United States the OAS convened an extraordinary meeting of the Inter-American Economic and Social Council at the seaside resort of Punta del Este in Uruguay. There was much talk of the necessity of national planning, and Latin American government officials saw that their United States counterparts were no longer sensitive to the notion of enlarged governmental action as their Republican predecessors had been. A group of experts was formed to review national development plans. Che Guevara was there in green fatigue uniform claiming that the Alliance was nothing but a reaction to the Cuban Revolution, "a device to domesticate the peoples of the hemisphere to the orders of imperialism." His chilling prophecy rang in the delegates' ears: "The Cordillera of the Andes will be the Sierra Maestra of America." [5]

Douglas Dillon, Secretary of the Treasury, pledged the government of the United States to contribute more than $1 billion a year to the grand cause, adding that Latin America could expect another $20 billion of foreign private investment in the next decade. He declared that the purpose of it all was clear: that the United States recognized this was a revolutionary task and that we were no strangers to revolution. [6]

The Charter of Punta del Este committed the nations of the hemisphere to twelve radical objectives, ranging from redistribution of national income and comprehensive land reform to expanded education, housing, and health services. Through it all ran the strong initiative of the United States that reforms required profound political, social, and economic change.

But the Alliance also had the support, indeed was in many ways inspired by, Latin American revolutionaries, particularly Eduardo Frei Montalva, President of Chile. For him its promise lay in two factors: "First, it established principles for hemispheric cooperation with a clear ideological orientation expressed by its forthright support for a democratic revolution in Latin America; second, it represented a change in the hitherto prevalent concept of financial and economic assistance given by the United States." It implied a cooperative relationship between the donor and recipient nations.[7] For Latin Americans like Frei the most significant impact of the Alliance was that for the first time the United States supported revolutionary change. Through both inadvertence and design, however, the United States gradually permitted other priorities to displace change on the scale of importance. In particular, it failed to confront or to dispose of the contradiction implicit in commitment to change and to stability.

By April of 1967 the dream had failed, but the presidents of the hemisphere met again at Punta del Este to attempt its

TABLE 7

U. S. Economic Aid to Latin America
(In Millions of Dollars)

	1969 (Est.)	1968	1967
Aid Loans and Grants	$270	$ 527	$ 545
Export-Import Bank Loans	200	230	469
Food for Peace	180	223	87
Social Progress Trust Fund*		2	2
Other U.S. Economic Aid	25	25	23
U.S. Contribution to IADB	300	300	250
Totals	$975	$1,307	$1,376

* Long-term, low-interest funds administered by the Inter-American Development Bank.

Source: *The New York Times*, August 1 and September 22, 1968.

renewal. This time the United States raised its pledge to $1.3
billion a year from 1967 to 1971. As will be seen from the
table below, the bulk of these funds were to come in the form
of loans, a source of resentment on the part of Latin Americans
who were feeling the increasing weight of debt.

It is quite apparent that the glorous vision of the Alliance for
Progress is now blurred and pitted. Surrounded and embittered
by mutual suspicion and recrimination, it has failed to produce
the change it sought. The unique dedication of the Alliance to
radical change, to revolution, has been all but smothered. With it
has gone the ideological initiative which the United States had
seized in 1961.[8]

A serious crisis of confidence exists. In 1968 the House of
Representatives reduced the foreign aid budget for Latin America from the $625 million requested for fiscal 1969 to $270
million, by far the lowest level since the Alliance began. Galo
Plaza Laso, secretary general of the Organization of American
States, and two of his senior aides have questioned the "willingness of the United States to meet its commitments." [9]

Despite the consistency of the objectives of the Alliance with
United States interests as we set them forth in the previous
chapter, it has failed to fulfill or to promote them effectively.
It is time to do something different. Before setting a new course,
however, let us review briefly why and how the Alliance has
failed.

In commenting on the Alliance it is easy for all of us to suc-
cumb to what Albert Hirschman calls *fracasomania*—"the urge
to proclaim as failure a new undertaking as soon as it is launched,
and before it could possibly yield its intended benefits." Americans in particular are given to expecting quick solutions to
knotty problems and to crying failure at anything less. Having
this frailty in mind, what can we say on the credit side for the
Alliance?

It has unquestionably started a trend of thinking, a debate,
perhaps, in the direction of radical change. Vital issues are
being talked about more than before; considerable reform legislation has been passed; some programs have been begun. Since
1960 tax revenues have increased some 25 per cent; inflation in

some countries has been restrained; university enrollment has increased by 80 per cent and high-school enrollment by 140 per cent.[10] The $7 billion of United States aid since 1960 has been paralleled by the investment of some $101 billion of Latin American public and private resources.[11] Men have laid roads, built schoolhouses and hospitals, constructed housing, cured diseases, distributed food, rendered technical assistance, trained teachers, and dispensed books. Financial assistance, incentives, and risk guarantees have aided the development of local and United States enterprise in a general way. A substantial portion of AID loans in this category have been made to banks and other intermediate credit institutions for sublending to business firms, farmers, and others. This is supposed to be "seed" capital. Considerable loan money has gone for urban housing in a losing effort to keep up with the flow of people from the country to the cities. Small amounts of funds have gone to engines of change as we have defined them: the American Institute for Free Labor Development has channeled money into trade unions; the International Development Foundation, with AID support, is assisting peasant organizations in Peru, Guatemala, and elsewhere; some change-oriented industries, cooperatives, and credit unions have received help; and some American universities, notably Harvard, Stanford, and Michigan State, have been supported to train new managerial elites. The bulk of AID funds, however, has been distributed according to the philosophy implicit in the Department of State's Year-end Review for 1967:

> An almost endless pageant of roads, dams, industrial and commercial buildings, schools, colonization projects, power plants and irrigation systems are eloquent reminders that people bent on self-improvement are no longer thwarted by handicaps.
>
> A pre-requisite for socio-economic integration is generally conceded to be the construction of physical infrastructure works. Hence the drive to speed the construction that makes possible a better working parnership of the Alliance nations.

In the first five years of the Alliance, according to the Department of State, Latin American nations invested $91 billion "toward their own accelerated development." Support from the United States amounted to more than $6.5 billion. Another $1.1 billion came from Europe; and $2.3 billion from international lending agencies.[12]

Although the policy of the Alliance was to have been inter-American from the beginning, by default and by design the United States has taken charge. Our domination of the effort has been only slightly diluted by the Inter-American Committee of the Alliance for Progress (CIAP). CIAP was formed by the Inter-American Economic and Social Council in 1963 at the recommendation of former Presidents Lleras of Colombia and Kubitschek of Brazil to provide for greater Latin American direction and control of the Alliance. The United States was given a permanent place on the committee, with six other members representing regional groupings of Latin American nations. It was stipulated that "a distinguished Latin American" was to be chairman of the committee. Carlos Sanz de Santamaria, former finance minister of Colombia, was selected. CIAP was to be the executive committee of the Alliance for Progress. Other agencies concerned with Latin American development were to advise it. These included the Inter-American Development Bank, the panel of nine experts ("the nine wise men") of the Inter-American Economic and Social Council, and the United Nations Economic Commission for Latin America. The committee was to recommend priorities for the allocation of development funds, but it was not given power to disburse funds. This power remained in the hands of the lender, principally the United States government.

CIAP has done well so far, producing valuable country studies, identifying major development problems, and recommending solutions. It has also led discussions with the Development Assistance Committee of the Organization for Economic Cooperation and Development (OECD) in an effort to increase European, Canadian, and Japanese participation in Latin American development. OECD grants and loans have amounted to about $100 million annually. Its effectiveness has remained limited, however, by the dominance of the United States, which in April 1966 provoked the resignation of the "nine wise men."

They complained that bilateral relations between the United States and Latin American governments had replaced the original idea of the Alliance.

Nonetheless, CIAP stands as the best effort so far to make the Alliance the partnership it was supposed to be. Its achievements are a tribute to the distinguished and progressive Latin Americans and North Americans who have composed it.

In spite of the dedication and diligent effort of some of the hemisphere's noblest and ablest men, the results of the Alliance have been sadly disappointing. The revolution which it sought has not occurred; and the revolution which is taking place is proceeding outside and in many ways in spite of its embrace. Indeed, on balance one cannot avoid the disturbing conclusion that after the columns are added the total effect of the Alliance has been to solidify the status quo, to entrench the oligarchs, to heighten the obstacles to change.

The reasons are informative.

First, the Alliance immediately confronted the combined opposition of the oligarchs and the Communists, who for different reasons sought the same end. Governments which might have sought to implement its provisions were thus immediately discouraged from doing so by the threat of force on the right and the left. Other governments lacked even the desire for change, but willingly accepted the assistance offered. They made the appropriate pledges but used the funds to maintain stability and retard the revolution, incidentally corrupting themselves in the process. Their arguments were principally that revolution would invite communism and threaten foreign investment. In this way they successfully appealed to the contradiction in United States purpose between stability and change. Eduardo Frei said what was lacking was a clear ideological direction and determination on the part of political leaders to bring about change. He observed that many Latin American governments have used the Alliance as a bargaining lever to get more United States aid with which to maintain the status quo; and that these governments nominally committed themselves to internal reforms which they later allowed to lie moribund or to be used for the benefit of those in power.[13]

As a result, the Alliance has found itself generally allied with the forces of the status quo. The Panamanian government was loath to allow AID money to go to Bishop McGrath's project in Veraguas Province—it was too radical, a "hotbed of Christian Democracy." In general, little AID money fuels the radical Church whether in Brazil, Bolivia, or the Dominican Republic. Consistent as these groups are with the aims of the Alliance, they are clearly in conflict with the ruling status quo.

Other disillusioned Latin American proponents of the Alliance have come to see it as a monstrous diversion, forged by governments to exert pressure on themselves. Having urged social change, they can say that the will to do it was present but the obstacles were too great.

Implicit in the procedures foreseen by the Alliance is the notion that experts, technicians, and government bureaucrats have the capacity for revolution. They don't, of course; and even if they did, they would hardly be a match for the skill and force of the Tolerant Oligarchy.

The second reason for disappointment with the Alliance relates to the first, but rests fundamentally on the failure of the United States and its officials to understand or to accept the priority of the Alliance's ideological commitment. We were somehow unable or unwilling to mean what we said. Our predilection for pragmatism, taking the path of least resistance, smothered the flame of purpose which President Kennedy had sought to ignite. When the teeth of our commitment to the Alliance began to press, we were unprepared to bite.

AID objectives and programs in Latin America are tied to the policies and capabilities of local governments. These are rarely efficient engines of change, and they are generally unwilling to support those which are.

In Guatemala in 1966 both the government and the American embassy had finally come to realize that rural change—a sharp increase in peasant motivation and organization—was a significant national requirement. The guerrillas were recognized as reflecting a deep-seated and radical political problem rather than being just another bunch of bandits. In that year AID allocation for rural development was raised from a negligible amount to

$500,000. The Ministry of Agriculture received most of this, spending it on jeeps, office equipment, and tractors for its Agrarian Reform Institute. An additional $75,000 was allocated by the ministry for "special projects"—community centers, water systems, and the like, mostly in rural municipalities. The remainder was used for training government workers for rural activity, with a small amount left to support the activities of the International Development Foundation, one of the very few United States organizations which is skilled and experienced in motivating and organizing peasants. We do not need to list again the familiar reasons why all but the last and smallest of these expenditures were irrelevant to our basic objective.

The case of Panama between 1963 and 1968 is comparable. There too the programs of government and AID, except in the most superficial sense, failed to fulfill the aims of the Alliance. They were not aimed primarily at structural change; they were heavily concentrated in Panama City; they largely ignored the rural part of the country; they aimed at gathering political support for the regime in power; they became tainted by corruption. The aims of the United States, as seen in the short run by the embassy and the AID mission, were not apparently inconsistent with those of the regime. Primarily concerned with a stable environment in the immediate vicinity of the Canal, the United States felt the concentration of funds in the city was justified, even though it was quite apparent that in the long run the urban problem was a rural one—one new house was being constructed for every five rural immigrants. And "getting along with the Panamanians" was given a clearly higher priority than achieving the purposes of the Alliance. Our AID program in Panama has thus amounted to a series of unrelated "projects": housing, water, and sewage in Panama City; urban savings and loan associations; culverts and bridges; a sea wall; enlarging the highway from Panama City to Tocumen Airport; and scattered building efforts throughout the country which have had little or no connection with existing or potential engines of change. The United States and Panamanian officials involved are not to blame. They are both parts of systems which have precluded anything different.

To penetrate this dilemma further we must reconsider the matter of interests and objectives, remembering the general United States interests set out in the previous chapter within the specific context of Veraguas Province.[14]

I

There is the argument that whatever the objectives of the United States, our policies and actions in a foreign country must be controlled by the government in power at any particular time. In a sense, this argument is obviously right; it cannot be our purpose to violate the sovereignty of another country. In another sense, it is wrong; it surely cannot be our purpose to feed corruption or to perpetuate that which we feel is against our national interest. Too often the argument is used to justify expenditures of funds for purposes which are irrelevant not only to our national objectives but even to those of the country itself, purposes which are purely bureaucratic in nature, formulated by a local governmental administrative unit or interest group which may have little understanding for or capacity to deal with the problems at hand.

Our AID mission thus tends to become an extension of the local governmental administration, in a sense nourishing its difficulties and sometimes delaying the establishment of more effective political structures. It is too easy to blame this situation on the local government or on local AID personnel. We must blame the highest echelons of United States political leadership, where the responsibility rests for the formulation of objectives, priorities, criteria, and commitment.

Partly because this dilemma is recognized locally, our foreign aid is frequently concentrated on material and technical projects which superficially are administratively clean and politically safe. The fact that these projects are sometimes irrelevant to the principal problems is not likely to be considered. It must be remembered that AID's predecessor agencies were firmly committed to the doctrine that they were in business to render technical assistance. In a very positive fashion they shunned what was thought to be "political." With the Alliance for Progress and the attempt to merge AID with the foreign service and the struc-

ture of our embassies abroad, this aversion to political considerations was somewhat diluted. But old notions die hard. That it is
a preposterous pretense to separate the injection of millions of
dollars from its political effects in what may be called a technical
fashion is still glossed over in many instances. For example, a
road, a bridge, or a hydroelectric station is too often considered to
be in and of itself a good thing. Frequently, the priority is not
fixed on whether the road or the bridge is located properly to bring
more of the population into the national political and market
system, or whether the hydroelectric station and its output are
so arranged as to bring power and light more cheaply to more
people.

The matter of schoolhouses raises the same issue but adds another dimension, namely, that of transferring our own national
experience to environments in which it is irrelevant. The American public-school system is regarded as part of the backbone of
American democracy. We presume, therefore, that broad public
education is in and of itself a good thing and a harbinger of
democracy. We seem to forget the unique levels of motivation
and opportunities for the use of education which have always
characterized the United States. We seem to forget that we stand
almost alone in the world in having never known the crippling
and deadening effects of feudalism. For education to bring democracy, it must be carefully combined and mixed with motivational elements.

In Veraguas, for example, the problem of education is substantially irrelevant to the number of existing schoolhouses; it
is rooted in the fact that the *campesino* sees no special purpose
in having his child in school on time, regularly, year in and year
out. He does not visualize for his child a life that is substantially
different from his own. When, however, twenty-five *campesinos*
joined together for that first cooperative effort in San Francisco,
and when they discovered that the only person in the village
who could keep the small accounts was the local priest, they
recognized in a remarkably short time the need for education.
As never before, they had their children in school on time and
overtime. They built an extension to the schoolhouse themselves, and would in fact have built the whole structure if none

had been there. They scoured the countryside to insure that their village had the best schoolteacher, and they even started to consider appropriate changes in the school's curriculum to make it more relevant to the children's needs. It would not be excessive to suggest that CEPAS has been more of a stimulant to education in Veraguas than has the school system. Today it is operating directly four highly successful vocational and agricultural schools.

Another problem which arises from the imprecision of our objectives is that we tend to confuse the world about the purposes of our bountiful aid. Our idealism is received with cynicism, and the worst is suspected, there being no clear, believable, and consistent purpose set forth. No one likes to receive charity, and a nation will go to great and often irrational lengths to deny that it has.

Let us consider the President's Economic Report of January 26, 1967, which states: "We will give first priority to fighting the evils of hunger, disease and ignorance in those free world countries which are resolutely committed to helping themselves."

Given the enormity of the task and the serious limitations of our contribution, it seems questionable whether this is a precise statement of our "first priority." It would seem that peace, the prevention of a nuclear holocaust, or human survival in general was of higher priority. As can be shown quite dramatically, the maintenance of peace may be quite irrelevant to hunger, disease, and poverty. Both Cuba and Viet Nam, for example, were relatively well off in these three respects. Their present threat to world peace does not derive from hunger, disease, or ignorance. The second part of the President's statement raises further questions. How do you tell when a country "is resolutely committed to helping itself," and is that what really counts? The purposes of our aid in Panama, for example, are presumably not unrelated to the maintenance of a stable environment around the Canal. Furthermore, where is the sense or justice in saying that if Latin American governments can't get the rich to pay, the poor will have to suffer?

The United States government, in the face of these dilemmas, has at least two alternatives: It can change its objectives so that they are compatible with current bureaucratic operating procedures of local governments, or it can develop new objectives, fix new priorities, and design new means for their fulfillment. On the assumption that the second alternative is the more desirable, it becomes necessary to clarify our new objectives and to understand precisely what their implementation entails. Assuming our new objective is the support of change rather than of the status quo, we have to understand change in the revolutionary sense.

A revolutionary process of structural change is and must be under way in Veraguas and similar areas. The political, social, and economic organization of the province is inadequate to meet the needs of the people. Serious structural vacuums exist. Inexorable pressures outside and inside the province are moving—perhaps slowly and obscurely, but incessantly—to fill the vacuums and to create new structures. This is a process which we can regard as certain to continue. Obstacles in its way tend to increase its intensity, and thus its potentiality as an invitation to aggression and a threat to peace.

It is, therefore, in the vital interests of the United States to promote the creation in Veraguas—as our example—of new political, social, and economic structures which can insure the fulfillment of the inevitable revolutionary process without violence, if possible. It is assumed that there are a variety of predatory powers who are eager to exploit the weakness and chaos that accompany such fulfillment.

The successful fulfillment of the revolutionary process and the creation of the necessary new political, social, and economic structures require the active participation of the people of the province. Theoretically, perhaps, new revolutionary structures could be imposed by the Panamanian government or by some other outside force, but given the realities of the situation this is not likely. There must be pressure within and from the province itself.

Such pressure requires among the people a measure of confidence, self-respect, hope, and vision which are only beginning to exist and are due mostly to the work of CEPAS-Juan XXIII. Such pressure requires an ideology, an organic vision of the problems of Veraguas in its being and in its becoming. It requires a sense of dignity, an ability to recognize and develop personal capacities, a sense of power within the environment. The *campesinos* must understand that there is an alternative to the "permanent poverty" which they are currently convinced is theirs. They must become less oppressed by a concern for sheer survival, less dependent on escape from that oppression through alcohol and superstition.

The fulfillment of these requirements demands motivation and organization. There is no direct relation between them and the fulfillment of a material or a technical need. That is to say, providing the *campesino* with food or a road or a social center has no necessary relevance to the critical factors stated above, which are motivational, spiritual, political, and ideological. In the words of Eric Hoffer: "You do not win the weak by sharing your wealth with them; it will but infect them with greed and resentment. You win the weak only by sharing your pride, hope or hatred with them." [15]

The key to the successful fulfillment of the objectives listed above, which we shall define as "development," is the sequence which was derived from the problems of the province and stated earlier. To repeat, this sequence is agitation, motivation, organization, and commitment.

The need on which this sequence is based should not necessarily be chosen on the basis of economic or technical criteria. Rather, the need chosen should be easily understood by the *campesino,* important to him, readily dramatized, and should require for its fulfillment a feasible, continuing, manageable task within the structure of the environment.

In Veraguas, for example, the need for rice-storage facilities was identified as being particularly useful according to these criteria. One of the early CEPAS precooperatives built a bin which allowed members to store their own rice rather than to pay the *tienda* for this service. The *tienda*-keeper's wife, recognizing, perhaps unconsciously or instinctively, the revolutionary political, social, and economic implications of this action, recruited a number of other women in the village and one night burned the bin down. The small and fragile organization could well have crumbled at this point, its members returning to the hopelessness from which CEPAS was seeking to extricate them. But, as it happened, CEPAS was able to encourage them at this critical moment and to provide a small supply of concrete blocks with which a new and better bin could be constructed. The incident was thus converted from an organizational minus into a definite plus, the new organization having confidence that it could not only change its environmental structure but could also withstand attacks upon the new structure.

Obviously, the significance of this event goes far beyond the need for a place to store rice. From the point of view of our development objectives the storage bin was significant in that around it a new organization or political institution was created with the capacity to meet many needs beyond that of storage. This new institution was a creator of new structure, the core of a new community, bringing confidence, power, and hope to those involved. The event also demonstrates the role of the agent of change or development, in this case CEPAS: leadership, competence, access to power (the capacity to provide concrete blocks), and the ability to protect. Finally, it demonstrates what is perhaps the most important role of matter in development: to strengthen the growth and power of a community or a political organization, or a development institution. Matter which falls outside such a purposeful receptacle is only accidentally useful to development.

The next objective thus becomes commitment to a community, which brings with it belief in the efficacy of cooperation, loyalty, and allegiance to the community, and a new sense of belonging. A variety of structural changes in political, social, and economic systems, such as the market and credit systems, are also effected.

From this flows the generation of indigenous leadership and the creation of new, local political and institutional receptacles which can usefully receive material and technical aid and make such aid useful for development. Whether these institutional receptacles are governmental or nongovernmental is of no real consequence; they must be *of* the community and in time will either significantly influence or in fact become "government."

In this way, the *campesino* develops a positive and useful identification with the nation. In fact, some might say that then and then only a real nation begins to exist. Confidence and participation in representative government develop at the local level, while at the national level there emerge administrative will and capacity to reach, assist, and represent the countryside. Continuing pressure comes to be exerted on the decision-making processes of the national government, with the result that higher priority is fixed on the problems of places like Veraguas. The motivation and capacity for rural action on the part of government administrative officials grows. The *campesino's* trust in and willingness to use his government increase in turn.

In conjunction with this framework it is possible to set a number of economic and social objectives which may carry with them special values. For example, in the declaration of the April 1967 meeting at Punta del Este, the several presidents agreed to "modernize the living conditions of our rural population, raise agricultural productivity in general, and increase food production . . . to promote education for development . . . to expand programs for improving the health of the American peoples." If one considers how these aims are to be accomplished in Veraguas, the microcosm we are using for a model, the preceding framework becomes relevant. Food production is a good example. It is quite plain from all I have said before that the problem of increasing agricultural yield is only partly solved by agricultural technology. It is also, and substantially, a problem of motivation and organization; a problem of land title, of the market, of credit systems; a problem of management, incentives, prices, economics, politics, and society.

2

Having attempted to clarify the objectives the United States should recognize in the development of Veraguas and similar places, let us now examine how they can be used and applied to determine programs.

Objectives are the measurements by which priorities and criteria for judging success can be set. If they are effective, therefore, they provide the basis for selecting between alternative programs. If they are not effective, such selection is necessarily haphazard and lacking in continuity and harmony; programs lack integration and purpose; development becomes marginal.

In the case of Veraguas, clear objectives help to clarify the task of program selection, provide direction for the expansion of projects, and even suggest new approaches which can be made.

There is no shortage of ideas for the development of the province. The following list includes some of those which have been seriously proposed, and serves to underline the importance of the objective-priority-criteria framework for making development decisions set out in the preceding chapters:

1. All-weather roads to open new areas of the province to greater participation in the economy.
2. A study of the mineral and forest resources of the province.
3. A study of the land—its fertility and appropriate seedings for it—to be used as a building block for further development.
4. Extension of low-cost electricity to rural areas.
5. Construction of a port.
6. Improvement and expansion of the two government agricultural schools in the province to train more students from Veraguas, undertake more experimentation, disseminate more information, and make more assistance available to the people of the province.
7. Provision of more technical and agricultural advice.
8. Encouragement of the land-reform agency to proceed with its work of parceling and selling off government lands so that individuals can become owners of the plots they work.
9. Governmental incentives to enterprises to locate or expand in Veraguas, through tax concessions, long-term loans, and the like.
10. Construction of a center in Santiago to interest passing tourists. The center would house a museum; provide information about the province, including its history

and places of particular interest; sell slides; show movies; be an outlet for native crafts, and be the focus of civic activities which it could also help to stimulate.

11. Improvement of the school system by construction of more schools, addition of new teachers, and a reorientation of the education available to make it more relevant to the peasants and their problems; also expansion of the National University's Santiago extension to teach agronomy, economics, and other subjects of immediate use to the people of the province.

12. Development of new industries, such as a rice mill, manufacture of wood and leather furniture, new lines of leather goods, tobacco and coffee processing, a slaughterhouse, or a food-processing enterprise.

13. Setting up of new commercial establishments such as a restaurant, office supply store, agricultural machinery store, construction company, repair shop for electrical equipment.

14. Opening a store in Panama City to sell Veraguan goods.

15. Persuading a traveling wholesaler to supply the *tiendas* in the countryside, reducing distribution costs while providing more variety in consumer goods.

16. Supporting and financing CEPAS-Juan XXIII and the associated cooperatives and organizations.

When we apply the framework set out above to this list, two projects emerge as being of highest priority: (1) the careful and imaginative support of CEPAS and its associated groups; and (2) the establishment of a food-processing enterprise either in association with CEPAS-Juan XXIII or independent of it.

The integrative nature of CEPAS and its affiliates is well exemplified by the fact that it could bear directly on all the ideas proposed above. If it were judged desirable to strengthen CEPAS, virtually all sixteen projects could be carried out by, with, or through CEPAS. The only limitation, apart from funds, would be managerial talent within the CEPAS organization.

CEPAS, as we have seen, deals directly with the *campesinos*.

One of its aims is to develop the capacity of peasants to deal effectively with the environment, and to help them prosper in many ways. Increasing and improving the rice harvest is one of its goals; the introduction of new crops is another. The same organization that performs these services could provide more efficient and effective transportation to the nearby cane mill. Transport of cane is now extremely expensive. As a result, production, mill profits, and *campesino* incomes are all low. The Juan XXIII cooperatives could own trucks, using them in season to haul sugar cane and at other times for general produce. Wider cooperation between CEPAS-Juan XXIII and large-scale commercial agricultural enterprises could help both groups by introducing better agricultural techniques and by motivating and educating the *campesinos*. CEPAS has already helped a farmer start a successful chicken enterprise. With a hundred chickens, he is now able to make $10 to $15 a week. CEPAS has helped him with credit and marketing, standing as an intermediary between him and his environment. It can also communicate his experience to others who may benefit from it. No less important is the political and cultural effect which a growing CEPAS can have, providing confidence, participation, involvement, access to power, competence, and protection. CEPAS, in short, fills the structural void in Veraguas in many ways.

It might, therefore, be appropriate for the government to arrange the introduction into Veraguas of matter and technique—roads, electricity, better schools, fertilizer—in harmony with the aims of CEPAS and its organizations. CEPAS will insure that the matter has a use, the technique, a demonstrator; and CEPAS itself will be nourished.

In spite of the fact that AID officials from Panama City as well as Washington have made frequent visits to Veraguas, have been duly impressed by the bishop and his work, and have left a wake of enthusiasm (with not a few hints of assistance), AID's assistance as of 1968 to CEPAS and its associated cooperative Juan-XXIII has been modest, to say the least. Total assistance has been two $10,000 loans, a small matching grant, and some used hardware. As we have noted earlier, a considerable percentage of the Panama aid package for 1967, which totaled about $30 million, was allocated for urban uses. Bearing in mind the objectives of the United States, the nature of the countryside—especially that of Veraguas, the most populous of the central provinces—and the future of Panama, there is a question whether the above balance of allocations was well advised. Similarly, it seems doubtful whether much of the $88 million AID commitment made to the Balaguer government in the Dominican Republic during its first eighteen months went to the engines of change in that country. Certainly none was received by FEDELAC, the country's most successful *campesino* organization.

Let us now consider a business investment in Veraguas, using our framework of objectives to reach a decision. While the investment must return a profit, the primary criteria by which we will reach a decision are those related to the objectives of the development discussed earlier. We shall compare and consider two proposals for enterprises in Veraguas which have been considered by AID and others in Panama, one for a slaughterhouse, the other for an integrated food-processing industry.*

The proposed slaughterhouse would process fifty head of cattle per day. It would be situated in Divisa, a small town at the juncture of Veraguas and the neighboring provinces of Coclé and Herrera. The enterprise would serve these three provinces and Los Santos Province. A capital investment of $300,000 would be needed, in addition to $100,000 for operating expenses. The slaughterhouse would probably be owned by an already-existing cattlemen's cooperative.

By using this slaughterhouse instead of existing facilities in Panama City, it is estimated that cattlemen would save as much as $6 per head in freight charges. Depending on its success, the enterprise could ultimately be expanded to include a sausage kitchen, curing cooler, smokehouse, beef-boning room, and canning facilities.

* Slaughtering cattle is indeed food processing. I draw a distinction here—perhaps somewhat artificially—between this particular proposed slaughterhouse, which, as we shall see, has a narrow development effect, and the more general, integrated food enterprise which we shall discuss further on.

Locating the slaughterhouse in Veraguas, it is argued, could help increase meat quality by reducing tissue shrinkage of live animals during shipping. It might stimulate the cattlemen of the area to produce more and higher-quality cattle. It could help create a balance to the slaughterhouse monopoly in Panama City; improve health of the stock by reducing transmission of diseases; unite the cattle producers around a central interest; lower beef prices by selling to a local market which as of now imports most of its beef; help the small farmer who wishes to market a few head of cattle; stimulate satellite industries such as meat-packing, freezing, tanning, or a blood-meal operation.

The slaughterhouse is a typical business project, having both merit and feasibility. It could be a profitable operation, and it might have many of the effects noted above. Measuring it as a development project, however, we find it has serious shortcomings.

It would have few of the political or social effects at which we are aiming. Its economic impact would be limited, since it would employ a relatively small number of people and influence only the cattle-owning population of the province. In Veraguas, the average herd is twenty head; of the 22,000 farms in the province, only 2.1 per cent have more than fifty head. The slaughterhouse would, therefore, have little effect in reaching the bulk of the province's people, and would have minimal importance for the owners of fewer than twenty head of cattle. It would provide little new motivation or organization and would not affect existing structures in any appreciable manner. It might even solidify entrenched power and have a negative effect on development.

On the other hand, it is likely that the establishment of a food-processing plant in the province could meet a number of our objectives. In Veraguas fruits and juices such as orange, lime, papaya, apricot, peach, or naranjilla might be produced. Corn, tomatoes, beans, pineapples, peas, or fruits might be canned. Preserves or marmalades of fruits could be processed. Soups could be made and packaged. Other products such as coffee, tobacco, plantain chips, yucca, or cashew nuts might be processed and sold. Another very real possibility in this connection would be to assist Juan XXIII in the construction of the rice mill mentioned earlier.

A food-processing plant of this sort in Veraguas would employ a number of laborers from the province in its own operations. It would build on the existing resources of Veraguas: land, crops, and people. The plant would stimulate supporting industries and services, such as a marketing organization and new or better transportation and roads, as well as a more flexible credit supply. Most important, a food-processing plant would affect a great number of people.

From studies of similar industries, we have learned that an industry that depends upon *campesinos* for supplies can have far-reaching influence. The relation between a plant purchasing raw material from peasants and the peasants is rarely a simple exchange of cash for goods. Usually, a number of political, social, and economic factors are involved as well. The plant carries out activities on behalf of the *campesinos* that would rarely be expected in the United States. For example, the cane mills in the interior of Panama, purchasing sugar cane from the peasants, find themselves doing far more than paying cash for cane received. The mills make loans throughout the year for seeding, cleaning, and harvesting the cane; they send out new seed types, introduce fertilizers, insecticides, and herbicides, and help finance peasants who want to purchase trucks for transporting cane. They pay trucking costs, including repair and gasoline bills, and then deduct these charges from the amount due the trucker. They then automatically deduct and pay the trucker the amount he is due from the *campesino* who sent in his cane. In some cases, this relationship is restrictive and hampers development in rural areas, but this model can be adjusted so as to be very helpful for development. The proposed food-processing plant could take on all the functions of the mills, but with enlightened management it could have a much more striking developmental effect. For example, whereas the cane mills only provide one "inspector" to assist and guide 250 peasants, a new firm could have a more extensive and better-trained organization to reach the peasants. Such a staff, trained to work with peasants, to teach agriculture, to visit the peasants' fields, to give talks or even movies in the peasant villages, would have a startling effect on the agricultural system.

Experience in Veraguas suggests that peasants are susceptible to change, that they desire to improve their lives, but that doubt and lack of knowledge, confidence, and opportunity often restrict them. As the work of CEPAS shows, with close attention and supervision, they are responsive to outside influences. The cost of developing a program such as this would not seem great compared to the long-term benefits whch would flow from it. Furthermore, such an enterprise could soon become self-sustaining and profitable.

Food-processing by its nature is often a decentralized industry; it is frequently better located where the food is grown than in the cities. The industry, therefore, helps to bridge the rural-urban gap, both in providing a source of employment to surplus rural labor and in slowing the migration to the slums. By increasing the number of wage-earners, it increases consumer buying power in the countryside, and thus it provides markets for industries serving rural needs.

By virtue of its power and importance relative to what is around it, the food-processing enterprise can have a profoundly beneficial effect on the total organization of the community in which it is located. This effect is by no means limited to the more efficient production of larger quantities of higher quality food. It can extend as well to the administration of local government, the judicial system, education, skill training, the removal of distortions in the credit and market systems, and the introduction of efficient, low-cost transport.

16

NEW STRUCTURES FOR THE
REVOLUTIONARY PROCESS

We have viewed the revolutionary process in Latin America, and have considered its relation to the interests of the United States. Between the two there is a gap, the dimensions of which are ill defined, obscured by traditional misperceptions of both process and interests. The task is to close that gap.

To do so requires the identification of United States power and purpose with that combination of change which is at once most promising and most consistent with our view of the good community. This is, after all, both the promise of the Alliance for Progress and the plea of the noblest and best leadership of Latin America.

The promise has gone unfulfilled and the plea unanswered, partly because of a miscalculation by both North Americans and Latin Americans of the nature and capability of government. The achitects of the Alliance were by culture and training imbued with the liberal, European-United States notion that governments adequately supplied with matter and techniques can be relied upon almost as a matter of nature to introduce changes to enhance the public good. Experience has shown, however, that governments, particularly those in prerevolutionary or prenational settings, are seriously limited in doing so, restricted by both will and capacity. This restriction derives from two characteristics of such societies: A majority of the people exist outside any significant relationship to this government, beyond its jurisdiction, reach or interest; and government tends to be the creature of oligarchic power-holders whose controlling interest is in maintaining the status quo. In the United States limitations on the capacity of local, state, or federal government to change urban black communities derive from corresponding characteristics.

But governments are not monoliths. They are composed of many parts, many kinds of flesh and blood. These include first of all political leaders. Some of them are revolutionary reformers —Frei, Lleras, and Betancourt, for example; others are technically oriented "modernists"—Somoza, Costa e Silva, Onganía. Governments are also bureaucracies, which as a rule are plagued by problems of inertia and commitment to old myths and interests. But invariably, in their midst there are those who are committted to change the old ways. Governments are armies, which themselves include a wide spectrum of purpose and competence. Governments are composed too of shadows cast by interest groups outside their formal organization: labor, businessmen, landowners, the Church, for example. So while it is true that generally in Latin America the complex whole of government is ineffectual as an introducer of change, it is also true that elements within it have both will and capacity for change. If these elements are to be successful in the way that the Alliance for Progress had envisaged they must be backed and prodded by outside engines of change.

In this context I recall a conversation with a high South Viet Namese official in 1966. We spoke of the problems of making South Viet Nam a coherent nation with unifying purpose. It was apparent that to this end he was eager to pursue long-delayed policies of land and credit reform. He seemed to understand well that the South was caught in a condition of revolutionary abortion, stopped halfway through a revolutionary process, a process which had been completed in the North, for better or for worse. Although those in control of the South were unwilling to accept the northern model of revolutionary change, they had failed to construct their own revolutionary alternative. Thus, many of the old and worn-out structures of colonial days lingered on. Furthermore, it seems painfully clear that the

United States actually encouraged the failure of the South to design a revolutionary alternative. As early as 1963, Don Van Sung, a prominent Viet Namese political figure, warned: "By emphasizing anti-communism rather than positive revolutionary goals and from lack of a better adaptation to the local situation, the United States has reduced its anti-communist efforts in Viet Nam to the maintenance of an administrative machine and of an army." [1]

I suggested to the Viet Namese official that revolutionary organizations in the countryside were needed which would, for example, break the hold of absentee Chinese mill owners and French rubber planters and lay the basis for more equitable ownership of land and the development of credit and markets for the farmers. The few organizations which had been working in that direction, such as the Tenant Farmers Union, had been decimated by Ngo Dinh Diem, with inadvertent United States help. The official agreed that revolution was a necessary prerequisite to nationalism, but he said, in effect: "What am I to do? A committee of powerful generals governs this country. They have far-flung interests. The revolution cannot start there. If it were to start in the provinces, then some of us in Saigon could perhaps be responsive."

In Colombia during the late 1920's and early 1930's peasants invaded land and seized *haciendas*, turning them into cooperatives. The landowners called for military repression, but in this instance the government refused to become involved, using the pressure of rural violence to force a land-reform law through the legislature.[2] In Viet Nam, however, the government could look to no such pressure from the countryside to start the process. For a time the Peoples' Action Teams were showing some promise of becoming such engines of change. Composed of young volunteers, these teams were given an unusually revolutionary brand of training by a capable and charismatic leader named Captain Mai. After training, they were returned to the villages they came from, prepared to organize and defend that village against all marauders—the army of South Viet Nam, the corrupt agents of Saigon as well as the Viet Cong—and to develop its political, economic, and social interests. As Captain

Mai began to make progress, he threatened the status quo. In 1966 he was branded a "socialist" and forced out.[3] (Such a sequence is, of course, common practice in Latin America and has been for decades.)

The most serious aspect of Mai's removal was not so much that it happened, but that the United States failed to perceive that it was symbolic of the forces and the circumstances which made the achievement of our objectives virtually impossible. We had committed ourselves to helping the South Viet Namese build a nation, but we had failed to see the essential revolutionary prerequisites for doing so, or at least we had failed to give suitable priority to these prerequisites. We also attributed legitimacy and capacities to the government of South Viet Nam which it did not have. We supplied it with virtually unlimited money and material to do what it could not possibly do. We thus corrupted it and all it touched. Although we used the word "revolution," we meant rather material inundation: the spewing forth into an unready countryside of vast quantities of matter, from tin roofs and pigs to schoolhouses and community centers. The fact eluded us that these things had little to do with the structural changes which were so necessary for the achievement of our objectives.[4]

The analogy between Viet Nam and Latin America is easily strained, but in some respects it is clear and pointed. In both places our vital interests have been regularly and dangerously frustrated by our failure to perceive the revolutionary precedents required for national organization and progress and by our naïve disposition to judge virtually any "government" as being capable of effecting those precedents. This is not to say that we have been unaware of the weakness and limitations of the governments with which we have been associated in either Viet Nam or Latin America. Rather, we have been unable or unwilling to conceive of ways of going around them to achieve our objectives, which, ironically, are in many ways their objectives also.

The hang-up lies principally in the well-worn admonition which is generally given sacred absolutism: It is forbidden to interfere—except now and then, as in the Dominican Republic —in the internal affairs of another nation, and, therefore, United

States efforts to introduce change, whether in Viet Nam or in Latin America, must be undertaken by, with, and through local governments.

This reasoning rests on the following assumptions.

1. All Latin American states are also nations.

2. All (except for Haiti and Cuba, which are outside our aid program) * have national governments which are presumably representative of the will of the people. That is, all governments are by some such standard legitimate. This assumption must be made, because aid and assistance to an illegitimate government would surely be as "interventionary" as aid to a group which might be seeking to change that government.

3. Aid to the government in power does not constitute support of the political party and interests which that particular government represents to the detriment of the opposition. If this were not the case, aid again would be clearly interventionary.

4. All governments have the will and capacity to comply with the terms and conditions of United States assistance, not only as set forth in the Alliance for Progress but as further stipulated by a wary Congress and fearful administrators.**

We have seen time and again the fallacies in these assumptions. And yet, we seem to be paralytically locked to their acceptance. The time has come when we must make quite plain to ourselves and others that millions of dollars of aid to a Latin American government may in fact constitute gross intervention on behalf of the groups in power and may be seriously damaging to groups who are not in power. Let us not mince words: Any foreign assistance is interventionary in one way or another. In addition, the withdrawal of assistance, once granted, is also interventionary. (This also applies to investment.) By pretending that we can provide aid without interfering in the internal affairs of another country we are in effect interfering haphazardly and

---

* Mexico is also off the aid list, but for quite different reasons.
** These terms and conditions frequently lead to the understandable change that we want to do over the foreign country in our image. In reality, we very often aim much higher, attempting to endow it with those ideals which we mythologically cherish—like unfettered private enterprise—but which we have been unable to sustain.

thoughtlessly, generally in such a way as to fix and stabilize the established elites. If we are unable to find a way around this dilemma, we are left with the real question whether governmental assistance does not in fact do more harm than good, in the long run setting back the processes of change which we have established are essential.

A new approach must be based upon a clear perception of what governments can and must do and what they cannot do. Governments in Latin America perform a wide variety of essential and useful services, sometimes with considerable efficiency, and in this performance they need and should receive increased assistance from outside sources. National administrative and legal systems must be sustained, money printed and regulated, public services rendered, and criminals curbed. Schools, hospitals, roads, dams, factories, communication systems, and transportation facilities must be built. Regional commercial, economic, political, and military agreements and institutions must be formed and strengthened. Governments are essential for the conduct of these necessary national and international activities.

We might add, incidentally, that the more representative a government is, the more successful it will be in carrying out these responsibilities, but this is not as simplistic as it is often made. It does not mean, for example, that so-called democracies do a better job or indeed are more representative than so-called dictatorships. The trappings of democracy and constitutionality frequently mask a variety of oligarchy which is hard to distinguish from and perhaps is even less representative than more blatant forms of authoritarianism.

Governments then—whether good or bad, representative or unrepresentative—are necessary for many things. Important as they are, however, they rarely can introduce the wide variety of radical change which is required. This change, in fact, in many cases would tend to subvert the very base upon which governments stand. Since United States interests require such change, our policy should strive to separate our assistance programs from local governments. It should seek to minimize the use of United States power and resources as a means to maintain the status quo. We must remove from ourselves the onus of sustaining the obstacles to change. This is as much a moral as a political necessity. Our policy should also seek to make a formal distinction between diplomatic recognition of a regime and approval or disapproval of that regime.

All this we must do not only out of loyalty to ourselves and our interests but also out of respect for those political leaders of Latin America, many of whom were prime movers in the Alliance for Progress, who themselves are keenly aware of the need for radical change of revolutionary proportions. These men often find themselves hobbled by their own governments, restrained in their efforts to introduce change by recalcitrant oligarchs and conservative bureaucrats, both of which groups are bolstered by our aid program. They are also impeded by insufficient organization and pressure for change outside of government.

I

Although the total thrust of a new foreign assistance policy should be directed at the fulfillment of the radical changes envisaged by the Alliance for Progress, the means to this end should in the light of the above considerations be seen in two quite separate types of programs.[5]

First, there are the programs of assistance designed to sustain, nourish, and improve existing local growth structures. Essentially supplemental in nature, such programs presuppose the existence of effective local structures capable of converting and directing economic inputs into a coherent, purposeful development scheme. They are, therefore, designed to serve and assist local government and those public and private institutions and enterprises which are generally favored by and necessary to government. Such programs include: health, education and public works; routine industrial development; training and assistance for military and police forces and civil administration; trade and tariff arrangements and export development.

These programs are in essence nonrevolutionary. They may well contribute to the gradual evolution of existing structures, but they are primarily aimed at improving the conditions of life within existing political, social, and economic structures. Programs of this sort, however, are by definition tied to national governments and therefore to the status quo; consequently, they may obstruct change. Such an effect should not be blamed on the United States but rather should be shared regionally.

There are other reasons why programs of this first type are best directed and coordinated by regional representatives and regional agencies. They are related to the commercial, economic, and political integration of the region, to the development of international transportation and communication links, to the preservation of regional order, and to the sustained and balanced regional economic growth. Furthermore, the United States is in an ineffective and distasteful position when it harasses and chides Latin American governments to make the most efficient use of large quantities of assistance (e.g., Chile). Latin American leadership would be not only better suited for the task but more acceptable; it would also be more sensitive to questions of priority, timing, concentration, and focus.

I therefore propose that all programs in this first category be carried out under the direction of the Inter-American Committee of the Alliance for Progress (CIAP), acting for the Organization of American States. To implement its programs CIAP would use the World Bank, the International Development Association, the Inter-American Development Bank, regional development banks, and such additional institutions as may be necessary. It would coordinate the foreign assistance activities of these institutions. For this purpose CIAP would have a regional office in each of the Latin American countries. This system of programs might be called the New Alliance for Progress. It would be financed by contributions from Latin American governments, the United States government, and European government members of the Organization for Economic Cooperation and Development (OECD).

It is apparent that assistance to the engines of change will not for the most part fall within this New Alliance. These engines might, as they do now, receive valuable technical and economic injections from their governments or from international governmental assistance organizations, but such assistance tends to be small, unreliable, and encumbered with stifling bureaucratic requirements. It is altogether insufficient for the vital task of change.

United States objectives, therefore, require a second and quite distinct system of assistance programs to find and fuel the critical combinations of engines of change so as to make the revolution as effective, as peaceful, and as useful as possible. Just as the first type of programs sustains local growth structures, the second assists the design and construction of such structures where they do not exist and helps new organizations of local power make existing structures more consistent with revolutionary impera- tives. It may appear that the two types of programs are con- tradictory. In a sense they are and must be. Our purpose, however, is to make the contradiction more precise and manage- able, to make the two sides complementary rather than con- tradictory. The vital interests of both the United States and Latin America lie in designing better ways of handling the existing contradiction. If this can be achieved, we will have pulled the teeth of violence from the jaws of revolution.

Programs of this second order are essentially nongovernmental. They seek to strengthen those organizations and institutions which can bring pressure to bear upon government and establish useful links with it. They are apart from government and in fact may often be hostile to the regime in power or to parts of that regime. They are the critical levers required to make the change process move, the means by which the first type of programs are given new direction, the essential forces required to weave a modern and lasting political fabric.

Implicit in all we have said about engines of change is that they will and must have purposeful direction. This direction must be well informed and well founded, guided by purposes and criteria which are set with objectivity and independence, derived from the community itself and not, as so often in the past, taken artificially from an alien environment. Programs to assist the development of purpose-making institutions in Latin America, therefore, fall naturally into the second group. They are by their nature local, aimed at a particular community, organization, group, or institution. There will be regional similar- ities and relationships in their conduct, and close regional cooperation would be desirable, but we have seen that the workings of our engines of change are fundamentally rooted in a particular place and a particular group of leaders and followers. It is not, therefore, necessary or perhaps even at the moment desirable to place them under regional supervision or direction. Eventually, we can hope that both types of programs can be merged within a new multilaterial framework. For the time being the second type will obviously be controversial; they must be handled with great care and delicacy, moving experimentally from small to larger undertakings. Even so, this new idea will be attacked; it would never survive the onslaught of the status quo if it were a part of a large international bureaucracy.

Congress should therefore establish and fund an American Foundation for the purpose of launching group two programs, using a diversity of nongovernmental institutes, centers, and organizations, representing a broad spectrum of United States interests and talents, each with special capability to work with and assist a Latin American engine of change or purpose-making institution. We should make the most of the pluralism of American society, accentuating its great and varied strength and employing it to connect the United States naturally to Latin American counterparts, presuming shared enthusiasm.

Before looking in more detail at how the New Alliance and the American Foundation would function, it is necessary to sketch quickly radical shifts in the organization of United States foreign affairs which our new interests and objectives and these resulting shifts in program demand.

An ambassador of the United States should once again confine himself strictly to being the representative of the President of the United States to the government of a foreign country and nothing more. This transition would be made possible by the replacement of the Agency for International Development and its foreign missions by the new structures mentioned. Ambassadorial representation should not imply approval or disapproval of the regime in power; it should merely be recognition of an existing state of affairs and condition of power. Although as the representative of the President the ambassador would be expected to make known the interests of the United States, it would not be his function—as it often is today—to seek to change the internal structures upon which the regime receiving his credentials rests.

As overseer of the AID mission and local grand master of the Alliance for Progress, the American ambassador is invariably expected to encourage the regime in power to change itself in some rather fundamental ways. United States (Alliance) assistance is at least theoretically predicated on such change. The ambassador, however, is rarely in a position to secure the changes sought even though they may be promised. He is, therefore, frequently in the ignominious and pointless posture of allowing money and material to flow under false pretenses, consoling himself and Washington with the dictum that he cannot meddle in internal affairs. On the other hand, if the government happens to be doing what by Alliance standards are the right things, the United States ambassador is virtually compelled to glow if not to crow about it. That is why in Chile, for example, the United States embrace of the reformist Frei government made that government the bloody target of both right and left, costing it the good will of the right with little compensatory gain from the left.

Such a replacement for AID would, of course, have other desirable effects. The size of United States embassies would be reduced and considerable dead weight on the wrong end of our balance of payments thus removed. More important, AID's replacement, partially by the New Alliance, would shift considerable responsibility for development planning and initiative back onto Latin American countries themselves. It would also increase Latin American self-scrutiny of both the purposes and priorities of development programs as well as their conduct.

A word belongs here about the Peace Corps. It is undoubtedly the most successful and rewarding United States initiative in the last decade, but even it stands threatened by the contradiction inherent in the commitment of the United States to both change and stability. Operating as they have, with and through local governments, Peace Corps volunteers in Latin America have felt the futility of attempting to introduce lasting institutional change. To the extent they have succeeded, they have frequently tended to encounter local governmental resistance, as well as increasing demands for control by United States ambassadors and embassies. Many in the Peace Corps have resisted embassy encroachment, arguing quite rightly that much of the Corps' validity and success derives from the distance it has managed to keep from the conventional United States diplomatic bureaucracy. At this writing, however, there are signs that those advocating Peace Corps independence are losing the battle and that embassy "coordination" is becoming increasingly prevalent.

A neat set of alternatives pose themselves under the scheme which I have advocated: The Peace Corps can continue as it is, risking increasing absorption by the traditional embassy structure; it can take a more radical course, emphasizing its commitment to change, and become an agency funded through the American Foundation, thereby increasing its distance from both the United States and local governments; or it can become an international organization, operating under the aegis of the New Alliance in Latin America and under similar regional auspices in the rest of the world. The first alternative seems to me to be unacceptable; it would almost certainly deny the Peace Corps its singular appeal to youth and its innovative dynamism. The second is undoubtedly impractical; the Peace Corps is too large and extensive to proceed regularly with any real degree of independence from local governments. The third alternative is therefore left as the most desirable. An internationalized Peace Corps is not a new idea, and the reasoning of this book would suggest that it is a sound one.[6]

Some may think it odd to suggest such a radical transformation of foreign assistance at a time when the existing program is in jeopardy and there has been a rebirth of isolationist sentiment in this country. A close look at congressional attitudes toward foreign aid, however, will show that the most serious and alarming criticism is coming from those who have long been its staunchest supporters. These men are disturbed because foreign aid seems to be failing by its own lights to achieve its own prescribed objectives.[7] In fact, as we noted earlier, some feel that it is indeed retarding long-term growth, especially in a political sense. It was congressional initiative—not that of

AID—which forced foreign assistance administrators to place greater emphasis on political development by adding Title IX to the Foreign Assistance Act several years ago. In this respect many leaders of Congress have been ahead of AID in realizing the necessity for a radically different approach. Whether the new approach is specifically the one I have suggested or a different one, it seems that the will of Congress is coming closer to the conceptions of interests and objectives upon which mine are based.

Only by some such new approach can we hope to arouse the national enthusiasm required to raise the level of United States foreign assistance to where it should be—at least 1 per cent of the gross national product and in time hopefully 2 or 3 per cent. Out of the total Latin American aid allocation, it might be appropriate to consider that 70 per cent would flow through the New Alliance system, with 20 per cent available for distribution by the American Foundation. The remainder might be distributed through the proposed overseas investment corporation or other routes mentioned below. Let us now consider in somewhat greater detail how these two systems would work in practice.

2

The New Alliance would be composed of an interrelated and expanded group of regional governmental institutions under the general and continuing coordination of CIAP, the Inter-American Committee of the Alliance for Progress. In 1967 CIAP became the permanent executive committee of the Inter-American branch of the United Nations' Economic and Social Council, as well as the chief organ of the Organization of American states for the consideration of all issues having to do with development—aid, internal reform, trade, and integration. CIAP at the moment appears to be the most promising form for bringing the ablest Latin Americans into a position of initiative and control over the development of the region. Under CIAP's general guidance, United States and perhaps European funds would be channeled into multinational regional organizations such as the Inter-American Development Bank, the World Bank, and the OAS itself for distribution in loans and grants to regional and national development institutions in Latin America. Special attention should be given to increasing the capacity of the Inter-American Committee for Agricultural Development (CIDA) to plan and press for rural reform and development. CIDA, one of the more neglected offspring of the Punta del Este Conference, may well have expired by the time this is in print; and yet it has conducted the most useful studies of Latin American rural conditions. It needs invigoration.

The task of insuring that these funds were being used honestly and efficiently would fall upon the international institutions themselves, which experience has shown are strict and tough in this regard—often more so than United States officials can or want to be. This proposal involves an expansion of those existing programs, which for the most part have worked well, and an extension and strengthening of Latin American control over these programs. The Alliance for Progress would continue as a true "alliance"; opportunities for regional growth and integrated development independent of United States pressures and influence would be increased; and yet the United States would maintain a useful relationship.

Funds and support from this network of regional institutions would flow much as they do now—loans, both hard and soft, grants for special projects, technical assistance and training—to governments and government-sanctioned institutions. In the past these have included business enterprises as well as labor union cooperative undertakings, ranging from housing to meat-packing.

But there would be some important and significant differences under the New Alliance, deriving largely from its regional rather than United States character. It would be more appealing to Europeans, and perhaps would even entice assistance from the Soviet Union. Training and technical assistance could be brought from many countries other than the United States. Israel in particular has much to offer.* Then, too, regional control of military and police assistance and training would seem to be a particularly salutary innovation, removing the United States from this sticky

* It is difficult today for AID to arrange for Israeli assistance to Latin America for a variety of reasons, not the least of which are the Arabs.

area and providing us with valuable political distance and
maneuvering room which we do not now have.

But perhaps the most important effect of the New Alliance
would be the added impetus which it would give to national and
regional planning and thus to the integration of Latin America,
first commercially and economically and then politically. We have
seen how damaging the close proximity of the United States and
its officialdom can be to Latin American initiative and purpose-
making efforts. We cannot help ourselves—it is in the nature of
things; we are large and powerful and our breath is heavy.
The closer we are to the processes by which Latin Americans
plan, establish priorities, identify their interests, and determine
actions, the more these processes will be distorted, dampened,
deadened, and defeated. We have long spoken about the necessity of "giving the Latin Americans the tools and letting them
do the job for themselves," but we have rarely acted accordingly.
Our AID programs have become an increasingly clumsy and
self-defeating exercise in almost the opposite direction.[8]

Supervision of the New Alliance at the country level would
be undertaken by regional, internationally directed personnel.
The New Peace Corps would work closely with New Alliance
country offices, helping to insure in particular that funds and
resources were channeled as effectively and efficiently as possible to the marginal masses who are so generally excluded from
the benefits of government programs. Peace Corps volunteers
would, in keeping with the argument of this book, be in the
forefront of creating the organizations and the motivation required to convert these resources into something of lasting value.

The steps necessary to the achievement of Latin American
integration require a measure of self-examination by Latin American leaders and nations that cannot take place if the United
States is looking over every shoulder. National purposes must be
defined; business interests must be identified; careful research
and investigations must be carried out, all within a context of
considerable fear and ignorance and an atmosphere of delicate
sensibilities. Much of the apprehension derives from the fear that
integration, once a dream of Latin American leftists, has become
the subversive plot of the United States and its corporations to

"exploit" the wealth and the people of the hemisphere on a regional rather than a national scale. No progress can be made until the means and resources are available in Latin American hands to assemble the brains, talent, and leadership, and to make the decisions necessary to achieve the essential goal of integration. Senator Jacob Javits has already suggested the importance of CIAP as the basis for effective integration machinery.[9] The New Alliance will have the vital effect of giving CIAP the importance it needs and deserves.

Emphasizing the regional organization of foreign assistance would also have its effect on business and investment. CIAP and the New Alliance, as part of their integration planning, could, for example, greatly strengthen and expand the work of multi-national investment companies such as ADELA (Atlantic Community Development Group). Organized in 1963–64 to attract world-wide investment capital to Latin America, ADELA is composed of almost two hundred industrial companies, banks, and financial institutions from Europe, the United States, Canada, and Japan. A catalyst for regional investment and enterprise, ADELA is attracting increasing outside investment in its projects, and has invested some $70 million of its own capital in a variety of Latin American development projects. It is a natural ally of CIAP and the Inter-American Development Bank in carrying forward the steps necessary to form the Latin American Free Trade Association (LAFTA).

We can see even in this brief review that much important work could be done by the New Alliance. Its purposes would be very much those of today's Alliance for Progress; we could hope that it would find new and better ways to achieve them. But we cannot expect rapid or radical change to result from its expenditures. Given the nature of the Latin American environment and the factors at work within it, we cannot expect even the New Alliance to move the revolutionary process fast enough for the protection of United States and Latin American interests.

It therefore becomes necessary to work the second route also and to establish the American Foundation.

The reasons for the Foundation would be close to the message of this book: revolutionary change is under way; it is inevitable;

it is in many ways essential and morally justified; the interests of world peace and of the United States require that this change be assisted. While it may require some conflict, the objective should clearly be to minimize violence. The objective of the Foundation would be to make the revolution peaceful; to make it effective; to make it consistent with broad principles of Latin American self-determination and with the best interests of the United States. In order to do so it would seek to bring to bear the material and technical resources of the United States to assist Latin American engines of change and associated purpose-making institutions, particularly universities. The activities of the Foundation would be essentially independent of the United States government and of Latin American governments.

The Foundation would be under the direction of a distinguished board of trustees. Members of the board and the Foundation's president would be appointed by the President of the United States and should represent a broad spectrum of North American as well as Latin American interests and points of view. In the initial years a majority of the board should be United States citizens. Members should be broadly committed to the purposes of the Foundation. Let it be emphasized here that the Foundation would be frankly an instrument of the United States to foster nongovernmental United States organizations which have the interest and the competence to find and fuel engines of change in Latin America. It might be indirectly an instrument of the United States government; but it certainly would not be part of it. Indeed, much of its validity would derive from its independence of government control. Its purpose would be to promote that change which is in the interest of the United States—as well as of Latin America—but which the United States government cannot promote.*

Acting in accordance with the principles of the Charter of Punta del Este and subsequent Alliance doctrine, the Foundation would identify a wide and varied spectrum of private United States groups and organizations which would have special capacity to identify, reach, and assist Latin American change engines

* Though it may seem farfetched, the Smithsonian Institution might offer something of an administrative model for the American Foundation.

in related areas of activity. The Foundation would, through grant and agreement, fund the activities of those United States institutions which could best establish a long and constructive relationship with change and purpose, making institutions in Latin America: organizations of the radical Church, peasant unions, trade unions, universities, and new varieties of local and multinational enterprises. Many of these are organizations and institutions which AID cannot reach at all today, or because of its governmental connection cannot reach effectively and efficiently. That they are important has been shown; that they can be reached by the United States is clear through the many activities of private United States groups in the past.

The Center for Rural Development in Cambridge, Massachusetts, for example, has been working in a small way—with grossly insufficient funds—with CEPAS in Veraguas and with FANAL (National Federation of Agricultural Workers) in Colombia. FANAL has not been thought important either by AID or by those in the Colombian government with whom AID makes its plans. That it is the only *campesino* organization in Colombia, a land ridden by rural violence for almost thirty years, apparently has not impressed the planners. In a small way the center has also assisted Bishop McGrath's operations in Veraguas at a time when AID was unable—because of local political circumstances—or unwilling to provide any more than token assistance.

The American Institute for Free Labor Development, the International Development Foundation, and the Cooperative League of the United States are private organizations which have been receiving funds from AID to carry on programs of this sort. These organizations have been unnecessarily impeded by their association with the United States government; they have from time to time unnecessarily embarrassed the government; they have been far less effective than they might have been if they were untied from government bureaucracy and embassy responsibility and allowed to follow their own natural ways.

AIFLD in particular suffers from being thought of as the tool of the United States government. Its difficulty, however, comes not so much from the fact that the bulk of its funds come from the United States government, through AID, but rather that AID and the embassy feel required to exert paralyzing administrative and policy control over it. Partly because of this attachment, AIFLD has become infected by something of the same disease that troubles so much of AID: It has a weakness for injecting money and material before receptacles are in place to insure an institutional effect; it has a way of putting up buildings, recreation centers, and the like for their own sake, without always making certain that wider, deeper, and better organization of working people results. It has also cut itself off from contact with a number of the more radical and effective worker organizations in Latin America, particularly in rural areas. Whether this constriction of its effectiveness was brought about because of its AID attachment or because of its own conception of the nature and future of the radical Christian labor and political movement in Latin America is hard to say. It might well be advisable to split AIFLD into several components, each concentrating on different areas of labor activities. This might improve its access and would also diminish its size alongside ORIT (Inter-American Workers' Organization), whose servant it is in part supposed to be. (ORIT has an annual budget of $323,000, compared with AIFLD's $5 million.) In any event, we can safely say that AIFLD, or any organization like it which is seeking to strengthen Latin American worker organizations, would do better as an independent entity working under a Foundation grant than as a government contractor under almost day-to-day supervision.

The Foundation would assist in the design and establishment of entirely new United States groups to promote the change organizations which we have described throughout this book: nonprofit and profit-making corporations for the opening of new lands in such areas as Maranhão, Brazil; turn-key operations undertaken by consortia of United States food and agricultural enterprises, to be turned over to local managers and interests, including cooperative organizations of the farmers who actually work the land.

Perhaps most important would be the role of the Foundation

in making possible direct ties between United States and Latin American universities, uncluttered by governmental considerations on either side. The Foundation could at long last halt the futile and mutually debasing efforts of the United States government in consort with some of our universities to make Latin American universities into replicas of our own. The basic problem of the university in Latin America is not that it is dissimilar from its United States counterpart, but rather that it has remained detached from and often ignorant of the community in which it exists. The need is not for it to become like its United States counterpart but to become more relevant to its own community.

Latin America needs above all else the study, the insight, the self-knowledge, necessary to formulate its own independent purposes and goals in respect to its universities. These must be arrived at by way of the discipline and detachment which only a great university can provide. It is perhaps presumptuous to suppose that there is any way in which the United States can help in such an important and precarious venture. But I believe that our Foundation, working with the best of North America's universities, could be of great use, if only in one pursuit: the support of greatly expanded research by Latin American scholars, with young counterparts and assistants from the United States, into the real nature and problems of their respective communities. Latin Americans should not come to the United States to study their region; we should go there to learn about their communities with them. American scholars have a good deal to offer in research: the idea itself, first of all—actually getting out into the streets, factories, and fields and asking questions. Getting dirty and hot in the pursuit of knowledge is an unfamiliar notion to many. Also, the techniques of research have been highly developed in recent years in North America; computer use and advanced methods of inquiry, for example. All this is essential to give the revolutionary process deep and intelligent purpose and direction, and also to hasten the progress. But it is extremely doubtful that such activities could be carried out under existing government-tied programs with all their bureaucratic overhead and political sensitivity.

But what happens when a Foundation-supported group encounters the status quo in Latin America and there is a conflict? How do you deal with the inherent problems of subversion in this suggestion? After all, we are bypassing government to introduce change to which government may be resistant.

Here is where the great advantage of separation from the United States governmental apparatus—the embassy and AID— becomes clear. Under our proposed scheme of things the ambassador would neither have to know about nor feel responsibility for Foundation-supported activities in his country of assignment. He might as a courtesy be informed of them, but no more.

Let us assume that the Center for Rural Development, with Foundation help, has been making good headway in training organizers with a peasant federation in Latin America. These organizers, as part of their work, establish a series of cooperatives producing tomatoes, corn, and rice. A large United States company, with Foundation assistance during the first year, enters into a 50-50 partnership with the federation in its entrepreneurial ventures, providing it with technical assistance and access to both domestic and internation markets. Another American company negotiates a similar partnership with the federation to produce cucumbers and manufacture and bottle pickles for off-season delivery and sale in the United States.

As the federation's income from these ventures grows, its ability to hire organizers and expand its activities increases. Organizing drives in the country's coffee areas are beginning and increased pressure is being brought to bear on the national land-reform institute to break up large land-holdings and distribute them to the peasants as the law promises.

The country's president, a progressive at heart, is delighted with the progress the federation is making, knowing that for the first time it is bringing new hope to the farmers in the country's congenitally troubled countryside. An important group of land-owners, however, are frightened and concerned; they come to the president to protest against the activities of the federation and in particular to complain about the activities of the United States group working with the organization.

The president has a number of options. He talks to the

United States ambassador, who quite rightly says that he has heard something about what those Americans were doing but that it is a private group; it has nothing to do with him or with the embassy. However, he will look into it. The president is satisfied with this answer for the time being; it allows him to keep his oligarchs cool. The ambassador investigates and reports back to the president, who may suggest that the activities be reduced somewhat or may in fact (at least secretly) wish the organizers godspeed. If the problem persisted and all other means to its solution failed, the United States group could be asked to leave the country. (My guess is that this would be a rare and unlikely outcome.) In the meantime, a good deal might have been accomplished.

For those who say this is unrealistic I would point out that West German government funds are given to a variety of nongovernmental institutions and organizations for development purposes in Latin America. Some of these funds undoubtedly end up assisting the organizations of the radical Church in Northeast Brazil. I strongly doubt, however, that the German ambassador is held responsible by the Brazilian government for these activities in the Northeast, which from time to time have caused it considerable discomfort.

United States entrepreneurial and investment activity should be stimulated both by the Foundation and by an expanded package of incentives and guarantees administered by the Department of Commerce. Here the report of the Watson Committee on Private Enterprise in Foreign Aid is still valid and useful. This report explored "methods for harnessing the vast nongovernment sector of the United States to the task of accelerating economic growth in the less developed countries." It recommended that a substantially broader role in international development be assigned to "business, labor organizations, agricultural groups, professional societies, educational institutions." [10] The proposal of the International Private Investment Council and of President Johnson's General Advisory Committee on Foreign Assistance Programs for a new development investment corporation also deserve serious consideration. To make the most of increased availability of government assistance for this purpose, American business will have to widen its sights and put its ingenuity to work along the lines suggested in Chapter 13.

The essence of this idea is that in our foreign assistance activities we stop behaving as though we were a statist monolith like the Soviet Union. Our greatest strength lies in our plurality of interests, points of view, and competences. We should not and need not stifle our plurality when we seek to achieve our objectives abroad. Let our natural forces go to Latin America; they will cause change with more smoothness and economy than Washington can imagine. In the process we will learn as well. We will certainly bring back revelations of purpose, understandings of motivation, and organization, which will help us to deal better with our own problems of direction and change.

By loosing a broad plurality of American forces in Latin America we will also be better able to avoid the kind of cultural imperialism which monolithic government-centered undertakings tend to spawn. A Christian Democrat friend described this when he said: "I'm not afraid of a Communist take-over in Latin America. My major fear is that we will end up as one more hunk of capitalist protoplasm, consuming well, with a higher standard of living but with no purpose in life, with nothing to contribute to the world, a warmed-over and inadequate version of the U.S." [11] I can see how much of our current AID effort kindles this fear. It is obvious, however, that this man's lament is entirely consistent with strong currents of thought today in the United States. We should be able to find some answers together to our mutual concerns about the future of man, his communities, and his institutions.

3

I hold no special brief for this particular combination of change in our foreign assistance programing. I am perfectly prepared to accept the possibility that the Foundation and the New Alliance may be ahead of their time or impractical in some other more substantial way. I have suggested them with a certain dogmatism because it seems to me clearer and more respectful to the reader to be forthright—even if it means being forthrightly wrong.* The point is not so much the specific formula as the change in national philosophy and commitment which must be confronted.

The argument of the preceding chapters is that America's crisis-oriented pragmatism is insufficient to deal with the ideological challenge presented by the revolutionary world. Our long preoccupation with communism has diverted us from using our great power and resources to lead in the building of new structures for a new order. Henry Kissinger advised us well when he wrote: "The challenge of our time is whether we can deal consciously and creatively with what in previous centuries was adjusted through a series of more or less violent and frequently catastrophic upheavals. We must construct an international order before a crisis imposes it as a necessity." [12] It is not so much a question of techniques as of attitudes: a willingness to submit to an intellectual and philosophical catharsis.

The traditional bureaucracies of government and business cannot be relied upon to perform this task. Neither can we look to the skills of the specialist and the technician. It will take the lonely courage of leadership; the imagination of the visionary; the moral purpose of the philosopher; the manipulation of the statesman; and the creativity of the prophet.

The challenge to government, then, is to recast our vision of the revolutionary world in general and Latin America in particular; to connect our moral purpose to that vision; to redesign our commitments accordingly; to reassess our resources in order to best meet our commitments; and to realign our bureaucracies in order to bring those resources to bear in the most effective manner. For example: It is our interest and purpose to increase levels of motivation and organization in rural Latin America as a part of our commitment to revolutionary change. It is also our interest and purpose to minimize the causes of war. Taking the case of unrest in rural Guatemala, we can postulate two alternative ways of proceeding. We could follow or espouse an essentially coercive policy of military intervention, or we could seek

---

* As Francis Bacon said: "Truth emerges more readily from error than from confusion."

the installation of engines of motivation and organization to achieve the same purpose. In this case the appropriate engine might be large-scale, integrated food-processing enterprises.

If we consider the bureaucratic implications of these alternative courses of action, it is clear that current United States governmental bureaucratic structure is such as to favor strongly the military approach rather than the more novel socio-political one. This is not because the former would be necessarily judged intrinsically better, but because of the way problems are normally assigned for solution in the United States bureaucracy. Habit and tradition have dictated that the Defense Department holds primary responsibility for "insurgency." We ourselves are not bureaucratically prepared to view the problem of violence in rural Guatemala in any other way.

This becomes manifest if we think about the second policy alternative again, in bureaucratic terms. With us, food and agriculture have traditionally been regarded as being under the jurisdiction of the Department of Agriculture, with the Agency for International Development of the Department of State obtaining certain jurisdiction in foreign agricultural activities. Now, if the National Security Council were considering a United States policy for operations in Guatemala, the Department of Agriculture would not be represented at all, and AID's representation would be marginal. Even if these two bureaucratic entities were members of the NSC, they would be expected to reflect their agricultural interests in technical rather than political-military terms. Thus, the possibility of utilizing food processing instead of guns and airplanes as a means of achieving our objectives would not even be considered by those with the power of decision. This automatic limitation of alternatives by virtue of domestic bureaucratic structure can only be remedied by concerted political action at the highest level.

If a decision were reached that integrated food processing in rural Guatemala offered a more effective way of meeting long-term interests than military action, then, of course, a wide range of problems of implementation follows. We are not now geared to using essentially private entrepreneurial resources in this area for the achievement of essentially governmental ends. Nevertheless, that such a gearing could be designed and effected seems obvious; in wartime, government and private business have integrated their activities with outstanding success in such fields as transport, communication, and construction.

The fundamental issue in this case boils down to two questions: How important is it to the government and people of the United States that the food-processing industry offer its managerial skills and technical competence to help bring organization, synthesis, and integration to disordered communities? And what is the order of priority of its doing so?

Presumably, if the priority were high enough it could be done on a far larger scale than at present. We have shown that the assessment of priority is hindered substantially by the bureaucratic organization of government. This can only be altered by major initiative on the part of political leadership.

There is also a need for similar initiative and leadership on the part of United States industry. United States companies are wary about entering into ill-defined relations with government. They would serve their own interest well, however, if they were to define more sharply the ways in which those interests are in conflict or in harmony with those of the United States government, foreign governments, and the revolutionary process. I have suggested that such an analysis would reveal substantially more harmony than might be supposed.

Business leaders of the United States have glimpsed the new challenges confronting them in this regard. George S. Moore, president of the First National City Bank of New York, has said: "Today's institutions—banking, business, public or private—cannot exist in modern society without reacting constructively to the goals of society and the economic, technological, social, and political forces that mold society." [13] Lammot du Pont Copeland, president of DuPont, has added that "business is a means to an end for society and not an end in itself." Sol M. Linowitz, formerly chairman of the board of Xerox Corporation and ambassador to the OAS, carried the same thought further when he spoke of business problems in the future being ones of "identity." "What should a corporation be?" he asked. "Which goals can it best seek to pursue? What meaning does it have for people and for the society of which it is a part? My own thesis is this: To realize its full promise in the world of tomorrow, American business and industry . . . will have to make social goals as central to its decisions as economic goals." [14]

These thoughts are at some variance with the more traditional notion that maximum profit is the chief goal of business. It is not that profits are bad or that they are not essential for the conduct of successful business; it is rather that they have become a less certain measure of success or criterion for judging long-term corporate growth and stability. The point is not, therefore, that businessmen have become suddenly more altruistic or that they are speaking differently; it is rather that they are perceiving the necessity of thinking in more philosophical, indeed ideological, terms about the direction of business.

As the modern large corporation becomes an increasingly important and efficient agency for the organization of social and economic life, it is forced, whether it wants to or not, to choose between alternative social and economic goals. It is forced to establish values and priorities which previously it was perfectly willing to leave to government or the Church or someone else. Its power and efficiency are thus driving it into essentially political goal-setting areas where it has never been comfortable. Its increasing ability to circumvent the national state will make even more urgent the requirement for new corporate purposes.

For both government and business, therefore, the most urgent needs in the future are likely to be in the area of philosophy and ideology; of goals, values, and purposes; of priorities, perception, and criteria. Here we may well find ourselves turning to the integral humanism of Jacques Maritain and to the notions of universal synthesis set forth by Pierre Teilhard de Chardin.

In *Humanisme Intégral*,[15] Maritain speaks of "three moments or aspects" of modern culture. During the first, which occurred during the sixteenth and seventeenth centuries, man sought a unified human order "conceived according to the Christian pattern inherited from preceding ages, a pattern which became forced and began to be corrupted." In the "second moment" (the eighteenth and nineteenth centuries) man demanded a culture to free him from "the superstition of revealed religion and to open up to his natural goodness the perspectives of a perfect security to be attained through the spirit of riches, accumulating the goods of the earth." The "third moment," in which we find ourselves today, witnesses the "materialistic overthrow of values, the revolutionary moment when man, placing his last end decisively in himself and no longer able to endure the machine of this world, engages in a war of desperation to make a wholly new humanity rise out of a radical atheism." In this third moment, says Maritain, in order to rule over nature man is forced to "submit himself more and more to technological and inhuman necessities. . . . God dies; materialized man thinks he can be man or superman only if God is not God."

Maritain sees salvation in what he calls "integral humanism." He envisages a return to an organic structure of society implying a new pluralism rather than the unity of the Middle Ages. He insists on the autonomy of the temporal order from both science and the Church, having as an objective "the conquest or realization of freedom . . . the freedom of autonomy of persons, a freedom that is one with their spiritual perfection." He seeks a society in which lives are regulated not by science but by wisdom. "We must choose," he says, "between the idea of an essentially industrial civilization and the idea of an essentially human one, for which industry is really only an instrument and is therefore subjected to laws that are not its own." Political and economic planning, therefore, becomes "a science of freedom proceeding according to the dynamism of means to ends and in continuity with the nature of the human being."

> Modern civilization is a worn-out garment. One cannot sew new pieces on it. It requires a total and, I may say, substantial recasting, a transvaluation of cultural principles. What is needed is a vital primacy:
>
> of quality over quantity,
> of work over money,
> of the human over the technological,
> of wisdom over science,
> of the common service of human persons over the individual covetousness of unlimited enrichment, and

of the common service of human persons over the State's covetousness of unlimited power.[16]

The thought of Teilhard de Chardin is in harmony with this view. Himself both a geologist and a theologian, he attempts a synthesis between science and religion. Mankind seems to be approaching "a critical point in social organization," says Teilhard. "The immense social disturbances which today so trouble the world appear to signify that Mankind in its turn has reached the stage, common to every species, when it must of biological necessity undergo the coordination of its elements." [17]

To borrow from Teilhard's image: It is as though we were beginning to become aware of some vast whirlpool ahead of us, the ripples of which we are feeling. They forecast and warn that there must be a synthesis in all things. A gigantic unity is being forced by this cosmic vortex. The barriers of race, nations, distance, sectors, and interests confront inevitable dissolution. But Mankind is not helpless in this universal grip. He can organize his response to the irresistible force, using it to magnify rather than to frustrate his capability. The way to the inevitable synthesis is threatened with conflict and turmoil; the ultimate unity will not come easily. The risk is great that the clashes it will cause will be so catastrophic as to obliterate all life in a unity of extinction.

A different vision is, however, also plausible: a vision of Man, growing in perception and love, organizing with sufficient speed and proper direction so that he will merge in harmony with the whirlpool's gigantic pull, strengthened by its forming force into a new and more glorious unity.

NOTES

CHAPTER 1

1. Roberto de Oliveira Campos, "Rising Expectations: With or Without Revolution," *Columbia Journal of World Business,* May–June 1968, p. 10.
2. See Samuel P. Huntington, *Political Order in Changing Societies,* Yale Univ. Press, New Haven, 1968, pp. 41–53.
3. Remarks to ambassadors and leaders of the Organization of American States in the East Room of the White House, March 13, 1961.
4. Huntington, p. 6.
5. "The Alliance That Lost Its Way," *Foreign Affairs,* Vol. 45, No. 3 (April 1967), The Council on Foreign Relations, p. 443.
6. Cambridge Univ. Press, New York, 1961, p. 39.
7. Huntington, p. 1.
8. See Alfred Stepan, "Political Development Theory: The Latin American Experience," *Journal of International Affairs,* School of International Affairs, Columbia Univ., Vol. XX, No. 2, 1966, pp. 224–5.
9. Walt W. Rostow, *The Stages of Economic Growth,* Cambridge Univ. Press, New York, 1960, p. 51.
10. "The Quality of Aid," *Foreign Affairs,* Vol. 44, No. 4 (July 1966), The Council on Foreign Relations, p. 601.
11. *The Anatomy of Revolution,* Alfred A. Knopf (Vintage Books), New York, 1938, pp. 31–2.
12. Huntington, p. 42.

CHAPTER 2

1. John P. Cole, *Latin America: An Economic and Social Geography,* Butterworths, Washington, D.C., 1965, p. 12.
2. *Latin America, Trends in Economic Growth,* Statistics and Reports Division, Agency for International Development, Washington, D.C., June 1965.
3. Henry J. Bruton, "Productivity Growth in Latin America," *American Economic Review,* December 1967, p. 1099.
4. "Rising Expectations: With or Without Revolution," *Columbia Journal of World Business,* May–June 1968, p. 14.

5. Cole, p. 99.
6. "Latin America: A New Exploration," speech before Naval Academy Foreign Affairs Conference, Annapolis, Md., April 1966.
7. I am indebted to Cole, pp. 101–27, for much of the material in this section.
8. Robert B. Keating, A Regional Transport Investment Program for Latin American Economic Integration, Inter-American Development Bank, Washington, D.C., July 1968, p. 7.
9. Ibid., see chart, p. 19.
10. Frank Bonilla, "The Urban Worker," Continuity and Change in Latin America, John J. Johnson, ed., Stanford Univ. Press, Stanford, Calif., 1964, p. 186.
11. Ibid., pp. 188–9.
12. Ibid., p. 190.
13. See Joseph A. Kahl, "Social Stratification and Values in Metropoli and Provinces: Brazil and Mexico," America Latina January–March 1965, VIII, No. 1, Rio de Janeiro, Brazil, pp. 28–34, quoted in Journal of International Affairs: Political Development in Latin America, School of International Affairs, Columbia Univ. See also Stepan, pp. 227–30.
14. Alexander T. Edelmann, Latin American Government and Politics: The Dynamics of a Revolutionary Society, Dorsey Press, Homewood, Ill., 1965, pp. 265–7.
15. Robert D. Crassweller, Trujillo: The Life and Times of a Caribbean Dictator, The Macmillan Co., New York, 1966, p. 4.
16. Edelmann, p. 266.
17. Emil L. Nelson and Frederick Cutler, "The International Investment Position of the United States," U. S. Dept. of Commerce, Survey of Current Business, September 1966 and September 1968.
18. Annual Report 1968, ADELA Investment Co. S.A., pp. 42–4.
19. Ibid., p. 216.
20. Lincoln Gordon, "Punte Del Este Revisited," Foreign Affairs, July 1967, p. 631.
21. United Nations, Yearbook of the International Trade Statistics, 1968.
22. Gordon, p. 632.
23. Ibid., pp. 633–4.
24. Isaiah Frank, "Issues Before the U. N. Conference," Foreign Affairs, January 1964, pp. 219–20.
25. John Gunther, Inside South America, Harper & Row, New York, 1966, p. 489.
26. Facts on Latin American Development Under the Alliance for Progress, U. S. Dept. of State, Washington, D. C.

27. *The Trade Union/Campesino Movement and National Development in Latin America,* Document #1, IFPAAW Inter-American Conference for Campesino Leaders, Caracas, Venezuela, February 1967, p. 1.

28. From a report of the National Economic Planning Council of the Government of Guatemala, reported in *The New York Times* by Henry Giniger, November 10, 1966, p. 24.

29. Cole, p. 129.

30. Gunther, p. 299, quoting a letter from Ambassador Tomic to *The New York Times.* Total export earnings in 1966 were $877 million (IMF, International Financial Statistics, June 1968, p. 76).

31. Speech to the First National Congress of Farm Workers, Santiago, Chile, July 15, 1966.

32. Alba, p. 192.

33. Document #2, IFPAAW Inter-American Conference for Campesino Leaders, 1967, p. 1.

34. Frank Bonilla, *Rural Reform in Brazil,* AUFS Report, Vol. VIII, No. 4 (October 1961), Brazil.

35. Gunther, p. 341.

36. *Ibid.,* pp. 356–7. Figures drawn from Charles Malpica, *Los Duenos del Peru,* 1965, Lima, Peru, and Samuel Shapiro, *Invisible Latin America,* Beacon Press, Boston, 1963.

37. CIDA, *Land Tenure Conditions and Socio-Economic Development of the Agricultural Sector,* Brazil, 1966, p. 171.

38. *The Dilemma of Mexico's Development,* Harvard Univ. Press, Cambridge, Mass., 1963, p. 77; see also Frank Brandenburg, *The Making of Modern Mexico,* Prentice-Hall, Englewood Cliffs, N. J., 1964, p. 275.

39. Edelmann, pp. 231–8.

40. See Vernon, p. 16, for valuable commentary on *ejidos.*

41. Edelmann, p. 237; see also Oscar Lewis, "Mexico Since Cardenas," *Social Change in Latin America Today,* Council on Foreign Relations, Harper & Brothers, New York, 1960, pp. 312–19.

42. John D. Powell, *The Politics of Agrarian Reform in Venezuela,* Ph.D. thesis, Univ. of Wisconsin, 1966, p. 183, updated to 1967.

43. Edelmann, pp. 247–8.

44. Edelmann, p. 240.

45. *Ibid.,* quoting Alberto Ostria Gutierrez, *The Tragedy of Bolivia: A People Crucified,* Devin-Adair Co., New York, 1958, pp. 169–70.

46. "Peru's Misfired Guerrilla Campaign," *The Reporter,* January 26, 1967, p. 36.

47. Gunther, p. 92.

48. *Ibid.*

49. References are to CIDA (Brazil), 1966; CIDA, *Land Tenure Conditions and Socio-Economic Development of the Agricultural Sector in Seven Latin American Countries* (Regional Report), CIDA UP—65/058 Rev., May 1966.

CHAPTER 3

1. *Alliance Without Allies*, Frederick A. Praeger, New York, 1965, p. 125.
2. *Ibid.*, p. 8.
3. *Dance of the Millions: Military Rule and the Social Revolution in Colombia*, 1930–1956, Univ. of Pittsburgh Press, Pittsburgh, Pa., 1957, p. 179, quoted in Edelmann, p. 71.
4. *Ibid.*, p. 191, quoted in Edelmann, p. 73.
5. Arturo Ulsar-Pietri, "No Panacea for Latin America," *Politics and Change in Latin America*, Joseph Maier and Richard W. Weatherhead, Frederick A. Praeger, New York, p. 67, 1964.
6. Barbara Ward, *Five Ideas That Changed the World*, Norton & Co., New York, 1959, p. 14.
7. Quoted in Hubert Herring, *A History of Latin America*, Alfred A. Knopf, New York, 1966, p. 158.
8. Charles W. Anderson, *Politics and Economic Change in Latin America*, Van Nostrand, 1967, p. 17.
9. Herring, pp. 243 ff.
10. *Ibid.*, p. 244.
11. *Ibid.*, p. 15; see also Samuel P. Huntington, "Political Modernization: America vs. Europe," *World Politics*, April 1966, pp. 409–11.
12. Frank Tannenbaum, quoted in Anderson, p. 22.
13. Anderson, pp. 37–8; see also Claudio Véliz, "Centralism and Nationalism in Latin America," *Foreign Affairs*, October 1968, pp. 68–83.
14. Anderson, p. 43.
15. *Ibid.*, p. 57.
16. *The Conflict Society*, Hauser Press, New Orleans, 1961, p. 20.
17. Edelmann, p. 327.
18. Gladys Delmas "Argentina Returns to Autocracy," in *The Reporter*, November 3, 1966, p. 35.
19. Alba, p. 54.
20. *Ibid.*, p. 84.
21. Tad Szulc, *Latin America*, Atheneum, New York, 1966, pp. 72–3.
22. Anderson, p. 108.
23. Huntington, *Political Order in Changing Societies*, p. 333.
24. Vernon, p. 189; see also Robert J. Alexander, *Prophets of the Revolution*, The Macmillan Co., New York, 1962, pp. 44 ff.

25. S. M. Lipset and Aldo Solari, *Elites in Latin America,* pp. 36–40; also United Nations Economic and Social Council, Economic Commission for Latin America, Provisional Report on the Conference on Education and Economic and Social Development in Latin America, Mar del Plata, Argentina, 1963, p. 250.

26. William P. Glade, Jr., "Revolution and Economic Development," in Glade and Charles W. Anderson, *The Political Economy of Mexico—Two Studies,* Univ. of Wisconsin Press, Madison, 1963, p. 43, quoted in Lipset and Solari, p. 39.

27. Huntington, *Political Order in Changing Societies,* pp. 315–34.

28. *Ibid.,* p. 309.

29. *Ibid.,* p. 327.

30. *Ibid.,* p. 330.

31. *Ibid.,* p. 333.

32. *Ibid.,* p. 334.

33. Speech at the First Latin American Meeting of Caritas, Santiago, Chile, February 1964, quoted in Joseph Gremillon, *The Other Dialogue,* Doubleday, Garden City, N. Y., 1965, p. 227.

CHAPTER 4

1. Paul Sigmund, *The Ideologies of the Developing Nations,* Frederick A. Praeger, New York, 1963, p. 5.

2. Kenneth Boulding, *The Meaning of the 20th Century,* Harper & Row, New York, 1965, p. 118.

3. Cole, p. 61.

4. *Ibid.,* p. 62.

5. *Ibid.*

6. Herring, pp. 17, 18.

7. Lipset in Lipset and Solari, p. 8.

8. The Macmillan Co., New York, 1933, p. 29.

9. *Ibid.*

10. 442 Documentos del Bachiller Eucero, quoted in Mackay, p. 43.

11. *Spain,* p. 37, quoted in Mackay, pp. 7–8.

12. Mackay, p. 10.

13. *Ibid.,* pp. 17–18.

14. *A Donde Va Indoamerica?* Biblioteca America, Santiago, Chile, 1936, trans. by and quoted from Sigmund, p. 286.

15. "A New Civilization for South America," *Berkshire Review,* Williams College, Williamstown, Mass., 1966, trans. and ed. by Prof. Frank S. MacShane, p. 13.

16. *Ibid.*

17. *Ibid.*

18. The Macmillan Co., New York, 1946, p. 15.

19. *Ibid.*, p. 16.
20. *Ibid.*, p. 17.
21. *Ibid.*, p. 58.
22. *Ibid.*, p. 59.
23. *Ibid.*, p. 62.
24. *Ibid.*, p. 91.
25. *Ibid.*, pp. 91, 92.
26. *Ibid.*, p. 98.
27. *Ibid.*, p. 43.
28. *Ibid.*, p. 44.
29. *Ibid.*, p. 45.
30. Everett E. Hagen, "How Economic Growth Begins: A Theory of Social Change," *Journal of Social Issues*, January 1963, p. 20.
31. *Ibid.*, pp. 21–2.
32. Lipset, pp. 5–6.
33. *Ibid.*, p. 7.
34. Aldo E. Solari, *Estudios Sobre la Sociedad Uruguaya*, Arca, Montevideo, 1964, p. 162, quoted in Lipset and Solari, p. 7.
35. Hagen, p. 24.
36. T. Lynn Smith, *Brazil: People and Institutions*, Louisiana State Univ. Press, Baton Rouge, 1963, p. 231.
37. Lipset, p. 9.
38. José Luis de Imaz, *Los que Mandan*, editorial, Universitaria de Buenos Aires, Buenos Aires, 1964, p. 160, quoted in Lipset and Solari, p. 9.
39. Lipset, p. 13, quoting Fernando H. Cardoso, *El empresario industrial en América Latina: Brasil*, Naciones Unidas Comisión Economica para América Latina, 1963, E/CN/12/642/Add. 2 Mar del Plata, Argentina, pp. 25–6; see also Thomas C. Cochran and Ruben E. Reina, *Entrepreneurship in Argentine Culture, Torcuato Di Tella and S.I.A.M.* Univ. of Pennsylvania Press, Philadelphia, 1962, pp. 226–8.
40. Lipset, p. 14.
41. W. R. Crawford, *A Century of Latin American Thought*, 2nd ed. rev., Harvard Univ. Press, Cambridge, Mass., 1961, p. 4.
42. Juan F. Marsal, "Latin American Intellectuals and the Problem of Change," *Social Research*, Winter 1966, p. 564 ff.
43. "The Limitations of the Expert," in G. B. de Huszar, *The Intellectuals: A Controversial Portrait*, The Free Press, Glencoe, Ill., 1960, pp. 168, 171, quoted in Marsal, p. 565.
44. Marsal, p. 568.
45. "Latin America and Japan Compared," in John J. Johnson, *Continuity and Change in Latin America*, Stamford University Press, Stamford, Calif., 1964, p. 245.

46. Lipset, p. 24.
47. Vernon, p. 156.
48. Lipset, p. 25.
49. *Ibid.*, pp. 31–2.
50. François Houtart and Emile Pin, *The Church and the Latin American Revolution,* Sheed and Ward, New York, 1965, p. 55.
51. Robert W. Burns, "Social Class and Education in Latin America," *Comparative Education Review,* 6 (1963), p. 232, quoted in Lipset, p. 19.
52. *Ibid.*
53. *Socio-Economic Progress in Latin America,* Sixth Annual Report (1966), Social Progress Trust Fund, Inter-American Development Bank, Washington, D. C., 1967, p. 36.
54. Social Progress Trust Fund Report, pp. 33–5.
55. Kalman Silvert, *The Conflict Society,* p. 109.
56. Edelmann, p. 134.
57. Covey T. Oliver, *Statement to House Foreign Affairs Committee,* Washington, D. C., March 21, 1968.

CHAPTER 5

1. Quoted by Samuel Eliot Morison, *The Oxford History of the American People,* Oxford Univ. Press, New York, 1965, p. 31.
2. George C. Lodge and Stephen F. Gudeman, *The Veraguas Report,* ICH 11G103, Graduate School of Business Administration, Harvard Univ., Boston, Mass., 1967, pp. 7 ff.
3. Brandenberg, *The Making of Modern Mexico,* p. 257.
4. George C. Lodge and Stephen F. Gudeman, *Aire Libre, S.A.,* ICH 13G20, Graduate School of Business Administration, Harvard Univ., Boston, Mass., 1966.
5. For comparable situations see Richard W. Patch, "Bolivia: United States' Assistance in a Revolutionary Setting," in Richard N. Adams et al., *Social Change in Latin America Today,* Vintage Books, New York, 1961, p. 127; Joseph R. Thome, unpublished report cited in Peter Dorner, "Interpretative Synthesis and Policy Implications of Land Tenure Center and Related Research," quoted in William C. Thiesenhausen and Marion R. Brown, *Survey of the Alliance for Progress,* Senate Committee on Foreign Relations, Washington, D. C., 1967, pp. 24–5; John D. Powell, "The Politics of Agrarian Reform in Venezuela: History, System and Process," unpublished Ph.D. thesis, Univ. of Wisconsin, Madison, 1966.
6. *Peasant Society in the Colombian Andes,* Univ. of Florida Press, 1962, pp. 224–5; see also Smith, especially quotations of Pedro Calmon, *Espirito de Sociedade Colonial,* São Paulo, 1935, pp. 197–9.

7. For an interesting parallel to Veraguas, see Theodore Schultz, *Transforming Traditional Agriculture,* Yale Univ. Press, New Haven, Conn., 1964, pp. 35, 176, 184–90.
8. "Counter-revolutionary America." *Commentary,* April 1967, pp. 31–2.
9. For an interesting and relevant study, see John D. Powell's report on the relationship between the Venezuelan Campesino Federation and land reform in that country: *The Peasant Union Movement in Venezuela,* Ph.D. thesis, School of International Relations, Univ. of Southern California, 1967.
10. See Schultz, p. 59, for comments on the "agricultural expert" in a different context.

CHAPTER 6

1. Helio Jagueribe, *Economic and Political Development,* Harvard Univ. Press, Cambridge, Mass., 1968, p. 4.
2. *On the Theory of Social Change,* The Dorsey Press, Homewood, Ill., 1962, pp. 297 ff.
3. Introduction to Frank Brandenburg, *The Making of Modern Mexico,* pp. viii–ix; see also John Womack, Jr., *Zapata and the Mexican Revolution,* Alfred A. Knopf, New York, 1968.
4. Y. S. Brenner in his perceptive *Theories of Economic Development and Growth* (Praeger, New York, 1966, makes a relevant comment. Speaking of economic growth or change, he says: "The most important factor then seems still to be the spirit of society. Alas, no one has so far shown as strong a social motive as private gain to stimulate incentives for economic progress, nor has anyone been able to attribute the outstanding technological progress in the Soviet Union to pecuniary gains. The whole problem of economic incentives is still a dark corner of human behavior."

CHAPTER 7

1. Reed Hertford, "Some Notes on Mexico's Agricultural Development," unpublished USDA briefing paper.
2. *Ibid.,* p. 2.
3. Clark W. Reynolds, "Agrarian Revolution in Mexico: A History of Agricultural Production and Productivity 1900–1960," unpublished, mimeographed, pp. 10, 34; Wolf Ladejinsky, "Traditional Agriculture and the Ejido," *Current Economic Position and Prospects of Mexico* (5 vols.), Vol. IV, Annex VII—Agriculture, Part II, mimeographed, IBRD, October 18, 1966, p. 42.

4. Reynolds, "Land Reform and Its Implications for Mexican Agricultural Development," mimeographed, pp. 2 ff.

5. P. 48.

6. *Ibid.*, p. 41.

7. *Ibid.*, p. 48.

8. *Ibid.*, p. 66.

9. Reynolds, "Agrarian Revolution," pp. 6, 23.

10. Reynolds, "Land Reform," p. 6.

11. Ladejinsky, p. 83.

12. *Ibid.*, p. 84.

13. *Ibid.*, p. 41.

14. Nathan L. Whetten, *The Role of the Ejido in Mexican Land Reform,* May 1963, p. 4, Land Tenure Center, Univ. of Wisconsin, p. 571, quoted in Ladejinsky, p. 51.

15. IADB, Social Progress Trust Fund Report, p. 375.

16. Powell, pp. 11, 14.

17. *Ibid.*, p. 69 ff.

18. *Ibid.*, p. 122.

19. *Ibid.*, p. 175.

20. *Ibid.*, p. 192.

21. See IADB Report, pp. 157–8.

22. A. O. Hirschman, *Journeys Toward Progress,* Doubleday and Co. Inc., Garden City, N. Y., 1965, pp. 40 ff.

23. Stefan Robock, *Brazil's Developing Northeast: A Study of Regional Planning and Foreign Aid,* The Brookings Institution, Washington, D. C., 1963, p. 48.

24. Hirschman, p. 42.

25. *Diagnosis of the Brazilian Crisis,* p. 148. Translated by Suzette Macedo. Berkeley, Univ. of Calif. Press, 1965. Translation of *Dialética de desenvolvimento.*

26. Robock, p. 9.

27. See Gilberto Freyre, "Misconceptions of Brazil," *Foreign Affairs,* April 1962, p. 455.

28. Gunther, pp. 94–5.

29. Hirschman, pp. 106 ff.

30. Robock, p. 4.

31. Hirschman, p. 128.

32. Gunther, p. 44.

33. "Brazil: Complex Giant," *Foreign Affairs,* January 1965, p. 303.

CHAPTER 8

1. For a useful summary of these events see the table in Alistair Hennessy, "The Military in Politics," in Claudio Veliz, ed., *Latin*

America and the Caribbean: A Handbook, Frederick A. Praeger, New York, 1968, pp. 373 ff.

2. Edwin Lieuwen, "Militarism and Politics in Latin America," in John J. Johnson, ed., *The Role of the Military in Underdeveloped Countries,* Princeton University Press, Princeton, N. J., 1962; pp. 138–9.

3. Lyle N. McAlister, "Changing Concepts of the Role of the Military in Latin America," *Annals of the American Academy of Political and Social Sciences,* 360, July 1965, p. 91.

4. John J. Johnson, quoted in McAlister, p. 91.

5. McAlister, p. 90.

6. See Robert D. Crassweller, *Trujillo: The Life and Times of a Caribbean Dictator,* The Macmillan Co., New York, 1966.

7. Fluharty, *Dance of the Millions,* quoted in Johnson, pp. 147–8.

8. Johnson, p. 120.

9. McAlister, p. 93, and Edward Glick, *The Nonmilitary Use of the Latin American Military,* Systems Development Corporation, Santa Monica, Calif., July 18, 1964.

10. John M. Goshko, *Washington Post,* February 5, 1968.

11. *Ibid.*

12. Henry Giniger, "Reforms Put Off in Guatemala," *The New York Times,* March 9, 1968.

13. *The New York Times,* "News of the Week in Review," April 16, 1967, p. E13.

14. Edward J. Mitchell, "Land Tenure and Rebellion: A Statistical Analysis of Factors Affecting Government Control in South Viet-Nam," RM-5181-ARPA, The RAND Corporation, Santa Monica, June 1967.

15. Alba, p. 178.

16. "The Latin American Military," Survey of the Alliance for Progress, A Study for the Subcommittee on American Republic Affairs of the Committee on Foreign Relations, U. S. Senate, October 9, 1967.

CHAPTER 9

1. Roque Dalton, "Catholics and Communists in Latin America: Some Aspects of the Present Situation," *Peace, Freedom and Socialism,* January 1968, p. 36.

2. Pope Paul VI, *Populorum Progressio.* The full text may be found in *The New York Times,* March 29, 1967, pp. 23–5.

3. Paul L. Montgomery, "Church Lends Its Support to Colombia's Land Redistribution Program," *The New York Times,* July 17, 1967.

4. *The National Catholic Reporter,* Vol. 4, No. 14, January 31, 1968, p. 7.

5. *The New York Times,* April 7, 1968.

6. *Ibid.,* March 31, 1968.

7. "Hour of Decision for Church, Cost of Change," *Confirmado,* Buenos Aires (Spanish), March 1969, pp. 12–14; see also "Laymen Give Support to Resigning Priests," *La Nacio,* Buenos Aires, April 11, 1969.

8. See articles in *El Popular* (Spanish),Montevideo, March 26, 1969, p. 5; April 1, 1969, p. 7; April 2, 1969, p. 2; April 3, 1969, p. 2; see also "Zaffaroni and Ferro Seek Lay Status, To Wed," *El Diario,* Montevideo (Spanish), March 27, 1969, p. 14.

9. Ivan Vallier, "Religious Elites: Differentiations and Developments in Roman Catholicism," in Lipset and Solari, p. 199.

10. Dalton, p. 36.

11. Goshko, "Bishops Move to the Left," *Washington Post,* March 11, 1968, Sect. A, p. 8.

12. Translated by the author from *A Strategy Against Poverty,* DESAL publication in Spanish, August 1966.

13. See Vallier in Lipset and Solari, p. 211, for relevant discussion.

14. Hart, p. 95. Telegram on file in the Ministry of Agriculture, Santo Domingo.

15. *Ibid.,* p. 101.

16. *Ibid.,* p. 102. Free translation of a telegram on file in the Ministry of Agriculture, Santo Domingo.

17. *Ibid.,* p. 103. Ref. Francisco Dorta-Duque, *Situacio Legal,* Oficina de Planificacion, Coordinación y Evaluación, Min. of Agriculture, Santo Domingo, April 20, 1967, and *El Carib,* Santo Domingo, April 19, 1967, p. 7.

18. Frederick B. Pike, "The Catholic Church and Modernization in Peru and Chile," *Journal of International Affairs,* Columbia University, Vol. XX, No. 2, 1966, p. 277.

19. Henry Giniger, "Guatemala Is a Battleground," *The New York Times Magazine,* June 16, 1968.

20. *The National Catholic Reporter,* January 31, 1968, Vol. 4, No. 14, p. 5.

21. Giniger, *The New York Times,* November 11, 1967, p. 24.

22. *Religion and the Rise of Capitalism,* Harcourt Brace & Co., New York, 1926.

23. Northrop, Chap. III.

24. *Reflections on America,* Charles Scribner's Sons, New York, 1958, p. 118.

25. Ricardo Arias Calderón, address to CICOP meeting, Boston, Mass., January 1966.
26. Vallier, p. 221.
27. Samuel Ramos, *Profile of Man and Culture in Mexico*, translated by Peter G. Earle, New York, McGraw-Hill, Inc., New York, 1962, pp. 77–8, quoted in Vallier, p. 222.
28. *Ibid.*
29. Thomas J. Hamilton, "Czech Urges Christian-Marxists Talks To Avoid a New Stalinism," *The New York Times*, April 12, 1968.
30. For an excellent summary of the attitudes of the Church toward revolution and violence in Latin America, see Bishop Marcos Mc-Grath, "Development for Peace," *America*, April 27, 1968, pp. 562–7.
31. Quoted in Juan Luís Segundo, S.J., "Christianity and Violence in Latin America," *Christianity and Crisis*, March 4, 1968, p. 31.
32. Translated from the Spanish, *El Tiempo*, Bogota, Colombia, Sept. 8, 1968, pp. 20–2.

CHAPTER 10

1. Gabriel A. Almond and Sidney Verba, *The Civic Culture*, Princeton Univ. Press, Princeton, N. J., 1963, p. 478.
2. Joseph R. Slevin, "Where AID Is Bearing Fruit," *Boston Globe*, May 27, 1968, p. 38.
3. See Ernst Halperin, *Nationalism and Communism in Chile*, MIT Press, Cambridge, Mass., 1965, p. 27, for the contrary argument.
4. Profs. William C. Thiesenhusen and Marion R. Brown, "Problems of Agriculture," Survey of the Alliance for Progress, A Study for the Subcommittee on American Republics Affairs, Committee on Foreign Relations, U. S. Senate, December 1967, p. 13.
5. George I. Blanksten, *Ecuador: Constitutions and Caudillos*, Univ. of California Press, Berkeley, 1951, quoted in Edelmann, p. 336.
6. For more on Latin American political parties and leadership, see Harry Kantor, *The Ideology and Program of the Peruvian Aprista Movement*, Octagon, New York, 1966, and Alexander.
7. Eduardo Frei Montalva, "Paternalism, Pluralism, and Christian Democratic Reform Movements in Latin America," in *Religion, Revolution and Reform*, William V. D'Antonio and Frederick B. Pike, eds., Frederick A. Praeger, New York, 1964, p. 37.
8. *Ibid.*
9. *Ibid.*
10. *Ibid.*, p. 36.
11. Paul E. Sigmund, "Christian Democracy in Chile," *Journal of*

International Affairs, School of International Affairs, Columbia Univ., Vol. XX, No. 2, (1966), pp. 334 ff.

12. See Halperin, p. 22.
13. Interview in 1966 in Chile.
14. Jaime Castillo Velasco, *El Problema Communista,* Editorial Del Pacifico, S.A., Santiago, Chile, 1955, p. 214; quoted in Halperin, p. 196.
15. See Halperin, p. 197, for comments on communitarianism.
16. "The Government Bureaucrats and Political Change in Latin America," *Journal of International Affairs,* School of International Affairs, Columbia Univ., Vol. XX, No. 2 (1966), pp. 289–308.
17. *Ibid.,* p. 296.
18. *Ibid.,* p. 306.
19. "Democratic Revolutions," *Commonweal,* October 29, 1965, p. 121.
20. Edward L. Burke, "The Christian Democratic Party in El Salvador," unpubl. thesis, Woodrow Wilson School of Public and International Affairs, Princeton Univ., October 1966, p. 29.
21. *Ibid.,* p. 22.
22. *Ibid.,* p. 23.
23. Juan de Onís, "University Shutdown in Chilean Strike," *The New York Times,* October 24, 1966, p. 18.
24. Allen Young, "Students Protest in Brazil," *Christian Science Monitor,* October 1966.
25. De Onís, "Student Unrest Grows in Brazil," *The New York Times,* September 18, 1966, p. 26.
26. Paul L. Montgomery, "Troops and Armor Massed in Rio to Forestall a Demonstration by Students," *The New York Times,* August 7, 1968, p. 12.
27. "School Abolished at Guatemala University," *The New York Times,* August 12, 1968, p. 9.
28. Darcy Ribeiro, "Universities and Social Development," Lipset and Solari, pp. 352–3.

CHAPTER 11

1. Halperin, "The Decline of Communism in Latin America," *The Atlantic Monthly,* May 1965, p. 37.
2. "Latin America," *Survey,* London, January 1965, p. 158.
3. *Ibid.,* p. 161.
4. See *Translations on Cuba, No. 567,* U. S. Dept. of Commerce, a translation of *Revolution en la Revolucion?* by Regis Debray, reprinted in the Spanish-language periodical *Politica,* February 1–14, 1967, Mexico City, pp. 1–32, especially p. 5.

5. UPI, "Castro Is Scored in Pravda Article," *The New York Times*, August 1, 1967.
6. Robert Scheer, ed., *The Diary of Che Guevara*, New York, Bantam Books Inc., 1968, pp. 15 ff.
7. Halperin, *Atlantic Monthly*, p. 37.
8. Robert Rogers and Ted Yates, "The Undeclared War in Guatemala," *Saturday Evening Post*, June 18, 1966.
9. "Insurgency in Latin America," p. 18.
10. Halperin, *Survey*, p. 165.
11. For a discussion of this see Rostow, *Stages of Economic Growth*, pp. 145–67, and Halperin, *The Problem of Feudalism in Latin America*, Center for International Studies, MIT, Cambridge, Mass., October 1967.
12. Che Guevara, *Guerrilla Warfare*, p. 15.
13. Debray, pp. 82–5.
14. *Ibid.*, p. 7.
15. *Ibid.*, pp. 17–21.
16. *Ibid.*, p. 39.
17. *Ibid.*, pp. 31–3.
18. *Ibid.*, p. 42.
19. *Ibid.*, p. 79.
20. *Ibid.*, p. 67.
21. *Ibid.*, p. 69.
22. *Ibid.*, p. 78.

CHAPTER 12

1. "Labor Policies and Programs," *Survey of the Alliance for Progress*, a study prepared at the request of the Subcommittee on American Republics Affairs by the staff of the Committee on Foreign Relations, U. S. Senate, July 15, 1968, p. 2.
2. Aníbal Quijano Obregón, "Contemporary Peasant Movements," Lipset and Solari, p. 322.
3. See George C. Lodge, *Spearheads of Democracy*, Harper & Row, New York, 1962, Chapter 1 and elsewhere.
4. Henry A. Landsberger, "The Labor Elite: Is It Revolutionary?" Lipset and Solari, pp. 287–8.
5. Robert J. Alexander, *Organized Labor in Latin America*, Free Press, New York, 1965, pp. 35–45.
6. *Ibid.*, pp. 50–3.
7. Norman Ingrey, "Confrontation Shakes Argentine Labor," *Christian Science Monitor*, April 3, 1967, p. 3.
8. Alexander, pp. 71–84.
9. *Ibid.*, pp. 104–10.

10. Brandenburg, p. 346.

11. Landsberger in Lipset and Solari, p. 264; Frank Bonilla, "The Urban Worker," *Continuity and Change in Latin America,* John J. Johnson, ed., Stanford Univ. Press, Stanford, Calif., 1964, pp. 193–200; Victor Alba, *Alliance Without Allies, op. cit.,* pp. 103–5.

12. For the importance of this phenomenon in South Viet Nam, see Samuel P. Huntington, "The Bases of Accommodation," *Foreign Affairs,* July 1968.

13. Landsberger, pp. 270–5.

14. *Ibid.,* p. 283.

15. See Serafino Romualdi, *Presidents and Peons,* Funk & Wagnalls, New York, 1967, pp. 110–21, for an interesting account of the birth of ORIT.

16. See Romualdi, *Presidents and Peons.*

17. "Labor Policies and Programs," p. 10.

18. Address at the Council on Latin America, April 2, 1965, quoted in Romualdi, p. 418.

19. The Regional Program for the American Institute for Free Labor Development, FY 1969, mimeographed, Washington, D. C., March 1968.

20. John D. Powell, "Peasant Union Movement in Venezuela," School of International Relations, Univ. of S. Calif. Presented as a paper at the conference on peasant movements held at Cornell Univ., Dec. 1966.

21. *Ibid.,* p. 6.

22. *Ibid.,* p. 7.

23. *Ibid.*

24. *Ibid.,* p. 15.

25. John D. Powell, *The Role of the Federación Campesina in the Venezuelan Agrarian Reform Process,* mimeographed, 1967, p. 39.

26. *Ibid.*

27. *Ibid.,* pp. 39–40.

28. Powell, *Peasant Union Movement in Venezuela,* p. 22.

29. *Ibid.,* p. 26.

30. *Ibid.,* p. 39.

31. Obregón in Lipset and Solari, pp. 313–17.

32. Huntington, *Political Order in Changing Societies,* pp. 359–60.

33. For another example, see Henry A. Landsberger, "The Role of Peasant Movements and Revolts in Development: An Analytical Framework," Bulletin, International Institute for Labor Studies, Geneva, Switzerland, February 1968, pp. 33–4. See the rest of this article for Landsberger's hypotheses concerning peasant movements, which are similar to my own. Also see Obregón in Lipset and Solari, p. 317.

34. Landsberger, *Bulletin,* pp. 79–81.

35. *Ibid.,* p. 81.

36. Address at Notre Dame University, "Religion and Social Revolution in Latin America," April 23, 1965.

37. Juaregui H. Arturo, "ORIT General Secretary Answers CLASC Attacks," Inter-American Labor Bulletin, August 1966. For a more detailed and vitriolic attack on CLASC see Jesse Friedman, "CLASC Unmasked," AFL-CIO Free Trade Union News, Oct. 1966, Vol. 21, No. 10. Friedman was at the time program director of the ORIT Institute, Cuernavaca, Mexico. Friedman's article was answered by Monsignor George G. Higgins, director, Social Action Department, National Catholic Welfare Conference. Commenting on Friedman's assertion that his criticism was "an objective analysis," Father Higgins wrote: "If that represents an 'objective' analysis of CLASC, I shudder to think of what Mr. Friedman might be tempted to say over a drink in a Cuernavaca bar if he happened to be in a somewhat more 'subjective' mood. In any event, he is kidding himself if he thinks that current U.S. interest in CLASC is limited to 'leftist intellectuals.' The next time he comes to the States I will be happy to put him in touch with a number of authentic anti-Communists who, rightly or wrongly, think that CLASC, with all its imperfections, has something to offer and the time has come for ORIT (with all of its imperfections) to get down off its high horse and start looking for ways and means of achieving at least a modicum of labor unity in Latin America."

CHAPTER 13

1. See Harvey Leibenstein, "Enterepreneurship and Development," American Economic Review, papers and proceedings of 80th Annual Meeting of American Economic Assoc., Cambridge, Mass., May 1968, pp. 72–83.

2. Raymond Vernon, "Conflict and Resolution Between Foreign Direct Investors and Less Developed Countries," *Public Policy,* Vol. XVII, Fall 1968, John F. Kennedy School of Public Administration, Harvard Univ., Cambridge, Mass., pp. 333–51.

3. Alex Inkeles, "The Modernization of Man," in *Modernization,* Myron Weiner, ed., Basic Books, Inc., New York, 1966, pp. 138–50.

4. Edward S. Mason, "Economic Development in India and Pakistan," Occasional Paper No. 12, Center for International Affairs, Harvard Univ., Cambridge, Mass., September 1966, p. 2H.

5. *Ibid.,* p. 54.

6. Walter P. Falcon and Carl H. Gotsch, "Agricultural Development in Pakistan: Lessons from the Second Plan Period," mimeographed, Development Advisory Service, Center for International Affairs, Harvard Univ., Cambridge, Mass., pp. 11–16.

7. See Emil L. Nelson and Frederick Cutler, "International Investment Position of the United States in 1966," *Survey of Current Business,* U. S. Dept. of Commerce, October 1968, pp. 19–32.

8. Interview with Antônio Marcôe Pimenta-Neves, managing editor, Folha de São Paolo, July 1968.

9. U. S. Rep. F. Bradford Morse and Timothy B. Atkeson, "United States Private Investment Under the Alliance for Progress: Policy Developments Affecting United States Private Investment in Latin America, 1960–1965," *Boston University Law Review,* Vol. XLVI, No. 2 (Spring 1966), pp. 153–4.

10. George C. Lodge and Lawrence G. Franko, *Venezuelan Insurance Bill* (D), Harvard Business School, President and Fellows of Harvard College, Cambridge, Mass., 1967, pp. 3, 4, 9.

11. *Business Week,* December 7, 1968, p. 106.

12. *Ibid.,* November 16, 1968, p. 120.

13. I have borrowed in this section from George C. Lodge, "Food Processing—Key to Economic Development," *Harvard Business Review,* September–October 1966. See also Ray A. Goldberg, "Agri-business for Developing Countries" in the same issue.

14. For an account of the way in which three such enclaves brought profound change, however, see Vernon, "Foreign Owned Enterprises in the Developing Countries," *Public Policy,* Graduate School of Public Administration, Harvard University, Cambridge, Mass., 1966, pp. 367–9. Vernon describes the pervasive effects of the guano industry in Peru, the foreign enclave economy in Mexico during the Porfirian era, and the foreign oil companies in Venezuela.

15. See Wayne G. Broehl, Jr., "The International Basic Economy Corporation," United States Business Performance Abroad Series, National Planning Association, Washington, D. C., 1968.

16. *Ibid.,* p. 278.

17. *Ibid.,* p. 64.

18. For a survey of current U. S. activity in this area, see John R. Moore and Frank A. Padovano, *U.S. Investment in Latin American Food Processing,* Frederick A. Praeger, New York, 1967. See also Dr. Peter Kuin's "Meeting Economic and Social Needs in a Variety of Countries," a pamphlet published by Unilever N.V., Rotterdam, for a concise and thoughtful account of how a European director of an international firm sees its role in development.

19. Miguel Wionczek estimated that in 1964 foreign investments in

Latin America amounted to only about 6 per cent of total invest-ment. Thirty-five per cent of the total was located in Venezuela; another 35 per cent in three countries, Argentina, Brazil and Mexico combined, and 10 per cent in Peru and Colombia together. The rest was scattered among a dozen smaller countries. (See Wionczek, "A Latin American View," in *How Latin America Views the U.S. Investor,* Raymond Vernon, ed., Frederick A. Praeger, N. Y., 1966, p. 4.) These figures undoubtedly minimize the influence of United States business in Latin America, however, since it probably con-trols as much as 40 per cent of the region's production in one way or another.

20. Wionczek, p. 4.
21. "Informe del ex-Presidente Lleras Camargo ante la OEA," *Com-mercio Exterior,* Mexico, February 1963, p. 402, quoted in Wion-czek, p. 9.
22. Wionczek, p. 13.
23. *Ibid.,* p. 18. See also Dwight S. Brothers, "Private Foreign Invest-ment in Latin America: Some Implications for the Alliance for Progress," in Cole Blaiser, ed., *Constructive Change in Latin Amer-ica,* Univ. of Pittsburgh Press, Pittsburgh, Pa., 1968, pp. 87–116.
24. See Frank Tannenbaum, "The Survival of the Fittest," *Columbia Journal of World Business,* March–April 1968; see also Peter Drucker, *The Age of Discontinuity,* New York, Harper and Row, 1968, Chapters 4 and 5.
25. *Ibid.,* p. 19.
26. "Economic Sovereignty at Bay," *Foreign Affairs,* October 1968, pp. 119–20.
27. See Simon Williams, "Private Investment in World Agriculture," *Harvard Business Review,* November–December 1965, for other thoughts on this subject.
28. *El Tiempo,* conference conclusions, translated from the Spanish, pp. 20–2.

CHAPTER 14

1. Francisco García Calderón, "Dictatorship and Democracy in Latin America," *Foreign Affairs,* April 1925, p. 469.
2. See Adolf A. Berle, *Power Without Property,* New York, Harcourt Brace, 1959.
3. Emilio Maspero, "Latin America's Labor Movement of Christian Democratic Orientation as an Instrument of Social Change," in *Revolution, Religion and Reform,* William V. D'Antonio and Frederick B. Pike, eds., Frederick A. Praeger, New York, 1964, pp. 172–3.

4. See George C. Lodge, "Revolution in Latin America," *Foreign Affairs*, January 1966, pp. 189–91.
5. Eric Hoffer, *The Ordeal of Change*, Harper & Brothers, New York, 1952, p. 12.
6. Increasingly, the Church in Latin America is speaking of those exceptions when violence becomes necessary to overthrow intolerable structures. "We cannot exclude the possibility of some specific situation in which violence against the established authority may be morally justified," writes Bishop Marcos McGrath "Development for Peace" (*America*, April 27, 1968). "History provides many such situations that were approved by the Christian conscience . . . I think it is safe to say that most Christians agreed in conscience with the armed opposition to the Batista regime."

CHAPTER 15

1. *The Economy of the Western Hemisphere*, Oxford Univ. Press, London, 1963; quoted from John P. Powelson, *Latin America: Today's Economic and Social Revolution*, McGraw-Hill Co., New York, 1964, p. 291.
2. Arthur M. Schlesinger, Jr., *A Thousand Days*, Houghton Mifflin Co., Boston, 1965, p. 202.
3. *Ibid.*, p. 203.
4. *Ibid.*, p. 205.
5. William D. Rogers, *The Twilight Struggle*, Random House, New York, 1967, pp. 35–9.
6. *Ibid.*, p. 37.
7. Eduardo Frei Montalva, "The Alliance That Lost Its Way," *Foreign Affairs*, April 1967, p. 439.
8. Ricardo Arias Calderón, a prominent Christian Democrat, described the change as follows in a conversation in Panama City in the summer of 1966: "Kennedy was in a way our last great illusion. With the communist take-over of Cuba our protected world ended. The feeling we had toward Kennedy was largely the result of this fact: the danger of Cuba gave us a feeling of need for protection and we felt that he had new, up-to-date ways of protecting us. Johnson is a cold shower, bringing us back to reality, which is probably a good thing." This comment is particularly relevant to earlier thoughts about the importance of tying policies into perceptible self-interest.
9. *The New York Times*, September 22, 1968.
10. Felipe Herrera, president of the Inter-American Bank, "Latin America: Reforms and Regionalism," *The New York Times*, January 22, 1968, p. 54.

11. *The New York Times,* October 20, 1968, p. 8E.
12. *Facts on Latin America's Development Under the Alliance for Progress,* April 1967, U.S. Dept. of State, Washington, D. C., pp. 1–2.
13. Frei, "The Alliance That Lost Its Way," p. 443.
14. In the following I am again drawing on Lodge and Gudeman, *The Veraguas Report,* pp. 49–62.
15. *The Passionate State of Mind,* Harper & Brothers, New York, 1954, p. 32.

CHAPTER 16

1. Edward G. Lansdale, "Viet Nam: Do We Understand Revolution?" *Foreign Affairs,* October 1964, p. 82.
2. Huntington, *Political Order in Changing Societies,* p. 358.
3. See John C. Donnell, "Pacification Reassessed," *Asian Survey,* August 1967, p. 571.
4. See Huntington, *Political Order in Changing Societies,* Chap. I.
5. See Raymond F. Mikesell, *The Economics of Foreign Aid,* Aldine Publishing Co., Chicago, 1968, pp. 257 ff. for a penetrating discussion of these two parts from an economic point of view.
6. See Seth Tillman, "Peace Corps: A New Way of Playing the Game," staff report (unpublished), Senate Foreign Relations Committee, 1967.
7. See Senator J. W. Fulbright's criticism of the AID program in Colombia (*The New York Times,* Feb. 2, 1969) and note his insertion into the *Congressional Record* (May 23, 1968, pp. S6307–S6310) of a speech by Teodoro Moscoso, first Coordinator of the Alliance for Progress, which incidentally is quite consistent with my proposals.
8. See Mikesell, p. 183.
9. Jacob Javits, "Last Chance for a Common Market," *Foreign Affairs,* April 1967, p. 452.
10. *Report of the Advisory Committee on Private Enterprise in Foreign Aid,* Agency for International Development, Washington, D. C., July 1965, pp. 1 ff.
11. Conversation with Ricardo Calderón, Panama City, July 1966.
12. "Domestic Structures and Foreign Policy," *Daedalus,* Spring 1966, p. 529.
13. *The New York Times,* July 3, 1966, pp. 1, 16.
14. Sol M. Linowitz, "The Demanding Seventies," speech before National Industrial Conference Board, Public Affairs Conference, New York, April 21, 1966.

15. New ed., Fernand Aubier, Paris, 1947.
16. Maritain, *The Social and Political Philosophy of Jacques Maritain,* Image Books, Doubleday, New York, 1965, pp. 229–74.
17. Pierre Teilhard de Chardin, *The Future of Man,* trans. by Norman Denny, Harper and Row, New York, 1964, p. 39.

INDEX

INDEX

A NOTE ABOUT THE AUTHOR

George C. Lodge was born in Boston in 1927 and graduated from Harvard College in 1950. He served as a reporter on the Boston *Herald* for four years and from 1954 to 1961 was with the Department of Labor, first as director of information and later as assistant secretary for international affairs. In 1962, he was the Republican candidate for the U.S. Senate from Massachusetts, and then joined the faculty of the Harvard Business School, where he is now associate professor of business administration. He is the author of *Spearheads to Democracy: Labor in Developing Countries* and contributes articles to *Foreign Affairs*. Mr. Lodge is married and the father of six children.

A NOTE ON THE TYPE

The text of this book was set on the Linotype in Fairfield, the first type face from the hand of the distinguished American artist and engraver Rudolph Ruzicka. In its structure Fairfield displays the sober and sane qualities of a master craftsman whose talent has long been dedicated to clarity. It is this trait that accounts for the trim grace and virility, the spirited design and sensitive balance of this original type face.

Rudolph Ruzicka was born in Bohemia in 1883 and came to America in 1894. He has designed and illustrated many books and has created a considerable list of individual prints—wood engravings, line engravings on copper, aquatints.

The book was composed, printed and bound by The Colonial Press, Incorporated, Clinton, Massachusetts. Typography and binding design by Arthur Beckenstein.

3 5282 00350 9034